BTEC FIRST
FOR ICT PRACTITIONERS

BTEC FIRST
FOR ICT PRACTITIONERS

RICHARD MCGILL
BERNADETTE FISHPOOL
MARK FISHPOOL

Hodder Arnold
A MEMBER OF THE HODDER HEADLINE GROUP

The author and publishers would like to thank the following for the use of photographs in this volume, Microsoft screenshots are copyright of Microsoft Corporation, Adobe screenshots are copyright of Adobe:

2.01 © Mark Evans / istockphoto.com; **2.07** © 2006 NVIDIA Corporation; **2.08** © 2006 NVIDIA Corporation; **3.02** © Peter Clark / istockphoto.com; **3.03** © Mariano Ruiz / istockphoto.com; **3.04** Photodisc / Getty Images; **3.05** © 2006 Wacom Europe GmbH; **3.06** DRS Data Services Limited; **4.01** Ebay.co.uk; **4.02** © Microsoft Corporation; **4.03** Napster.co.uk; **4.04** © Converse 2006; **4.05** RSPCA online 06/04/2006; **4.06** Copyright Guardian Newspapers Limited 2006 / top image: Andrew Parsons/PA/Empics, bottom image: AFP PHOTO/RAMZI HAIDAR/Getty Images; **4.16** BP plc; **4.17** Ebay.co.uk; **5.02** Image courtesy of The Advertising Archives; **5.03** Helene Rogers / Alamy; **5.04** Photo By Sipa Press / Rex Features; **5.06** Swerve / Alamy; **5.13** Art To Part, Inc.; **5.14** Photo Courtesy of Z Corporation; **5.15** ©Saxpix.com/age footstock / Superstock; **5.16** www.purestockX.com; **5.17** © nick free / istockphoto.com; **5.18** Royalty Free Photodisc; **5.19** © Valerie Loiseleux / istockphoto.com; **6.12** © Jon Feingersh/zefa/Corbis; **6.15** ©2000-2006 Belkin Corporation; **6.16** ©2000-2006 Belkin Corporation; **6.17** ©2000-2006 Belkin Corporation; **6.18** ©2000-2006 Belkin Corporation; **6.20** ©2000-2006 Belkin Corporation; **6.24** Maplin Electronics; Image used with the permission of http://www.build-your-own-cheap-computer.com; **Close up of the CPU socket on a motherboard;** © Norman Chan / istockphoto.com; **Photo of CPU Scoket on a Motherboard** © Scott Rothstein / istockphoto.com; **PS 2 Port** © Dino Ablakovic / istockphoto.com; **Serial Port** © Dino Ablakovic / istockphoto.com; **Parallel Port** © Matthew Stanzel / istockphoto.com; **12.05** Nonstock / Jupiter Images; **12.7** © Bryant Tonkin / istockphoto.com; **14.02** © Sandy Jones / istockphoto.com; **14.03** © © Dainis Derics / istockphoto.com;

14.04 Test Tools Europe Limited; **14.05** Test Tools Europe Limited; **14.06** © John Clines / istockphoto.com; **14.07** Maplin Electronics; **14.08** Maplin Electronics; **14.09** Maplin Electronics; **14.10** Maplin Electronics; **14.14** Winford Engineering; **16.01** Alan King / Alamy; **16.03** Bluetooth SIG; **16.04** ©2000-2006 Belkin Corporation; **16.07** © 2001-2006 Sony Ericsson Mobile Communications AB; **16.10** © Jim Orr / istockphoto.com; **16.13** © Mike Blake/Reuters/Corbis; **16.15** © Mike Blake/Reuters/Corbis; **16.16** © 2001-2006 Sony Ericsson Mobile Communications AB; **16.17** © 2000-2006 Belkin Corporation; **17.01** © Jim Sugar/CORBIS; **17.03** © PCP / istockphoto.com; **17.09** © Nikolay Iliev / istockphoto.com; **17.12** ACE STOCK LIMITED / Alamy; **17.13** Helene Rogers / Alamy; **17.14** Dan Lockton/Creative Commons; **18.01** © Copyright 2006 ATI Technologies Inc.; **18.02** © 2006 Wacom Europe GmbH; **18.03** © Canon Europa N.V. and Canon Europe Ltd 2002-2005; **18.04** © 2006 SanDisk Corporation; **18.05** © 2006 Hewlett-Packard Development Company, L.P.; 18.06 © Canon Europa N.V. and Canon Europe Ltd 2002-2005; **19.15** © Andresr / istockphoto.com; **Sony Playstation 2, with control pad** © Judith Collins / Alamy; **Microsoft Xbox with control pad** © Alan King / Alamy; **Gamecube with control pad** © Judith Collins / Alamy; **Nintendo Wii** Nintendo; **Xbox 360 with controller** Xbox 360 with controller; **Nintendo gameboy advance SP** Photo By Steve Meddle / Rex Features; **Gamepark GP2X** KT Corporation; **Sony PSP** © Se7en Imaging/Nigel Ash 2005 / Alamy; **Desktop PC with speakers attached** © Nicholas Monu / istockphoto.com; **Playstation 3** © 2006 Sony Computer Entertainment Europe; **20.07** FPG / Taxi / Getty Images; **20.17** Photo by Martin Lee / Rex Features; **20.19** John Powell Photographer / Alamy; **20.20** © KMITU / istockphoto.com; **20.24** Test Tools Europe Limited; **21.09** © João Saraiva / istockphoto.com;

Orders: please contact Bookpoint Ltd, 130 Milton Park, Abingdon, Oxon OX14 4SB. Telephone: (44) 01235 827720. Fax: (44) 01235 400454. Lines are open from 9.00 – 5.00, Monday to Saturday, with a 24 hour message answering service. You can also order through our website www.hodderheadline.co.uk.

British Library Cataloguing in Publication Data
A catalogue record for this title is available from the British Library

ISBN-10: **0 340 927 666**
ISBN-13: **978 0 340 663**

First Published 2006
Impression number   10 9 8 7 6 5 4 3 2 1
Year   2012 2011 2010 2009 2008 2007 2006

Cover photo © Getty Images
Typeset by Fakenham Photosetting Limited, Fakenham Norfolk
Illustrations by Anthony Jones © Art Construction.
Printed in Great Britain for Hodder Arnold, an imprint of Hodder Education, a division of Hodder Headline Plc, 338 Euston Road, London NW1 3BH by Martins the Printer, Berwick Upon Tweed.

CONTENTS

Appendices

Full copies of the grading grids that appear at the end of each unit are included on the companion CD. These can be printed and used to monitor your progress.

ACKNOWLEDGEMENTS

The writers would like to thank the following:

Mark Fishpool

Matthew, Rebekah and my wife, for inspiration.
Hamish, Norman, Manny, Mike and John, for leading the way.

Bernie Fishpool

Christopher, Josie and my husband, for encouragement and endless support.
Grateful thanks to Eric Russell-Brown of Stroud College for help and support on Unit 19.

Richard McGill

Kath, Verity and Jan of Filton College, for their help and support.
Vanessa, for her continued patience and understanding.

The **writing team** would also like to thank Stephen Halder and Paul Lee at Hodder for their support during the development of this book and Alison Austen for her tireless work in editing the script. Also Eddie Allman, Mike Rich and Judith Tope at Edexcel for hints and tips along the way.

Mark and Bernie Fishpool (Editors)
Spring 2006

INTRODUCTION

During 2005 Edexcel rewrote their BTEC First qualification for IT Practitioners, taking into consideration invaluable feedback from various professional bodies, schools, colleges and employers.

Both its academic and vocational themes have been thoroughly revised to reflect more appropriately the changing needs of employers in the IT sector and the expectations of learners studying in both schools and further education colleges. Accordingly, part of its new structure includes a mixture of 30 and 60 guided learning hour (GLH) units and vendor units from industry leaders such as Microsoft®, Cisco® and CompTIA®.

The new BTEC First qualification (encompassing both a Certificate and a Diploma) links firmly to its sector's National Occupational Standards (NOS) and is supported by its Sector Skills Council (SSC).

Both qualifications have been accredited to the National Qualifications Framework (NQF) at level 2.

BTEC First Certificate for ICT Practitioners

In order to achieve the BTEC First Certificate for ICT (Information Communication Technology) Practitioners, you must pass units which total 180 GLH.

Your choice of units must include one 60 GLH core unit (Unit 1: Using ICT to Present Information), plus other specialist units totalling 120 GLH.

BTEC First Diploma for ICT Practitioners

In order to achieve the BTEC First Diploma for ICT (Information Communication Technology) Practitioners, you must pass units which total 360 GLH.

Your choice of units must include two 60 GLH core units (Unit 1: Using ICT to Present Information and Unit 2: Introduction to Computer Systems), plus other specialist units totalling 240 GLH.

This book includes vital material which is designed specifically to help you study (and complete) a number of popular unit combinations for both the Certificate and Diploma qualifications.

Units covered by this book

This **book** covers the following units:

Compulsory Core Units	GLH
Unit 1: Using ICT to Present Information	60
Unit 2: Introduction to Computer Systems (*)	60
Specialist Units	**GLH**
Unit 3: ICT Project	60
Unit 4: Website Development	60
Unit 6: Networking Essentials	60
Unit 7: Software Design and Development	60
Unit 8: Customising Applications Software	60
Unit 10: Spreadsheet Software	30
Unit 11: Numerical Applications	60
Unit 12: Installing Hardware Components	60
Unit 13: Software Installation and Upgrade	60
Unit 16: Mobile Communications Technology	30

* Considered a Specialist unit for BTEC First Certificate

The **companion CD-ROM** covers the following units:

Specialist Units	GLH
Unit 5: ICT Supporting Organisations	60
Unit 9: Database Software	30
Unit 14: Technical Fault Diagnosis and Remedy	60
Unit 15: Providing ICT Technical Advice and Guidance	60
Unit 17: Security of ICT Systems	30
Unit 18: ICT Graphics	60
Unit 19: Installing and Maintaining Home Entertainment Systems	60
Unit 20: Telecommunications Technology	60
Unit 21: Doing Business Online	60

Vendor units **not covered** either by the **book** or **companion CD-ROM** are as follows:

Specialist Units	GLH
Unit 22: Core ICT Hardware[1]	60
Unit 23: Operating System Technologies[1]	60
Unit 24: Supporting Users and Troubleshooting the XP Operating System[2]	60
Unit 25: Supporting Users and Troubleshooting XP Desktop Applications[2]	60
Unit 26: IT Essentials[3]	120

[1] CompTIA®
[2] Microsoft®
[3] Cisco®

ASSESSMENT AND GRADING

Assessment for this qualification is undertaken through a series of coursework-based assignments. Your tutors will either use assignments developed by Edexcel or will write assignments for you to do that meet grading criteria. These assignments, and the work you provide, are marked and checked by your own centre and are then checked through external verification with a representative from Edexcel.

This qualification will now be awarded on a points system, although your certificate will show achievement at Pass, Merit or Distinction. To monitor your own progress as you undertake the course, each unit has a monitoring sheet for you to use. A full set of master grids that you can print off and use is included on the companion CD.

Each time you complete an assignment, your tutor will identify which **grading criteria** you have been awarded. You can tick off your achievement on the relevant unit sheet. Using this mechanism you will be able to identify which grading criteria you still have outstanding at each level (Pass, Merit and Distinction). You must **always remember** that to achieve a particular grade you must have been awarded **all the grading criteria available within a grade**. For a Pass, all Pass criteria must have been achieved. For a Merit grade, all Pass and all Merit criteria must have been achieved. For a Distinction grade, all Pass, all Merit and all Distinction criteria must have been achieved.

Once a unit has been completed, you will be awarded a number of points. This will be dependent on whether the unit was a 30- or 60-hour unit. Please see the following points table:

Size of Unit (GLH)	Pass Grade	Merit Grade	Distinction Grade
30	3	6	9
60	6	12	18

(Table reproduced from the Edexcel Qualification Specification)

The point score for each individual unit is reported to Edexcel at the end of your course. The points are then added together to give a **total score**. This will be the overall grade that you achieve for the qualification. It is known as your **qualification grade**.

Qualification grade

This table shows the overall grade that will be awarded for your qualification:

Qualification	Pass Grade	Merit Grade	Distinction Grade	Distinction*
BTEC First Certificate (54 points maximum)	18–29	30–41	42–53	54
BTEC First Diploma (108 points maximum)	36–59	60–83	84–95	96–108

(Table reproduced from the Edexcel Qualification Specification)

As you can see from this table, for outstanding performance you can now be awarded a Distinction* (similar to the A* that can be awarded at GCSE).

A First Certificate or First Diploma are equivalent to GCSEs and, depending on which qualification you achieve, will be considered as follows:

BTEC First Certificate grade		GCSE grade equivalent
Pass	P	C B
Merit	M	B A
Distinction	D	A A*
Distinction*	D*	See note below

(Table reproduced from the Edexcel Qualification Specification)

BETC First Diploma grade		GCSE grade equivalent
Pass	P	C C B B
Merit	M	B B A A
Distinction	D	A A A* A*
Distinction*	D*	See note below

(Table reproduced from the Edexcel Qualification Specification)

Note: At the time of writing, the points for BTEC Distinction* grade were still to be confirmed on the DfES School and College Achievement and Attainment Tables.

Further information can be found on the Edexcel website at www.edexcel.org.uk. For example, you can look at the unit specification and guidance given to your tutors. Your centres have been advised by Edexcel to keep up to date with the latest guidance provided on the website. In addition, your tutors have access to support materials on www.edexceloncourse.org.uk.

UNIT GRID

A unit grid has been provided that maps the content of individual units and shows where the authors have made direct links between different units. This means that you will find direct references made to the content of other units in the book. In addition, Unit 7, for example, is annotated with a C against Units 2, 8 and 9. This means that the link is **conceptual**. There are ideas and concepts in the unit that can be reapplied to the other units listed. This may also occur with other units. Finally, some units are annotated with an E. This means that Edexcel identified links between units in the Unit Specification, which have not been developed in this book.

Unit	1	2	3	4	5	6	7	8	9	10	11	12	13	14	15	16	17	18	19	20	21
1 Using ICT to Present Information	▓			✓	C		✓	✓	E	✓			✓		E	✓		✓			✓
2 Introduction to Computer Systems		▓				C		✓				✓	✓	E		✓	✓	✓			
3 ICT Project	✓	✓	▓	C			✓		✓	C							✓				
4 Website Development			C	▓	C													✓			C
5 ICT Supporting Organisations	✓		✓	✓	▓				✓	✓							✓				
6 Networking Essentials		✓		✓		▓							✓			✓				✓	
7 Software Design and Development		C	✓				▓	C	C	✓											
8 Customising Applications Software	✓						✓	▓	✓	✓											
9 Database Software	C		✓				✓	✓	▓	✓											
10 Spreadsheet Software	C		✓				✓	C	✓	▓											

Unit	1	2	3	4	5	6	7	8	9	10	11	12	13	14	15	16	17	18	19	20	21
11 Numerical Applications	✓									✓											
12 Installing Hardware Components		C				C							C	E	E						
13 Software Installation and Upgrade		C	C		C							C					C				
14 Technical Fault Diagnosis and Remedy	✓	✓					✓			✓		✓	✓		C						
15 Providing ICT Technical Advice and Guidance	✓	C				C	✓					✓	C	C							
16 Mobile Communications Technology	✓	✓			✓	E						✓					✓			✓	
17 Security of ICT Systems	✓	✓		E		✓						✓	C								
18 ICT Graphics	C	C		✓	C																
19 Installing and Maintaining Home Entertainment Systems												✓				✓				✓	
20 Telecommunications Technology	C	C				C										✓			C		
21 Doing Business Online	C	C	✓	✓	C												C				

✓   denotes direct links made between units

C   suggests a conceptual link between units

E   denotes additional links in content identified by Edexcel but not highlighted in this book

USING ICT TO PRESENT INFORMATION

INTRODUCTION

In order to succeed it is important for organisations to communicate effectively. This means communicating both internally (between the departments inside the company) and externally (with other bodies, such as customers and suppliers).

To do this, organisations use a variety of software packages (depending on which particular features they need to use), and a range of document types in accepted business formats.

This unit explores the way that organisations use ICT to present information by introducing you to standard document types and common features of applications packages, such as Microsoft Word®, Excel® and PowerPoint®.

Learning outcomes

On completion of this unit you should:

1 understand the purpose of different document types
2 understand the basis for selecting appropriate software to present and communicate information
3 be able to use commonly available tools and techniques in application packages
4 be able to review and adjust finished documents.

RECORDING YOUR PROGRESS

In order to achieve each unit you will complete a series of coursework activities. Each time you hand in work, your tutor will return this to you with a record of your achievement.

This particular unit has 11 criteria to meet: 6 Pass, 3 Merit and 2 Distinction.

- For a **Pass**: you must achieve **all** 6 Pass criteria.
- For a **Merit**: you must achieve **all** 6 Pass and **all** 3 Merit criteria.
- For a **Distinction**: you must achieve **all** 6 Pass, **all** 3 Merit **and both** Distinction criteria.

So that you can monitor your own progress and achievement in each unit, a recording grid has been provided (see the **Progress check** section at the end of this unit).

Understand the purpose of different document types

While historically the term **document** has been understood to mean something physical (for example, paper-based) that contains writing, the birth of digital documentation has seen the definition change. Now **document** is simply defined as any text that contains some information, without specifying the format. This section will clarify the modern categorisation of documents and explain their purpose.

Types of documents

Key term

Short formal: document types included in this category are memos, letters, emails, order forms, invoices, agendas, minutes. All these documents are included under this heading for two reasons:

a) They tend to be relatively short (no more than one or two pages in length).

b) There is a traditionally accepted basic format which dictates what should and should not be included.

Memos

Memos have traditionally been used by organisations to communicate between departments. This is because, unlike a letter, there is no need to include the recipient's (person receiving the memo) postal address. In larger organisations it is also likely that when completing the **From** and **To** details, the person's name and department will be included, and possibly even their office location, for example:

From: Rajhit Singh, Accounts (Room 3, Building 1)

To: Andrew Gustavson, Human Resources (Room A4, Building 3)

With inter-office memos, the level of detail should be sufficient to ensure that the memo will reach its destination.

Microsoft® Word has a number of memo templates from which you can choose.

MEMO	
From: Person sending the memo	Date: today's date
To: Person who will receive memo	Reference: any relevant file or typist details
Subject: heading, or title of the memo	
The content is now written here. Once the content is finished, there is no need to sign the document.	

Fig. 1.1 Typical memo layout

Letters

Letters are almost always used by organisations to communicate with the outside world. As with memos, they have a set structure that should be used. Most organisations personalise their stationery with a formal letterhead that includes the company's name, address and telephone number; usually, it also includes a graphical or WordArt image as a company logo. Microsoft® Word has a number of letter templates from which you can choose.

MyCompany Limited

123 London Road
MyTown
MT99 1ZZ
04156 978371

Insert the date here

Insert any reference information, such as file details or writer/typist

Name of recipient
Address in full
Postcode

Dear Sir or Name

Here you insert the content of the letter. Once the letter is finished you need to formally close it, with either Yours sincerely or Yours faithfully. Which you use will depend on whether your letter started with Dear Sir or someone's name. As a rule, Dear Sir letters are closed with Yours faithfully, otherwise it will be Yours sincerely.

Yours faithfully/Yours sincerely

Name of sender
Title if appropriate

Fig. 1.2 Typical letter layout

Emails

It is becoming increasingly common to send emails both inside the organisation and outside to customers and suppliers. Clearly, to be able to do this, you first need to have a relevant email address. In many cases initial contact is by letter and subsequent contact is via email, particularly between organisations. The main advantage of email over letter is that email is more or less instant.

As designated (special) software is used to communicate via email, the format is defined by the software you are using (although some features can be changed by the user).

The layout is not dissimilar to the structure of a traditional memo, with the user required to input To, Cc, Subject and the email main text.

'Cc' traditionally stands for **carbon copy**. In the days of typing memos rather than sending emails, a piece of carbon paper would be placed between two sheets of paper before the memo or letter was typed. When the carbon paper was removed, the second sheet acted as a copy of the first. This copy could later be used for filing purposes or could be sent to someone else. With an email, if you need someone else to see a copy of the email, you simply key their email address into the Cc panel on the email. The original recipient (the person the email was sent to) can see the contents of the Cc panel and will know who else has seen the email. For this reason, Cc no longer stands for carbon copy; now it stands for **circulation copy**.

You will also see on emails that you can list recipients in a Bcc panel. Bcc stands for **blind circulation copy**. This means that the person to whom the email was originally sent does not know that a copy of the email has been sent to someone else.

Each email is automatically tagged with the user's identification, so the recipient always knows who the email is from.

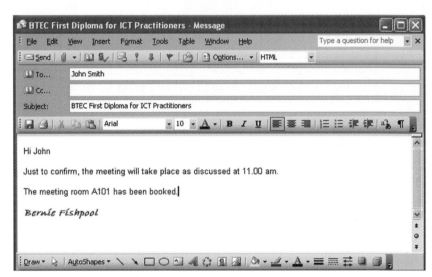

Fig. 1.3 Typical email layout

Order forms (often referred to as purchase orders)

While templates for order forms are also available on the Internet, many companies create their own. These templates have common features:

- name and address of the company placing the order
- name of the supplier from whom they are ordering
- details of what is being ordered, with quantity, description and price.

Finally, the order will list any special instructions (e.g. the delivery address may well be different from the invoice address).

PURCHASE ORDER  123 London Road
MyTown
MT99 1ZZ
04156 978371

Order Date: date order placed

Supplier Details

> Supplier's details, including name, address and postcode

Delivery Address

> Full address and postcode of where the goods should be delivered to

Quantity	Description	Price (per unit)	Total
		Total	
		VAT	
		Grand Total	

Special Instructions: sometimes organisations can say exactly when they want goods delivered

Fig. 1.4 Typical purchase order layout

Invoices

Invoices are used by organisations to ask for payment for goods they have provided. They are very similar to purchase orders in terms of their construction, but **Special Instructions** at the bottom of the order are replaced by **Payment Instructions**, and all organisations that are VAT-registered must include their VAT Registration Number on their invoices.

VAT (value added tax) is a tax that companies have to charge over and above the base price of their goods. Company A **charges** its customers VAT on goods that they buy. Company A also **pays** VAT to company B when it buys from them (after all, Company A is Company B's customer!). Company A pays the difference between what it is paid by its customers and what it has paid to its suppliers to the government. It is a way of the government generating revenue. For example,

Sales VAT	£21,000
VAT paid on purchases	£10,000
Difference	£11,000 – the government receives this amount

INVOICE

MyCompany Limited

123 London Road
MyTown
MT99 1ZZ
04156 978371

Invoice Date: *date invoice sent*

Customer Details

Customer's details, including name, address and postcode

Quantity	Description	Price (per unit)	Total
		Total	
		VAT	
		Grand Total	

Payment Instructions: 30 days from date of invoice

VAT Registration Number: 999 9999 99

Fig. 1.5 Typical invoice layout

In the event that the sales VAT is less than the VAT paid on purchases:

Sales VAT	£10,000
VAT paid on purchases	£21,000
Difference	£−11,000 – the government pays this back to Company A

Agendas

In its simplest form, an agenda is a list of **formal discussion points for a meeting**. The agenda itself is distributed to all those who are expected to be attending to the meeting *before* the actual date. This is done to ensure that everyone who is coming to the meeting knows in advance what will be discussed.

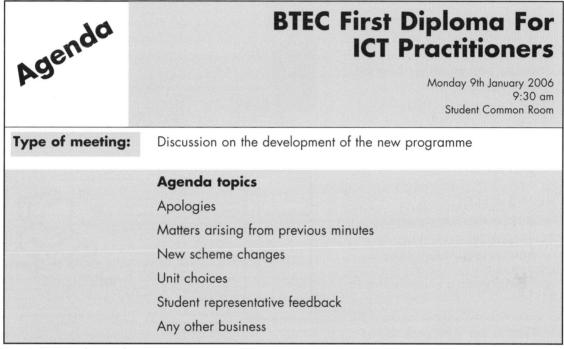

Agenda

BTEC First Diploma For ICT Practitioners

Monday 9th January 2006
9:30 am
Student Common Room

Type of meeting: Discussion on the development of the new programme

Agenda topics

Apologies

Matters arising from previous minutes

New scheme changes

Unit choices

Student representative feedback

Any other business

Fig. 1.6 Agenda template

The above agenda was created using the Agenda Wizard in Microsoft® Word. Traditionally, the items that will always exist on an agenda are:

- **Apologies**: where those who should be attending the meeting and who are unable to do so are excused for their absence.
- **Matters arising from previous minutes**: the minutes of the previous meeting are read and agreed as an accurate reflection of that meeting   if there was no previous meeting, this will clearly be omitted.
- **Individual discussion points** for this particular meeting.
- **Any other business (AOB)**: where those attending have an opportunity to add any issues that have arisen since the agenda was written, or to contribute ideas for discussion that were not originally considered when the meeting was set up.

Minutes

Once a meeting has taken place, a formal record is created. Using the agenda items as a basis for the content, issues and agreed actions are reflected under each of the subject headings. The completed minutes are sent to each person who attended the meeting (and those who sent their apologies). These minutes will then be discussed at the start of the next meeting.

Key term

Extended formal: document types included in this category are articles, newsletters, reports and user guides. All these documents are included under this heading because they tend to be longer than two pages in length. In addition, while there is an anticipated content, organisations can effectively present these documents in any way they choose.

Articles

Articles are **pieces of writing on a given subject.** These can be found in newspapers, magazines and journals. An article usually has a heading, and may contain subheadings if it is of sufficient length and complexity.

Newsletters

Modern software has a range of interesting templates that can be used to create eye-catching newsletters. Newsletters are usually distributed to people who share a common interest – for example, a BTEC First Diploma ICT Practitioners Newsletter could be circulated to everyone undertaking the course, to give them information about events, dates, times and changes in timetables.

Figure 1.7 is a representation of a basic newsletter template available in Microsoft Publisher®.

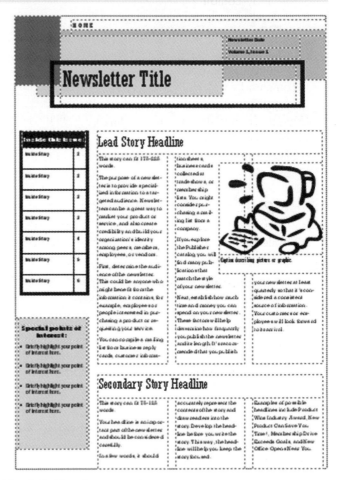

Fig. 1.7 Newsletter template

Reports

Reports are regularly used by organisations to **communicate an issue** or series of issues in a readable format. Often bound in the style of a book, the report will have:

- title page
- list of contents with relevant page numbers
- brief introduction to the report's contents
- main body containing the essence of the report (usually subdivided into sections, each with a heading)
- conclusions drawn from the evidence contained in the report
- recommendations for further actions
- appendices (any additional information that might help readers to understand the report)
- bibliography (a list of any sources used in the creation of the report – books, journals, websites).

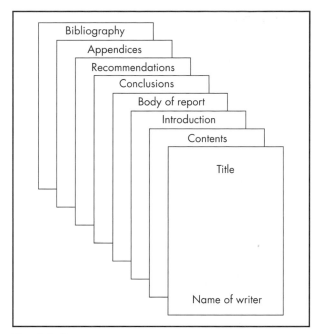

Fig. 1.8 Report structure

User guides

These days, most equipment comes with a user guide. For equipment such as microwave ovens and mobile phones, this is represented as a hard copy (paper booklet), while some software packages have a user guide on a CD or one that can be accessed through the Internet.

User guides generally have instructions on all aspects of the item, to include:

- setting up instructions
- description of all the item's features
- troubleshooting guide where users can look for help if a problem develops.

User guides must be written in such a way that anyone can understand them. Frequently, modern user guides are written in multiple languages, which reflects the needs of a global market.

Graphical documents include illustrations, charts, flow charts and diagrams. There is clear evidence that software to support graphical documents is becoming increasingly complex and sophisticated.

Illustrations

The term **illustration** covers a number of different types of image. It could include photographs, line drawings and descriptive drawings. In basic terms, an illustration is some sort of image that is used to give a **visual representation** of something, thereby making it more easily understood.

Charts

Most spreadsheet applications now include functionality to create charts. Charts are considered to be visually easier to understand than plain text. Look at the following two examples and decide which is easier to understand – the **table of information** (on the left) or the **chart** (on the right)?

Gadgets for U Financial Statement			
	Sales	Costs	Profits
April 2005	£24,256.00	£13,098.24	£11,157.76
May 2005	£26,075.20	£14,080.61	£11,994.59
June 2005	£28,030.84	£15,136.65	£12,894.19
July 2005	£30,133.15	£18,381.22	£11,751.93
August 2005	£32,393.14	£19,759.82	£12,633.32
September 2005	£34,822.62	£21,241.80	£13,580.82
October 2005	£35,867.30	£21,879.06	£13,988.25
November 2005	£36,943.32	£27,707.49	£9,235.83
December 2005	£38,051.62	£28,538.72	£9,512.91
January 2006	£39,193.17	£29,394.88	£9,798.29

Fig. 1.9 Table of financial data

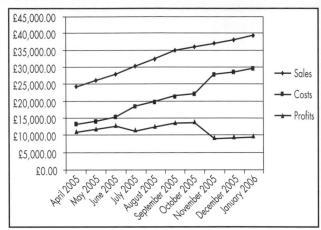

Fig. 1.10 Graphical representation of table

Although the two images give you the same information, the graphical image (the chart) makes the comparison easier to see and, therefore, easier to understand.

Flow charts

Flow charts are used frequently in computer program design, in project management and in manufacturing, to represent the fundamental components of processes. When you consider processes at the most basic level, many processes consist of

Flow charts themselves use a number of shapes to represent different actions. These symbols are commonly used to draw business functions.

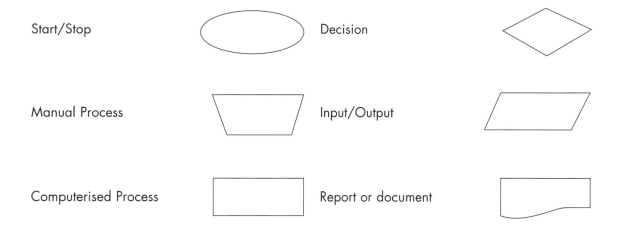

Start/Stop		Decision	
Manual Process		Input/Output	
Computerised Process		Report or document	

Thus, the previous diagram represented using more accurate shape notation would be:

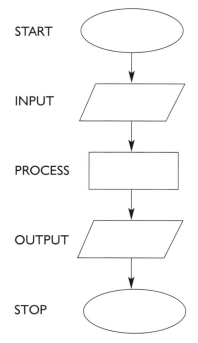

START

INPUT

PROCESS

OUTPUT

STOP

Notice that the flow chart is not written left to right, but **top to bottom**.

This is only an overview of some of the basic shapes used in flow-charting – there are many more. (See Unit 7: Software Design and Development, for flow-charting in programming.)

Diagrams

A diagram is a simplified representation of what can sometimes be a complex idea or concept. It is often a drawing which contains labels, for example a diagram of the human eye in a biology book (the eye is drawn with arrows and labels showing the different parts of the eye).

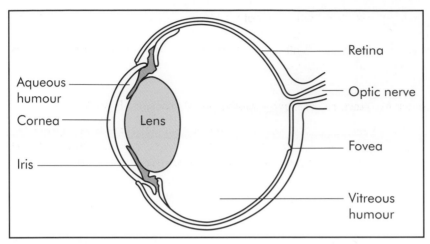

Fig. 1.11 The Human Eye

Promotional documentation would include advertisements, leaflets and, with the growth in Internet technology, web pages. Promotional documents are used to gain publicity for a product, an issue or an individual or group.

Advertisements

While software exists that allows organisations to create eye-catching and varied advertisements, it is on the Internet where there has been most development, particularly in terms of how sophisticated animated images have become, changing colour, font type or font size, and in terms of user interactivity.

Pop-ups are advertisements that generally appear without any direct action by the user. What happens is that where a pop-up has been attached to a web page, opening the web page will automatically activate the pop-up also, typically displaying in a new window. Usually written in JavaScript, these pop-up advertisements sometimes capture email addresses, which organisations can then use for more targeted email activity. (For more on JavaScript see Chapter 7: Software Design and Development.)

Leaflets

Leaflets are often folded pieces of printed paper that contain one or more advertisements.

These documents are then distributed free of charge, either handed out to passers-by, or posted through letter boxes by paid distributors, or by larger organisations such as the Royal Mail.

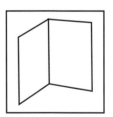

Fig. 1.12 Leaflet

Web pages

World Wide Web (**WWW**) pages are used in many different ways, to advertise products, services, individuals or organisations. In addition, they are used to sell products (Doing business online – see Unit 21) or simply to provide information. **Search engines** are used to seek out information on a particular subject. The principle is simple: writers of pages that can be accessed on the web create a **meta tag**, which is not visible to the user, but which carries a description of the article's contents and a number of keywords. When the user enters key (or search) terms into the browser, the software will search these meta tags and list all those pages that are relevant because they contain those key terms. The HTML script for a meta tag would look something like this:

<META name="Computer Architecture" content="motherboard processor RAM">

Not all Internet documents have meta tags, and not all search engine software is set up to use this information inside a web page. However, with the increasing amount of information on the World Wide Web, it is likely that the use of meta tags will become more and more important to reduce search times.

(For more information on web pages and the use of HTML tags, see Unit 4: Website Development.)

Presentations traditionally relied on technology such as the OHP (overhead projector), using OHTs (overhead transparencies or acetates). The development of Microsoft PowerPoint® has meant that many organisations have replaced their overhead projectors with new LCD (liquid crystal display) projectors, which displays enlarged computer-generated images on a screen. Using Microsoft PowerPoint® software also allows users to embed moving images and links to Internet pages or other files in an electronic slide show.

Other presentation technologies that have been developed in recent years include the interactive electronic whiteboard, which is increasingly replacing the old-fashioned whiteboard in classrooms. These boards, just like their predecessors, allow users to draw and write on the surface. The advantage of the new electronic version is that teachers can display images from the computer and annotate (write on) them using a special pen.

Informal documents include mobile phone messages (known as texting, or txting) and creative writing.

Texting

The numbers on a mobile phone keypad are used to select letters of the alphabet. Clicking these develops a message.

Using the above keypad as an example, to select the word 'hello', the user would press:

H	4 twice
E	3 twice
L	5 three times
L	5 three times
O	6 three times

Punctuation is usually stored on key 1, and 0 is used to create a space.

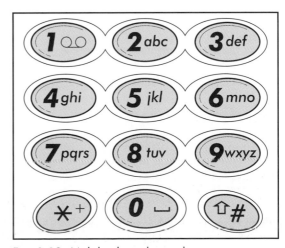

Fig. 1.13 Mobile phone keypad

Common words are also often abbreviated to reduce the number of key presses required to construct the message. Common abbreviations include:

Abbreviation	Meaning	Abbreviation	Meaning
PLS	please	WU?	what's up?
THNX or THX	thanks	CUL8R	see you later
U	you	B4	before
4	for	MYOB	mind your own business
HRU	how are you?	N1	nice one
L8R	later	NVR	never
CU	see you	2NITE	tonight
X	kiss	GR8	great
XLNT	excellent	RUOK?	are you ok?

These are examples of some of the abbreviations currently in use. It should be remembered, however, that while these may be appropriate in text messaging, they should always be written **in full in formal documents**.

(See Unit 16: Mobile Communications Technology, for the social impact of texting.)

Creative writing

While software products are being developed that assist writers in organising their writing projects, most novelists simply use word-processing packages such as Microsoft® Word to develop and store their stories, poems and novels. A simple advantage of using word-processing software over traditional typewriters is the **cut** and **paste** facility of products such as Microsoft® Word. Allowing writers to move sentences, paragraphs or even whole chapters of books makes both writing and editing much more feasible and enjoyable. Additionally, functionality such as spellcheck, grammar check, word search and replace and thesaurus makes them much more attractive tools to use.

Audience types

When creating documents, users should consider whether the **intended audience** is an individual or a group of people. This will have a bearing on which software is used to create the document (this concept is considered more fully in the next section of this chapter), and how many copies are ultimately made of the document either electronically or as paper copies.

Appropriate communication

In developing appropriate documents computer users should always consider the following.

Meeting user need

Documents should be created at a level that suits the target reader. For example, **terminology** (special language) might need to be adjusted to suit the intended audience. Where the Earth might be described to a four- or five-year-old child as being 'round', it is more likely that the term 'a sphere' would be used with readers who are older.

Writing for the younger reader means:

- simpler language
- shorter sentences
- large fonts.

Older readers can deal with:

- more complex ideas
- more complex language
- longer sentences
- smaller fonts.

Specialist tools

Some computer software includes functionality that can carry out a **readability test** on a paragraph, section or page. Using a scoring system, the **grammar** and **style** of a document, length of words used and how the ideas are organised, are assessed to predict how readable the text actually is. The results obtained from the test give an indication of the appropriateness against **educational reading ages**. This is merely an indicator, however, and should *not* be relied on as an absolute fact.

Netiquette

Netiquette is a term that has been created from the words **net** (from Internet) and **etiquette** meaning acceptable behaviour. Effectively, netiquette sets out rules for what is and is not **acceptable conduct** on the Internet. These rules are unofficial because, ultimately, they are not usually enforceable. Breaches of netiquette, however, have seen users being ejected and banned from chat rooms by their moderators. Furthermore, some users consider that sending **spam** (unwanted email) is bad netiquette, as is typing everything in CAPITALS – which is considered to be the same as SHOUTING!

Summaries

In the traditional sense, summaries are **brief statements** that offer the reader the main points of a document or article. The document would be read by the author or another individual, who would extract the important issues, including the key conclusions. This summary would then be accessed by individuals who wished to learn the main points of a document to enable them to decide whether they wish to read it in full. More recently, however, functionality has been built into software that creates automatic summaries based on the text of word-processed documents.

Templates

With the development of software applications, increasing numbers of templates have become available. For example, if you consider Microsoft® Publisher, which is designed to be used solely to find ways of presenting information and data in various written formats, the range of available templates includes:

- advertisements
- certificates
- brochures
- business cards
- calendars
- flyers
- gift certificates
- greetings cards
- invitations
- labels
- letterheads
- CVs.

These templates themselves are offered in a range of styles, which can be chosen by the user for different applications.

Appropriate choice of application package

The ability to choose the appropriate applications package for a given situation from a user perspective is something that can easily be learned. However, choosing the appropriate applications package from an organisational perspective can be more difficult, particularly when it comes to having to weigh up **features** against **cost**. In addition, some applications have minimum computer specifications that are needed for the programs to run correctly. When purchasing software, these requirements should be checked before buying the package, otherwise organisations might find themselves having to upgrade systems merely to accommodate the software. An example of this would be where a program requires 512 MB of RAM (**r**andom-**a**ccess **m**emory) to run correctly and the computer has only 256 MB.

Selecting appropriate software

Most software applications have been designed to help users to present information in a specific way. This section looks at the appropriateness of specific software options to meet user need.

Text-based (text editors, word processors)

Use: large volumes of text

Typically, these packages are used for word-processing, where large volumes of text need to be keyed in and manipulated. Microsoft® Word is by far the most commonly used software in this category, although applications such as Microsoft® WordPad (which contain significantly fewer features) are often available as part of the operating system.

Free word-processing software can also be downloaded from the Internet.

Graphics software (graphic tools in packages, stand-alone graphic packages)

Use: creating and manipulating images

Many of the generic applications packages contain graphic tools. For example, Microsoft Excel® has functionality to create charts and graphs. Microsoft® Word has WordArt functionality, which enables users to create interesting displays based on specific words:

Creating such displays merely requires the activation of WordArt and for users to key in the phrase or word they wish to display.

Alternatively, stand-alone graphic packages also exist, such as CorelDRAW® or Adobe Photoshop®. In the case of Photoshop, the product has been developed to work with photographic images. CorelDRAW®, on the other hand, is used for a number of different image applications.

(For further information, see Unit 18: ICT Graphics.)

Presentation software

Use: presenting ideas and concepts to an audience

Products such as Microsoft PowerPoint® now have competitive alternatives, such as Presentation Builder. These products create electronic slide shows, a sequence of individual slides which the presenter can move between to provide visual support to a verbal presentation. In addition to the development of specialist software, the Internet has seen an emergence of companies offering to create these presentations, for those who do not have the IT skills, as a commercial service.

Other technologies (texting on mobile phones, email, multimedia)

Texting software has clearly been developed by organisations such as Orange and Vodafone to support this activity on mobile phones. More sophisticated software also has email and multimedia capabilities.

In terms of regular computer usage, Microsoft Outlook® is the most commonly used email software package, although, as with other categories, free downloads do exist (e.g. Mozilla Thunderbird).

Multimedia software applications include editing software for TV and radio, as well as for the film industry. As this is a highly specialist market, these applications (such as Adobe Premiere® Pro) tend to be expensive.

Features

This term is generally used to describe the properties of an application, as well as some of its functionality, and it covers a range of categories, including the interface, input and output options, automation facilities, **shortcuts** and integration compatibility with other applications. This section provides an overview of the terminology.

Interface as WIMP, GUI

Key Term

WIMP is an abbreviation of windows, icons, menus and pointing devices and is used to describe systems which have these features.

The opposite of this is command line functionality, where every instruction that the user had to input was physically keyed in using some sort of specialist language. Today it is more common to refer to a WIMP interface as a GUI interface, where GUI stands for graphical user interface, implying that users interact with the computer through the manipulation of scroll bars, buttons, icons and other visual tools. While GUI is a relatively generic term that covers many different features, the term WIMP is more specific about which aspects of the interface are available.

Voice recognition and output options

Voice recognition systems allow computers to capture and interpret words spoken by the user, converting them into text or acting on them as commands. These systems require a microphone as an input device, and, once calibrated (set up to respond to the speech patterns of a particular user), the user activates the software and talks to the machine. A commercial example is Dragon NaturallySpeaking®.

Once a document has been created it can be similarly output using the computer's speakers, where a computerised voice reads back the text. This is clearly a very useful tool for the visually impaired or physically challenged.

Integrated packages and compatibility

It has become increasingly necessary for packages to have **integration capabilities**. This means that something created in one package can effectively be copied and pasted into another document, possibly in a different package. To fulfil this concept, Microsoft® developed and marketed Microsoft® Office, which contains word-processing, spreadsheet, database, publishing and presentation capabilities. Prior to this development, these products were sold individually and were often incomplete without each other – together they form a complete business solution.

True integration will allow users to copy and paste a series of records created in Microsoft® Access into a table in Microsoft Excel®, Microsoft® Word or Microsoft PowerPoint®, while maintaining font and layout. If these products were not compatible, pasting the data might result in nonsense appearing on the screen.

Similarly, when new versions of products are developed, manufacturers include functionality that allows files created in previous versions to be opened, saved and manipulated in the new version. This is called **backwards compatibility**. Often this functionality does *not* work in reverse – a file saved in a later version might not be opened in an earlier version. With most current versions of Microsoft® Office (this includes Office 2000, ME and XP) there are few such compatibility issues.

(For more on selecting software see Unit 13: Software Installation and Upgrade.)

Variety of outputs (audience notes, speakers' notes, different file formats)

With some software a file can be output in a number of different formats. Examples of this would be Microsoft Excel®, where data can be output as an image or as tables of information; or, more interestingly, Microsoft PowerPoint®, where a presentation can be printed as a set of original slides, a set of handouts, or where only the speakers' notes are printed, without any of the slides themselves.

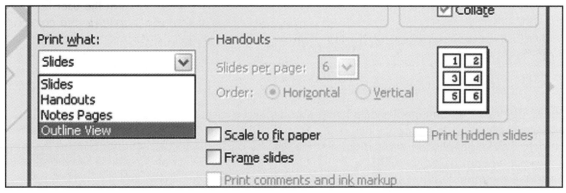

Fig. 1.14 Print dialogue box in Microsoft Powerpoint®

If the user selects to print the presentation as handouts, s/he will be asked whether there should be 2, 3 or 6 slides visible on each page. Remember, the more slides you include on a single page, the smaller the writing will be, and where 6 slides per page is selected, it is possible that parts of slides may be hard to read.

Automated procedures (wizards)

Some of the functionality in an application is accessed by way of a wizard. Wizards are like mini applications in their own right. Once activated, these applications walk users through a series of steps to reach a specific target. An example of this is the Label Wizard in Microsoft® Word, which sets up the printing of labels dependent on user choices. Similarly, the Query Wizard in Microsoft® Access helps users to quickly interrogate database records. These procedures can also be done manually (in other words, without the assistance of the wizard). However, the process would take **longer** and might require the user to have **specific knowledge or abilities**.

Shortcuts and inserting special characters

Shortcuts can be developed as a series of key presses for a given purpose. Some shortcuts are set as defaults inside software applications. For example, holding down the **CTRL** (control) key and pressing **P** will usually bring up the **Print** dialogue box. Some common shortcuts are as follows:

Shortcut	Action
CTRL + B	**Embolden**
CTRL + U	<u>Underline</u>
CTRL + I	*Italic*
CTRL + C	Copy
CTRL + V	Paste
CTRL + X	Cut
CTRL + N	New page
CTRL + H	Find and replace

These shortcuts can be complemented with user-defined shortcuts. The default for **CTRL + E** in Microsoft Word® is to centre the text being typed. In the event that the user frequently types in French, they might choose to reassign (change the use of) this key combination to insert the **é** character when pressed; or **CTRL + A**, which is defaulted to select all, could be reassigned to insert the German character **ä**. The alternative to using a shortcut is inserting the symbol or character using the **Insert Symbol** option on the menu, then selecting the relevant character from a range of special characters offered.

Allowing the user to assign shortcuts is what effectively **personalises** an application for a user or a group of users. (See Unit 8: Customising Applications Software, for more information.)

Use of templates

As stated earlier in this chapter, templates are used to create documents in a set style and format. Most software packages have some sort of template functionality.

Mail merge

Mail merge is an important feature of modern word-processing applications. It gives the user the ability to send the **same** correspondence to a number of **different recipients**, without having to manually change the name and address of each recipient before each print. The document is usually created in Microsoft® Word, with the names and addresses being **imported** (brought in) from other packages, such as Microsoft® Access or Microsoft Excel®, although Microsoft® Word has its own mini-database functionality that will accommodate lists of names and addresses keyed in directly.

Information

This can be categorised in two main ways, either by 'type' or by how 'structured' it appears to be.

Types (e.g. text, numbers, images, graphics, charts, tables)

Information is defined as **data that has been processed** to enable it to be viewed in a given way. In some cases, data stored in one way can be manipulated to be displayed in another (we have already seen this earlier in the unit, when we considered spreadsheet data viewed as a table or a graph).

Basic information may be categorised as:

Type	Description
Text	Letters of the alphabet, although this can often include numbers and symbols
Number	Whole numbers (integers) or numbers with a decimal part (real numbers)
Image	Photographs
Graphic	Drawings, including line drawings and diagrams
Chart	Pie charts, bar charts
Table	Rows and columns of information, sometimes separated by lines (like this table)

Structured and unstructured information

Unstructured information is a collection of **disorganised facts**, **figures or ideas**. It becomes structured when it has been **interpreted and organised** in such a way that it has **meaning**.

Finding information (ICT sources and non-ICT sources)

Information can be found in a variety of sources.

Non-ICT	ICT sources
Books	E-books
Newspapers	Websites
Trade journals	Databases
Official documents	Audio-visual
Visits	Newsgroups
Magazines	Forums

This is not an exhaustive list, but it does represent the most likely sources of information that ICT practitioners will access. Non-ICT sources will require users to physically find the information, whereas search engines can be used to find online information. However, many of the non-ICT sources are now being catalogued using sophisticated computer systems which can create indexes.

Checking validity of information

It is important to understand that all information should be treated **with caution**. Although it is likely that published sources (books, newspapers and journals) are accurate because these will have been checked, the fact that there is little or no policing on the Internet means that information drawn from this source should be checked for validity before assuming it to be reliable. Comparing any suspect data with using a printed source, such as a book or a journal, will reassure users that the information is valid. Checking information on a number of websites may seem ideal, but it is not. This is because some websites are created by **cutting and pasting** from other websites, and it is just as likely that incorrect as well as correct information could be duplicated and made popular as 'fact'.

Using commonly available tools and techniques in applications packages

Most software packages have **formatting and editing tools**. Because of the number of these tools, they are usually activated from a menu or toolbar. These toolbars can be switched on or off (made visible or removed) within most software through the *View* tab on the main menu bar. Some examples follow.

Formatting text (characters, paragraphs, pages)

The **Format** toolbar is used to manipulate aspects of the displayed text.

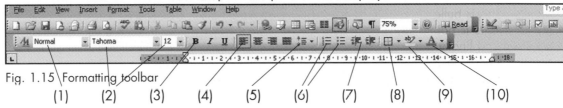

Fig. 1.15 Formatting toolbar

    (1)   (2)   (3)   (4)   (5)   (6)   (7)   (8)   (9)   (10)

(1)   The Normal tab offers the user a choice of normal text or a variety of heading and subheading styles. Simply selecting from the dropdown menu enables the user to switch between different styles.

(2)   Font type and size. There are a variety of fonts on offer, and more can be downloaded and added to the available font library. Sizes can also be adjusted. For example:

Font style Tahoma   Size 12

Font style Times New Roman   Size 22

(3)   Bold, Italics and Underscore. Clicking on one (two or all) of these changes the subsequent text accordingly. Users can also highlight whole sentences or paragraphs and activate these formatting options separately.

FONT COMIC SANS MS SIZE 12

(4)   Justification can be adapted as follows:

This text is left justified.

This text is centred

This text is right justified

Text that is **fully justified** is straight on both the left-hand and right-hand sides. This can be seen in this particular example, where sufficient text has been written to demonstrate the option.

(5)   This option adjusts line spacing.

Single line spacing is where a line appears immediately under the previous line of text. This will continue to be the case unless the enter key is pressed twice to force a clear line.

Double line spacing is where there is a clear line immediately below a line of text, before

the next line of text appears.

(6)   Bullet points are used to list items in a document. The advantage of using this technique in a document is that it draws attention to the individual items. In fact, this section itself is a list of bullet points. The points can be numbered or bulleted for effect.

1)   This is bulleted list of points. Here is point 1.
2)   Here is point two.
3)   And finally point three.
•   This is an alternative way of displaying bulleted points.
•   Here is the second point.
•   And finally the third.

Fig. 1.16 Bullet point optionality

(7)   These options allow users to indent paragraphs, or reduce the amount that a paragraph is indented. Activating the icon with the arrow facing right increases the amount of the indent; clicking on the other icon, with the arrow facing to the left, decreases the indent.

(8)   When activated, this icon places a border line around text.

(9)   The next icon allows users to highlight words, paragraphs or whole passages of text. This makes the relevant text stand out and is an alternative to emboldening it or placing it in italics.

(10) The final icon shown changes the colour of the font. When the drop down menu beside

the icon is clicked, approximately forty colour choices are offered. Users can select alternatives by clicking on more colours.

Editing text (e.g. insert, edit, delete, copy and paste)

The **Edit** toolbar has fewer icons than the formatting toolbar. Working from left to right, the icons are as follows:

Fig. 1.17 Edit toolbox

The scissors icon activates the **cut** option. This will **delete** any text that is highlighted and store it on the clipboard (a temporary area in the computer's RAM).

The two pages icon signifies the **copy** option, and when the icon is clicked, whatever is highlighted is also placed on the clipboard. Unlike the cut option, the original highlighted text remains.

Clicking on the clipboard icon will paste the text/table/image held in memory to wherever the cursor is.

The final icon, which looks a little like a paintbrush, is the **Format Painter**. If selected, this option will allow you to copy a highlighted object's format to another object (e.g. copy a word's format to another word).

Inserting images, files, symbols or page breaks is straightforward, as the insert function has a menu list all to itself on the main menu bar. Inserting text into a paragraph is also very easy. Simply move the cursor to the relevant position and begin to type. However, there are times when users begin to type and the computer appears to be writing over the text that is already present, rather than inserting it. This is usually because the **INS** (Insert) key on the keyboard has been pressed to toggle the **OVR** option on the status bar at the bottom of the window.

This means that the computer is **overwriting the text** rather than inserting. Pressing the Insert key again will remove the option and allow the user to insert text.

Fig. 1.18 Status bar

Fig. 1.19 Autoshapes

Formatting and editing graphics (e.g. basic shapes, images, charts, tables, draw, resize, align, rotate and flip)

This option is located on the **Drawing** toolbar. From this dropdown menu a number of different basic shapes can be selected for insertion by the user. The flow chart shown earlier in this unit was created using these options. The star shown on the next page was selected from the Stars and Banners option. Simply click on the required shape, then move the cursor to the start position, hold down the left mouse button and drag, then release.

The Drawing toolbar also contains options on manipulating images. For example, the star shown to the right has been **flipped horizontally** (see below) using the Draw menu on the Drawing toolbar.

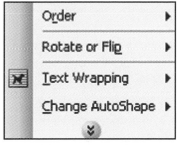

Fig. 1.20 Draw, options menu

Images can also be rotated using the same menu.

Advanced tools

Other tools can be found on the relevant toolbars within applications. Put simply, these tools include features such as:

Tool	Use
Crop	Crop allows users to extract part of an image without its surrounding detail.
Paste Special	In Microsoft® Word, Paste Special permits users to insert images in documents but treat them as independent objects. In Microsoft Excel®, however, Paste Special enables users to select the nature of the content from a list of options. (This will be discussed in Unit 10: Spreadsheet Software.)
Paragraph Styles	These include headings, titles, subheadings or captions, which help readers make sense of documents. Whichever style is chosen, users should ensure that the application of the style is consistent throughout the document.
Animation	Animated files can also be inserted into documents, though this is more likely to be done in Microsoft PowerPoint® presentations, which are shown electronically. Clearly, any animation included in a Microsoft® Word document would no longer be animated when the document is printed.
Tracking	This feature enables users to track changes made to documents. Whether detail has been inserted, deleted or modified is noted, along with details of when the modifications were made. Sometimes it is also possible to identify who made the changes. Also called 'markup'.

Combining information

Documents are more interesting when information is combined. As such, it is common for users to copy and paste information from websites, scanned documents and other files into integrated documents. In the event that this is done, however, there are some key issues that should be observed:

- Users should check that the font colour, size and type is **consistent** throughout the combined document.
- **Styles** should be made consistent, so that if one heading is in bold and italic font, the next heading of the same type is not shown in italic and underscored.
- **Paragraph indentation** needs to be checked to ensure that any indented sections are indented to the same point.
- Users should check that **justification of the document** is the same throughout the document.

If these items are checked, a combined document will look as if the whole document were created at the same time. The same rules are also applied to web pages.

Presentation techniques

While some of these issues have been covered in previous sections, it should be understood that decisions on the following aspects of documents are usually left to the discretion of the user, although some organisations do have a **house style** that they expect their employees to adopt.

Choice of font and size

The font should be chosen carefully and users must ensure that whichever font is chosen is **legible**, of a **suitable size** to be read by most people and that **all text is present**. This is particularly important in Microsoft Excel®, where, if the font is not an appropriate size (or the columns have not been correctly adjusted) the data may not be fully visible, and this in itself could be misleading. Take this example from Microsoft Excel®:

	A
1	1.23E+10

Fig. 1.21
Exponential

In this instance the column is not wide enough to accommodate the number. Excel accommodates this by displaying the number using **scientific notation** (also called **exponential**).

Similarly, there can be problems with dates.

In the above spreadsheet example the date has been inserted in **cell A1**. This can be seen in the bar above **column C**. Unfortunately, the font is too big and the column cannot accommodate the data. It displays hash symbols instead.

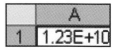

A1	▼	_fx_	01/03/2006
	A	B	C	D
1	########			
2				

Fig. 1.22

Use of colour

While the colour of backgrounds can be changed easily in most software applications, users should bear in mind that if a colour printer is not available, any colours will be displayed in shades of grey (**greyscale**) which could present visual problems for readers.

Different layouts (e.g. columns, tables)

In normal use, Microsoft® Word displays text as a single column. In other words, it writes between the margins, moving from one line to the next as the width of the page becomes full. However, it is also possible to select to display the text as two or even three columns, just as you might see in a newspaper.

In normal use, Microsoft® Word displays text as a single column. In other words, it writes between the margins, moving from one line to the next as the width of the page becomes full.	However, it is also possible to select to display the text as two or even three columns, as you might see in a newspaper.

In normal use, Microsoft® Word displays text as a single column. In other words, it writes between the	margins, moving from one line to the next as the width of the page becomes full. However, it is also possible	to select to display the text as two or even three columns, as you might see in a newspaper.

Creating columns is a simple process. Type in the text, highlight the area you want to display in columns, then select the **Format** menu and **Columns**. All that remains is to key in the number of columns required.

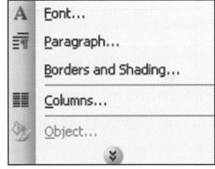

Fig. 1.23 Format menu

Headers and footers

Headers and footers are frequently used in documents, particularly for identification information.

The footer shown below displays:

- filename of the document
- page number.

BFD Unit 1.doc	25

Fig. 1.24

Other information that can be included in a header or footer includes:

- author's name
- date
- document revision number.

It is also common for organisations to include a small version of their company logo in the header.

Accessing headers and footers is done through the **View** dropdown menu, and using the mouse to **toggle** (move) between the two.

Fig. 1.25 Header and footer menu

Advanced techniques (e.g. tables of contents, indexes)

It is essential in a multi-page document to include a **contents page** and/or an **index** to ensure that readers can find what they need easily.

Contents pages tend to be organised with sections listed in the order in which they occur in the text.

Indexes, however, are more likely to include the same headings, but be organised in alphabetical order. This can be very useful and is the reason why some published books include contents pages at the **beginning** of the book and an index at the **back**.

Information storage

To ensure that information is readily accessible once stored, users should observe the following rules:

- Files should be stored in a relevant format. For example, Microsoft® Word files are stored with a .doc extension. Similarly, Microsoft Excel® files are stored with a .xls extension and Microsoft® Access with .mdb.
- All software applications save files with a specific extension. These extensions should not be amended as doing so might make them unreadable by the software.

File management (e.g. naming files, folder structures, moving and deleting files)

Files should first be given sensible names so that they can be retrieved easily. For example, calling a file **File 1.doc** might seem reasonable when it is created, because it is likely that the user will initially remember what it contains. However, will the user still be able to remember the file's content a week or a month later? Possibly not! As such, it is more appropriate that the filename should give the user an indication of what the file contains. For example, the following image has been created to be used in this book. It has been named **directory.bmp**.

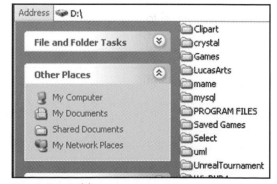

Fig. 1.26 Folder structure

The .bmp extension instantly tells the user that the file is a **bitmap** file (a kind of image). The name **directory** describes the content. This file is an image of a folder structure.

The above image shows the first level of a folder structure for files stored on a drive designated D:\.

Each of the individual folders, when opened, may well contain other folders.

Once opened, the files contained in the folder will be visible.

File details (name, size, type, date modified)

Files have a name, size, type and modification date. This can be seen by accessing the file manager and hovering the mouse pointer over a file, to view the file's **properties**.

This image displays the .pdf file properties. It states that the file (entitled Unit 1.pdf) is an Adobe Acrobat® document, modified on 11 March 2006 at 16.09 p.m. The file size is 350 KB.

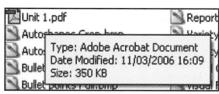

Fig. 1.27 Adobe file properties

Further information about the file can be displayed by hovering the mouse pointer over the file's name, clicking the right mouse button and selecting properties. The properties display will have information not seen in the condensed version shown above. It will give the full **pathname** of the file (e.g. D:\mydata\Unit 1.pdf), the **date created** and will allow the user to change the icon if required.

Be able to review and adjust finished documents

Review

It is important for users to review documents they have created and, to this end, there is a series of criteria against which the success of document creation can be measured.

Use of media

You are also asked to reflect on whether the media that was used to present the information was the most appropriate one. Should the **document** really have been a **presentation**? Should the **diagram** have been a **photograph**?

Feedback from other people

In terms of the document created, it is often sensible to ask for feedback from others. This is particularly useful when creating documents like **user guides** or **questionnaires**, in fact, anything that is likely to be viewed and used by a number of people. Sometimes when we ask questions or write instructions, we may understand what is meant, but others might not interpret our words in the same way: it is possible that what is written is **ambiguous**. It is always useful to check that others interpret things as the writer intended. When creating software from scratch (in programming, for example), getting relevant feedback from users in an important part of the testing phase.

User requirements check

If a user has created a document on behalf of someone else it would be usual to ask the user to confirm that the document has met their original requirements. For example, secretarial staff and administrators usually get the signatories of letters to read them before they are signed and distributed. In the same way, originators of reports will read and approve these before they are printed, photocopied, bound and distributed. This is good practice and ensures that errors in documents are quickly identified and eradicated.

Quality (e.g. proofreading, accuracy, functionality, aesthetics, spellchecking, grammar checking, thesaurus)

As part of the quality process there are other checks that should be made, in addition to asking the originator to read the document:

Issue	Description
Proofreading	It is important that users proofread documents they create. This process should quickly eradicate careless or semantic (meaning) errors – for example, where the word 'fare' (cost of using a bus) has been confused with 'fair' (reasonable or just). Rereading the document and checking the use of words in context is vital to ensure that the document has the correct meaning.
Accuracy	While applications such as Microsoft® Word, Microsoft Publisher® and Microsoft PowerPoint® have functionality that can be used to check the accuracy of grammar and spelling, Microsoft Excel® does not have the ability to check any numbers input into the spreadsheet. These must be checked manually to ensure that they are accurate.
Functionality	Does the document do what it is intended to do? For example, if an invitation has been created using Microsoft Publisher®, does it contain the event details, the date, time and location of the event?
Aesthetics	Does the document look professional, eye-catching or interesting (whichever is appropriate)?
Spellchecking	Has the spelling been checked electronically, in addition to the document having been proofread?
Grammar checking	Has the document been checked for grammar errors? This, again, can be done electronically, although it should not be done to the exclusion of proofreading.
Thesaurus	The thesaurus is probably one of the most useful functional tools of word-processing software. Sometimes, when creating a lengthy document, it is difficult for users to think of alternative words. Take the example of the word **house**. The thesaurus offers the following alternatives: residence, dwelling, abode, to name but a few. This allows the user to say the same thing, using an alternative (yet appropriate) word.

Explaining decisions and actions taken (e.g. choice of package, choice of techniques and tools, layout)

For the purposes of the BTEC First Diploma for ICT Practitioners, learners will need to be able to explain decisions they have taken, or their reasons for specific approaches. They will have to justify their choice of package for a particular use, choice of techniques, such as style, use of particular images, and so on.

Case studies

This book will use three typical businesses to help illustrate how ICT is used within organisations. All three companies, though very different, do frequent trade with each other!

You will see these businesses discussed in some of the units, and may be asked to use this information to answer some questions at the end of unit chapters.

Business #1

Steve Hodder runs a small skateboard company (Steve Hodder Skateboards – SHS). He is a sole trader (this means that he owns the company and has no partners – he does, however, have three employees who work for him). The company sells both off-the-shelf skateboards (pre-built ones) and skateboards made to meet particular customer requirements (custom-built ones). They also sell the skateboard components and have recently expanded their stock base by adding a diverse range of accessories, including a range of specialist DVDs, music CDs and phone covers and cases.

While its primary business is selling direct to the public (they do not as yet have a website or online selling capabilities, although a consultant is looking at this for them), the company has recently started to organise skateboard events and competitions, sponsored by Diskount Video Discs (DVD) and We Cell Phones (WCP).

Business #2

Diskount Video Discs is a private company (a limited company with a small number of investors that is privately owned). It has three local branches. Primarily retailing DVDs and CDs to the general public, they already have a website and customers can buy in store or online.

With seventeen employees (including part-time and administration staff), this company is expanding and has recently agreed to sponsor some of the SHS events. They also purchase their phones from We Cell Phones.

Business #3

We Cell Phones (WCP) is a PLC (public limited company – anyone can own shares in a PLC). With lots of shops throughout the UK and a large number of employees, this company sells phones and accessories to the general public and exports some products abroad.

With a successful online business in addition to its shops, this company supplies phones to both

DVD and SHS. While DVD's staff use the phones to support the business activities, SHS use the phones and sell them on to the general public.

We Cell Phones has been sponsoring local music, indoor sport and some charity events for many years and has recently become involved with SHS as the major sponsor for the first outdoor skateboarding competition to be held in the county.

All three companies have a mutually beneficial relationship and are happy to be working together in a number of different ways.

QUIZ

1. Name three documented ways in which WCP, SHS and DVD might communicate.
2. Which documentation method will Steve Hodder use to communicate with his staff?
3. Name four of the main components of a report.
4. What is an agenda used for?
5. Give two formatting techniques that can be used on text.
6. Why is a graphical image sometimes better than a table of numbers?

ANSWERS

1. Letter, email, newsletter, invoice, order
2. Email or memo
3. Title page, Contents, Introduction, Body of report, Conclusions, Recommendations, Appendices, Bibliography
4. To advise those attending a meeting about what will be discussed
5. Colour, size, font style, alignment
6. Because a visual representation can be easier to interpret.

COURSEWORK GUIDANCE

To pass this unit, you need to able to show that you can differentiate between different types of document. You'll need to show that you know when to use a specific document type and why. You will also need to demonstrate an understanding of which software applications support which types of document.

On a practical level, you will need to show that you can use basic document tools and techniques, including importing images and using them alongside text to provide information.

Part of the unit requires you to understand that documents should be well presented – that aspects of your documentation should be consistent, clear and businesslike. It should go without saying that the same level of care and attention should be applied to your own work. Checking your work is particularly important – and this is a good target to set yourself right at the beginning of the course.

Unit links

This unit has direct links to the following:

Unit 4 Website Development
Unit 5 ICT Supporting Organisations
Unit 7 Software Design and Development
Unit 8 Customising Applications Software
Unit 10 Spreadsheet Software

Unit 13 Software installation and upgrade
Unit 16 Mobile Communications Technology
Unit 18 ICT Graphics
Unit 21 Doing Business Online

Edexcel also show links to:

Unit 9 Database Software
Unit 15 Providing Technical Advice and Guidance

Further reading

Etherington, S., *Formatting and Printing* (Dorling Kindersley, 2003) ISBN: 0751364290

Hayward, A., *Essential Computers: Introducing Flash* (Dorling Kindersley, 2001) ISBN: 0751335835

Sherman, J., *Basic Computer Skills Made Simple: XP Version* (Made Simple, 2003) ISBN: 0750661372

Watson, J., *Designing Documents* (Dorling Kindersley, 2002) ISBN: 0751346322

Watson, J., *Drawing with Word* (Dorling Kindersley, 2002) ISBN: 0751346349

Progress check

As suggested at the beginning of this chapter, this grid should be used to monitor your progress. It shows how many Pass, Merit and Distinction criteria you need to achieve to be awarded that particular grade in the unit. When your coursework has been marked, your subject tutor will indicate which criteria you have achieved.

To record your achievement, simply tick the criteria awarded to you when each assignment is returned (you may be given three assignments for this unit U1.01, U1.02 and U1.03 – the last column may not be used).

	Assignments in this Unit			
Assignment	**U1.01**	**U1.02**	**U1.03**	**U1.04**
Referral				
Pass				
1				
2				
3				
4				
5				
6				
7				
Merit				
1				
2				
3				
4				
Distinction				
1				
2				
3				

What follows is a completed example of the progress check grid for this unit to show you how is should be used.

	Assignments in this Unit			
Assignment	**U1.01**	**U1.02**	**U1.03**	**U1.04**
Referral				
Pass				
1	√			
2	√			
3		√		
4		√		
5			√	
6	√			
7				
Merit				
1	√			
2		√		
3	√			
4				
Distinction				
1	√			
2				
3				

You will see above that you only need to show evidence in the white boxes. The greyed out boxes do not apply for this unit (there is no P7, M4 or D3 criterion).

Using this system for this unit, you would be able to see that you have achieved a Merit, as you have not been awarded D2 (Distinction criterion 2).

While a copy of this grid (adapted to suit the requirements of each unit) is included at the end of each unit, there is also a master copy on the companion CD that can be printed and used. The CD copy also allows you to record your key skill achievement against Literacy, Numeracy and ICT objectives.

INTRODUCTION TO COMPUTER SYSTEMS

INTRODUCTION

With the continued miniaturisation of the microprocessor and the falling costs of hardware components through improved mass production, computer systems can be found everywhere – from the humble kitchen microwave oven through to life-saving medical equipment in the local hospital.

An important aspect of becoming an ICT practitioner is being able to recognize the hardware components that are used to build such systems, how to work with them and understand how they operate through their software programs.

Learning outcomes

On completion of this unit you should:

1 know different uses of computers in homes and businesses
2 be able to explain the use of common types of hardware in a personal computer system
3 know how to select software for a specified user
4 be able to safely connect hardware devices and configure software for a specified user.

RECORDING YOUR PROGRESS

In order to achieve each unit you will complete a series of coursework activities. Each time you hand in work, your tutor will return this to you with a record of your achievement.

This particular unit has 14 criteria to meet: 7 Pass, 4 Merit and 3 Distinction.

- For a **Pass**: you must achieve **all** 7 Pass criteria.
- For a **Merit**: you must achieve **all** 7 Pass and **all** 4 Merit criteria.
- For a **Distinction**: you must achieve **all** 7 Pass, **all** 4 Merit **and all** 3 Distinction criteria.

So that you can monitor your own progress and achievement in each unit, a recording grid has been provided (see the **Progress check** section at the end of this unit).

Key terms

Hardware: physical components in a computer system (e.g. keyboard, mouse, monitor)

Software: instructions which tell the computer what to do (e.g. Microsoft Windows®, Microsoft Word®)

Different types of computer

There are many different types of computer system which are used both at home and at work. It is important to appreciate the different types available.

Personal computer (PC)

A PC usually consists of a base unit, monitor, keyboard and mouse.

Although the base unit may be orientated horizontally or stand in a vertical **tower**, it contains all of the computer's major **hardware** components (e.g. **motherboard**, central processing unit, or **CPU**, and **memory**).

The monitor is used to display **output** from the computer's graphic (or video) card; monitors (sometimes called a VDU – visual display unit) can be either **CRT** (cathode ray tube)-based or **TFT** (thin-film transistor)-based. Because of their smaller desk footprint and reduction in emitted heat and radiation, TFTs are quickly becoming the most popular form of display device.

Fig. 2.1 A typical desktop PC

The keyboard and mouse represent basic **input** devices. Modern designs are often **cordless**, using **wireless technology** to communicate with the base unit.

Server

A server is usually much more powerful than a standard desktop PC; it typically has more memory, multiple processors and a number of hard disks. Components in a server have to be extremely reliable as the hardware is designed to run with little rest; battery-backed units called uninterruptible power supplies (**UPS**) keep the machine running temporarily when the main electrical power is lost.

Generally, a server's job is to provide other computers on a network with files, applications or services.

Servers that are dedicated to running specific services are named accordingly, for example:

- **mail server** provides users with centralised email facilities
- **print server** provides users with shared printing
- **file server** provides users access to shared data
- **web server** provides users with access to web pages.

Falling costs have now placed server technology within the reach of the home market and it is not unusual to find server technology being used domestically.

Mainframe

An older term, a mainframe is a large and expensive computer system that typically runs a large corporation or government department. They are often capable of supporting hundreds or thousands of different networked users simultaneously.

In November 2005, the most powerful known 'supercomputer' was the IBM BlueGene/L, used at the US Department of Energy in Livermore, California. It contains 131,072 processors and can perform 280.6 TFlop/s (TFlop = teraflop, a measurement of decimal number calculations per second).

Mobile devices

Mobile devices such as personal data assistants (**PDA**s), notebooks and laptops also contain PC-style components. Typically, their performance is geared towards greater power efficiency than a normal desktop PC. Because of this, components in mobile devices such as these are often less powerful and offer much lower power consumption, which makes them ideal portable processing platforms.

Embedded devices

Other household devices also have microprocessors; these are commonly called embedded devices. Telephones, washing machines, microwave ovens and games consoles all contain similar components to that of a more traditional computer system, although generally they are much less powerful (i.e. slower processing, less memory, limited input and output, etc.).

The primary difference with these types of computer system is that they are often dedicated to performing a specific function (e.g. the microwave cooks food), and the selection of hardware and its programming reflects these reduced needs.

Data representation

Decimal

Decimal (or **denary** as it is sometimes known) is the number system we use to count. In decimal, all numbers are expressed as quantities of powers of 10, and we use the digits 0 through 9. For example, 267 is actually:

Hundreds (100s)	Tens (10s)	Units (1s)
2	6	7

The general consensus is that we count in tens because we have ten fingers. But computers do not have ten fingers, of course! Instead, computers consist of millions of two-state electronic switches, and, importantly, each switch can be either on or off. This leads us to the binary number system.

Binary

The **binary** (or **base 2**) number system can ideally represent these switches, as only two different digits can be used: 0 and 1. Binary numbers use the powers of 2 to build numbers. For example, the denary number 13 would be written in binary as 1101:

8	4	2	I
I	I	0	I

(In other words, 13 = 8 + 4 + 1)

Inside the computer system **all data** is represented in binary, no matter what **kind** of data it actually is – music, pictures, video, text, and so on.

Here are some other examples:

32	16	8	4	2	I		
I	I	0	I	I	0	=	**54** denary
	I	0	0	0	I	=	**17** denary
	I	I	0	0	0	=	**24** denary

It is useful to remember that odd binary numbers will **always** end in a 1.

Bits

Computer memory is grouped in a particular way. You have probably already heard the terms bytes, kilobytes and megabytes.

The smallest unit of computer memory is the **bit** (short for binary digit). A bit can only store 1 binary digit, **either** a 0 or a 1.

0	or	I

Collecting bits together can form bigger units.

Bytes

A byte is a collection of 8 bits. A simple example would be:

0	0	0	0	0	0	0	0

Another example would be:

0	0	I	I	I	0	I	0

A byte gives us **256** different binary combinations (0–255 in denary).

A byte is seen as a significant amount of storage because it is big enough to store a **single** alphanumeric character (e.g. 'A' or 'z' or '7') when using an appropriate **character set**, such as **ASCII** (American Standard Code for Information Interchange).

Sometimes 4 bits are collected together to form a smaller unit called a **nibble**.

Kilobytes

Although in the metric system 'Kilo' is used to represent 1000, in computing, a **kilobyte** is actually **1024** bytes, which can also be written as 2^{10}, or, in full, as $2 \times 2 \times 2 \times 2 \times 2 \times 2 \times 2 \times 2 \times 2 \times 2$.

Although in the 1970s and 1980s a computer system's main memory was impressively stated in kilobytes, it is now seen as a rather small measurement. Modern computer systems tend to use kilobytes when referring to the size of small data files on a disk drive.

You may see kilobyte abbreviated in ways such as **kb**, **KB**, **K** or **k**. For example, all the following represent 5 kilobytes: 5kb, 5KB, 5K and 5k.

Megabytes

Again, although 'mega' is often used to describe 1 million, in computing it actually represents 1,048,576, or 2^{20}. It is also the same as 1024 kilobytes.

Megabytes are typically used to describe quantities of main memory (**RAM** – random-access memory) and larger file sizes.

A single megabyte is generally enough to store:

- a single photograph (no compression, but good quality)
- a minute of music (compressed)
- text from a typical-sized book.

Megabytes are formally abbreviated as **MB**, but you might hear them referred to informally as **meg** (e.g. Her PC has 512 megs of RAM.)

Gigabytes

A gigabyte is the next storage unit commonly used. It is often used to describe the size of backing storage (e.g. a 100-gigabyte hard disk).

Again, although the term 'giga' is used to describe 1 billion, in computing, it actually represents 1,073,741,824, or 2^{30}. It is also the same as 1,048,576 kilobytes, or 1024 megabytes.

A 4.7-gigabyte digital versatile disk (DVD) is capable of storing a 2-hour movie.

Gigabytes are formally abbreviated as **GB**, but, again, you may hear them referred to informally as **gig** (e.g. His PC has 30 gigs of space free on the hard disk.)

Terabytes

A terabyte is the next storage unit commonly used, particularly for hard disk storage on servers and mainframe computer systems.

While the term tera is used to describe 1000 billion, in computing, it actually represents 1,099,511,627,776 bytes, or 2^{40}.

Terabytes are formally abbreviated as **TB**.

Larger units

Larger units of storage are available, but are not in common usage. These larger collections include (in ascending order): Petabyte (**PB**), exabyte (**EB**), zettabyte (**ZB**) and yottabyte (**YB**).

Memory unit summary

Unit	Bits	Bytes	Kilobytes
Bit	1	–	–
Byte	8	1	–
Kilobyte	8,192	1024	1
Megabyte	8,388,608	1,048,576	1024
Gigabyte	8,589,934,592	1,073,741,824	1,048,576
Terabyte	8,796,093,022,208	1,099,511,627,776	1,073,741,824

Logical representation

A computer system can be viewed in a logical way, which is to say that we can **imagine** how it is connected rather than concentrate on the actual **physical** details.

A logical representation of a PC system can be shown in this simple **block diagram**:

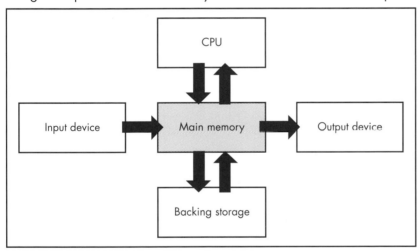

Fig. 2.2 A simple block diagram of a PC system

This diagram shows a simple relationship between the subsystems that form a typical PC.

- **input device** allows the user to manually enter data (e.g. a keyboard)
- **main memory** temporarily stores data entered by the user (i.e. the RAM)
- **CPU** processes data transferred from main memory, returns results (i.e. the processor)
- **output device** displays results of the processed data as information (e.g. on a monitor)
- **backing storage** more permanently loads and saves data (e.g. hard disk).

Users

Clearly, with the popularity of computers in the home and the workplace, the uses a computer system is put to are quite varied, and just as varied are the skills of its users.

Users can generally be divided into either IT (information technology) users or ICT practitioners, and although these are slowly becoming blurred, you are currently learning how to become a practitioner.

IT user

An IT user has basic proficiency using the computer system to achieve a set aim; this may typically be using a word processor, spreadsheet package or database. Most users at home fall into this category, as do employees who use basic IT to support their job.

IT users depend on easy-to-use interfaces in order to accomplish their tasks. They often have little technical appreciation of how the computer system actually works.

ICT practitioner

An ICT practitioner often has enhanced skills; for example, they are familiar with the hardware in a computer system or can program and develop web pages or build a network.

There are other common titles used in the workplace:

- **helpdesk support**: an employee assisting IT users with their technical problems
- **technician**: an employee diagnosing and fixing faults in hardware or software
- **administrator**: an employee managing a computer system or network.

Because of the professional demands of such jobs, ICT practitioners are generally higher paid and have to gain commercial (e.g. Microsoft®, Cisco®) and/or vocational qualifications, such as the First Diploma, in order to perform their roles satisfactorily.

Field experience (that is, successfully doing the job for real in the workplace for a number of years) is also a vital factor.

User interface

On a typical computer system, user interfaces come in two different varieties: **CLI** and **GUI**.

Command line interface (CLI)

CLIs are perhaps the oldest form of interface. They have the following characteristics:

- keyboard input
- short command names
- limited user help
- basic error or diagnostic message
- text display.

Perhaps the most famous CLI is **MS-DOS**® (Microsoft® disk operating system), whose appearance still exists as a **command prompt** in versions of the Microsoft Windows® operating system.

Figure 2.3 shows a typical view of a CLI.

A CLI can be used to input commands which the computer system typically executes when the **Enter** key is pressed. Erroneous commands usually generate a brief message indicating a

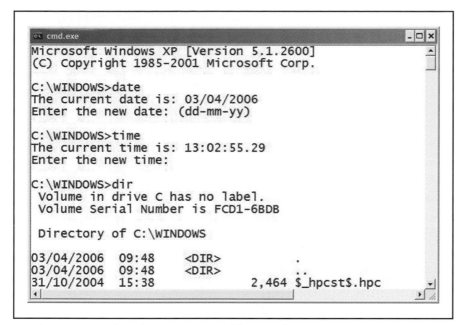

Fig. 2.3 A screenshot of a CLI (command line interface)

potential problem, but they are rarely user-friendly and often require technical knowledge to unravel.

While the CLI is often seen as an unfriendly environment where complex commands have to be remembered by the user, the trained practitioner can achieve rapid results with only a few keystrokes.

SCORECARD

- Not user-friendly
- Not very attractive
- Limited help for the user
- Limited input techniques (usually only keyboard)
- Error messages often unhelpful
+ Fast response, even on slower equipment
+ Proficient users can perform complex tasks quickly
+ Commands can be linked together to form automated scripts for regular jobs

Operating systems such as Unix® and various Linux® distributions make very effective use of their command line interfaces.

Graphical user interface (GUI)

A GUI (often pronounced 'gooey') is based on an earlier notion of a **WIMP** (windows, icons, menus and pointing devices) system, as developed in the early 1970s.

A GUI creates a user-friendly media-rich environment for users to explore, work and play within. Perhaps the most familiar GUI is the one presented by Microsoft Windows®, as shown in Figure 2.4.

Fig. 2.4 A screenshot the Microsoft Windows® XP desktop

The Apple Mac® OS X also makes extensive use of a GUI, as shown in Figure 2.5.

Fig. 2.5 A screenshot the Mac® OS X desktop

GUIs use a combination of pictures (icons), sound (beeps and tones) and natural 'point and click' selection with a mouse to enable the user to perform both simple and complex tasks.

In the older MS-DOS® CLI, to see the **contents of a hard disk** we would need to type:

DIR C: and press **Enter**.

In Microsoft Windows® we simply **double-click** on the hard disk **icon**, as demonstrated in Figure 2.6.

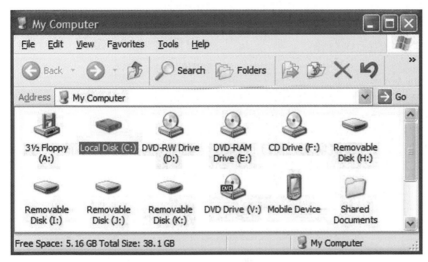

Fig. 2.6 Accessing the hard disk using a GUI

SCORECARD

- Complex GUIs may require faster processing
- Can be slow to respond
- Requires more hard disk space to install
- Uses more system resources (processor, memory, etc.) to run
+ User-friendly
+ Configurable environments to suit user's preferences
+ More comprehensive input device support
+ No need to remember complex instructions
+ Some basic operations take longer to complete than CLI alternative

Other interfaces are specialised because they may use different input techniques or output devices.

Examples of these may include **voice recognition** as an input tool (e.g. to state destination in a computer-controlled lift) or **biometric** reading of a fingerprint to open a computer-locked door or power on a notebook PC.

Hardware

Motherboard

As noted, the primary hardware component inside a computer system is called a **motherboard**. The motherboard is where all of the other components are **plugged in** or **connected**. This particular type is called **ATX** (advanced technology extended).

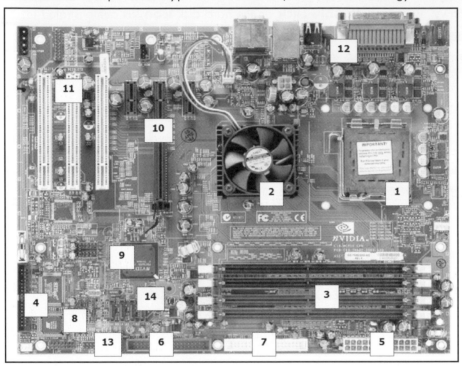

Fig. 2.7 A typical motherboard

Key

1. **Processor socket**: where the CPU is fitted
2. **Northbridge chip**: manages data traffic between faster motherboard components (RAM, CPU and AGP)
3. **RAM slots**: where memory is fitted
4. **FD (floppy drive) connector**
5. **Power socket**: where power from PSU (power supply unit) is connected
6. **IDE primary connector (PATA)**: connects to hard disk, CD-ROM, DVD, etc.
7. **IDE secondary connector (PATA)**: connects to hard disk, CD-ROM, DVD, etc.
8. **Basic input output system (BIOS) chip**
9. **Southbridge chip**: manages traffic between slower motherboard components
10. **PCI-Express slots** replacing older **Accelerated graphics port (AGP)**. PCE-E sockets are frequently used for newer graphics cards
11. **Peripheral component interconnect (PCI) expansion slots**

12 **External device connectors** (see Figure 2.8 for more detail)
13 **Front panel connector pins**: for connecting motherboard to case
14 **SATA (Serial ATA)** – modern connectors for hard disks, replacing **PATA**.

CPU

The CPU is the brain of the computer. The speed of the processor's internal clock is measured in hertz (Hz); this is a measurement of frequency.

For example, here are some commercial **CPU descriptions**:

AMD Sempron™ 2800+ 64Bit Architecture	1.6 GHz	Socket 754
Intel® Celeron® D 326	2.533 GHz	Socket 775
Intel® Pentium® 4	3.2 GHz	Socket 478

As you can see, modern processor speeds are measured in **gigahertz (GHz)**. It is tempting to compare processor power only in terms of **raw speed**, but this is not always accurate. A processor may have a faster clock speed, but may be **less efficiently constructed**. For example, a slower 64-bit processor may be able to process data **more efficiently** than a rival 32-bit processor with a faster clock speed. This is because the 64-bit processor can handle bigger chunks of data per clock 'tick'.

Motherboard 'chipset'

This is a combination of the microprocessors used in the Northbridge and Southbridge. Some chipsets are favoured because they are seen to have better performance or greater reliability when building systems. Some motherboards do not have a Southbridge, preferring to delegate its job to a group of smaller sub-processors.

RAM

Random-access memory, or RAM for short, is the **main memory** used by the computer when it is processing.

Data is stored here temporarily, as when the power is removed the data is lost; this is what we call **volatile** storage.

Modern RAM comes in the form of slim memory 'rails'. By far the most common form is the **DIMM** (dual in-line memory module). A special form of DIMM called **DDR** (double data rate) is even more efficient at retrieving and storing data, although this has recently been eclipsed by **DDR2** and **DDR3**, which are even faster.

RAM is often a key factor in good computer system performance and it is frequently better to add RAM generously to a system in order to ease an operating system's reliance on hard disk space as 'virtual' memory (which is slower).

Although suffering the occasional upwards blip due to demand outstripping supply, RAM prices have been consistently falling for the past few years.

By 2006, 512 MB of good quality, fast DDR RAM costs less than £25; that is roughly 5p per MB.

Floppy drive

Based on Sony technology originally dating back to 1983, the 3½-inch floppy diskette is probably one of the most recognisable forms of external backing storage. Although other disk formats have challenged it, few have been so popular. Floppy drives are a magnetic storage medium.

By the turn of the twenty-first century, however, the limited capacity of 1,474,560 bytes (roughly 1.44 MB) is seen as too small for many modern applications, and new computer systems are being built without floppy drives. Some notebooks and laptops keep their physical footprint small by excluding internal floppy drives; however, it is possible to connect external floppy drives if required.

Flash memory drives which connect via a universal serial bus (**USB**) are now set to replace them in everyday use.

By 2006, a floppy drive now costs as little as £5 and a single floppy disk as little as 15p.

Hard disk

Unlike a floppy drive, with removable media, hard disks are fixed inside the computer system's case. Like floppy drives, they are also a magnetic medium.

Hard disk units are more expensive than floppy drives, store vast amounts of data and spin at speeds of around 7200 **rpm** (revolutions per minute). Additionally, they access data (reading and writing) much, much faster (see data transfer table on page 54 for comparison).

Hard disks are often called **IDE** drives; this is because they have integrated drive electronics – circuits built into them which perform the basic task of controlling the drive's read/write heads and motor. Some texts also describe such drives as being **ATA** (advanced technology attachment), which is also correct.

By 2006, a 200 GB IDE drive can be purchased for approximately £60; this is roughly 1/10p per MB.

Optical technology

Unlike magnetic media, such as floppy disks and hard disks, optical drives such as **CD** (compact disc) and **DVD** use laser light to read data. As such, they are not prone to the corruption of magnetic interference.

Drives and discs can be **read-only** (e.g. **CD-ROM** and **DVD-ROM**). Such disks and drives cannot be used for recording as they have been officially manufactured. The drives will not be capable of writing any data.

Recordable and **rewritable** drives and disks exist for both CD and DVD technology. Some common formats are listed below:

- **CD-R**: compact disc recordable
- **CD-RW**: compact disc rewritable
- **DVD-R**: digital versatile disc recordable
- **DVD-RW**: digital versatile disc rewritable

Optical disc storage

Disc Type	Format	Storage capacity	Notes
CD-DA	Compact disc digital audio (i.e. a Music CD)	Typically 74 minutes of audio	
CD-ROM	Compact disc read-only memory	650 MB/700 MB	
CD-R	Compact disc recordable	650 MB/700 MB	
CD-RW	Compact disc rewritable	650 MB/700 MB	
DVD-5	Digital versatile disc, single layer, single-sided	4.7 GB	DVD±R/RW
DVD-9	Digital versatile disc, double layer, single-sided	8.5 GB	DVD±R
DVD-10	Digital versatile disc, single layer, double-sided	9.4 GB	DVD+R
DVD-18	Digital versatile disc, double layer, double-sided	17.1 GB	DVD+R

A newer optical technology called **Blu-ray** is also starting to appear on the market. Its first mainstream usage is likely to be within Sony's next gaming console, tentatively named the PlayStation® 3. Although it has the same 12 cm diameter as a DVD, it is thought capable of storing up to **200 GB** of data.

Flash storage

Since around 2002 the use of flash devices for storing data has become increasingly popular, although the technology was originally invented by IBM as early as 1998.

A flash device can also be known by a number of other names, including thumb drive, pen drive and USB stick. Being small and highly portable, they are commonly placed on key rings or lanyards.

A flash device is essentially a plastic casing containing a small printed circuit board (**PCB**), a flash memory chip (whose contents are electronically alterable) and a USB connector. When the device is plugged into a computer system's USB port, the device is recognised, drivers are loaded into memory and the device becomes usable as a regular disk drive.

As noted earlier, flash storage devices are rapidly becoming the preferred method of removable storage, although such electronic components are susceptible to electrostatic discharge (**ESD**), so should be treated carefully when not in use. Flash devices are available in sizes up to 64 GB.

By 2006, a high-quality 128 Mb flash drive costs approximately £7; this is roughly 5p per MB.

Input devices

Many different input devices exist. The purpose of any input device is to capture data and translate it into a machine-readable format (i.e. binary) so that it can be processed.

The most common input devices are listed below:

- **telephone handset** for **VOIP** (voice over internet protocol) phone calls
- **keyboard** for manual data entry of alphanumeric data
- **mouse** for point and click selection or drawing
- **joystick** for playing games
- **trackball** for precision operations, popular for **CAD** (computer-aided design) applications
- **graphics tablet** for hand-drawn computer graphics
- **scanner** for digitising images for editing or combining with text
- **digital camera** (also including **webcam** and **video camera**) for capturing still or moving images or video conferencing
- **touch screen** for simple user selection of basic menu choices, commonly used in public information terminals.

Some input devices employ **direct data capture** techniques, which bypass the user's need for **transcription** (e.g. reading and keying in) and **reduce** input errors.

Common direct data capture devices include:

- **Bar code reader**: as seen in high street shops when purchased goods are scanned for their stock information.
- **OMR**: (optical mark reader): a device which reads pencil marks on a specially printed pro forma. Multiple-choice exams are a common application of this technology.
- **OCR**: (optical character recognition): a method of reading and recognising printed characters when a page of text is scanned. Initially, OCR relied on special fonts, but modern technology can interpret handwriting with a high degree of accuracy. A similar technique is used with PDAs and tablet PCs.
- **Microphone**: for recording sounds and voice-recognition control.

Most input devices can connect to a modern PC using an external connector, typically USB.

Output devices

While it is true to say that the most common form of output device is the monitor, other output devices exist:

- **printer**: either laser or inkjet-based, used for mass printed output
- **plotter**: either flatbed or drum, used for printing technical line diagrams
- **speakers**: to output sound effects and play music
- **CAM** (computer-aided manufacture) tools: to control computerised manufacturing (e.g. automated lathes).

Again, most output devices connect simply to a modern PC using an external connector, typically USB for printers and plotters, while speakers connect to the sound card. (For more on printing devices see Unit 18: ICT Graphics.)

Internal expansion

It is common to add functionality to a computer system by plugging in new expansion boards. In fact, this one was of the first major selling points of the original IBM PC.

The most common type of expansion slots are:

- **ISA** (industry standard architecture), mainly obsolete as at 2006
- **PCI** (peripheral component interconnect)
- **AMR** (audio modem riser)
- **CNR** (communications and network riser)
- **ACR** (advanced communications riser)
- **AGP** (accelerated graphics port, sometimes referred to as advanced graphics port)
- **PCI Express**, phasing out PCI and AGP

Modern expansion slots tend to support the following types of expansion:

Type of expansion	ISA	PCI	AMR/CNR/ACR	AGP	PCI Express
Sound card	👍	👍	👍		
Modem (**mo**dulator **dem**odulator)	👍	👍	👍		
Network **i**nterface **c**ard (**NIC**)	👍	👍	👍		👍
Graphics card	👍	👍		👍	👍
Firewire card		👍			👍
USB card		👍			👍

A modern motherboard tends to have a variety of different quantities and types of expansion slot. Many of these types of expansion card are now **fully integrated into the motherboard** itself, reducing the importance of expansion slots somewhat. These all-in-one motherboards are quite popular with the hobby-builder and businesses.

(For more on expansion, see Unit 12: Installing Hardware Components.)

External connections

Although some devices are connected internally via motherboard expansion slots, other devices are simply plugged into the back of the motherboard via **ports** and **interfaces**.

Figure 2.8 shows a **rear view** of a motherboard, with its connectors.

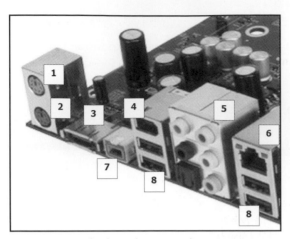

Fig. 2.8 A motherboard's external connections

Key

1 6-pin PS/2 mouse port (usually green)

2 6-pin PS/2 keyboard port (usually purple)

3 External SATA (Serial ATA) connector – a way of connecting modern hard disk technology which is replacing the older PATA (Parallel ATA) connection. SATA connectors are usually on the motherboard itself although external drives are becoming more popular.

4 6-pin Firewire 400 (also known as IEEE 1394, to connect video cameras, etc.)

5 Integrated sound card connectors: Analogue line-in (blue), analogue headphones or speakers (green) , analogue microphone (pink), S/PDIF (orange) for digital output and analogue output for rear speakers (black).

6 RJ45 connector for an Ethernet cable (to connect to a network, this is an integrated network interface card). Modern boards will use faster Gigabit Ethernet ports.

7 9-pin Firewire 800 (also known as IEEE 1394b)

8 USB ports (x 4). These are often paired. Modern USB ports are version 2.0.

The connections available on the back of a motherboard vary greatly from manufacturer to manufacturer and from model to model.

Some connections (PS/2 connections, older 9 and 25 pin serial and 25 pin parallel ports) are deemed to be 'legacy' (i.e. historic) technology. Currently, it is possible to buy motherboards which are legacy-free; they rely solely on USB ports for keyboard, mouse and printer connectivity.

If there is a blue 15-pin **VGA** (video graphics array) connector present it would indicate that the motherboard has an **IGP** (integrated graphics processor).

Data transfer speeds

The speed at which data is transferred can be measured and compared in order to design efficient and well-performing computer systems. When a component works slowly it creates a bottleneck for data movement.

Data speeds are often shown in two different formats: 2 Mbps or 2 Mbits/s. To simplify things, we will treat these as the same. In this case, we could say that data is travelling at 2 megabits per second.

The following comparative grids can be used to make basic components selections.

Connection types

Type	Data speed
9-pin serial	115,00 bit/s (maximum)
Parallel port (IEEE 1284)	2 Mbit/s (practically) 4 Mbit/s (theoretically)
USB 1.1	1.5 Mbit/s (low) 12 Mbit/s (full)
USB 2.0	480 Mbit/s (hi-speed)
Firewire (IEEE 1394)	100 Mbit/s 200 Mbit/s 400 Mbit/s (fastest)

Expansion slots

Type	Data speed	Frequency
ISA (16-bit)	2 Mbytes/s	8.33 MHz
PCI	133 Mbytes/s	33.33 MHz
AGP 1.0x	266 Mbytes/s	66 MHz
AGP 2.0x	533 Mbytes/s	133 MHz
AGP 4.0x	1066 Mbytes/s	266 MHz
AGP 8.0x	2133 Mbytes/s	533 MHz
PCI Express (x1)	500 Mbytes/s	
PCI Express (x16)	8 Gbytes/s	

RAM

Module	Type	Frequency	Bandwidth
PC100	SDRAM	100 MHz	0.80 Gbytes/s
PC133	SDRAM	133 MHz	1.07 Gbytes/s
PC1600	DDR200	100 MHz	1.6 Gbytes/s per channel
PC2100	DDR266	133 MHz	2.1 Gbytes/s per channel
PC2700	DDR333	166 MHz	2.7 Gbytes/s per channel
PC3200	DDR400	200 MHz	3.2 Gbytes/s per channel
PC2-3200	DDR2-400	100 MHz ×2	3.2 Gbytes/s
PC2-4200	DDR2-533	133 MHz ×2	4.2 Gbytes/s
PC2-5300	DDR2-667	166 MHz ×2	5.3 Gbytes/s
PC2-6400	DDR2-800	200 MHz ×2	6.4 Gbytes/s

Backing storage

Media	Data transfer rate
Floppy disk	500 Kbytes/s
Hard drive ATA 100	100.00 Mbytes/s
Hard drive ATA 133	133.00 Mbytes/s
Hard drive (Serial ATA)	150.00 Mbytes/s to 300 Mbytes/s
CD-ROM ×1	0.15 Mbytes/s
CD-ROM ×52	7.8 Mbytes/s
DVD-ROM ×1	1.39 Mbytes/s
DVD-ROM ×12	16.62 Mbytes/s

Connectivity

Apart from linking systems via parallel, serial or USB cables, modern connectivity to a computer system is achieved with either a **modem** or an **NIC** (network interface card).

A modem is typically used in **dial-up** connections via telephone lines. Its job is to convert the computer system's digital signals into the analogue signals used on the older telephone system. Another modem at the receiving end would then reverse this operation to allow the server (or other workstation) to read the incoming data.

Outside of commercial applications, modems were originally used to connect enthusiasts to (now) primitive-looking **bulletin board services** (BBS), and then, towards the mid-1990s, to the Internet itself. These types of temporary connection are called **narrowband** services, and, at the time, could be very expensive, as billing was based on every second of time actually spent connected.

Modems were not fast, the fastest connections being around just 56 Kbit/s. The slowness of dial-up connections readily became apparent as more and more websites became graphically intensive – a dial-up user could wait many, many minutes for a page to load. The gradual shift to broadband connections changed all this.

Broadband connections can be achieved using an NIC and a **cable modem**. The cable modem is typically connected to another cable modem at the user's **ISP** (internet service provider) via a cable television infrastructure; this is generally called 'cable Internet access'. An NIC typically works at 10 or 100 Mbits/s.

Another broadband solution is asymmetric digital subscriber line (**ADSL**). This is a form of data communications technology that enables faster data transmission over standard copper telephone lines than the older dial-up modem can provide. In order to connect to an ADSL service, an ADSL modem must be connected to the computer system. This can be achieved via USB or a standard NIC. The cable modem's location has to be typically within a range of 3 miles (5 km) of an ADSL-enabled telephone exchange.

(For wireless technologies, please see Unit 16: Mobile Communications Technology.)

Systems software

It is important to get systems software right when building a computer system. Perhaps the most important types of system software is the operating system (**OS**).

The relationship between the OS and the hardware is shown in Figure 2.9.

Although the BIOS performs **basic hardware management**, the more complete and featured OS is needed to act as a **bridge** between the applications software and the BIOS layers.

We have already touched on the features of an OS when looking at the command line and graphical user interfaces.

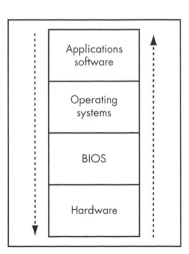

Fig. 2.9 Relationship between the OS and hardware

However, an operating system has more jobs to do than just provide an interface for the user!

A typical OS is responsible for:

- **disk defragmentation** (to regroup files which have become 'split up' on a disk)
- **hardware management** (including drivers to allow the computer to talk to its devices)
- **memory management** (allocating memory for different programs to use)
- **disk filing system** (for organising file storage on a hard disk)
- **task scheduling** (for running other programs and services)
- **network support** (to support network communications and sharing of network resources).

Additionally, there are other **utility programs**, which also form part of the systems software suite and naturally complement the operating system.

These utilities include:

- **diagnostic tools** (to discover and repair system faults)
- **disk repair** (to mend corrupted or damaged data files)
- **anti-virus** (to remove viruses and protect against future infection)
- **file managers** (to copy, rename, move, delete large numbers of files)
- **program development environments** (to create bespoke programs in languages such as C, Visual Basic, C++, Java).

Applications software

Applications software, when used in conjunction with an operating system, performs **specific tasks** for the user.

There are many different types of applications software, but the common ones include:

- **office software** (e.g. word processor, spreadsheet, database, presentation)
- **business and industrial software** (e.g. **CAD** – computer aided design, **DTP** – desktop publishing)
- **communication software** (e.g. email, chat programs, instant messaging etc)
- **educational software** (e.g. **CAL** – computer-aided learning, **VLE** – virtual learning environments)
- **games**
- **specialist** (e.g. speech recognition, route planners).

Knowing what type of software to install on a computer system can be difficult. The core aims should be to know:

- user's requirements (what they actually need to do)
- The hardware and operating system being used (what the computer can run).

Both these factors will help determine which application software to install. Three basic options may be available:

- **commercially available solution**: a package bought off the shelf in a shop, by mail order or online
- **tailored solution**: a commercial package which has been tweaked or customised to perform certain tasks required by the user
- **bespoke solution**: a solution which has been created specifically for the user by a paid developer.

The advantages and disadvantages of these different options can be seen in the following table:

	Advantages	**Disadvantages**
Commercially available solution	Available immediately Large user base Support available	Compromises have to be made Does not meet needs very well
Tailored solution	Quick to implement Product is well tested, as based on an existing product	Some compromises are made Does not meet some needs
Bespoke solution	Will meet user's needs exactly Professional product May give business advantage	Can be expensive Not immediate (takes time) Support will cost extra Training will be needed

Compatibility

Checking compatibility between hardware and software is a vital factor when building a computer system.

An **OS** typically has requirements which must be met by the **hardware** before installing.

An **applications software** package also often has technical requirements that must be met by the **hardware and the OS** before installing.

Hardware requirements typically involve:

- **processor**: is it fast enough?
- **memory**: is there enough RAM to run the software?
- **graphics card**: is it powerful enough to display the correct images?
- **hard disk**: is there enough space left to install the program?
- **optical drive**: for installation media
- **internet access**: for online updates, registration or connectivity.

It should be remembered that there will be both a **minimum required** and a **recommended** list of requirements. The minimum requirements will get the program actually **running**; the recommended requirements get it **working acceptably well**. An application's requirements usually also require a specific version of the OS in order to run (e.g. Microsoft Windows® XP with service pack 2), as well as the more common hardware list.

Here is an example **minimum requirements** list:

> **Here's what you need to use Windows® XP Home Edition**
>
> - PC with 300 megahertz (MHz) or higher processor clock speed recommended; 233-MHz minimum required; Intel Pentium/Celeron family, AMD K6/Athlon/Duron family, or compatible processor recommended
> - 128 megabytes (MB) of RAM or higher recommended (64 MB minimum supported; may limit performance and some features)
> - 1.5 gigabyte (GB) of available hard disk space
> - Super VGA (800 × 600) or higher resolution video adapter and monitor
> - CD-ROM or DVD drive
> - Keyboard and Microsoft Mouse or compatible pointing device

Source: http://www.microsoft.com/windowsxp/home/evaluation/sysregs.mspx

While Microsoft Windows® XP will run on this computer system specification, the hardware is rather modest and would not give the optimum user experience.

Health and safety

Although Unit 12: Installing Hardware Components tackles this subject in more detail, it is useful to touch on the important health and safety issues here.

When installing new hardware you should:

- use an anti-static wrist-strap when installing components
- only use the correct tools
- be careful when using tools
- be careful of sharp edges inside computer cases when installing network cards
- switch off mains sockets before plugging in mains cables
- only switch on a mains socket when all mains cables are in place and plugged in
- do not leave trailing cables that can be tripped over.

Other factors which could pose problems include manual handling, where there is guidance from the UK's **HSE** (Health and Safety Executive), recommending maximum **safe loads** and recommended **postures** for lifting, lowering, pushing and pulling heavy equipment.

Additionally, health and safety issues also apply to IT users, particularly with regard to:

- **DSE** (display screen equipment) – for workstation ergonomics, user's posture and reduction/prevention of eyestrain
- **RSI** (repetitive strain injury) – a soft tissue injury typically resulting from poor posture, bad ergonomics, stress, and repetitive motion.

Most organisations would have a **risk assessment** procedure and a local **Health and Safety officer**, who would ensure compliance with any relevant legislation.

Configuration of software

As you are probably aware, modern software is highly customisable; it can be altered functionally and aesthetically to suit a user's personal tastes.

The following list contains some common customisations:

- **appearance** of the user interface (the 'skin' or theme)
- use of **short cuts** (to popular files or programs)
- **toolbars**
- **automation** of common tasks (e.g. macros, wizards)
- **privacy** settings
- **input** settings (e.g. keyboard repeat rate, mouse sensitivity, voice control)
- **display** settings (e.g. screen resolution)
- **audio feedback**
- **accessibility** settings
- **additional functionality** via optional plug-ins.

Personalisation

Most computer systems, no matter how big or small, permit personalisation – letting the user tweak the appearance of the software to reflect their own likes and dislikes. This is particularly true for a GUI.

Common customisations of the GUI include:

- desktop arrangement of icons
- wallpaper image
- mouse settings
- date/time setting
- screen saver
- task bar settings
- shortcuts.

Let us examine one of these in more detail. The **screen saver** is an **animated picture** or text display that prevents '**burn-in**' on CRT monitors (where non-moving images permanently mark the phosphorous coating on the screen and leave a 'ghost'). The screen saver is perhaps one of the most personal choices a user can make, often displaying their favourite film star, sports hero or family pet.

Modern screen savers also incorporate **passwords** – this is useful if a workstation is left unattended in an open-access environment (e.g. an open-plan office), as it prevents others from accessing the machine without permission.

Screen savers can be installed via a removable media (e.g. floppy disk) or downloaded directly from the Internet. In Microsoft Windows® XP, access to the Screen Saver settings is via the **Display Properties** dialogue box.

Fig. 2.10 Microsoft Windows® XP Display Settings dialog

Commercial screen savers are also available for download, although some (from less reputable websites) often contains viruses and Trojan Horses, so care should be exercised before installing.

(Other customisations are covered in Unit 8: Customising Applications Software.)

Security

There are many threats to data stored on a modern computer system.

Some threats are accidental in nature:

- **user error**, such as accidentally deleting a file or program
- **media failure**, such as floppy disks or CDs suddenly not reading properly
- **hardware failure**, such as a hard disk not being recognised by the BIOS.

Some are the result of **malicious actions**:

- **viruses**: programs which corrupt files or hijack services
- **spyware**: programs which send sensitive user data
- **data theft**: data being stolen by physical or networked means
- **physical theft or damage**: breaking or stealing hardware devices or components
- **hacking**: professional or amateur attempts to disrupt computer systems to which they have no legitimate access.

A number of malicious actions are legislated under the **Computer Misuse Act 1990**.

Data loss can be prevented by:

- **anti-virus software**: software to prevent virus infection or execution
- regular **backup** of data: a regular procedure to make an official copy of important data
- use of **firewall**: hardware or a program which filters unwanted network data
- **physical security**: locks, secured card-swipe doors, anti-tamper devices, video surveillance, etc.

(Although covered briefly here, the subject of security is discussed in more detail in Unit 17: Security of ICT systems.)

Working Practices

For the ICT practitioner, the task of installing new hardware or software follows standard procedures that are typically laid down by their organisation as **best practice**.

This would typically include:

- **assessing and minimising risks**: observing Health and Safety regulations
- **obtaining resources**: hardware, software or paperwork required
- **recording relevant information**: logging actions performed
- **communicating progress**: keeping interested parties informed of how the job is progressing, any problems encountered or changes of plan
- **communicating outcomes**: telling interested parties what impact the installation has on the system (good or bad).

(For more detail on working practices, please refer to Unit 12: Installing Hardware Components and Unit 13: Software Installation and Upgrade.)

☆ **Activity**

In order to run new accounting software for completing his tax returns, Steve Hodder of SHS has decided to update his personal PC. He has been given two competitive quotes and specifications from two local companies.

Using your computer systems expertise, examine the two specifications and decide which purchase is better value for money (VFM).

> QUOTE I
>
> - Microsoft® Windows® XP Home Edition
> - AMD Sempron™ 64 3000+ processor
> - 512 MB DDR RAM (PC3200)
> - 160 GB SATA 7200 spm hard drive
> - On-board Direct 2D/4D graphics
> - 17" Viewsonic VE710B TFT LCD monitor
>
> **Price:** £499.00 inc. VAT

QUIZ

1. Convert the following denary numbers into binary:
    a) 19
    b) 120
    c) 340
2. Convert the following binary numbers into denary:
    a) 10110
    b) 101111
    c) 101010
3. How many bytes in 2 KB?
4. How many bits in 4 bytes?
5. How many kilobytes in 4 MB?
6. Match the description to the correct units:
    i)   A measurement of data transfer   a) Hz
    ii) A measurement of hard disk rotation   b) MBit/s
    iii) A measurement of memory capacity   c) rpm
    iv) A measurement of frequency   d) MB
7. Which expansion slot is faster: ISA, PCI or AGP?
8. Name 3 typical utilities.
9. Meeting which hardware requirement usually yields better results: minimum or recommended?
10. Name 2 common IT user Health and Safety issues.

ANSWERS

1. (a) 10011
    (b) 1111000
    (c) 101010100
2. (a) 22
    (b) 47
    (c) 42
3. 2048 bytes

4. 32 bits
5. 4096 kilobytes
6. i   = b
    ii = c
    iii = d
    iv = a
7. AGP
8. Diagnostic tools
    Disk repair
    Disk defragmentation
    Anti-virus
    File management
    Program development environment
9. Recommended
10. DSE, RSI

COURSEWORK GUIDANCE

To pass this unit you will need to show that you understand the different aspects of computer systems, that you can identify different computer types and their purposes, describe the role of command line and GUI operating systems, and specify applications software to meet user needs.

In practical terms, you will be asked to demonstrate that you can connect computers and peripherals and that you can configure software for a given user.

You will need to be able to show that you can work safely and that you understand the security and legal issues surrounding the use of computers.

Part of working with computer systems is that you can demonstrate solid skills, but also that you can demonstrate thoroughness through careful checking of your work.

Merit and distinction criteria for this unit are centred on justifying your choices and evaluating aspects of computer systems.

Unit links

This unit has direct links to the following:

Unit 6   Networking Essentials
Unit 8   Customising Applications
             Software
Unit 12 Installing Hardware
             Components
Unit 13 Software Installation and
             Upgrade
Unit 16 Mobile Communications
             Technology

Unit 17 Security of ICT systems
Unit 18 ICT Graphics

As one of the two core units for the programme, it should be understood that this unit underpins all other units in the scheme.

Edexcel also show links to:

Unit 14 Technical Fault Diagnosis and
             Remedy

●●●Further reading

MacRae, K., *The Computer Manual: The Step-by-Step Guide to Upgrading and Repairing a PC* (Haynes Group, 2002) ISBN: 1859608884

Rathbone, A., *Windows XP for Dummies*, 2nd edn (Hungry Minds Inc., US, 2004) ISBN: 0764573268

White, R. and Downs, T., *How Computers Work* (Que, 2003) ISBN: 0789730332

Progress check

To record your achievement, simply tick the criteria awarded to you when each assignment is returned (you may be given three assignments for this unit, U2.01, U2.02 and U2.03 – the final column may not be used). There is a full copy of this grid available on the accompanying CD. The copy will also allow you to record your key skill achievement against Literacy, Numeracy and ICT objectives.

	Assignments in this Unit			
Assignment	**U2.01**	**U2.02**	**U2.03**	**U2.04**
Referral				
Pass				
1				
2				
3				
4				
5				
6				
7				
Merit				
1				
2				
3				
4				
Distinction				
1				
2				
3				

A completed sample of this document (for reference purposes) can be found at the back of Unit 1.

ICT PROJECT

INTRODUCTION

A project is an activity that results from an organisation identifying a need or failure in its processes and systems. This activity is temporary and lasts until the replacement systems are in place and have been evaluated.

Sometimes the solution to a problem is to simply purchase an application (**off-the-shelf** package), such as accounting package from Sage. The project team should investigate whether a suitable package already exists and, if so, how much it costs. In the event that there is a close off-the-shelf match, but the application needs a little modification to be exactly right, this is known as a **tailored** solution. The final electronic option is to create a product completely from scratch (**bespoke**), using programming or web design software. It is important for project developers to consider a fourth option, which would be to create a manual solution (one with paper records and files). Computerisation might well be the best solution, but it should not automatically be assumed that this is the case. Ultimately, the project will have a budget and a timescale which need to be observed. In most situations a project is undertaken by a team of developers who work together to investigate, design, build and test a solution. In the case of this unit, however, there will only be one developer – YOU!

In general, projects are fun because they provide an opportunity to watch products grow from the kernel of an idea, through development, to eventual completion and implementation.

Learning outcomes

On completion of this unit you should:

1 understand use of models and activities involved in projects and some key factors that influence them

2 be able to identify requirements for a particular project, gathering relevant information as required, and create a project plan

3 be able to execute a project and monitor progress within identified resources and timescale

4 review a project and test the new product or system.

Understand the use of models in project development

Key term

Models: a project model is effectively a **recipe for undertaking a project**. Consider it in terms of a cake recipe. The recipe has a list of ingredients (for a project, this will be a list of the resources needed to complete the project) and a method (series of steps to follow).

A project model therefore is a **set of steps** that you will need to go through to **ensure** the **successful completion** of the project.

There are many project models, which vary considerably in their complexity. The simplest model is known as **plan-do-review**.

Simple models

In considering the plan-do-review model it is often helpful to visualise it as a **cycle**.

The project needs to be fully **planned**, taking a number of factors into consideration. Once the planning has been undertaken, the **implementation** (doing) phase starts, and the solution is formally developed. Finally, the solution is **uploaded** onto the client's system and **used** for an agreed period. It is then **reviewed** (evaluated) against a set of criteria.

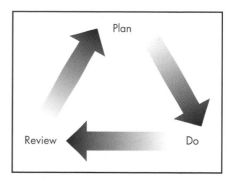

Fig. 3.1 Project model

It is possible that the use and evaluation of the developed solution might lead to new plans being needed:

- There may be a need to further **enhance** the current solution (because some additional minor functionality is needed).
- The solution may become completely **inadequate** (too much needs to be changed or added).
- **Technology has advanced** (the organisation would like to take advantage of this).

The whole process may well begin again!

In order to be able to plan the project, the project itself needs to be **defined** (that is, it needs to be identified and described).

Choosing a project can be a difficult decision to make, but it is likely that you will either be given an idea for a project or you will be allowed to choose what you would like to do. If you are allowed to choose, you could select a project that simply sparks your interest, or a real project for an organisation or individual. Whatever project you select, you should agree it with a tutor, as he or she will help you to monitor your own progress.

As a guide, when you choose a project you should:

- Consider your **strengths** and **weaknesses** (e.g. you may be a good programmer, have excellent Microsoft Office® or website skills, or have technical skills that would enable you to advise on the implementation of a network).
- Choose something that really **interests** you.
- Ensure that the project is **realistic** (that it can be done **within the identified constraints** – constraints are the **limits** within which you will develop the project, such as time, money, skills, available technology, which will be discussed later).

Factors that influence projects

There are a number of **internal and external factors** that you should consider when you are planning a project. These factors include internal issues, such as the skills that are available to support the project:

- **technical skills**: there is little point in choosing to work with software or a programming language you have never seen!
- **transferable skills**: such as time management, planning skills, communication skills
- **external issues**: such as resources you have available to you, including money, hardware, software, and so on
- **training of staff**: do the client's staff already have any related skills, or will these need to be learned?

Money

Most organisations have a limited budget when it comes to project development. It is usual that the developer (you) will be given an idea of how much the organisation can afford to spend. You have to calculate whether it is possible to develop a solution within the budget allocated. All aspects of the project need to be evaluated in terms of financial cost:

- **upgrades to hardware**: is a new computer required or can parts of existing systems be upgraded
- **upgrades to the operating system**
- **software**: this will include any development costs for bespoke systems
- **installation costs**: including cabling for electrical points or networks.

At this stage, if the finance allocated seems insufficient, you would have to return to the client and ask for more, justifying the need for the extra expenditure.

Timescales

As with finance, the organisation will have an idea about how quickly the solution needs to be implemented. The more complex the solution, the longer it will usually take to implement. There is also a notion that the longer the project takes to develop, the more the solution is likely to cost, as more work will be required. Calculating the cost and the timescales involved is easier once the requirements of the project are known.

From a development perspective, the plan that is ultimately created should contain:

* **milestones**
* dates when **interim reviews** will take place
* **handover date**.

Requirements

Purpose of project

A project usually begins either with an idea or because an organisation has identified a problem or inadequacy in current practices that needs to be rectified. This is known as the **project proposal.**

The idea or problem is usually discussed by managers and/or users until, finally, a project proposal is identified and put into words. It is extremely important that you get a proposal **signed**, as being a true reflection of the problem or idea. The reason for this is to ensure that all those who are involved in the project (both you and the client) have an **accurate record** of what has been agreed. It is then less likely that further down the line you will be told, 'But that's not what we meant…!'

Why a solution is needed

The solution needs to be **justified** and this is done in terms of the **business benefits** that the organisation will gain from implementing the project. The following are some of the benefits that could be gained from a solution:

* **improved customer service**: for example, a quicker response to customer requests
* **cost savings**: fewer staff can process more work
* **extra sales revenue**: due to better marketing information (being able to analyse customer information can help organisations target products more effectively)
* **improved cash flow** position: invoices go out faster
* **better stock control**: less money tied up in superfluous stocks
* **improved staff morale**: jobs are made easier
* **less duplication of effort**: delivery note and invoice created simultaneously by the system rather than having to type one after the other
* **better management information**: computerised systems have the ability to produce information faster than manual methods, so managers can identify problems earlier.

Who it is for

The anticipated **users** of the system need to be **identified**, in terms of the **likely number** of users. Which **functional areas** (e.g. sales, purchasing, manufacturing) of the organisation that will make use of the system also need to be established. This will give you an indication about how much data will be input and output from the system and how much data will need to be stored, searched and manipulated (**volume of data**).

Inputs and outputs

You will need to establish what **inputs** the system will need to handle and what **outputs** the user will expect the system to produce.

What data will be **input** into the system? For example:

- **customer details**: names, addresses, telephone numbers and contacts
- **supplier details**: names, addresses, telephone numbers and contacts
- **sales orders**: customer details, quantity, description and price of items ordered, sales representative ID
- **purchase orders**: supplier details, quantity, description and price of items ordered
- **stock information**: part number, part name, description, cost price and resale price, quantity in stock, minimum stock level.

What data will be **output** from the system? For example:

- **customer lists**: a list of all the company's customers
- **single customer information**: using a search facility
- **supplier lists**: a list of all the company's suppliers
- **single supplier information**: using a search facility
- **sales delivery notes**
- **sales invoices**
- **sales analysis**: customer buying patterns, sales representative performance
- **stock levels**: how much of each item is in stock
- **stock exception reports**: low stock or high stock, reorder instructions.

At this stage, the actual specifics of the information are not required, just an idea of what will go into the system and what will be required of it.

Processes

Calculations will clearly be required on orders and invoices, first calculating the total of the order or invoice, but also calculating VAT.

Key term

Value added tax

This is a tax which is charged by all businesses that have a turnover in excess of £58,000 per year. This is known as the VAT threshold. This figure is reviewed each year by the government.

(For further information, see Unit 1: Using ICT to Present Information.)

The term **processing** also includes any other activities that take place using the stored data. Examples would be **using criteria** to **search** data (printing a list of customers in a specified location) or **ordering data** in a **defined way**. Processing is usually what generates the outputs from the system.

Timescale

This is found by working backwards from the final deadline (the point in time by which the organisation would like the system up and running) to the start date.

Documentation

Most organisations expect a developer to provide documentation to support the system. This documentation is likely to be from two perspectives: **user** and **technical**.

The first thing you need to understand about documentation is that it needs to look professional. Poorly presented documentation makes clients doubt the **quality** of the product. This means that the documentation should not contain any spelling or typing errors. It should be interesting to look at and easy to navigate, so a contents page, for example, is a must. Below is a list of usual contents for each of the documentation types.

User documentation

- **How to access the program**
- **Basic instructions** for using each of the features (both for inputs and for any reports that the system generates)
- Separate instructions for any **advanced functionality**
- A **troubleshooting guide** – what to do when things go wrong
- A **glossary** of error messages, what they mean and what users should do if they see such a message
- **FAQ** – frequently asked questions.

The user documentation is easier to read if it includes images. As such, it is usual to include screen captures. Apart from anything else, it improves the appearance of the document.

Technical documentation

This is a formal record of the system and is used to support its maintenance. The typical contents would include:

- **Basic structure of the tables or files** that the system uses (these are created during the design activities)
- **Printouts of macros** (or sometimes of programming code in the case of bespoke solutions)
- **Validation routines**
- **Structure of queries and reports**
- **Inputs masks** (if appropriate)
- **Security routines** (e.g. passwords).

Constraints

Any constraints that may be relevant to the project are identified. Money and timescales have already been considered earlier in this unit.

Other constraints could also exist, such as **lack of skills** – the developer or development team might need to do additional research in order to implement some aspects of the project.

From an organisational perspective, there could also be issues such as:

- **training**: how much time will users lose from doing their own jobs while they receive training?
- **space**: is there sufficient space to accommodate new equipment, or will there be a need to reorganise the working environment?
- potential **redundancy of staff**: could such staff be used elsewhere in the organisation?

Capacity

- You should understand the **amounts of data** that will need to be **processed** by the system.
- **How many users** will be using the system at any one time?
- **How much data** will need to be stored?

These considerations will have a physical bearing on the computer hardware employed. This will be investigated as part of the **gathering information** phase of the project.

Usability

Decisions need to be made about the systems usability from three perspectives: **ease of use, access and disability, interfaces.**

Ease of use

If the organisation has an existing computer system, it is likely that there will already be employees with IT user skills. Alternatively, there might be no one in the organisation who has any real skills in this area and **training** will need to be provided. Either way, you need to decide how basic the system will need to be to accommodate those who are going to use it. In general, ease of use refers to how easy it will be for users to interact with the system and execute tasks.

Access and disability issues, and user interfaces

If there are less able users in the organisation, this might have an impact on the types of hardware that are purchased. A mouse (see Figure 3.2) might need to be replaced with a trackball (see Figure 3.3). Users may require ergonomic keyboards (see Figure 3.4) or a graphics tablet (see Figure 3.5).

Fig. 3.2 Mouse

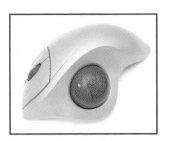

Fig. 3.3 Trackball

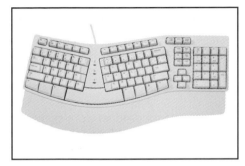

Fig. 3.4 Ergonimic keyboard

Fig. 3.5 Graphics tablet

There are clearly other devices that can be used to **access the system** and **capture data** that might also need to be considered, such as **OMR readers**. These readers are designed to process pen (or pencil) marks that are situated in predetermined positions on forms.

The client may want a system that has a command line interface (CLI), as shown in Figure 3.7.

This type of interface requires users to respond to **prompts** and **key in responses** via a **keyboard**.

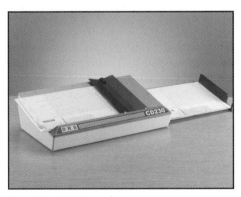

Fig. 3.6 OMR reader

Most modern systems use what is known as a **WIMP** (windows, icons, menus, pointing devices). These systems are much more visual in nature and are **easier to navigate** and use.

An additional way of interacting with a system is through **voice recognition**. This requires a microphone and specialist software that converts words that are spoken by the user into text. There are also a series of keywords and phrases that the user must learn (and use) to manipulate the text.

Fig. 3.7 Command line interface example

The project

The plan-do-review model gives you a basis for project management and product development. This in itself needs to be broken down into a number of activities, as explored below.

Planning activities

Once a project has been selected, the next step is to write an **outline proposal**. This should reflect what the actual project is to do and why (**justification**). The description should explain the problem and what a solution would be designed to achieve. Using the skateboard company as an example:

> The proposal is to develop a stock system for Steve Hodder Skateboards (SHS). The system is needed to enable the organisation to monitor the movement of stock. This will allow the company to calculate how much money is invested in stock, and which items sell best and worst (so that they can consider stocking more of those items that sell well and fewer of the items that sell less well).

Notice that in the above proposal no indication has been given about **how** the problem will be solved. It **does not** identify any particular solution (such as Microsoft Access® or Microsoft Visual Basic®). It merely **suggests** that the answer to the organisation's difficulty may well be a stock system. At this stage, it is not even indicated that this will be an electronic (computerised) solution.

Consider alternatives

The next step in the process is to **consider** possible **alternative solutions**. These alternatives are likely to be an electronic system or a manual one.

Electronic options: in the first instance, you need to check to see whether an **application** already exists that will fully satisfy the user's requirements and solve the problem. Such a solution would already have the right structure and would only require the input of the company's data to implement it. If such a product exists, it will be offered as one potential alternative. You should remember, however, to check that the application is compatible with your client's system – there is not much point in buying software that runs on Microsoft

Windows® XP, if the client only has Microsoft Windows® ME. To ensure that there will not be any difficulties, you should always check that the specification of the machine is at least the same, or better, than the software requires.

The second potential electronic solution is to create a **tailored system** using products such as Microsoft® Office. This would be considered a tailored solution because the developer has to manipulate the software to create the final solution (for example, s/he needs to create tables, queries, forms, reports and a menu system in Microsoft® Access, prior to the input of data).

The third electronic solution would be to create a **bespoke** solution (a product programmed from scratch, using a language such as C, Visual Basic or Java).

Manual option: depending on the problem, it is possible that the solution might be to implement a **manual solution** (physical paper records). However, while this is certainly a valid option, it is unlikely to provide a long-term solution to the problem.

To compare the possible solutions, it may well be useful to create a table of information about the investigation into the four alternatives. Doing so will better enable a comparison to be made.

	How expensive is the solution?	How much develop-ment time is required?	Do I have the skills to develop this alternative?	What are the hardware requirements?	Will the solution solve the problem?
Off-the-shelf application	Expensive	Zero	Not applicable	No change required	Mostly
Tailored application	Moderate	4 months	Yes – good skills	Minimal upgrade	Yes
Bespoke	Expensive	9 months	Yes – some skills	Minimal upgrade	Yes
Manual	Inexpensive	3 months	Yes	Not applicable	Only in the short term

How the decision is made ultimately will depend on the organisation's priorities. Clearly, if the decision is to have an **electronic** solution in **less than 6 months**, that automatically discounts the bespoke and manual options. Once this has been decided, the project can move forward.

The other aspect of the project that might need to be considered is what the company already has in terms of computer hardware and software. To establish this, you will need to gather information.

Gathering information

You should consider the following:

- **Does the organisation already have any computers?** If yes, how many and what are their specifications? Will they have the capacity to run the proposed solution?

- **Will the solution need to be networked?** If yes, does the organisation already own any technology? Is there cabling in place or will this need to be installed?
- **Does the organisation have any software?** (This includes both operating system and any other software that might be needed to make use of data in your solution.) If yes, what is it and will there be any compatibility issues?
- **How much money does the company have to spend on the project?**
- **What will the system need to do?** What processes will it need to execute?
- **What data will need to be stored?** How will the data need to be manipulated (e.g. queried or reported)?

To answer these questions, you will need to gather information from the organisation using a number of alternative techniques: **questionnaires**, **observation**, **interview** and **market research** are the most common. Each of these techniques has advantages and disadvantages.

Questionnaire

Questionnaires are **documents** containing a series of **directed questions**, which need to be answered by **respondents** (in the case of a project, the respondents – the people who fill in the questionnaire – would be the eventual users of the system). The data is then collected and analysed and conclusions are drawn based on the user responses.

SCORECARD

+ Useful where you need to ask a large number of potential users a series of questions
+ Each person is asked the same questions, which makes analysing the answers much easier
+ Respondents will feel at ease when completing the questionnaire, particularly if the questionnaire is anonymous
+ Questionnaires are particularly useful for gathering facts that are quantifiable (you can estimate how many times something occurs, for example)
- Questions must be simple and their meaning clear so that they cannot be misinterpreted
- If the questionnaire was completed anonymously the developer might not be able to seek clarification for any unclear responses
- It is difficult to ensure that the respondent is actually telling the truth

Observation

This is where the developer or another member of the project team physically **observes an employee** while they are working, so that they can establish exactly what the employee does, how they do it and who they work with in order to accomplish the task.

Interview

Interviews are conducted to establish users' **needs** and **thoughts** on the development of the solution.

Market research

With some systems it might be appropriate to undertake **market research**. This is particularly useful if the solution is likely to be made available to a **range** of businesses (e.g. all schools or sports clubs). Alternatively, the software might be intended for the **general public**, in which case, research would need to be undertaken with potential buyers.

Market research is usually undertaken by **specialist research companies** who are paid to survey the public (you may have seen them in your town or city). They usually have the right structure and techniques to reach a large number of **respondents** and the ability to handle and **interpret** the data gathered.

Defects in information

All techniques do have one thing in common. The **data is not always reliable**. As such, most organisations that are undertaking fact-finding exercises **do not rely on a single technique**. They are more likely to use a number of different strategies to check the validity of the information gained. For example; while a questionnaire might be used to gather information from a large number of users, it is likely that the developer and his/her team will also interview and observe some of the users as well. You should consider very carefully which techniques you will use and in what combination you will use them.

Any information that is subject to analysis should also be checked carefully before it is used to support decisions made when developing the project.

Preserving (upholding or keeping) confidentiality

A developer should always be aware that organisations may well have **sensitive information** that needs to remain **confidential**. It is absolutely vital that developers and members of the team treat this information with respect and that they do not divulge anything to a third party (anyone outside the organisation).

Once the above information has been obtained, calculations are made to establish exactly how much the system will cost, and this price will be compared with the allocated budget so that decisions can be made about whether to proceed. If the project is to continue, the developers will need to produce a **project plan**.

Produce project plan

To move the project forward, the next step is to create a project plan. This is where all the **tasks** that will need to be undertaken are **identified**. Developers should always carefully consider these tasks and whether they should be **broken down into smaller tasks**. Either way, the tasks should include the following:

- analysing the current system (gathering information)
- designing a solution
- developing the solution
- testing the solution
- reviewing and evaluating the solution

It is often useful to write up the project plan as an **ordered list**. The list should have the tasks shown in the order that they should be undertaken; it should indicate **milestones** (or **deadlines**) by which the different tasks should have been completed; it should identify any **resources** that are required to achieve the task; and a column for you to include any comments about the task or anything else that should be considered.

Task	By when	Resources needed	Comments

Ensure that the plan is **realistic!** The plan should contain **recovery** or **catch-up time** that will be available if there is a problem during the development. Remember also to include sufficient time to **test your product**. Most developers will agree that the time allowed for testing should be about 50 per cent of the total development time. This is because testing has a number of phases that should be considered to ensure a robust product.

Do not forget that when the project plan is created, it should contain:

- **specific milestones**: points where tasks should have been completed
- **interim review dates**: where you and the client get together to review progress
- the **final date** on the project plan: this should reflect the final **handover date**, as previously agreed with the client.

Once complete, the plan should be **checked by the client**. In the case of a First Diploma project, the plan should be checked with a tutor, who will effectively act as the client.

Gain permission to proceed

It is important to agree a project plan to ensure that it is realistic. The client will want to know **how much** the project is going to **cost**, both in terms of the solution being developed and any changes the developer wants to make to the existing hardware. Most importantly, the client will want to know when the product will be **ready to use**.

Make sure you have the **client's permission** to proceed with the project (otherwise you might be working for nothing!).

Design a solution

The design phase of the project is probably one of the most important. This is because errors during design will obviously lead to errors during development. The design will usually include consideration of the following aspects:

- **what** data is to be stored
- **how** the data will be stored: in tables, in files
- **how** the data will be queried and reported: what information needs to be extracted from the product
- **user interface**: colours, layout of screens
- **report layouts**.

The design is documented using a combination of text and images, is presented to the client (sometimes with a **prototype** of the product) and is agreed before implementation begins.

Data table

A **data table** records the actual data that the solution will store, from a structural perspective. Take Microsoft® Access as an example. Microsoft® Access data is stored in tables (for further information see Unit 9: Database Software). These tables contain **rows** and **columns** into which the data is input. When the user opens the table to input the data (if not using an input form), the headings at the top of the column will indicate what the content of each column should be. In the first column of the table shown below you can see that the user will enter the course code, and in the next the course title. What you can not see from this view is the data type expected or the size of the data entry area (how many characters can be keyed in). This information is held in the table's **structure**.

Course code	Course title	Duration of course
E101ITP	BTEC First Diploma for ICT Practitioners	1 year
E102BUS	BTEC First Diploma in Business	1 year
E103ITP	BTEC National Diploma for ICT Practitioners	2 years
E104BUS	BTEC National Diploma in Business	2 years
E105ITP	BTEC Higher National Diploma for ICT Practitioners	2 years
E105BUSI	BTEC Higher National Diploma in Business (IT)	2 years
E107BUSM	BTEC Higher National Diploma in Business (Management)	2 years

The data table is a formal document that will reflect the structure of the table. It specifies the **names of each part of the record** (you will see that each record has a code, a title and a duration). These are known as **identifiers** or **field names**. Everything about each of these is recorded in the data table, as shown below.

Field name	Description	Type	Length	Format	Validation/ Input Mask
Course code	Unique identifier for course	Alphanumeric	12	Letter, 3 numbers, letters	Must not be NULL (empty)
Course title	Full course title	Text	35		
Duration of course	Length of course	Text	8		

For bespoke solutions, the data table is still used to reflect the contents of any files that the program accesses, as well as any data that is temporarily stored inside the program as the program runs (see Unit 7: Software Design and Development, for more on this topic).

Diagrams

Sometimes it is helpful for developers to create diagrams that represent what a program does. If programming in Visual Basic, for example, the technique is known as **storyboarding**. Alternatively, with a syntax-based programming language such as C++, Pascal or Java, traditional diagramming centres on concepts such as **structure diagrams** or **flow charts**.

Both storyboarding and structure diagrams are well-known industry standard techniques that allow programmers to walk through the design of the program (the sequence of actions). For Microsoft® Access style solutions, it is common to create flow charts. A flow chart (as seen in Unit 1: Using ICT to Present Information, page 11) is a visual image of a **sequence of steps** in a process. Flow charts could be used, for example, to represent what a macro is designed to do. At the beginning of this chapter we explained that there are many different models for developing projects, and each of these has its own version of diagramming, although, in principle, many of them are actually the same.

Other design phase considerations will be any **validation routines** that need to be set up (e.g. the user needs to input a number between 1 and 10). A routine is designed (often represented visually) which shows the validation process whereby the input is received, then checked, and if the input is not within the relevant boundaries the number is **rejected** and the user is asked to **input the number again**.

(For more on diagramming techniques used for designing programs, see Unit 7: Software Design and Development.)

Any queries and reports are defined: they are named and described (including their purpose).

Finally, any **security issues**, such as the use of passwords, are recorded. The developer might decide to password the whole program and then to also password certain tables, input forms or the display of a query or report, so that only authorised users can see parts of the data. The example here would be that only managers and those in the personnel department might be allowed to see employee salaries. As such, all other users would be prevented from seeing this information. (For further information on this subject, see Unit 17: Security of ICT Systems.)

Once these aspects have been written up or drawn (as in the case of diagrams), the developer is ready to move forward to the **doing** or **implementation** phase of the project.

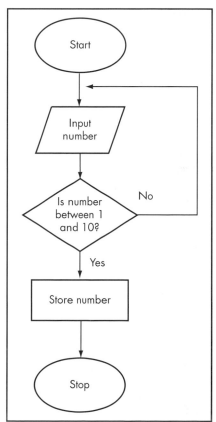

Fig. 3.8

Doing (or implementation) activities

Produce a solution

Producing a working solution can be both frustrating and rewarding, because although it is good to see the product growing, it can be a time-consuming activity! In addition, it is not unusual for developers to realise that they have forgotten how to do something when they come to try to implement part of the functionality, for example, not being able to remember how to set an input mask in Microsoft® Access, write a macro in Microsoft Excel® or a loop in a programming language. As such, it is often useful to have **access to books related to the software** being used in development, or to the Internet so that use can be made of online tutorials and other help files.

Do not forget that your tutors are also a useful resource to support this phase, as are other learners.

Monitor progress

While production is under way the developer also **monitors progress**. This is part of the reason why the **plan** was created at the beginning of the project. The plan (shown on page 79) contains a **comments column**. It was suggested in the planning section that this column should be used by the developer for noting any additional information about tasks that the developer felt necessary.

Here is a short section from a completed project plan, dealing solely with course information:

Task	By when	Resources needed	Comments
Create an input form for course details	End of week 3		Check alignment of input boxes
Create validation routine on duration column	End of week 3	Help with validation routine	Validate to ensure that the user can only enter 1, 2 or 3 years
Create a query that allows the user to search for specific course information based on a course code	End of week 4		This will need an input box to enable the user to key in which course s/he wishes to search on

This form could then be added to during development, to record progress.

Task	By when	Resources needed	Comments
Create an input form for course details	End of week 3		Check alignment of input boxes **Still some alignment problems, revisit later**
Create validation routine on duration column	End of week 3	Help with validation routine	Validate to ensure that the user can only enter 1, 2 or 3 years **Validation routine did not work and I needed tutor help to fix the problem – this has put the project behind schedule**
Create a query that allows the user to search for specific course information based on a course code	End of week 4		This will need an input box to enable the user to key in which course s/he wishes to search on

The alternative to adding detail into the comments column would be to add another column called something like **progress check**, and to use this to record both positive and negative comments on development experiences. This effectively becomes a **work log**.

Task	By when	Resources needed	Comments	Progress Check
Create an input form for course details	End of week 3		Check alignment of input boxes	**Still some alignment problems, revisit later**
Create validation routine on duration column	End of week 3	Help with validation routine	Validate to ensure that the user can only enter 1, 2 or 3 years	**Validation routine did not work and I needed tutor help to fix the problem – this has put the project behind schedule**
Create a query that allows the user to search for specific course information based on a course code	End of week 4		This will need an input box to enable the user to key in which course s/he wishes to search on	

Monitoring progress is essential for three reasons.

1) The developer can see whether they are keeping on track.
2) The developer can use this information when evaluating the project.
3) The developer can look back at this documentation at a much later date and learn from past mistakes when undertaking future projects.

As mentioned earlier in the chapter, the original project plan should have included interim reviews with the client (or tutor). The developer will often create an **update report**, which will be presented to the client during the interim review. Try to make this report positive rather than negative.

Finally, in the **work log** shown above the developer has included comments about problems experienced with the creation of the validation routine. As testing is a significant part of the project, it would be useful to record the activity undertaken to solve the validation problem to evidence testing. Screen captures are an excellent way of evidencing **interim testing**, particularly if the screen captures include error messages.

Testing and fixing of problems

As mentioned earlier, the testing phase of a project is one of the most important if the developer wants to be sure that the client is going to get a good product. It is usual to test the product in a number of ways:

Visual checking: the user interface should be checked for errors. User prompts and dialogue should be checked thoroughly for typing errors. Clearly this has a huge bearing on how professional the product seems to be. 'Plaese inpet nimber' for 'Please input number' will not impress the client! Ask others to look at the user interface, as they will often spot errors that the developer misses.

Test for functionality: This is where the developer has a list of things the solution is supposed to do and s/he tests the product to make sure that all the required functionality is there and that it works.

Test for logic: In the case of a solution that has been programmed using a programming language such as Visual Basic, C++ or Java, the program logic is tested. For example, if a statement (which selects one particular action) is tested to see what happens if the condition is met (in other words, if it is true) and what happens if the condition is not met (if it is false). A loop condition (where a section of code is designed to repeat or not to repeat, dependent on a specific set of circumstances) is tested to run again or not to run again.

Validation routines: Any inbuilt validation routines are tested. It is common to put validation on a field in a database, for example, to ensure that the value is not left blank. An example of this would be where a sports club is issuing discount vouchers dependent on a member's age (20 per cent discount for senior citizens, 30 per cent for those under 18). Clearly, the important data here would be the member's date of birth. Without this piece of information, the program would not be able to issue the right voucher. A developer would validate the age field to be within certain boundaries and also to be present.

Calculations: Any calculations that the solution executes **MUST** be tested using an alternative method. This could be mental arithmetic, using a calculator or making use of spreadsheet facilities.

Using sample data: It is usual to test a solution using sample data. This can either be data that has been provided to the developer by the client or sensible data that the developer has made up. There needs to be sufficient data input into the solution to test it properly. For example, during the design phase it was suggested that two queries could be developed, one to filter and list the customers by location, the other to search for a customer by name. Clearly, if only one customer has been input into the product, the developer will not be sure whether the program really works or not. To do this properly, at least 20 records should have been input, with at least 3 different locations. This data will then also allow the user to test the search facility for a specific customer. When testing data, developers should include:

- **normal data**: data which makes sense and is likely to be input
- **extreme data**: data which is unlikely, but may be input, for example, a member over the age of 110 years
- **erroneous data**: data which makes no sense and may be input, for example symbols or letters instead of a number, or vice versa.

This is done to find out what the program will do under these circumstances.

The developer will record all aspects of testing in a test log. This will include:

- **Date** of test
- **purpose** of test

- testing **strategy** (how the test is being carried out)
- **results** of the test
- **actions** required.

This can easily be made into a table, which can be added to as the tests are executed.

Date of test	Purpose of test	Testing strategy	Results of the test	Actions required
01/03/2006	Test validation on duration field	Input the following values: 3, 5 B, *, 0, 11 2195, – 433	Accepted 11 accepted! Rejected	Change value in validation range
01/03/2006	Test validation on duration field	Input the following values: 11	Rejected	

Notice that the second time the test was carried out, the only input value tested was 11, as this was the one that had caused the problem during the previous test.

The above tests may be undertaken by the developer (unless there is a testing team available). Once they have been completed successfully the solution is then offered for user testing. It is likely at this stage that the user will input more of his/her own data to give the product a thorough test. It is also likely that a number of potential users will use the system. The developer should get feedback from the users at this stage. It is often useful to develop a questionnaire that the user can have at his/her side when they test the product, to record their thoughts. They should be asked to consider the product from the following perspectives:

- **Does the solution have all the required functionality?** If not, ask them to identify what is missing.
- **Is the solution easy to navigate?** If not, how could it be improved?
- **Is the interface attractive and user-friendly?** If not, how could it be improved?
- **Any other comments** – offer the user to add any comments s/he wishes, in case something is spotted that the developer has missed.

While much of this testing has to be done at the end of the project, there are aspects that can be undertaken on an ongoing basis as the product develops. This is known as **interim testing**.

For example, when the queries are created, the natural thing for the developer to do is to input some data and **test them straightaway.** If this is done, record the test in your test log.

Using a combination of **interim** and **final testing** will tend to help developers find problems earlier in the process and eradicate them before they form part of a more devastating problem.

Review activities

Once the product is deemed to be fully **functional and complete**, you will **upload** it to the client's system and users will begin to use it.

The developer will need to be available in the initial stages so that any bugs that are identified can be dealt with quickly. For example, if the VAT as calculated by the solution does not appear on the invoice, if the AutoCounter is not working or a heading is only partially visible on a report, clearly this has an **immediate effect** on the **system's efficiency** and **usability**. It would thus need to be addressed immediately.

During this early use stage the developer can already begin the review process. Part of the activity for this phase will be evaluating the **appropriateness of the project plan**, including a consideration of whether or not the **timescales** were appropriate. The developer will need to evaluate critically whether s/he made good use of the resources available. To do this, the plan is pulled apart and analysed in terms of how it contributed to the success or failure of the project. The developer will learn lessons from this analysis that can be taken forward to the next project.

Shortly after implementation, the developer will seek **user acceptance** from the client. This is basically where the client confirms that everything is working as expected. Quite often this is the point where the developer receives his/her final payment.

Once the system has been running for an agreed period of time, the client and the developer will meet again to review the product. At this stage the developer can ask for feedback about the **impact of introduction** of the new system or product on the organisation. In other words, is the system realising the benefits that were anticipated at the start of the project?

Maintenance

While any **bugs** in the system must be eradicated quickly, it is possible that some bugs might not be found immediately because they are in **timed events** which do not happen frequently.

For example, VAT returns are sent to the Inland Revenue on a quarterly (every three months) basis. This return reflects the amount of VAT the organisation has collected on its sales, less the amount of VAT the organisation has paid on its purchases. The difference is paid to the Inland Revenue (assuming that the sales VAT is greater than the purchasing VAT – if this is not the case, then the organisation will receive a rebate instead).

What is more likely to happen once the system has been running for a while is that the organisation will identify **enhancements** that it would like to see. Sometimes these will be things that the organisation had not considered originally. On other occasions they might be things that could simply be done better – for example, when the user is using an input form, on pressing Tab between the boxes, the boxes are not accessed in sequence. This is known as the tab order on a form, and, while being incorrect it would not prevent the system being used, but it might be an irritant for the user.

Ultimately, if the number of enhancements (or size of the enhancement) becomes excessively large, the requests will become a proposal and the whole project cycle will begin again.

Recap

At the beginning of this unit, we described the project model as plan-do-review. Having now gone through the whole unit you will see that this is actually more like an overview of the whole project cycle because there are several parts to planning, doing and reviewing.

Figure 3.9 is a copy of a diagram that has been borrowed from Unit 7: Software Design and Development – it basically brings together all the aspects of a project in a visual way:

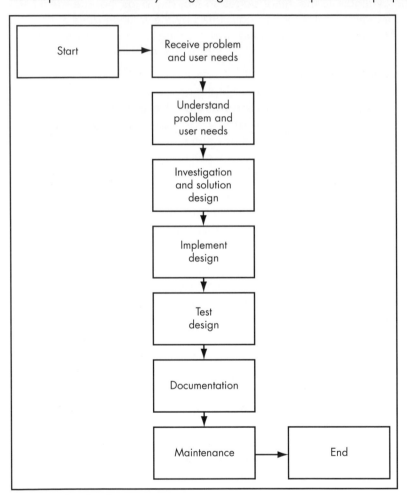

Fig. 3.9 The development process

Activity

SHS currently has a computer system that handles basic company information. It contains customer and supplier details and basic stock data. As the company is now expanding into competitions, it has decided to invest in software that will allow it to create posters, flyers and newsletters.

The company has a relatively old machine with the following specification:

- Microsoft Windows® 2000 professional
- AMD Athlon™XP 2000 processor
- 256 Mb PC2700 RAM
- 30 GB 7200 Rpm PATA hard disk
- 15" CRT monitor

(For more information on this type of specification, see Unit 2: Introduction to Computer Systems).

The company also has a budget of £500.00.

Identify two alternative software options that will have the functionality that the user requires, and recommend one of them as a realistic option.

NB: as software and hardware specifications will change dramatically in the next two years, no answer is given to this activity. You should use the Internet to find relevant software and compare its minimum specification with your machine specification and budget.

COURSEWORK GUIDANCE

As with other units, when undertaking your project you will be given a deadline to meet. This is realistic and is what would occur in the real world. From the outset you will need to use this time effectively. Most new developers forget just how long the different tasks will actually take (they underestimate). Plan early and stick to your plan as closely as possible.

To ensure success, make sure you follow the steps provided in this unit. If you undertake the steps in the right order, think carefully about each one and ensure that each is undertaken enthusiastically, you will ultimately achieve your goal.

Monitor your progress carefully against the deadlines you have set yourself and seek early support from your tutor if you feel that the project is not going as well as it should. Make sure you record your progress regularly – even the problems and mistakes made.

You need to ensure that your product is professional, well presented and does what the client originally requested. Ensure that you check your final solution thoroughly.

Ultimately, be realistic about your project – do not try to do too much!

Unit links

This unit has direct links to the following:

Unit 1   Using ICT to Present Information
Unit 2   Introduction to Computer Systems

Unit 4   Website Development
Unit 7   Software Design and Development
Unit 9   Database Software
Unit 10 Spreadsheet Software
Unit 17 Security of ICT Systems

Further reading

Butterick, R., *Project Workout: A Toolkit for Reaping the Rewards from All Your Business Projects* (FT Prentice Hall, 2005) ISBN: 0273681818

Heathcote, P. M., *Successful IT Projects in Access* (Payne-Gallway Publishers, 1999), ISBN: 0953249069

Maylor, H., *Project Management*, 3rd edn (FT Prentice Hall, 2002), ISBN: 0273655418

Progress check

To record your achievement, simply tick the criteria awarded to you when your project is returned. There is a full copy of this grid available on the accompanying CD. The copy will also allow you to record your key skill achievement against Literacy, Numeracy and ICT objectives.

Assignment		U3
Referral		
Pass		
	1	
	2	
	3	
	4	
	5	
	6	
	7	
Merit		
	1	
	2	
	3	
	4	
Distinction		
	1	
	2	
	3	

A completed sample of this document (for reference purposes) can be found at the back of Unit 1.

WEBSITE DEVELOPMENT

INTRODUCTION

Things are very different now; we have seen significant changes since 1989, when English computer scientist Tim Berners-Lee sat down and wrote the proposal that would establish a worldwide standard for the creation, transfer and hyperlinking of multimedia documents over the Internet.

For a growing number of people, the World Wide Web is quickly replacing traditional newspapers and television as their primary information source. It is also used as a portal to online 'chat', music downloads, online shopping, electronic banking, home entertainment, navigation, academic research and remote working. Websites have, quite simply, changed the way the world works.

In this unit you will learn the fundamentals of web page design and how to build your own multi-page websites using best practice.

Learning outcomes

On completion of this unit you should:

1 understand purposes of websites and the laws and guidelines that concern their development

2 understand the principles of multi-page website design

3 be able to create a multiple-page website.

RECORDING YOUR PROGRESS

In order to achieve each unit you will complete a series of coursework activities. Each time you hand in work, your tutor will return this to you with a record of your achievement.

This particular unit has 10 criteria to meet: 5 Pass, 3 Merit and 2 Distinction.

- For a **Pass**: you must achieve **all** 5 Pass criteria.

- For a **Merit**: you must achieve **all** 5 Pass and **all** 3 Merit criteria.

- For a **Distinction**: you must achieve **all** 5 Pass, **all** 3 Merit **and both** Distinction criteria.

So that you can monitor your own progress and achievement in each unit, a recording grid has been provided (see the **Progress check** section at the end of this unit).

Purposes of a website

Broadly speaking, websites fall into two basic categories:

- **commercial**
- **non-commercial**.

Commercial

This type of website is created as a tool for creating **more money** for its creators, through **advertising** their **services** or **products.**

In the early twenty-first century, most businesses have their own websites. These websites are generally listed in any literature that the business produces or placed on the product itself, encouraging customers to visit.

Some websites are **password-protected** and require **payment** in order to **access** their content (e.g. music file downloads such as Apple's iTunes®).

Others provide **secure online shopping facilities** and these sell any manner of goods, from holidays to houses to sweets, and so on.

Online auction houses, such as **eBay**, are also commercial websites.

Some sample **commercial** websites can be seen in Figures 4.1–4.4.

Online **gambling** websites have also become popular in the last few years, although they have caused some ethical concerns due to the **potential addictiveness** of the services provided.

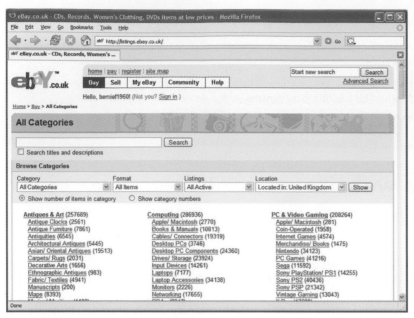

Fig. 4.1 eBay: a commercial website devoted to online auction

Fig. 4.2 Microsoft® Xbox 360™: a commercial website devoted to advertising the console.

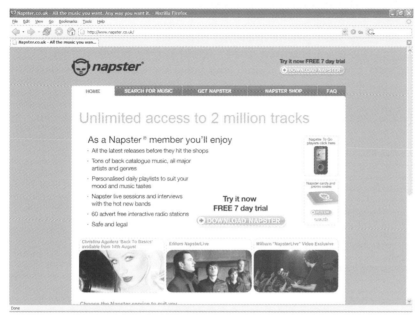
Fig. 4.3 Napster®: a commercial website devoted to online music

Fig. 4.4 Converse, a fashionable American company specialising in Athletic and Lifestyle footwear

Non-commercial

These types of website are created for **non-profit-making reasons**. Generally, they continue to exist through the creator's **own finance**, use of **third party advertising**, **sponsored links** or **donations** from generous visitors who value the resources provided.

Typical examples of non-commercial websites include:

- **personal pages**: about the creator, can include an online diary or **weblog** (often just called a **blog**)
- **advice** and **guidance**: 'how to' pages
- **fan** or **review sites**
- **clubs** and **societies**
- **charities**
- **educational**
- **governmental** (local or national).

Fig. 4.5 The RSPCA (Royal Society for the Prevention of Cruelty to Animals) website

Websites which exist as an information resource **within** an organisation are often called **intranets**. Unlike the company's **external** website (often called its internet **presence**), these can also be considered non-commercial and are not normally accessible by the general public. They are used for sharing policy documents, internal telephone directories, company news, and so on.

Meeting the client's need

When designing a website for another person or organisation it is vital to consider their **needs**. The website should not be created as an exercise for fulfilling your own personal tastes or creative flair, but as a **direct reflection of what the customer actually wants**.

Common concerns that the client may have are as follows:

Accurate and current information:
- Is the information on the website correct and as up to date as possible?
- How easy will it be to maintain the website and keep the information current?

Clear navigation:
- Is it obvious how to move around the website, from page to page?
- Can visitors get at the information they want quickly (within 2 or 3 clicks)?
- Can the visitor easily find their way back to the home page?

Fast download speeds:
- Will the website load quickly on slower narrowband (i.e. dial-up) computer systems?
- Have linked images been compressed where possible? If not, should there be a choice in content (low or high graphics versions)?

Suitability of language:
- Is the language grammatically sound, with no spelling errors (which can detract)?
- Is the language appropriate to the expected visitor (not too technical or unprofessional)?
- Are there pages available in different languages (this is very important for multinational companies)?
- Is there language present that may anger, insult or offend?

Choice of images:
- Are the images used suitable and do they match the accompanying text?
- Are the images of a suitable photographic or artistic standard?
- Are the images the right size?
- Are the images likely to anger, insult or offend (especially in the global market)?

Appropriate formatting:
- How effective is the page layout?
- Are the fonts and colour appropriate (e.g. using corporate colours)?
- Can font size and colours be changed easily to assist accessibility for visitors with reading or cognitive difficulties?

Laws and guidelines

Laws and **guidelines** are vital considerations when planning a website.

Although legislation varies greatly from country to country, and is therefore sometimes difficult to apply to resources (such as web pages) that are available globally, some particular legal acts are worth our attention.

UK Data Protection Act 1998

As discussed in other units, this legislation ensures that **personal data** is:

- processed fairly and lawfully
- obtained for specified and lawful purposes
- adequate, relevant and not excessive
- accurate and up to date
- not kept any longer than necessary
- processed in accordance with the 'data subject's' (the individual's) rights
- reasonably securely kept
- not transferred to any other country without adequate protection.

Although originally published in 1984, the 1998 revisions incorporate the EU's (European Union) 'Directive 95/46/EC on the protection of individuals with regard to the processing of personal data and on the free movement of such data'.

Theoretically, this act applies to **any data held on an individual**, not just that which is published on a website. Websites that display an individual's information or collect registration information need to be checked against these criteria.

UK Copyright Designs and Patents Act 1988

By definition, a copyright is the exclusive legal right to use an idea or expression, as denoted by the © symbol.

In British law, the **initial** owner of a copyright is assumed to be the original author of a work. However, if a work (e.g. a website) is created in the course of employment, then the **author's employer** is the owner of copyright.

On the WWW, problems occur because it is easy for authors to 'borrow' text or images from another website in order to incorporate them into their own. The use of **images** is particularly awkward, since a web-published photograph is typically the copyright of the photographer (or the company who paid them to take the photograph) and should **not** be used **without** their permission.

The UK has a concept called '**fair dealing**', which grants some **exclusions** to copyright for the purposes of academic or review purposes, especially where the work is non-profit. In either case, an acknowledgement of the copyright holder should be made publicly. In the USA a similar **fair use** ruling has been made, which many website authors, particularly those with non-commercial websites, attribute to their use of copyrighted images.

You should therefore be careful about 'borrowing' text or images from other sources (printed or online) without checking their permitted usage first. If in doubt: ask!

Digital Millennium Copyright Act 2000

Commonly known as the **DMCA**, this is a copyright act in the United States that criminalises the **creation** and **sharing** of any **technology** that can circumvent measures taken to protect copyright. The act was introduced, to some controversy, in 1998 by the Clinton administration.

In 2001, the EU passed the **EU Copyright Directive (EUCD)**, which is, in many ways, a piece of legislation with similar goals.

The supervisory role of the W3C

The **World Wide Web Consortium (W3C)**, headed by Tim Berners-Lee, also publishes **guidelines** and **standards** for web page creation to ensure that pages are interoperable (work together) across many different computer systems.

In particular, they have working parties working on:

Hypertext markup language (HTML): standards for what is considered to be valid HTML syntax. At the time of writing, the current version of the HTML standards is version 4.01, although its successor XHTML has already been introduced and is becoming more widely used.

Website designers and Web browser designers are encouraged to fully support these standards as they improve compatibility and the overall user experience.

Web Accessibility Initiative (WAI): Many users have visual, physical, auditory, speech, cognitive or neurological disabilities that impair their ability to use the Web. The WAI working party strives to improve web accessibility by removing the barriers that prevent people with such disabilities from using (and contributing to) the Web.

Importantly, WAI also advises on accommodating users with technical disadvantages (e.g. those with slow connections), who may also find modern website design a barrier to their enjoyment.

It should also be remembered that employers may have **internal guidelines** for the creation of web page content, particularly for their own intranet.

Web page content should also be checked for **accuracy**; if content is **incorrect**, or, worse still, **libellous** (saying things about someone that are untrue and damaging to a person's reputation), individuals or companies may pursue the author for **legal damages** in a court of law. These damages can be costly.

Principles of website design

Construction features

Most web pages are constructed from a **set of similar features**. Figure 4.6 shows a sample page from the Guardian's **online news service**.

Let us discuss a few of the more common construction elements.

Hyperlinks

As discussed, a hyperlink is the standard technique used to connect one resource to another. The resource may be another page, another place on the same page (an **anchor**), a separate image, a spreadsheet, an animation or even a piece of music.

A web browser can remember a page from a previous visit and **colour-code** hyperlinks, as follows:

- **Blue** means **unvisited** – the user **has not** clicked this link before.
- **Purple** means **visited** – the user **has** clicked this link before.

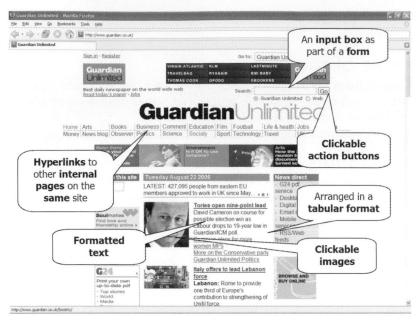

Fig. 4.6 Guardian newspaper online front page

This is not guaranteed, however, as **browsers** can **override** these colour settings and so can individual **web pages**, by using particular formatting in the **HTML.**

Hyperlinks use **uniform resource locators** (**URLs**) to specify the resources they connect to across the Internet. In theory, this resource could be anywhere in the world – as long as the URL is correct and the resource actually exists.

Here are some sample URLs:

http://www.bbc.co.uk/weather/ukweather/temperature.shtml

http://www.microsoft.com/windows/default.mspx

http://www.sainsburys.co.uk/home.htm

Frames

Frames have a somewhat **mixed reputation –** they are liked by some web designers and disliked **intensely** by others. The use of frames allows the designer to **split** a **physical browser screen** into a number of different **panes**. Each pane can show a **separate** (but linked) web **page**.

Figure 4.7 illustrates this.

When a **link** is selected on the **left-hand menu**, its associated page (e.g. 'page2.html') can **replace** page1.html in the **largest** frame.

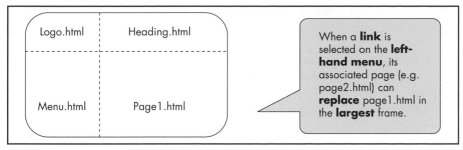

Fig. 4.7 Frames

When a **link** is selected on the **left-hand menu**, its associated page (e.g. page2.html) can **replace** page1.html in the **largest** frame.

Hot spots

A popular web page technique is to use **hot spots**.

The first type of hot spot is concerned with areas of a web page which **naturally draw the eye** of the visitor. These areas (**top-left** and **right-hand edge**) are useful to place important **logos**, **key information** or **advertising**.

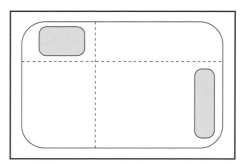

Fig. 4.8 Hot spots on a web page

The second type of hot spot is concerned with **images**, particularly those that are intended to be used as an **image map**. An image map is a picture which is **divided** up into several **different areas**, or hot spots. When the user clicks on a hot spot, it acts as a **hyperlink** to a different page or resource.

Consider the image in Figure 4.9, the SHS logo.

Fig. 4.9 SHS logo

We can use this image as an intuitive 'menu' system by drawing shaped hot spots on various areas to link to different pages of merchandise in our case study's skateboarding shop. (See Figure 4.10).

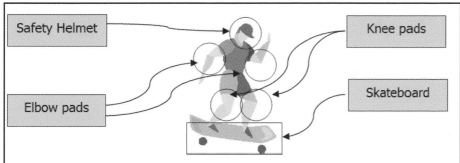

Fig. 4.10 Identified hot spots on the SHS logo

If the user clicks on the 'safety helmet' hot spot, it will hyperlink to safety-helmet.html. And should the user click on the elbow pads, it will hyperlink to 'elbow-pad.html', and so on.

In order to create an image map, we have three basic choices:

1. We can create an image map using a paint program and manually write the HTML code necessary (this is tricky).
2. Alternatively, we can use a commercial image-map maker, such as Boutell's Mapedit program (http://www.boutell.com), which is specifically designed for the job (see Figure 4.11).

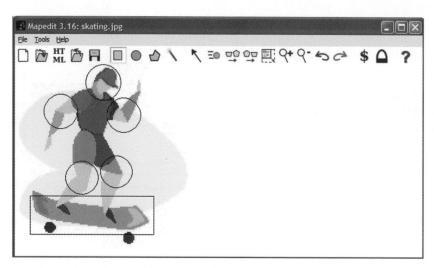

Fig. 4.11 Mapedit at work, creating the hot spots

3. Or we could use a full HTML editing suite, such as Adobe Dreamweaver®, which incorporates an image-map maker.

Perhaps the simplest technique for now is to use the image-map maker, Mapedit.

Here is the **simple HTML code** that is produced from an utility like Mapedit:

```
<img src="skating.jpg" usemap="#skating" alt="" style="border-style:none" />

<map id="skating" name="skating">

<area shape="circle"#safety helmet

 coords="75,15,15" href="safety-helmet.html" title="safety helmet" />

<area shape="circle"#elbow pads

 coords="39,39,14" href="elbow_pads.html" title="elbow pads" />

<area shape="circle"#elbow pads
```

```
   coords="92,42,14" href="elbow-pads.html" title="elbow pads" />

<area shape="circle"#knee pads

   coords="57,94,14" href="knee-pads.htm" title="knee pads" />

<area shape="circle"#knee pads

   coords="86,89,13" href="knee-pads.html" title="knee pads" />

<area shape="rect"#skateboards, decks, trucks and wheels

   coords="13,109,117,141" href="skateboard.html" title="skateboards, decks, trucks and
   wheels" />

</map>
```

This code could now be inserted into a suitable page for Web browser testing, as shown in Figure 4.12.

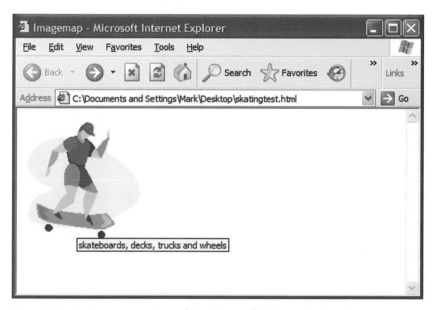

Fig. 4.12 An image map at work in Microsoft Internet Explorer®

The hot spots **do not**, of course, show up on the actual image. In Figure 4.12, the mouse cursor is **hovering over** the 'skateboard' hot spot and it is showing the suitable **alternative text**, and, when clicked, would load the appropriate page all about skateboards.

Email links

A clickable **email hyperlink** is a common sight on a web page. When the email link is clicked, the user's email client, with the target email address pre-filled (sometimes the subject, too), will appear.

Here is the HTML needed:

```
<a href="mailto:me@mysite.co.uk?subject=An example">Contact us.</a>
```

Figure 4.13 shows the web page view.

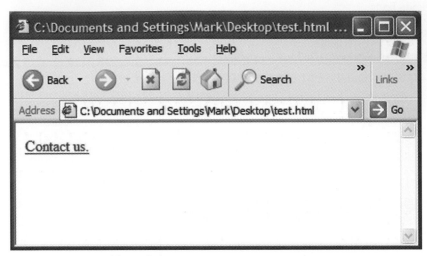

Fig. 4.13 An email hyperlink

And when **clicked**, the user's default email client will appear (as shown in Figure 4.14).

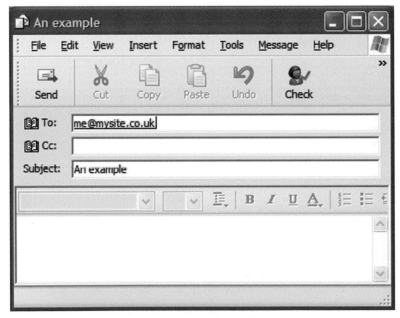

Fig. 4.14 User's email client with details pre-filled

Many modern commercial websites prefer to use **form-based** email submission instead, as these do not typically rely on the user being on their own PC, with their personal email software installed and running. This would allow users to send emails from PCs in public places (e.g. libraries, hotels, schools, conference centres).

Website design

When it comes to designing a website, good planning and forethought cannot be valued highly enough! There are many different techniques available to plan a website; perhaps the most commonly used is the **storyboard**.

A storyboard is used to plan the website pictorially, showing each page as a **named thumbnail** with the **inter-page navigation** clearly shown.

Let us explore the storyboard approach through a sample case study: SHS, a small skateboarding company, is looking to create a commercial website on which they can advertise

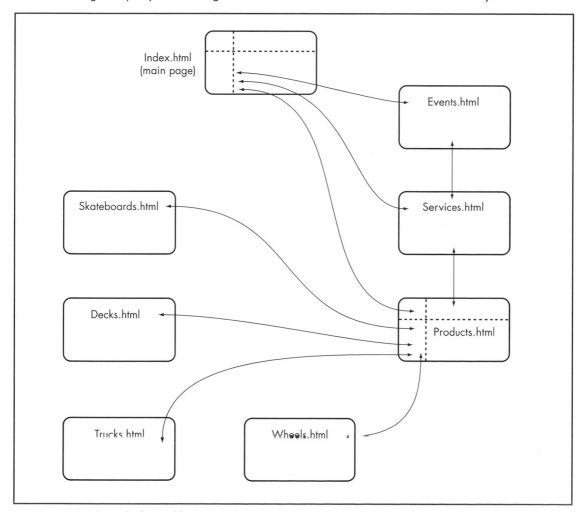

Fig. 4.15 Storyboard of possible SHS website

their **products**, **services** and details of local and national **events**. The company sells **skateboards**, **decks**, **trucks** and **wheels** from various manufacturers. They have asked for an easy-to-use site, with simple navigation.

Figure 4.15 presents a potential solution.

After a plan has been created – and amended, if needed – it should be possible to sketch out the pages in more detail, **taking information from the client** to help **populate** the pages. When sufficient detail has been collected, **sample draft pages** can be shown to the client for **feedback**.

More considerations

Other design considerations include the organisation's '**house style**'; this includes use of corporate colours, logos, catchphrases, and so on.

BP solar's home page is a good example of this: a clean, minimalist design, using their logo and corporate colours (green and yellow) to good effect (as shown in Figure 4.16).

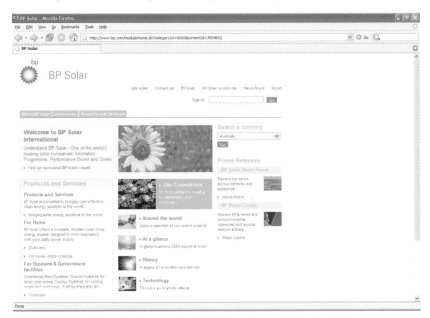

Fig. 4.16 The BP solar home page

It is always useful to remember that a company's commercial website is an extension of their presence in the marketplace. The large sums of money some organisations spend on their websites is testament to just how effective they feel their website actually is in attracting new customers.

Another important design aspect, though it may seem odd, is **continuity of layout**. The better websites use a **tried and tested** layout, with which users quickly become **familiar** and **comfortable**. Sites with **consistent layout** are generally **easier to navigate** and encourage people to explore, since they feel reassured that they are unlikely to 'get lost' in a maze of poorly organised or bewilderingly different pages.

Adding interactivity to the web page

There are many different ways that you can add interactivity to a web page, although perhaps the most common way to achieve this is to use a **form**. A form is an HTML component that can be used to collect data from the user.

Forms use combinations of familiar interface elements, such as **text boxes**, **buttons**, **radio buttons**, **checkboxes** and **drop lists**, to collect all manner of data. Some forms are used to process queries, while others are used to permit data entry via the keyboard. A good example of a form in action is shown in Figure 4.17.

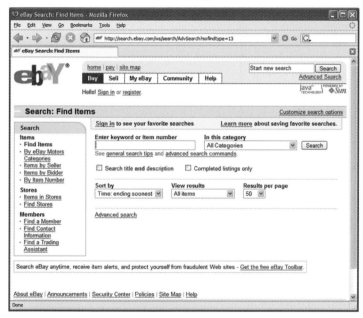

Fig. 4.17 eBay's advanced search page © eBay Inc. 2006

Creating websites

Web development software

You can develop web pages in a number of different ways. The most common techniques are explored below.

Text editor

A basic text editor (such as Microsoft® **Notepad**) can be used to create a simple web page by directly keying in the HTML code. Some more advanced text editors recognise HTML files by their extension (either .htm or .html) and can produce a form of 'syntax highlighting', which helps the designer read the HTML code more easily, different parts of the HTML being coloured differently.

Some web designers take great pride in the fact that they have created their (quite often complex) page using such a basic tool, often placing a 'built with Notepad' message on the page itself!

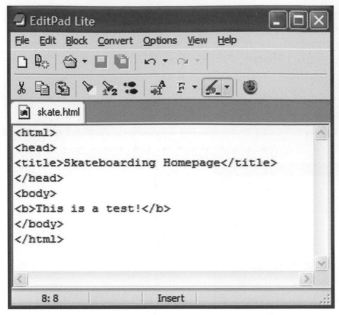

Fig. 4.18 A text editor being used to create a web page

HTML editors

HTML editing **suites** come in various **sizes**, **prices** and levels of **complexity**. Most are **WYSIWYG** (what you see is what you get) tools that allow the designer to create the page **visually** and the program then **writes** the **equivalent** HTML. These tools make effective use of the **drag-and-drop** approach to modern software design.

Suites typically also have **W3C validation** (for HTML standardisation), comprehensive support for JavaScript, Java and **CSS** (cascading style sheets) for formatting. They also assist the **management** process (by **organising** the pages into a complete interconnected site), and can **upload** to a **host** server for **publishing** and **submit details** to search engines.

Popular editing suites include:

* Adobe (formerly Macromedia®) Dreamweaver
* Microsoft FrontPage®

- CoffeeCup HTML Editor
- Quanta Plus.

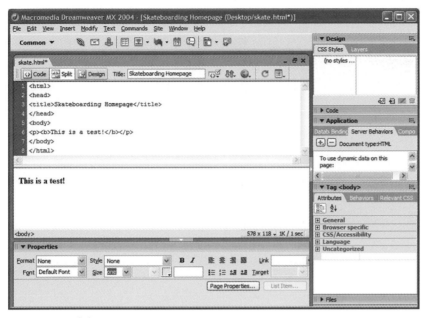

Fig. 4.19 Adobe Dreamweaver in use

SCORECARD

+ Fast, WYSIWYG drag-and-drop design means quick assembly of pages and sites
+ You do not have to learn HTML
+ Comprehensive help systems and samples usually provided
- Can be expensive
- Can be complex to use, especially for advanced features
- Can require more powerful computer system in order to run

Other applications

General-purpose, office-based applications, such as Microsoft® Word, Microsoft Excel® and Microsoft PowerPoint® can also **export** their data in an HTML format, effectively creating web page content very easily. Generally, this is performed through the **File->Save as type** menu option, and obviously demands very little HTML skill from you.

Adobe Flash® is also a popular tool for creating web page content, especially those rich in **multimedia** (pictures, sound, music, animation or video) and requiring more **advanced levels of user interaction**. In order to view Flash animations, a Web browser needs a Flash Player installed (these are **free** to download).

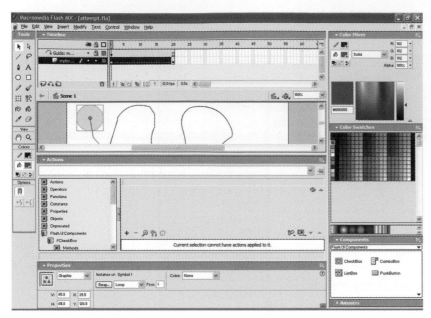

Fig. 4.20 Adobe Flash in use

Server scripting

It is also possible for **Web servers** to generate web page content **dynamically**. This is achieved when a server-side scripting language, such as **PHP** (PHP hypertext pre-processor) or **ASP** (active server pages), is used to interrogate databases based on submitted user queries. Such scripts write HTML, which is then sent back to the client's computer system.

The advantage of this is simply that up until the user's query was submitted, the HTML page **did not exist**, **reducing the storage** for all possible combinations that might exist if they had to be coded manually. More importantly, since the HTML is generated directly from a **live database**, the page content is likely to be **extremely current**. A common example of this would be **online shopping search facilities** that query stock databases for availability of particular items.

Formatting and editing HTML

Key term

HTML is a markup language and, as such, describes the **content** of a page and how it is structured.

HTML uses a number of special **tags** to identify its different sections. Most tags have a **start tag** and an **end tag** (e.g. **<HTML>** and **</HTML>**). Here are some **basic** HTML tags to get you started:

Start tag	End tag	What it means
<HTML>	</HTML>	Start and end of an HTML document.
<HEAD>	</HEAD>	Start and end of a HTML document's head(er); it contains information such as its title and keywords that may be useful to search engines.
<TITLE>	</TITLE>	Placed usually within the <HEAD> and </HEAD>, every HTML document **must** have a title to identify its content. The title is the text usually displayed in the **Web browser's title bar** when the page is loaded.
<META>	None!	Meta tags are used to describe the document itself rather than its content. A simple example would be: <META name="Author" content="U N Owen"> This specifies the author's name.
<BODY>	</BODY>	This represents the start and end of the document's main body; it is easiest to think of this as the central canvas of the HTML page.
<P>	</P>	Starts and ends a paragraph of text.

Note that HTML is not case sensitive.

```
<html>

<head>

<title>Skateboarding Homepage</title>

<META name="Author" content="U N Owen">

</head>

<body>

<p>This is a test!</p>

</body>

</html>
```

You can key this short HTML document into a **basic text editor** and it should then open successfully in a suitable web browser. **Remember to save the file as 'skate.html'.** Figure 4.21 shows the HTML file loaded into Microsoft Internet Explorer®.

Fig. 4.21 Our quick web page – notice the title bar

Combining information

Information on a web page can be collected from a number of different sources. Common sources include:

- scanner
- microphone
- digital camera (still picture or video)
- application package data (e.g. a spreadsheet)
- original artwork
- music or sound effects
- animations
- clip art.

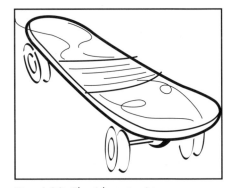

Fig. 4.22 The 'skate.jpg' image

For example, if we wanted to include a **clip art-style image** (e.g. 'skate.jpg'), we would need to add the appropriate tag to our HTML. You can use the HTML **<IMG>** tag to insert previously created pictures.

This is how you can place images onto your web page:

The 'alt' **attribute** is used to supply an **alternative text description** of the picture. This is seen as **good practice** as it enables users to know what the image is if they are unable to display it on their system (through personal choice – they have images disabled – or through browser limitations – it might be a text-only Web browser).

As you can see in Figure 4.23, the alternative description appears over the picture when the mouse pointer hovers over it.

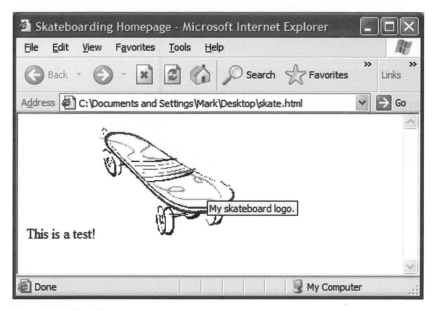

Fig. 4.23 The 'skate.jpg' image, now on our web page

Formatting example

Modern web page **formatting** is achieved using **CSS** (cascading style sheets), which is the preferred technique. It is possible to keep the content of a web page in one file (the .html) and the formatting in another (a .css file). Although it is not within this book's scope to cover all forms of CSS formatting, the following example demonstrates how it works.

Here is the **revised** HTML (skate.html). Note the new **stylesheet** link:

<html>

<head>

<title>Skateboarding Homepage</title>

<meta name="Author" content="U N Owen">

<link rel="stylesheet" href="mystyle.css">

</head>

<body>

<H2 align="center" *class="style3">*Skateboarding!</H2>

<H2 align="center"><img src="skate.jpg" alt="My skateboard logo." align="top">

</H2>

<p align="center"* class="style2"*><span* class="style1"*>The world of Skateboarding awaits you... </span><H3>

</p>

</body>

</html>

And the connected '**mystyle.css**' file:

.style1   {font-family: Arial, Helvetica, sans-serif}

.style2   {color: #000000}

.style3   {

        font-family: Arial, Helvetica, sans-serif;

        color: #FF0000;

        font-weight: bold;

        }

These CSS instructions create three styles of formatting: style1, style2 and style3:

- **Style 1** specifies a particular font family.
- **Style 2** specifies the colour black.
- **Style 3** specifies a particular font family, the colour red and to use bold.

(**RGB** (red green blue) colour codes are discussed in more detail in Unit 18: ICT Graphics.)

Here is the resulting appearance in a Web browser:

Fig. 4.24 The CSS-formatted appearance of the new page

CSS can also be used to change the **background colour** of the page.

.style1	{font-family: Arial, Helvetica, sans-serif}
.style2	{color: #FFFFFF}
.style3	{
	font-family: Arial, Helvetica, sans-serif;
	color: #FF0000;
	font-weight: bold;
	}
.body	{background-color: #000000;}

The results can be seen in Figure 4.25.

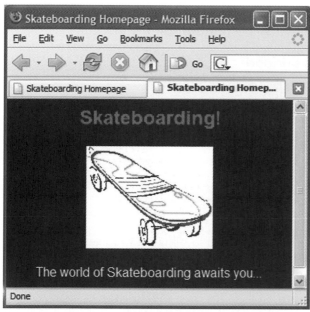

Fig. 4.25 Now with a black background!

Checking and reviewing the website

Once the website has been created, it is necessary to check it to see that it is **fit for purpose**. It is common to use a **simple checklist**, including page size, image size, internal links, external links, content, formatting and special requirements.

Page size

The page should display comfortably on the most common desktop resolutions as used by most users. Currently, this is **minimally 800 pixels × 600 pixels**, although **1024 × 768** is not uncommon.

A design decision will have been taken to either display contents **absolutely** (i.e. fix them in size) or allow them to **shrink** or **expand** as needed. The best way of checking this is to view the pages on a combination of different Web browsers, operating systems and desktop resolutions. This will approximate the audience diversity of hardware and software to a reasonable degree.

Image size

This is another concern as **large**, **uncompressed** images can take a **long time** to load on slow (**narrowband**) connections. You may have had this irritating experience at some point during your Web surfing!

It is often said that Web surfers have little patience when it comes to waiting for pages to load – if it takes too long, they will go elsewhere. For a commercial website, this means **losing a potential customer** (and their **money**).

If large, high quality images are needed, it should be possible to allow the user to **preview** these with either a **lower quality sample** or a simple **thumbnail**. The user can then decide whether they want to wait while a larger file downloads. This gives them **more control** and the Web servers a **reduced workload**!

Internal links

Internal links are links **within the same page** (anchors) or to another page within the same suite of pages. These need to be tested before publishing, as non-working internal links can be very irritating and frustrating for the casual visitor.

HTML editors such as Microsoft FrontPage® have an automated 'internal link' facility which identifies such defects.

External links

External links are typically hyperlinks **to other pages**, often to different Web servers, which may or may not be available from time to time. External links should be **checked regularly** to ensure that the URLs for a resource have not changed.

A number of sites also place an **advisory note** on their site as a **disclaimer** to indicate that they are **not responsible** for the content of another site they are linking to.

External links can be saved as **favourites** or **bookmarks** in the vast majority of Web browser applications.

Content

- Does the content reflect the requirements of the client?
- Is the content accurate and representative?
- Is the content up to date?
- Is the content appropriately presented?
- Do interactive elements, such as input forms, Javascript, Java applets, work correctly?

Formatting

This is particularly important if the website is being built for a client, particularly as a commercial site.

- Does it use appropriate imagery, company logos, and so on?
- Are the corporate colours and general colour scheme correct?
- Does the site allow for accessibility issues?
- Are the fonts that are used appropriate?
- Is the layout clear, or cluttered and confusing?
- Is the navigation system clear and easy to use?

Special requirements

It is quite common for resources on a website to require **additional software** (often called **browser plug-ins**) in order to experience particular files or embedded web page objects. Flash animations, video clips, Java applets and Adobe Acrobat® **PDF**s (portable document format) are by far the most common.

If you are using these types of objects to enhance your site, it is usually **good practice** (and **courteous**) to supply the **necessary external links** for visitors to **download** the appropriate software needed if they do not already have it installed.

Getting feedback

A simple fact: **visitor opinions matter!**

A popular technique for gauging visitor opinion is to use **feedback forms**. These invite the visitor to express their opinions of the website; sometimes it is actually encouraged through offering some attractive incentive – a free prize draw, for example.

Common questions on a feedback form might include:

- User's email address (for mailing notices regarding future website updates)
- User's occupation (helps to discover what demographic is using the site)
- User's age
- How often they visit the site over a specific period of time
- User rating of various features (typically on a poor, ok, good, excellent scale)
- Which features they find the most (and least) useful
- How they find the site's navigation (can they quickly find what they are looking for?)
- What improvements they would like to see
- How they discovered the website (this helps with marketing and advertising).

As noted, visitor feedback is an important factor when determining how well a website is working and what, if any, improvements can be made.

Publishing the website

There are a number of different ways that you can publish a website.

On an intranet

Publishing web pages on an organisation's intranet is not normally difficult. If security is exceptionally relaxed in the company it may be possible to simply drag and drop the files to the appropriate Web server's directory. But this is unlikely and a very insecure arrangement! Typically, the company will employ an intranet manager to oversee publishing and routine maintenance. The easiest option would be to send them a CD or email attachment which includes all the necessary HTML files, graphics and any other assorted media in the form of a single archived file (such as a .zip).

Since archives can retain the folder structure from the original files, when the files are unzipped into an appropriate Web server folder, the files and their sub-folders are automatically recreated. All that would then be necessary would be for the intranet manager to hyperlink the new pages to the existing intranet site.

On the Internet

This is somewhat more difficult, but there is a general order in which steps should be taken.

1. Select a **hosting company** for suitable **web space**.
2. **Purchase a suitable domain name** for your website (e.g. www.btec-first-ict.co.uk). This can cost as little as £3 for an entire year. Obviously not all combinations are available for purchase (they may already be in use); a domain registration company will allow you to check the availability of your preferred name.

   Some hosting companies also sell domains, so it is possible to purchase a **complete** domain name + Web space **package**.

   If you purchase the Web space and domain **separately**, it is necessary to request that the domain name is **re-pointed** towards your Web space. Be warned, this can take time and often requires an additional fee.
3. **Upload** your website pages, graphics, and so on, to your Web space, usually via **FTP** (file transfer protocol) client or a Web-based interface.
4. **Register** the page with a number of **search engines**. The hosting company may help you achieve this.

Since the Web space you have purchased is yours to use as you see fit (within the usage agreements stipulated by the hosting company), it is possible to perform full file and folder management, moving, copying, deleting and renaming files as you require.

Figure 4.26 shows a typical online hosting page, listing its different package deals.

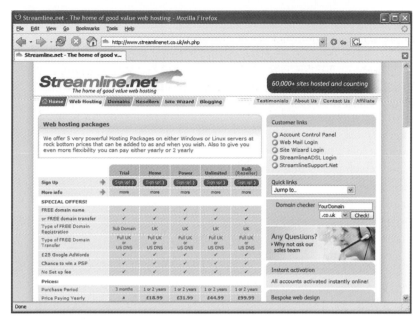

Fig. 4.26 A sample Web hosting company © Streamline.net 2006

☆ **Activity**

Build a simple multi-page website for SHS, using the storyboard plan presented earlier in this unit (page 105). You will need to collect suitable text and images from other sources to get started. It may also help to examine other commercial sites, such as Vapourised (www.vapourised.com), for ideas on content, suitable colours, fonts and navigation techniques. If possible, attempt to follow best practice by separating the content (.html) and the format (.css).

Present your website to your peers or your tutor for feedback. Evaluate your website, based on your own feelings and the feedback provided. How can it be improved?

QUIZ

1.   What is HTML?
2.   Give three design considerations when creating a website.
3.   Explain the purpose of the following HTML tags:
        a.   <HEAD>
        b.   <TITLE>
        c.   <IMG>
        d.   <P>
4.   What software can be used to upload your website pages to your host's server?
5.   Why is a form used?
6.   If an image has different clickable areas, what is it called?
7.   What is the HTML technique that splits a page into a number of different panes?
8.   Name two pieces of legislation that are connected to web page creation.

ANSWERS

1. Hypertext markup language – a language used to define the content and basic layout of a page.
2. Meet user needs
   Appropriate content
   Good navigation
   Accessibility
   Download speed
3. a. <HEAD> – start of a document's head section
   b. <TITLE> – used to specify web page's title in the browser's window bar
   c. <IMG> – used to insert an image
   d. <P> – used to start a paragraph
4. An FTP client.
5. To collect data from the user.
6. An image map.
7. Frames.
8. UK Data Protection Act 1998
   UK Copyright Designs and Patents Act 1988
   DMCA 2000
   EUCD 2001

COURSEWORK GUIDANCE

To achieve this unit you will need to demonstrate an understanding of the theory that underpins website development. In particular, you will need to show that you have gained a solid understanding of terminology. You will need to be able to evaluate different styles, constructions and design objectives of websites, by discussing actual commercial and non-commercial sites. You will also need to show that you have an understanding of the law in relation to websites.

In practical terms, you will need to design and create a multi-page website, and you will be asked to demonstrate that you understand how to upload and maintain a multi-page website.

For the higher grades, you need to be able to explain construction features of websites, suggest how websites could be improved and discuss the concept of interactive websites.

Finally, as part of the Distinction criteria you will need to evaluate techniques you have learned and used as part of the unit.

Unit links

This unit has direct links to the following:

Unit 3 ICT Project

Unit 5 ICT Supporting Organisations
Unit 18 ICT Graphics
Unit 21 Doing Business Online

●●●Further reading

Custro, E., *Creating a Web Page in HTML* (Peachpit Press, 2004)
ISBN: 032127847X

Hester, N., *Creating a Web Page in Dreamweaver 8* (Peachpit Press, 2006)
ISBN: 0321320228

Online Training Solutions, *Microsoft Office FrontPage 2003 Step by Step* (Microsoft Press US, 2003) ISBN: 0735615195

Vandome, D., *Dreamweaver MX 2004 in Easy Steps* (Computer Step, 2004)
ISBN: 1840782811

Copyright Designs and Patents Act 1988
http://www.opsi.gov.uk/acts/acts1988/Ukpga_19880048_en_1.htm

Digital Millennium Copyright Act (DMCA) 2000
http://www.copyright.gov/legislation/dmca.pdf

EU Copyright Directive (EUCD) 2001

http://europa.eu.int/eur-lex/pri/en/oj/dat/2001/l_167/l_16720010622en00100019.pdf

Office of the Information Commissioner http://www.ico.gov.uk/

UK Data Protection Act 1998 http://www.opsi.gov.uk/ACTS/acts1998/19980029.htm

Vincent Flanders' 'Web Pages that Suck' http://www.webpagesthatsuck.com

World Wide Web Consortium (W3C) http://www.w3.org/

Progress check

To record your achievement, simply tick the criteria awarded to you when each assignment is returned (you may be given three assignments for this unit, U4.01, U4.02 and U4.03 – the final column may not be used). There is a full copy of this grid available on the accompanying CD. The copy will also allow you to record your key skill achievement against Literacy, Numeracy and ICT objectives.

		Assignments in this Unit			
Assignment		**U4.01**	**U4.02**	**U4.03**	**U4.04**
Referral					
Pass					
	1				
	2				
	3				
	4				
	5				
	6				
	7				
Merit					
	1				
	2				
	3				
	4				
Distinction					
	1				
	2				
	3				

A completed sample of this document (for reference purposes) can be found at the back of Unit 1.

NETWORKING ESSENTIALS

INTRODUCTION

This unit helps you to understand why networks are used by organisations and how they help to coordinate activities carried out. They also improve communications throughout an organisation and allow resources to be used more efficiently by promoting sharing.

But there are also disadvantages with using networks, particularly in the complexity they bring to the existing technology, along with the specialised skills and ICT professionals needed to configure and operate them.

Additionally, networks are always a source of concern regarding security, as they can be a point of entry for unauthorised people who wish to access information inside an organisation to make changes or to see it before it is made public.

The roles of the servers in business client/server networks is shown and compared with the simpler peer-to-peer networks that are becoming increasingly common in our homes.

By the end of this unit you will also appreciate the functions of the various hardware devices and software components used, how they interact and be able to assemble simple networks.

Learning outcomes

On completion of this unit you should:

1 understand the use of computer networks
2 understand the features and services of local and wide area network technologies
3 understand network hardware and software components and how they are connected and configured
4 be able to set up and use a simple local area network.

RECORDING YOUR PROGRESS

In order to achieve each unit you will complete a series of coursework activities. Each time you hand in work, your tutor will return this to you with a record of your achievement.

This particular unit has 11 criteria to meet: 6 Pass, 3 Merit and 2 Distinction.

- For a **Pass**: you must achieve **all** 6 Pass criteria.
- For a **Merit**: you must achieve **all** 6 Pass and **all** 3 Merit criteria.
- For a **Distinction**: you must achieve **all** 6 Pass, **all** 3 Merit **and both** Distinction criteria.

So that you can monitor your own progress and achievement in each unit, a recording grid has been provided (see the **Progress check** section at the end of this unit).

Understand the use of computer networks

Let us look at how networks are used and, in particular, how they allow resources to be shared in an organisation. Afterwards we will consider some of their associated disadvantages.

Communication

Networks are used to help people inside an organisation communicate in these ways:

- **internal communications** between people, teams and departments
- **external**, between **customers** and information sources **outside** the organisation
- to help enable standard ways of working to **coordinate** the efforts of staff.

Internal communication

Individuals use email to **send** and **receive** messages, often with **attachments**, which are documents or files sent at the **same time** as the email. The network can help team-working by:

- providing **shared space** on the network where **files** can be kept so any of the team can use them
- using **groups** in **email address books** so an email can be sent to everyone in the team by choosing the name of the group
- setting up intranet pages so that team members can access them to help keep them **up to date** with changes and news relevant to the business
- permitting 'shared' applications, allowing users to work together on the same document even though they might be apart physically.

Functional areas, such as payroll or marketing, can use the network to help communicate their needs to other members of the organisation, for example, they may post up onto the intranet when the next cut-off date is for pay claims or cheque runs. A searchable and up-to-date telephone directory is also another popular intranet item. Marketing may post up recent releases to the press so that employees can be kept informed.

External communication

Organisations need to communicate with people and others from **outside** as well as inside. Customers may place **orders** via the Internet, which then sends order information to the sales department through the network. The network may then be used to inform the customer that the goods **have been sent** and when to **expect delivery**. Some customers might need to use this form of communication to resolve problems, such as goods arriving broken, or even not at all!

Having good **public relations** (PR) is always important to an organisation. This is another area where the network can help by providing up-to-date information for the website, which helps to enhance the organisational image. (For more detail on commercial websites, read Unit 4: Website Development.)

Research is often needed by the organisation for many reasons, including checking the product ranges and pricings of rival organisations and to help determine their own range of products and prices.

The Internet is an information resource used by most organisations, with their network providing their employees with access to it.

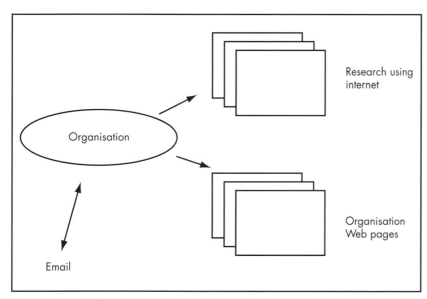

Fig. 6.1 External communication

Standard ways of working

Many organisations have **standard ways** of working to help their staff improve **productivity** and **work quality**. This can be done by using the network to:

- **coordinate** and **collaborate** with other staff by using shared disk space, so documents are kept up to date and work is shared between team members
- **inform** staff using online newsletters, emails and intranet
- **carry out research** using **historical data**, so that old data records can be used to find trends and help predict future customer demands.

Key terms

Coordinate: to organise staff or other resources so they do not duplicate effort and they produce results that are ready at the correct times. Without coordination, projects are delayed and cost more than they should, as several people might do the same task or not complete an important task (needed by others) by a specific deadline.

Collaborate: to work together on a project or task. With collaboration, a project is broken down into parts, which are then allocated to the members in the team. Collaboration can be very effective as each person can complete tasks which they are particularly good at.

Intranet: while the Internet spans the world, an intranet is a private 'internet' for use by the organisation, with web pages being made available from a local Web server. These may have sensitive information that is not for prying eyes (i.e. the organisation's competitors).

Managing resources

A resource can be almost anything that is useful to the organisation. Resources include:

- **information**, such as customer records, which the network can make available to every member of the organisation that needs it
- **hardware**, such as shared printers or scanners
- **software**, such as Microsoft Office® productivity suites
- **staff in teams**, who need the network to communicate and share files.

These are all factors to be considered when setting up and running the network.

CASE STUDY

Steve Hodder runs a small skateboard shop (SHS). As the business has grown, so have their computer systems. At first there was only one PC, which was used for everything, particularly:

- writing letters
- accounting
- producing price lists
- calculating the cost of products.

Then a second PC was used to run the till. It had a barcode scanner attached so they could scan products to help keep track of sales.

The third PC was purchased to run a bespoke program that was commissioned so that customers could enter details of a custom-built skateboard to find out how much it would cost.

These computers made working a lot more productive, but there were disadvantages, especially when data needed to be transferred from one computer to another:

- Records of sales had to be copied to a USB flash drive so they could do the accounts on the office PC.
- Details of custom-built skateboards had to be copied, using the USB flash drive, to the office PC so the orders could be built.
- Work done on the till PC during quiet times in the shop had to be copied to the office PC later.

The shop consulted with an ICT professional, who recommended they purchase a small network to link the PCs together. Their consultant ICT professional installed the network for them, trained them how to use it and set up a backup routine, so if a disaster happened to their systems the data would be safe.

The network has been a great success, saving the shop time and improving their response to customers.

Information

Information is the lifeblood of modern organisations. Many types of information are important to an organisation; these include such things as sales data, payroll hours and production costs.

Networks allow information to be stored so that it is available to those staff members who **need** it. Staff members **who do not need** it should be **denied access** to it by the network.

Networks give **rights** to users when they log on. These rights may mean that the user:

- is **not able to see** data on the network (no access)
- **may be able to see** data but **not change it** (read-only access)
- has **full rights to see and change data** (read/write, also called full access).

It is vital that information on the network is **controlled** to ensure that it is available to the people who need it and that the data is kept **safe**. Every organisation should keep data safe using backups.

> **Key term**
>
> **Backup**: when the data is copied to CD, magnetic tape or other media and then kept in a safe place. Sometimes IT specialist companies provide 'data warehousing' facilities, which store data off-site for other organisations.

Information that is spoilt is often referred to as being **corrupted**. Corruption can be caused by users entering bad information or faults which occur with hardware or software while they are being used. Backups should be made **regularly** so that if the data is corrupted, a recent **good copy** of the data can be **restored**.

Hardware

Hardware is a resource that can be managed by the network so that components are shared by users and used appropriately.

Printers are hardware devices that many organisations share through the network. They can be managed by ensuring that a number of users in different physical locations are able to print through them.

The network will manage access to hard disk storage, to ensure that **sensitive files** are not seen by users who have no need to see them. Similarly, files that are shared will be made available to every user who needs to use them.

It is also possible for a server to monitor other computer systems remotely, keeping track of processor usage, available hard disk space and applications running.

Software

Some organisations purchase their software with a **site license**. This allows many users to work with the software.

(Other types of license are discussed in Unit 13: Software Installation and Upgrade.)

Staffing

Staff are perhaps the most valuable resource an organisation has. They can be made more effective by using the network to **share information** and coordinate their efforts.

ICT professionals are also needed to set up and run the network. Configuring a network so it delivers everything to everybody, while making sure users are not able to or change private information, is very skilled work. There is an ongoing need for ICT practitioners to deal with the day-to-day issues and problems found when running the system, such as resetting a password or clearing a print queue so that users can print again.

Related legislation

There are laws concerning how companies operate and keep the workplace safe which are discussed throughout this book. As discussed in other units, the **Data Protection Act (DPA) of 1998** is particularly important to networks, as it concerns the duties companies have when keeping data on computer systems. In particular, the act requires that data kept on computer systems are:

- fairly and lawfully processed for specified purposes. Data cannot be obtained from other systems and then used for a purpose it was not registered for
- adequate, relevant and not excessive. The data must only be enough for the specified purpose; it is illegal to hold extra detail that could be used for another purpose in the future
- accurate and, where necessary, kept up to date. Any old or inaccurate data must be corrected
- kept for no longer than necessary. If the specified purpose is completed, the data must be destroyed
- processed in line with the rights of the individual
- kept secure. Data needs to be protected from hackers and other ways the information could be acquired by third parties
- not transferred to countries outside the EU unless there is adequate protection for the information.

Organisations running a network holding such data **must** keep **within** this law.

Disadvantages

Networks bring many, many benefits with them. It would be very difficult, if not impossible, for most organisations to survive without them. However, there are disadvantages to networks, including:

- **slowing down** of **response times** when computers need to log on or access distant information
- **disruption of the organisation** when the network is being installed (particularly the cabling)
- **increased complexity** and costs because networks add to the number of ICT components needed to make the systems function
- technical ICT staff can be **difficult** to find and **expensive**
- **security issues** – connecting computers together always carries the risk of someone **hacking** into the system to view or purposely corrupt data.

(For more on security issues, please see Unit 17: Security of ICT Systems.)

Slowing down of response times

A computer used as standalone will typically run faster if it is not connected to a network. This is because the network **adds** to the processing a PC needs to carry out, such as:

- **logging on to the network**, when secure data needs to be exchanged between the PC and a network file server to check that the PC and user are allowed on to the network
- **keeping the network connection open**, which will require some activity from programs running but not seen by the user
- **opening and saving files held on a file server** some distance from the PC, which is certain to slow the system down compared to using a hard disk inside the system box
- **running programs** that would not be required if the PC was standalone, such as an **email application**.

Increased complexity and costs

A standalone computer system is quite simple to set up and operate. There is not much hardware and for most PCs it all connects to the system unit.

A networked computer system is much more complex to **set up** and **operate**. There are many more **hardware components** to install to connect computers together and to control the network. **Cabling** and **switches** (or **hubs**) are needed if the network is wired. **Wi-Fi** wireless access points (WAP) and appropriate wireless network cards are needed for cable-free networks (which generally cause less physical disruption). Server computers are needed to control the network and to provide resources such as disk space, Internet connectivity, Intranet and shared printing.

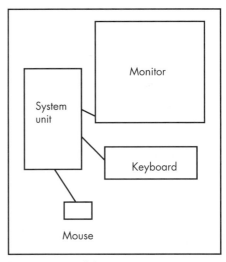

Fig. 6.2 Standalone computer

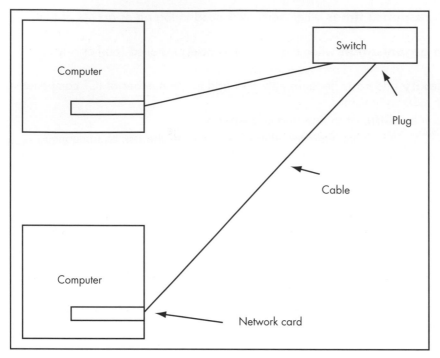

Fig. 6.3 Networked computer system

All this complexity means that networks cost more to run than standalone systems. The extra equipment is an obvious cost. Expertise needed in running the network means employing specialist ICT professionals, which adds to the cost.

Key terms

Hubs and switches are both devices that seem do a similar job, connecting computers together. They each have a number of ports where network cables can be plugged in.

Hubs are cheaper, simpler in construction and are typically used to boost the data signals coming in and send them out to all other ports.

Switches make judgements about data signals coming through them, based on the intended destination of the data. Switches are therefore a little smarter and can decide which port to send data to; this reduces network congestion.

Staff skills

Lack of staff skills may be a disadvantage as it costs money to **train** staff and to pay someone else to **cover** their workload as the training takes place. Even so, this may not be the best way of addressing skill shortages, as **experience** is a useful tool when used to avoid costly mistakes when setting up (and running) a network.

This leaves an organisation with the need to employ extra ICT professionals with the experience and skills needed to run the network, adding to the cost of the system. This is often achieved by employing **short-term contracted staff** (contractors) through an **external agency**.

Security issues

The data held on the network is the most valuable (and irreplaceable) part of the system. If there is unauthorised access to data then private (and confidential) information will be revealed or, worse still, changed. This can have consequences such as:

- a member of staff increasing the amount they are paid
- exam results changed
- product information made known to competitors to their advantage
- company performance details released too early, which affects their share price.

There are many, many more possible outcomes.

The importance of information held on a network needs to be recognised with **adequate security precautions** made to ensure that it is only **seen** by those who **need** to use it. For example, many modern organisations would quickly fold if they lost data such as how much is owed by their clients.

Features and services of network technologies

This section looks at the features and services of both LAN and WAN technologies. A **LAN** connects computers **on a site**, whereas a **WAN** connects sites **together**.

Features

The features of network technologies include:

- the **topology**, meaning how the cabling joins the computers together
- the **type of network**, particularly whether it is controlled by server computers
- **network access methods** – how the data signals are sent and received through the cables
- **data rates** – the speed data travels through the cabling
- **security** – how the network is protected from hackers and other risks.

Topologies

There are several types of topology available to designers of networks, including star and bus.

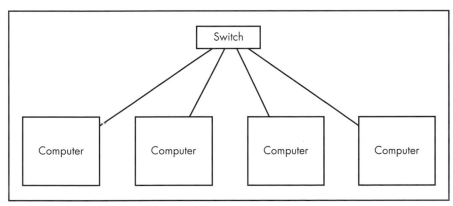

Fig. 6.4 Star topology

The **star** is perhaps the most common topology for modern networks. It provides **good speed** between components and is **quite robust**; if a part of the network breaks, usually the rest of the network will **continue to function** as normal. It is likely that you will be able to build and configure this type of network in your classroom with little difficulty, using some PCs, cables and a hub or switch.

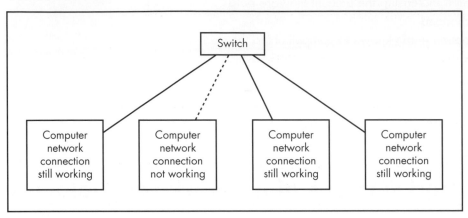

Fig. 6.5 Break in star topology

This topology is **very scalable**; it is easy to **connect the switches** together to form a **bigger network**.

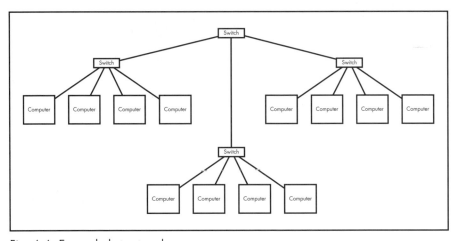

Fig. 6.6 Expanded star topology

The star topology is good over **medium distance** because each switch acts as a signal booster. Without boosting, the signal in a cable can **degrade** and become **corrupted** before it reaches its destination.

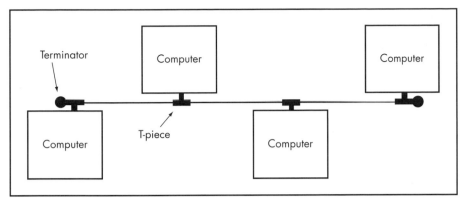

Fig. 6.7 Bus topology

The **bus** topology is an **older method** of connecting computers together that is becoming less popular because it can be **unreliable** and **difficult to trace cabling** faults.

Each computer network connection is to a T-piece, with the T-pieces cabled together. At each end of the cable there is a terminator, to keep the signal inside the cabling.

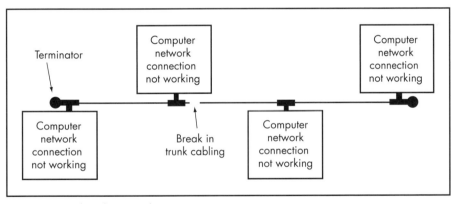

Fig. 6.8 Break in bus topology

If there is a break or problem in the trunk (or main) cabling, all computers will lose network capability. This is a problem with this topology, made worse because it is not easy to find where the problem actually occurs.

One method of finding a fault in the cabling of a bus topology is to do a 'binary chop' to divide the cable into two and then find out which half is still working. This is repeated with the half that does not work, and so on, until the fault is found.

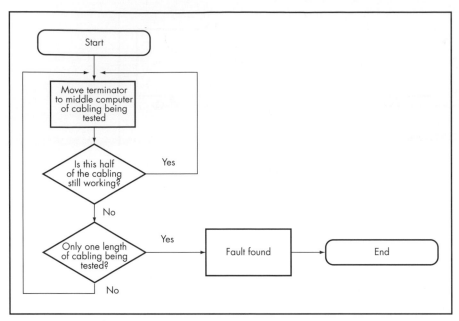

Fig. 6.9 Binary chop

Types of networks

There are two main types of network:

- **peer-to-peer** for small business or home
- **client/server** for most businesses.

> **Key term**
>
> **Peer-to-peer**: in a peer-to-peer network there is no server in overall control of the network. Each computer in this type of network has equal rights and responsibilities. They are all viewed as peers, hence the name, peer-to-peer. These types of networks work best where the users know each other and there are no security issues. They are not really suitable for larger organisations where there is much more need to safeguard and protect important data.

Client/server networks are the type used by most businesses. The clients are workstations used to log on to the servers which control the network.

Server computers are often PCs which are made to be more **reliable** and have lots of **RAM** and **disk space**. More reliability is often built in by **duplicating components** such as the **power supply** and hard disks. If a power supply breaks, the other can keep the server running until a replacement is fitted.

Servers with several hard disks often use **RAID** (redundant array of inexpensive of independent disks) technology, which divides data between the disk drives. RAID does this in such a way that the data is not corrupted, even if one of the disks breaks down. Many **RAID** systems allow **hot-swappable drives**, so a broken hard disk can be taken out of the server **without switching off the server**, then a new drive fitted with the server still running. RAID can then rebuild the new drive from the others.

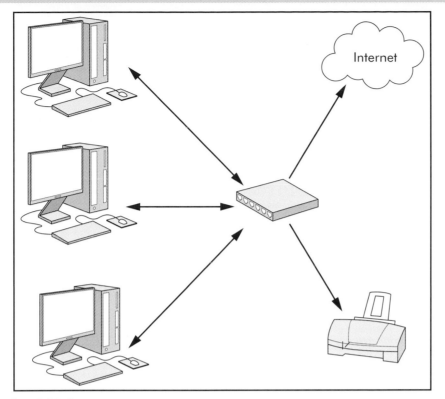

Fig. 6.10 Peer-to-peer

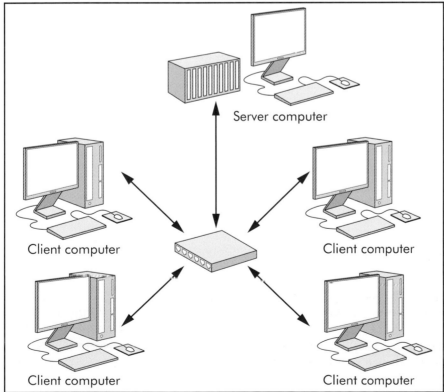

Fig. 6.11 Client server

Client/server networks can be very secure as the servers exercise full control over who logs on to the network and the rights that each registered user has.

Network access methods

Both star and bus topologies can use **CSMA/CD** (carrier sense multiple access with collision detection) as the method for transmitting data through cabling.

> **Key term**
>
> **CSMA/CD** is a method where a computer wanting to transmit some data through the cable listens first to find out if any other computer is transmitting. This is called carrier sense. If there is nothing in the cable, the computer transmits. This is **multiple access**, where many computers can use the cable at the same time.
>
> Unfortunately, sometimes two (or more) computers transmit at the **same time**. The resulting situation is called a data **collision** and ends up with all transmissions spoilt. Each computer will **detect** the collision and then each stops its transmissions, waits a **random** amount of time, then **retransmits**.

Data rates

The **data transfer rate** is how quickly data can travel through the network, often measured as megabits per second (Mbps). 1mbps means that a million **bits** are transmitted in one second (or over 100,000 characters per second).

Ethernet (bus)	10 Mbps
Ethernet (star)	100 Mbps
Wi-Fi	54 Mbps
Gigabit Ethernet	1000 Mbps

> **Key term**
>
> A **bit** is a 1 or 0 inside a computer system. When data is transferred between systems, a bit could be a voltage (1) or no voltage (0). The speed data is transferred at is usually measured in the number of bits that move every second. You must always remember that bits are usually grouped into bytes (with 8 bits to the byte), with each byte representing a piece of data such as a character (e.g. B or E). This means that the data transfer speed usually appears much faster than it really is, as it is the bytes that matter.

Security

Security is an important feature of any reliable network. Security needs to protect the network from hacking and keep its data safe. Protecting a network from hacking can be achieved by:

- making users **change** their **passwords** regularly
- keeping workstations in **secure rooms** so only users authorised to use them can enter the area
- **restricting log-ons** to business hours so nobody can log on in the evening, at night or during unexpected periods (e.g. public holidays)
- **backing up** the data regularly

- **firewalls**
- **anti-virus** software.

Any network is vulnerable to damage if a disaster happens to the premises, such as:

- fire
- flood from water pipes breaking (pipes are often in the ceiling)
- building collapse from vehicle, plane or earthquake impact
- theft.

Backups are kept so that even in one of these extreme situations, the network and data can be restored. Some companies keep their backups on site, but this is only wise if there is a fireproof safe for storage. It is much better to keep the backups off-site, as previously mentioned.

An organisation should always try restoring data from backup to ensure it can be done. It is not a good idea to leave this untested until the first time it is needed for real: it might not work!

Services

Services are the useful things the network does for the organisation, such as:

- communication between departments and users
- file transfer to share documents
- allowing access to databases
- allowing access to printers
- allowing access to the intranet
- allowing access to the Internet.

Fig. 6.12 Video conferencing

Communication

Communication is a crucial service offered by the network. Many users and organisations depend on email to quickly and easily send messages between users and departments. Emails can have attachments so documents can be sent with the message.

Some organisations use **video conferencing** (see Figure 6.12), where the network enables a meeting between users who are in **different locations**, often thousands of miles away.

Conferencing uses **webcams** and **microphones** connected to the computers of people in the meeting so that they can **see** and **hear** each other.

SCORECARD

+ Links people who are physically far apart
+ Unlike a telephone conversation, you can see and hear the person you are talking to
+ More personal than a telephone call
+ Reduces travel costs
- Hardware can be expensive
- Fast (broadband) connection required
- Cannot keep eye contact and observe body language, which are part of human communication skills.

Instant messaging-style applications are also popular communication tools.

File transfer

File transfer happens all the time in a network. Every time a user opens a document on a file server or another workstation it is transferred temporarily to their application, then can be saved back to its original location.

Networks can also move or copy files to other computers as email attachments or using file management software such as Microsoft Windows® Explorer.

Access to databases

Users in every part of the organisation must be able to **see** or **update** data they have rights to.

Here we can see a number of important databases which are being accessed across the network by different departments. The network delivers these databases to user workstations and ensures they have the correct rights.

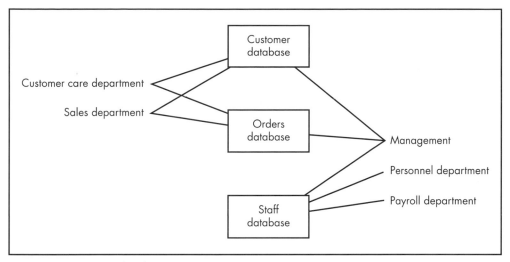

Fig. 6.13 Access to databases

Protocols

A protocol is a particular standard that is used when computers communicate, so that they can understand each other and exchange data safely and reliably.

The protocol usually starts with a communication between the devices to confirm that they are allowed to talk to each other. This may involve a log-on and password. Often the protocol then negotiates the **speed of the connection** and any **error trapping**. The error trapping is needed because whenever data is transmitted there is a possibility that some of it might get **corrupted**.

Error trapping **identifies** any part of the transmission that is spoilt, so that corrupted parts can be **retransmitted** by the sender.

Common protocols include:

- **TCP/IP** (transmission control protocol/Internet protocol) is one of the most common protocols. It allows computers to find sites and communicate data through the Internet.
- **HTTP** (hypertext transfer protocol) is another Internet protocol. It is used by web browsers to request Web pages and images from distant Web servers.

There are many, many others!

Data security issues

Data security is a main concern of ICT professionals who administer networks. They need to ensure that these issues are addressed:

- access control, so only authorised staff can log on and can only see and change the data they are allowed to
- virus protection to ensure viruses are detected and destroyed
- backup and recovery to allow the network to be rebuilt if a disaster hits it
- hacking is not possible
- firewalls to filter out viruses and threats from the Internet.

Access control

Access control is needed to ensure that only authorised staff are able to log on to the network. Access control may be:

- **physical**, where there is a swipe card or door code for the room where the workstation computers are located
- **logical**, the log-on procedure for the network.

Access control reduces threats to the network by only allowing authorised people to use the network.

Virus protection

There are a lot of computer viruses in our modern world, any of which can do damage to valuable data or alter a computer's configuration so that it is no longer usable. Anti-virus software is essential for networks to detect and destroy viruses. Such software usually needs to regularly download up-to-date virus lists ('signatures') from the manufacturer's website to maximise protection.

Viruses usually come from the Internet or from infected files brought in by users who do not know they are infected. Some organisations have procedures that either prevent users from bringing in their own files on removable media or insist upon such files being virus-checked before being used.

Most networks have a firewall where they connect to the Internet. The firewall is a hardware device or software that can block viruses from entering the network.

Hacking

Hacking is when a person who is not authorised to log on to a system finds a way in. Some people hack for the challenge and excitement, others because it gives them an opportunity to alter data held on a system.

Some hackers who expose weaknesses in the security of systems are occasionally employed to advise on how to make the systems more secure. Others may be legally prosecuted for their actions.

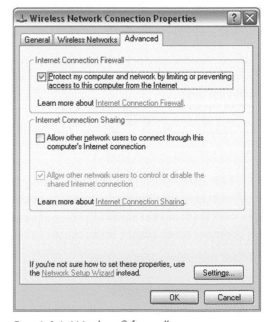

Fig. 6.14 Windows® firewall

Firewalls

A firewall is a method of preventing or blocking viruses from entering a network system. A firewall may be hardware or software.

The Microsoft Windows® operating system includes a software firewall that is found in the properties of an LAN or high-speed Internet in the Network Connections folder in the Control Panel (as shown in Figure 6.14). Many broadband modems have a hardware firewall included as part of the device.

Network hardware and software components

Every network is made from a number of hardware and software components. The hardware connects the computers together, the software makes it work.

Hardware and technologies

This section explains some types of hardware and technologies used in networks.

Network cards

The network interface card (**NIC**) connects a computer to the network. The connection may be:

- through cabling to a switch, hub or another computer
- a radio connection, using Wi-Fi to a wireless access point (**WAP**).

Some typical network cards are shown in Figures 6.15–6.18.

Network cards usually fit into a PCI slot inside a PC, and many notebooks use network cards in their **PC card** slot. As noted in Unit 2: Introduction to Computer Systems, many modern PCs have NICs or wireless built in. (For a more detailed look at Wi-Fi, please see Unit 16: Mobile Communications Technology.)

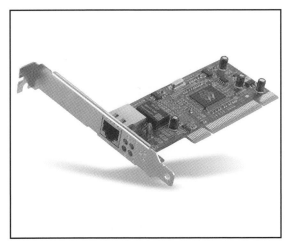

Fig. 6.15 PCI cabled Network Card

Fig. 6.16 Cabled Network PC Card

Fig. 6.17 PCI wireless Network Card

Fig. 6.18 Wireless Network PC Card

Workstations

A workstation is a modestly specified computer (typically a PC) which connects to the network and enables staff members to work using the network. In a client-server network, the clients are effectively the workstations.

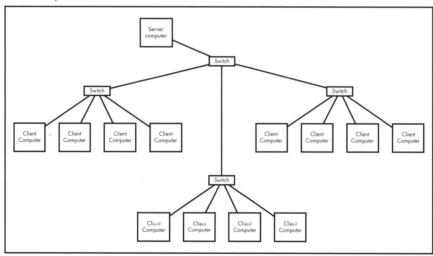

Fig. 6.19 Client server with workstations

Servers

A server is a powerful computer that controls part of a network. In a client-server network, the clients use services the server provides.

There can be several types of server in a network, for example:

- **mail server**: provides users with centralised email facilities
- **print server**: provides users with shared printing
- **file server**: provides users with access to shared data
- **web server**: provides users with access to web pages.

A print server may either be a computer configured to control the printers or a **dedicated device** which connects a printer to the network. A dedicated print server has ports (connections) for both the network cable and the printer. The circuits inside a dedicated print server translate the network data signals into printer data.

Modems

Fig. 6.20 A dedicated print server

DSL modems are used for broadband connection. They are also called broadband modems.

Broadband technologies

There are different technologies for broadband, including:

* **ADSL** (asynchronous digital subscriber line) is a type of **DSL** (digital subscriber line), and for most people the difference is not important. This is what we know as a broadband connection.
* **ISDN** (integrated services digital network) is an older technology that was used by businesses for a fast digital connection between sites.

Virtually every new broadband connection will be ADSL, although some organisations still have ISDN.

Peripherals

Computer systems need peripherals such as printers and scanners. Networks allow peripherals to be shared. This can make peripherals a lot more cost-effective as the organisation needs fewer of them. An office with 10 workstations might have just 1 or 2 printers. Without a network, there would probably be 10 printers, or 1 for each user.

Routers

Many different routes may be available; the router tests the speed and reliability of different routes, then chooses the optimal route for use. Many DSL modems have a router as part of the circuitry.

Hubs and switches

Hubs and switches look the same and both are used to plug in the cables from several computers to connect them together in the network.

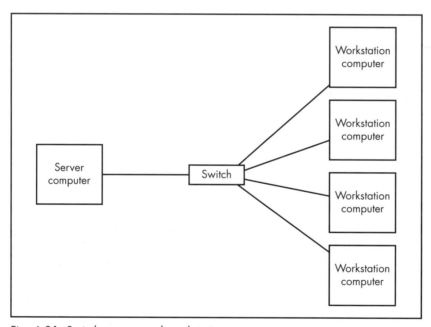

Fig. 6.21 Switch, server and workstations

As already mentioned, a switch is usually more expensive than a hub because it performs a more complex task.

Many large organisations use their switches to form a tree structure to connect the many computers in the network together. Faster cabling is used between switches to help the system work better.

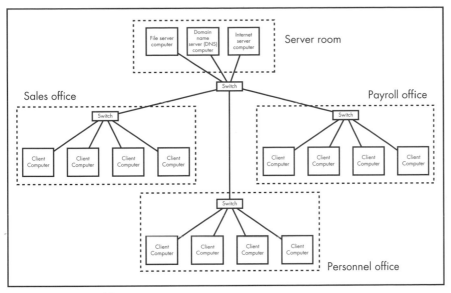

Fig. 6.22 Tree cabling

Uninterruptible power supply (UPS)

A lot of networks are needed 24/7 (24 hours a day, 7 days a week, i.e. all the time). Such networks use a lot of technology to help deliver this availability, including UPS, so if there is a power cut, the system will keep running. A computer can sense when the power starts to drop off, then very quickly change its power source to the UPS. Many UPSs use rechargeable batteries for their power. Large computer systems may use a battery-powered UPS to keep the power flowing, then start up diesel-powered electricity generator(s) to run the systems until mains power is restored.

Connectors and cabling

There is a lot of choice about how computers are connected together in a network.

1. **Fibre-optics** is an optical technology that uses light to transmit data through cabling with lots of strands of glass or plastic inside the cable. This is a fast transmission which can carry a lot of data. Fibre-optic cables can transmit data over 50 miles or more before the signal needs boosting, making them very useful in public systems such as those run by BT. The main use for this technology is to connect different sites together.

2. **Microwave and satellite technologies** are used for long-distance communication. Microwaves are used for transmitting telephone calls and other data between communications towers. Your evening news is often sent back to the television studio via satellite, by vans using

Fig. 6.23 A communication tower or mast

microwave transmitters. Microwaves are also the technology behind Bluetooth™ and Wi-Fi, and both allow wireless transmissions between devices.

3. **Cabling** is commonly used to connect computers together in a network. Most modern networks use a star topology, often with category 5 (cat 5) cabling to connect the workstations to a hub or switch. Cat 5 cabling is **UTP** (unshielded twisted pair); this reveals how the wires inside the cable are arranged. **STP** (shielded twisted pair) cables are **more expensive** and more difficult to work with, but are **faster** and more **reliable**. **Shielding** is when the wires inside a cable are **wrapped in metal** to protect them from **electromagnetic interference**, which can be produced by mains electricity cables.

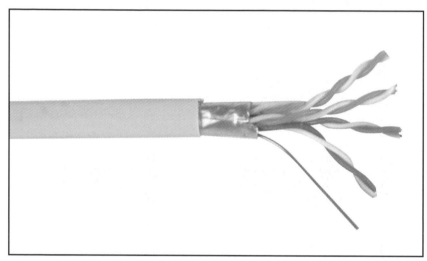

Fig. 6.24 STP cable (metal sheathing visible)

4. A **leased line** may be used by an organisation that wants to have a fast, reliable connection between computer systems in different cities. A leased line is a dedicated line as nothing else is attached to the line.

5. An **analogue line** is the traditional telephone line for voice calls. Modems can be used with these lines to allow computers to pass data through them as sound. **Digital lines**, such as **ISDN**, were developed for transferring data between computers using digital signals instead of sound signals. A modern ADSL broadband connection combines digital and analogue signals with a filter used to split these signals for the telephone handset and the DSL modem. (For more details on analogue and digital signals, see Unit 20: Telecommunications Technology.)

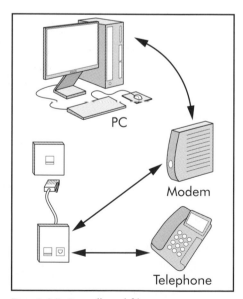

Fig. 6.25 Broadband filter

Software

Many types of software are needed for network usage, including:

- **Internet browser** to show web pages
- **firewall** to reduce virus risk
- **email** to allow user–user communications
- **FTP software** to upload or download files
- **network operating system** to enable the network to function.

Internet browsers

An Internet browser is a very popular software application that makes the Internet very easy to use. Microsoft Internet Explorer® is a browser that is part of the Microsoft Windows® operating system. There are many other browsers available, such as Mozilla Firefox® and Netscape Navigator®.

The browser takes the HTML files that make up a web page, then renders them so that they can be seen properly on the screen.

Firewalls

As discussed above, many computers use a **software firewall** to filter and (if necessary) block data trying to get in (and out of) a network. They are particularly effective when used to protect a computer system against unwanted data arriving from the Internet.

Popular software firewalls include: Zone Labs ZoneAlarm®, Sygate Personal Firewall and Norton Internet Security™.

Email

Email software such as Microsoft Outlook®, Hotmail or GroupWise allow users to send messages to each other. Email software usually includes an address book where the email addresses of people the user communicates with regularly are kept. This makes it much easier to use email, as the address book shows these people by their names rather than their email addresses. Address books also allow groups, so an email can be sent to several people at the same time.

FTP software

> **Key term**
>
> **FTP** (file transfer protocol) software is used to download or upload files to another computer. Uploading is when the file is **sent** from a computer **to** another by a user. Downloading is when a file is **copied down** from another computer **by** a user.

FTP functionality is included in applications that produce websites, such as Microsoft FrontPage® or Dreamweaver, to upload the pages to the Internet.

Network operating system

Networks need a network operating system (NOS) to enable the computers to communicate with each other. Operating systems such as Microsoft Windows® or Linux include peer-to-peer NOS functions to allow simple networking. Client/server NOSs are more expensive and complex. Microsoft Windows Server® and Novell Netware® are examples of a fully featured NOS.

Faults

Faults occur in networks and need to be resolved. Some ICT professionals specialise in this and are able to use their experience in solving new problems.

Here are some examples of commonly occurring faults and how to identify them:

- **network card failure** will stop a computer from using the network; another workstation will work if the cable is plugged into it
- **break in cable** will stop a computer from using the network; another workstation will not work if the cable is plugged into it
- **hardware failure** in hubs and switches which break network connections.

Setting up and using a simple local area network

Many ICT practitioners started their networking experience by setting up a network in their own home. More and more households have several computers. Home networks can be useful for sharing the Internet connection and printing.

Preparation

Before starting to set up a network it will be useful to check that everything needed for the network is available.

Collect components

The network will need components such as:

- **cabling**, which may be purchased, complete with the plugs. Many organisations use cable from a reel, cut it to the right length, then crimp the plugs to each end
- **network interface** cards to connect the computers to the cabling
- a **switch** to connect the cabling together
- **software** to allow the computers to communicate.

Check software licensing

Software **licensing** should be checked to make sure that it covers enough workstations. If not, some of the workstations may not be able to log on to the network.

When software is installed you will **agree to a license to use it**. It will be **illegal** to break the terms of the license.

Set up

Setting up a network involves:

- **setting up the hardware** so the computers are connected to each other
- **installing software** to allow the network to work
- an appreciation of **Health and Safety** to keep yourself and others safe
- knowing how to escalate problems so problems that are beyond your experience can be resolved.

Hardware

Once all the network components are gathered together, a start can be made. The first step will be to set up the hardware.

Computers need to be assembled, each with a keyboard, monitor and mouse. Network cards must be installed and connected to the cabling. Cabling will be connected to a switch or hub (as shown in Fig. 6.26).

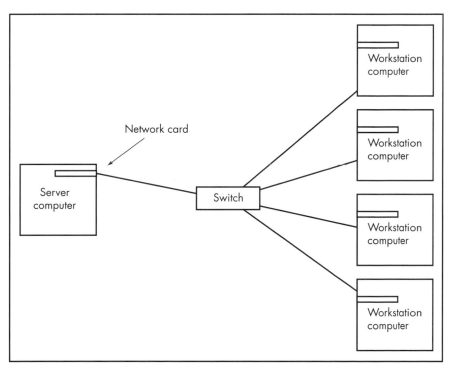

Fig. 6.26 Simple network

Software

The software must be installed on each computer.

If it is to be a client/server network the server should be installed and configured first. The client software can then be installed and set up on each workstation in order to log them on to the server.

Health and Safety

Your health is important, so Health and Safety issues need to be understood:

- use an anti-static wrist-strap when installing components
- only use the correct tools
- be careful when using tools
- be careful of sharp edges inside computer cases when installing network cards
- switch off mains sockets before plugging in mains cables
- only switch on a mains socket when all mains cables are in place and plugged in
- do not leave trailing cables that can be tripped over.

Knowing how to escalate problems

If something does not work, **reread the instructions** and check that you have done everything that is asked for. If it still does not work, **seek help** from someone with more experience. This is called **escalating** a problem and is how you gain experience. Make sure that if a problem is escalated you **understand how the problem was resolved**.

Testing

When a new system is set up it needs to be **tested properly** before handing over to users. Systems that are not tested often do not work properly end up wasting **user time** and **diminish your reputation**.

Testing should be **structured** so that sensible tests are carried out in a sensible order. Structured testing will **record the result** of each test (e.g. work records).

Functionality

The functionality of the system needs to be tested. Each computer should:

- **boot up** without error messages
- **connect** to the network
- be able to **use shared services** such as the Internet
- be **able to print**.

User interface

The user interface is the appearance of the screen. This should be set up so that icons that will not be used are deleted. Icons should be placed on the desktop for any applications that are installed.

Use

The computers will need to be used to confirm the features work and to give you hands-on experience of these.

Communication

You should be able to use the network to communicate with other computers on the local network or the Internet.

Transfer files

You should be able to transfer files between computers on the network.

Other features

Other features of the network should be used, such as allocating:

- users on to the network
- users' rights to parts of the system, such as the control panel (specifying which settings the user can and cannot change)
- disk space to users (this is often called a quota)
- which software applications or utilities the user can run.

☆ **Activity**

Steve Hodder of SHS has contracted you to plan out his new network for him.

You have been asked to produce:

1. A brief description of the type of network you recommend, with the roles of each computer explained.
2. A floor plan of the shop and back office, showing the computers and their potential cabling.
3. An explanation of how the data will be kept safe in the new system.
4. A list of the networking equipment (hardware) and software that will be needed in order to create the network. All items on the list should be correctly priced so that Steve has an idea of how much the network installation is going to cost (excluding your fees, of course).

QUIZ

1. What form of communication occurs between departments inside an organisation?
2. What form of communication is between a department in an organisation and one of their suppliers?
3. What type of user 'right' permits the changing of a document on the network?
4. What type of user 'right' allows a document to be opened on the network, but not changed?
5. What do we call information that has been spoilt?
6. What is the name given to a routine where data is copied to another place to keep it safe?
7. What is the name of the law passed in 1998 to protect the rights of people who have information stored on computer systems?
8. What does LAN stand for (L**** A*** N******)?
9. What does WAN stand for (W*** A*** N******)?
10. What is the name given to the topology shown in Figure 6.27?

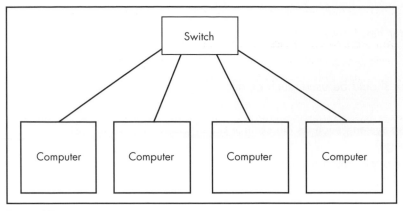

Fig. 6.27

11. What is the name given to the topology shown in Figure 6.28?

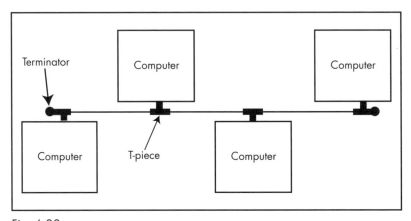

Fig. 6.28

12. What name is given to the type of network with no controlling computer?
13. What name is given to the type of network where a central computer controls the system?
14. What is the name given to a standard that is used when computers communicate so that they can understand each other?
15. What is the name given to the protocol used by Web browsers to format and display the files which make up a website?
16. What is the name given to the protocol used by computers to find sites and communicate through the Internet?
17. What type of access control has a swipe card for a room where workstation computers are located?
18. What type of access control requires users to log on to the network?
19. What is the name of a hardware device that blocks viruses from entering a network?
20. What device sends and receives computer data through a telephone line?
21. What does UTP stand for (U********* T****** P***)?
22. What is the name given to a dedicated line used by organisations wanting a fast, reliable connection between computer systems in different cities?

23. What is the name of the hardware to split broadband signals out for a telephone handset and DSL modem?
24. What type of software allows users to send messages to each other?
25. What type of software allows users to download or upload files to another computer?
26. What is seeking help from someone with more experience called?

ANSWERS

1. Internal
2. External
3. Read/write (also called full access)
4. Read-only
5. Corrupted
6. Backup
7. Data Protection Act (1998)
8. Local area network
9. Wide area network
10. Star
11. Bus
12. Peer-to-peer
13. Client server
14. Protocol
15. HTTP
16. TCP/IP
17. Physical
18. Logical
19. Firewall
20. Modem
21. Unshielded twisted pair
22. Leased line
23. Filter
24. Email
25. FTP
26. Escalation (or escalating the problem)

COURSEWORK GUIDANCE

As a largely practical subject, it is important that you know and understand theory before trying to apply it vocationally. As such you will be asked to describe how networks can improve communications in organisations, how they are used to manage resources, the advantages and disadvantages of their use in managing resources (for example the sharing of printing facilities).

You will need to demonstrate that you have understood LAN and WAN concepts and be able describe hardware and software components.

The Merit criteria asks you to compare network benefits with non-networked alternatives, explain how security threats can be minimised and asks you to demonstrate your understanding of troubleshooting by asking you to provide this kind of support.

For Distinction criteria you are asked to compare and evaluate features of LAN and WAN systems and explain how the network you will create as part of the practical can be extended.

The practical element of this unit will ask you to demonstrate that you can set up, use and test a simple LAN.

Unit links

This unit has direct links to the following:

Unit 2 Introduction to computer systems
Unit 4 Website Development
Unit 13 Software Installation and Upgrade
Unit 16 Mobile Communications Technology
Unit 17 Security of ICT Systems
Unit 20 Telecommunications Technologies

Further reading

Comer, D., *The Internet Book: Everything You Need to Know About Computer Networking and How the Internet Works* (Prentice Hall, 2000) ISBN: 0130308528

Hayden, M. and Habraken, J., *Sams Teach Yourself Networking in 24 Hours* (Sams, 2004) ISBN 0672326086

Rackley, S., *Networking in Easy Steps*, 3rd edn (Computer Step, 2003) ISBN 184078170X

Progress check

To record your achievement, simply tick the criteria awarded to you when each assignment is returned (you may be given three assignments for this unit, U6.01, U6.02 and U6.03 – the final column may not be used). There is a full copy of this grid available on the accompanying CD. The copy will also allow you to record your key skill achievement against Literacy, Numeracy and ICT objectives.

		Assignments in this Unit			
Assignment		**U6.01**	**U6.02**	**U6.03**	**U6.04**
Referral					
Pass					
	1				
	2				
	3				
	4				
	5				
	6				
	7				
Merit					
	1				
	2				
	3				
	4				
Distinction					
	1				
	2				
	3				

A completed sample of this document (for reference purposes) can be found at the back of Unit 1.

SOFTWARE DESIGN AND DEVELOPMENT

INTRODUCTION

Software design and development is concerned with solving problems by designing, implementing, testing and documenting reliable solutions.

Every piece of software that is used in the world today has been produced as the direct result of fulfilling an original user requirement, no matter whether the software is a Web browser, media player or operating system.

This unit will take you through the journey of building your own solution to a given problem, using appropriate software components.

Learning outcomes

On completion of this unit you should:

1 understand the software development process
2 be able to design and produce a software component using an appropriate programming language and environment
3 be able to debug and test a solution
4 be able to document the solution.

RECORDING YOUR PROGRESS

In order to achieve each unit, you will complete a series of coursework activities. Each time you hand in work, your tutor will return this to you with a record of your achievement.

This particular unit has 11 criteria to meet: 6 Pass, 3 Merit and 2 Distinction.

- For a **Pass**: you must achieve **all** 6 Pass criteria
- For a **Merit**: you must achieve **all** 6 Pass and **all** 3 Merit criteria
- For a **Distinction**: you must achieve **all** 6 Pass, **all** 3 Merit **and both** Distinction criteria.

So that you can monitor your own progress and achievement in each unit, a recording grid has been provided (see the **Progress check** section at the end of this unit).

Key term

Software: instructions which tell the computer what to do, also called a program.

Development Process

Typically part of creating an electronic solution for any ICT project, the complete development process is best described by the diagram shown in Figure 7.1 (although this can be abbreviated to **plan-do-review**).

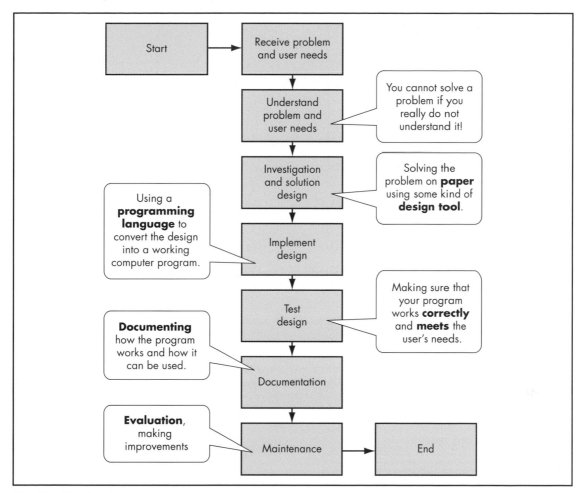

Fig. 7.1 The development process

Problems usually arrive at the developer in the form of a **broad outline description** from the **client** or **target end user**. The description is often sufficient to give an idea of what the problem essentially is, but not enough to start designing a solution confidently. The recommended step is to draw up a list which describes the **user's needs** and **the problem requirements** and helps **investigation**.

Requirements list

This list is best compiled by creating a **labelled grid** (as shown in Figure 7.2).

Input	Data storage
Processes	**Output**

Fig. 7.2 Requirements list

This grid can be used to record the results of your investigations into the problem. Let us start by looking at an example problem.

CASE STUDY

Steve Hodder Skateboards (SHS) is a local company that offers a membership scheme for their customers, giving a discount based on the type of membership 'medal' bought. The membership scheme has three different medal rates:

Bronze: £10 per year, giving 5 per cent discount on purchased goods
Silver: £20 per year, giving 8 per cent discount on purchased goods
Gold: £40 per year, giving 10 per cent discount on purchased goods.

The company would like a simple program that will allow the user to select their medal type and the number of years required, and will output the total price and the discount given.

Let us place this information into our empty requirements grid. The first place to start is to work out what **inputs** are required.

Input Type of medal Number of years	Data storage
Processes	**Output**

The next step is to work out what kind of **output** is required.

Input	Data storage
Type of medal Number of years	
Processes	**Output** Total price % Discount to be given

At this point we can see what is needed for input and what will need to be output.

The **data storage** and **processes** are the missing link – **how** we get from the input to the output.

Data storage

Encompassing **small data items** and **larger data structures**, data storage includes:

- any value mentioned in the problem
- any value calculated
- any value needed to process
- any value which will be output.

Sometimes it is difficult to get the data storage correct. Do not worry – you can always **add** or **remove entries** from it as your understanding of the problem improves.

Using these rules, we can redraw the grid with the appropriate **data storage**:

Input	Data storage
Type of medal Number of years	*Type of medal* *Number of years* *Total price* *Discount % to be given* **Medal price** **Medal discount**
Processes	**Output** Total price % Discount to be given

You will notice that we have **copied** the **inputs** and **outputs** into the **data storage** quarter, as well as **adding** entries for the **medal price** (£10, £20, £40) and the associated **medal discount** (5 percent, 8 percent and 10 percent). The next step is to work out what the **processes** should be.

Processes

Working out the **processes** is typically the difficult bit – these are the actual steps required to **convert** the **input** into the **output**. Generally speaking, you will find that the more complex a problem is, the more complex its processes will become in order to solve it. The processes are actually the core of the solution, where the ideas are placed that solve the problem. It is quite common not to get this right first time!

Let us try to redraw the grid once more, adding the processes:

Input Type of medal Number of years	**Data storage** *Type of medal* *Number of years* *Total price* *Discount % to be given* **Medal price** **Medal discount**
Processes Select the right discount % for the selected medal Select the right medal price of the selected medal Calculate total price (number of years x medal price)	**Output** Total price % Discount to be given

Solution design

Once we understand the user's needs and have a requirements list, we can start to **design a solution**. One of the earliest considerations to make is to determine whether or not the **software component** we are about to design is a **standalone program** (i.e. a complete solution) or part of a larger system (a **module**).

In the case study given, it appears to be a standalone program.

Designing

At this point, perhaps, it is necessary to introduce the concept of **programming constructs**, since they will form the heart of any solution we build.

A construct can be thought of as a type of 'building block', and all programs (no matter how complex) are built from **different combinations** of three blocks (sequence, selection, iteration).

Sequence

A **sequence** occurs when actions are performed **one after another** (i.e. step by step).

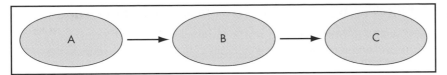

In this example, the action list will **always be A, B and C.**

Selection

A **selection** occurs when a **decision is made** that **determines** which of two (or sometimes more) **possible** actions are taken.

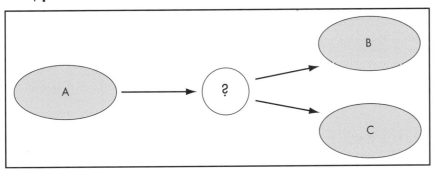

As you can see in this example, **either Action B or Action C is followed – not both**. This would mean that the actions list could either be **A, B** or **A, C.**

Iteration

Iteration is a fancy name for a **loop**; something that **happens repeatedly**. In programming, loops generally repeat **until told to stop**; this is usually achieved with some kind of **decision** or **condition.** Sometimes the decision is placed **after** the actions. We call this **post-conditioning**.

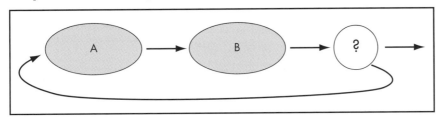

Because of this, the actions in a post-conditioned loop **always work at least once.**

Sometimes the decision is placed **before** the actions. We call this **pre-conditioning**.

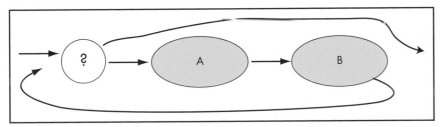

In a pre-conditioned loop, the actions **may never** be processed at all!

You may be wondering why we have both pre- and post-conditioned loops. The answer is simple: there are some occasions when one technique is more appropriate to use than the other.

How do you know when to use each type? Common sense and experience will help, as we shall see!

As mentioned, in order to build a program we often need to use collections of these different constructs, often 'gluing' them together to form a working solution.

QUIZ

Examine the following construct diagrams and work out the different combinations of actions that are possible.

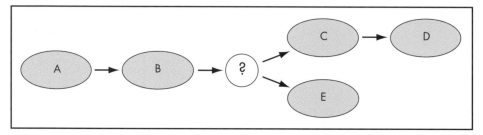

ANSWERS

A, B, C, D
A, B, E

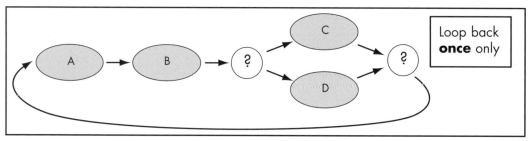

ANSWERS

A, B, C, A, B, C
A, B, D, A, B, D
A, B, C, A, B, D
A, B, D, A, B, C

Design tools

There are many different **paper-based design tools** which can be used to design a solution. Here are the most common that could be considered:

- pseudo code
- flow chart
- storyboard
- structure charts.

After a design has been created on paper, it should be possible to work through its logic and actions to see if it would work. Good solutions can then be implemented using a suitable programming language; poor solutions mean a return trip to the drawing board for another attempt!

Pseudo code

Pseudo code is a way in which we can write solutions using an ordinary **natural language**. The common convention is to use English, but other languages are equally valid. The main thing to remember is not to use any specific programming language terms; try to keep the wording as simple as possible!

We can describe any everyday process using pseudo code. For example, **making a cup of coffee**:

1. Get cup
2. Boil kettle
3. Put coffee in cup
4. Put sugar in cup
5. Add boiling water
6. Add milk
7. Stir.

However, this makes certain **assumptions**: that the cup is clean, that the kettle is full, that the kettle is plugged in, that the person wants milk and sugar, and so on.

We can refine the pseudo code using simple **constructs**; let us insert a **selection** to clean the cup if it is dirty.

1. Get cup
2. if cup is dirty
    2.1 wash the cup
  else
    2.2 use clean cup
  end if
3. Boil kettle
4. Put coffee in cup
5. Put sugar in cup
6. Add boiling water
7. Add milk
8. Stir.

Notice that there is now a **decision to be made** and that there are two **different actions** we could follow, depending on the state of the cup.

Let us take our **Skateboarding case study** and try to write it in pseudo code. Here is the **requirements grid** again:

Input	Data storage
Type of medal	*Type of medal*
	Number of years
Number of years	*Total price*
	% Discount to be given
	Medal price
	Medal discount
Processes	**Output**
Select the right % discount for the selected medal	Total price
Select the right medal price of the selected medal	% Discount to be given
Calculate total price (number of years x medal price)	

The pseudo code might look like this:

1. Ask customer for type of medal required

2. Input type of medal

3. Ask customer for number of years required

4. Input number of years

5. Select the right % discount for the selected medal

6. Select the right medal price of the selected medal

7. Calculate total price = number of years × medal price

8. Output total price

9. Output discount to be given.

This is generally fine and gets a **reasonable** solution, but we could **refine** it a little to give more help when we are ready to **implement**. The pseudo code that needs work are steps 5 and 6:

5. Select the right % discount for the selected medal

6. Select the right medal price of the selected medal

Just how do we go about selecting the right values to use? The answer involves going back to our constructs again; we need to use some **selections**.

Here is a revised version of the pseudo code, with steps 5 and 6 refined in such a way that it should be possible to convert it to a suitable programming language:

1. Ask customer for type of medal required

2. Input type of medal

3. Ask customer for number of years required

4. Input number of years

5. if medal = bronze
     5.1 discount = 5%
  else
    if medal = silver
       5.2 discount = 8%
    else
       5.3 discount = 10%
    end if
  end if

6. if medal = bronze
     6.1 medal price = £10
  else
    if medal = silver
       6.2 medal price = £20
    else
       6.3 medal price = £40
    end if
  end if

7. Calculate total price = number of years $\times$ medal price

8. Output total price

9. Output discount to be given

This is now in enough detail for the programmer to implement using a suitable programming language. Notice that there are no specific language instructions in this pseudo code; the programmer would need to work out how to 'input' and 'output' values in their chosen language.

☆ **Activity**

Write **pseudo code** for the following everyday problems:

1. Calculating and outputting the mean average of three whole numbers input by a user.

2. Converting an input measurement in centimetres to inches (there are 2.54 cm per inch) and outputting the result.

3. Adding together two input whole numbers and asking the user to guess their sum. If the user is wrong, output the correct answer. If the user is right, output a 'congratulations' message.

Flow charts

Flow charts are for most people a familiar (and popular) **visual tool** for describing the steps needed to solve a process. (You may already have read about this in Unit 3: ICT Project.)

Flow charts use a particular set of symbols, which are shown in Figure 7.3.

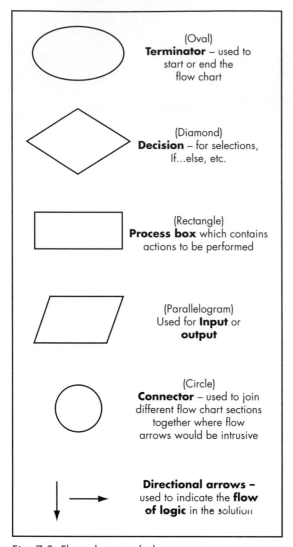

(Oval)
Terminator – used to start or end the flow chart

(Diamond)
Decision – for selections, If...else, etc.

(Rectangle)
Process box which contains actions to be performed

(Parallelogram)
Used for **Input** or **output**

(Circle)
Connector – used to join different flow chart sections together where flow arrows would be intrusive

Directional arrows – used to indicate the **flow of logic** in the solution

Fig. 7.3 Flow chart symbols

As a **visual tool**, flow charts are often preferred to the more text-based approach that pseudo code provides. However, flow charts representing complex solutions often become **large** and **unwieldy**.

Let us put some of these symbols together to **make the cup of coffee**; we'll use the **refined version** that checks to see if the cup is dirty.

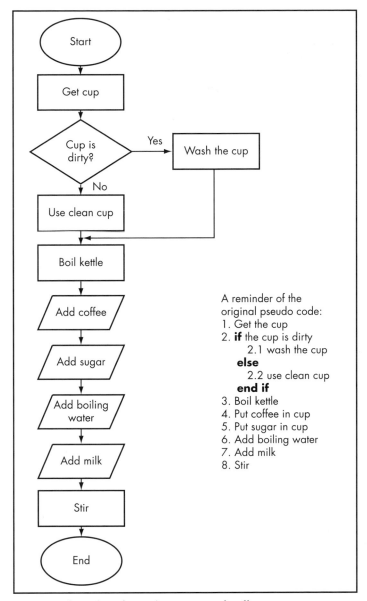

A reminder of the original pseudo code:
1. Get the cup
2. **if** the cup is dirty
    2.1 wash the cup
  else
    2.2 use clean cup
  end if
3. Boil kettle
4. Put coffee in cup
5. Put sugar in cup
6. Add boiling water
7. Add milk
8. Stir

Fig. 7.4 Flow chart for making a cup of coffee

We can also now attempt to flow chart the **Skateboarding case study** problem; be warned though, it is a bit more complex!

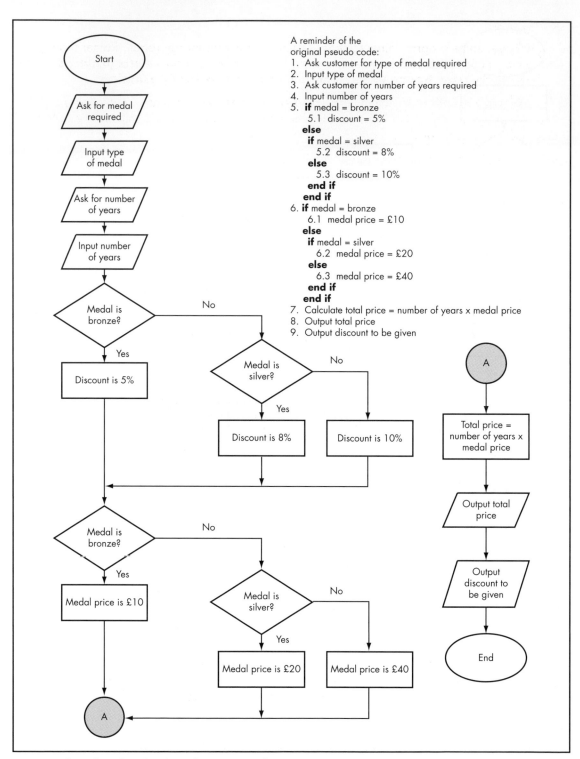

A reminder of the
original pseudo code:
1. Ask customer for type of medal required
2. Input type of medal
3. Ask customer for number of years required
4. Input number of years
5. **if** medal = bronze
    5.1 discount = 5%
  else
    if medal = silver
      5.2 discount = 8%
    else
      5.3 discount = 10%
    end if
  end if
6. **if** medal = bronze
    6.1 medal price = £10
  else
    if medal = silver
      6.2 medal price = £20
    else
      6.3 medal price = £40
    end if
  end if
7. Calculate total price = number of years x medal price
8. Output total price
9. Output discount to be given

Fig. 7.5 Flow chart for Skateboarding case study

Storyboards

As we will see, some programming solutions require a more visual approach. Rather than describe the solution as a series of steps, it should be possible to produce **storyboards** which describe what the **user hopes to see** when the program is **actually running**.

In this way, it is possible to show the **expected on-screen appearance** of the program before it is written and plan how it will work. The actual mechanics of the solution (i.e. what kinds of decisions and calculations it makes) may not be described at this point.

Here is an example storyboard for the **Skateboarding case study:**

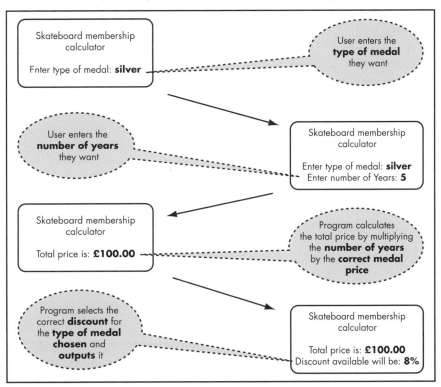

Fig. 7.6 Storyboards for Skateboarding case study

If the developer is intending to solve the programming using a visual language (e.g. Microsoft Visual Basic®), it should be possible to sketch out the basic buttons, textboxes and forms needed. It will also be possible to explain what actions should be performed when certain events occur (e.g. when a button is clicked).

Another advantage to this type of design tool is that the target user gets an idea of how the final program will look when running. This will enable them to make suggestions, improvements or corrections if the developer has misunderstood the original problem.

Structure charts

Unlike flow charts which demonstrate the **logical flow** of a solution, a structure chart is designed to show the **underlying construction** of the solution. It is very good at demonstrating the actual **constructs** (sequences, selections and iterations) which have been 'glued' together to build the solution. Also in direct comparison to flow charts, structure diagrams only make use of lines and rectangles.

Each construct is drawn using a slightly different notation: sequence, selection, iteration.

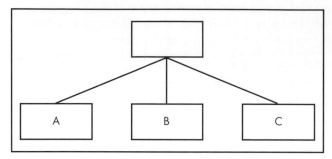

In this example, the **sequence** reads A, B and then C.

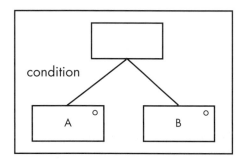

In this example, the **selection** shows that it is either A or B, not both. Notice the use of the small 'o' in the top-right corners of each **o**ption to demonstrate that it is a selection rather than a sequence.

It is useful to remember that the **action to perform** if the **condition is true** always goes on the **left**.

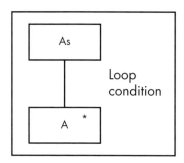

In this example, the **iteration** is indicating that As (plural) is actual made out of 'A' occurring a number of times, in fact, as many as the loop condition allows. The small asterisk (or star) in the top-right corner of the box signifies that the box is to be repeated.

Let us put this new tool into practice by revisiting the cup of coffee solution (see Figure 7.7).

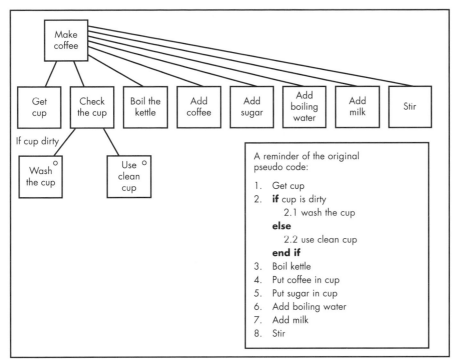

Fig. 7.7 Structure diagram for making a cup of coffee

You may notice that this diagram is a little more compact than the flow chart version; this is simply due to the different notation used. Flow charts tend to grow **vertically**, while structure diagrams tend to grow **horizontally** (unless they are really complex). Remember this when starting to draw yours!

Another tip is to remember that planning the design should be a spontaneous activity and that it should occur first (i.e. **before** the actual programming is performed).

Often, a hand-drawn flow chart or structure diagram is preferred to no sign of planning at all. **Remember this when submitting work for this unit.**

☆ **Activity**

Now use a **visual design tool of your choice** to solve these same problems:

1. Calculating and outputting the mean average of three whole numbers input by a user.

2. Converting a measurement input in centimetres to inches (there are 2.54 cm per inch) and outputting the result.

3. Adding together two input whole numbers and asking the user to guess their sum. If the user is wrong, output the correct answer. If the user is right, output a 'congratulations' message.

Let us produce a structure diagram for the **Skateboarding case study** problem; again, be warned, though, it is even more complex!

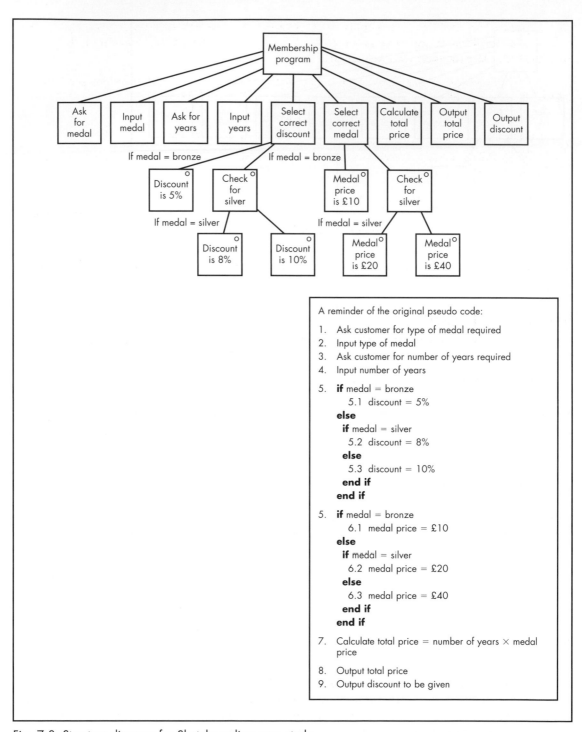

Fig. 7.8 Structure diagram for Skateboarding case study

At first glance, this looks far more complex. However, when examined carefully you should be able to see the different **constructs** which have been used to create this solution; in this example, only **sequences** and **selections** are used.

Structure diagrams are particularly useful when dealing with procedural languages such as **BASIC** (beginner's all-purpose symbolic instruction code)**, PASCAL** or **C**.

> **Key term**
>
> **Procedural languages** are used to solve problems by stating the actions required step by step.

If you plan to use other languages, particularly those which are visually oriented, such as Microsoft Visual Basic®, Borland® Delphi® and Sun Java™ you will find this design technique far less helpful and may be advised to use the storyboard approach instead.

As already noted, once a design has been put together and it has been examined to see if it meets the user's needs and the requirements list, it is possible to move on to the implementation stage.

Implementation

Implementation requires **converting your design** (no matter which technique you use) into a **recognised programming language**.

You may recall from Unit 2: Introduction to Computer Systems that computers only understand **binary**. In order for your programs to be run they have to be **converted** into binary (sometimes called 'machine code') by another program called a **translator.** Although there are many types of translator, the most common is called a **compiler**, and each programming language has its own version.

Over the last 50 years, there have been literally **hundreds** of different programming languages created. Some languages have since fallen out of favour with professional developers or been superseded; others cover very specific 'niche' markets (e.g. programming vending machines). A number of languages are popular within the industry because they are **fast to work with** and generally produce **reliable** and **robust** (not likely to 'crash') solutions.

As a new programmer, it is worthwhile getting a quick overview of a few different languages.

C

C is one of the older languages which could be considered for implementing your solutions, dating back to the early 1970s. It was created by Dennis Ritchie for use on the Unix™ operating system.

It is still a very popular general-purpose language, particularly for engineers interfacing hardware with computer systems, as it permits a fair degree of low-level (i.e. processor) control. Another advantage is that there are many different C compilers available, targeting code for a number of different operating systems and hardware configurations. This fact makes C a very **portable** language.

Here is a simple C program:

```c
#include <stdio.h>

int main(void)

{

        printf("Hello, BTEC First Diploma student!\n");

        return 0;

}
```

Microsoft Visual Basic®

Microsoft Visual Basic® is a **RAD** (rapid application development) tool used on Microsoft Windows® operating systems to create a range of different applications. As the name suggests, RAD languages encourage a **fast development environment**, and Microsoft Visual Basic® (often referred to as just 'VB') offers just that. Microsoft Visual Basic® programs are developed in **drag and drop** fashion, allowing the user to build a Windows®-compliant interface in a matter of minutes.

The big drawback with Microsoft Visual Basic® is typically its **speed** and **reliance** on the Windows® operating system in order to run. However, it is easy to get to grips with and proves itself a useful first language for many developers. Microsoft® has recently developed the language further into its VB.NET incarnation, which effectively superseded Microsoft Visual Basic® version 6.0.

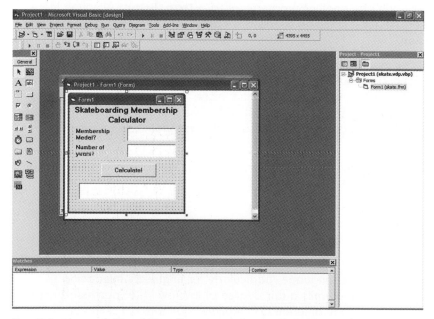

Fig. 7.9 Microsoft Visual Basic® version 6.0 at work © Microsoft, 2006

PASCAL

PASCAL is named after the seventeenth-century French mathematician and philosopher, Blaise Pascal. It was developed in 1970 by Niklaus Wirth as a language particularly suitable for **structured programming** (as demonstrated in the structure diagrams shown earlier, Figs 7.7 and 7.8) and **procedural solutions**.

Although PASCAL has a **standardised ISO** (International Organization for Standardization) version, many different versions exist. A popular RAD-based extension of PASCAL called Delphi has been created by Borland and competes with Microsoft Visual Basic® for the title of premier visual development tool on the Microsoft Windows® platform.

PASCAL itself is very rarely used for commercial solutions, but has found a lot of favour in schools, colleges and universities for teaching the principles of programming.

JavaScript

JavaScript is the Netscape Communications Corporation's name for its version of the ECMAscript language. JavaScript's most common usage is to provide **automation** and **interactivity** to **web pages**. As such, it is often included within the **HTML** (hypertext markup language) files which are downloaded from the Internet to a user's computer system.

Despite its name, it is only distantly connected to Sun's Java language. However, in common with Java, JavaScript's syntax (rules) is very much derived from C.

Language comparison table

Language	Advantage	Disadvantage
C	• Well established • Popular in industry • Portable • Efficient • Some C compilers are free • Standardised	• Syntax can be difficult to learn • Development can be slow • Case sensitive
Microsoft Visual Basic®	• Uses RAD approach • Quick, visual results for the new programmer • Friendly drag-and-drop development • Auto-corrects case used when keying code	• Relies on Microsoft Windows® • Slowly being phased out by VB.NET • Generally not fast • Generally not very efficient

Language	Advantage	Disadvantage
PASCAL	• Encourages good programming practice • Good for new programmers • ISO standard • Not case sensitive	• Not really used in industry, better as an educational tool
JavaScript	• JavaScript interpreter is present in most Web browsers (free) • Can be unpredictable as it can vary when run under different Web browsers	• Can be difficult to find and fix errors (debug) • Limited in scope • Can stop when error is encountered • Generally not fast • Case sensitive

So, which should you use? Ultimately, the choice of programming language has as much to do with the target user's expectations as the skills and knowledge of the actual developer (you!). At this level, any of the languages listed above represents a reasonably good trade-off between **functionality**, **ease of development** and **potential quality** of the end product.

Development environment

Modern programming languages use an integrated development environment (**IDE**). A modern IDE often incorporates the following facilities:

Text editor	Allows the developer to **key in** the program code. This works in a similar way to a word processor; however, there is unlikely to be a spellcheck function.
Compiler	Checks the code for errors and produces the necessary **machine (code) binary** for the program to run. It can also report a **list of errors** for the developer to fix.
Debugging facilities	Helps the developer to locate and fix the errors in their program. Common debugging facilities that we will see are **watches**, **breakpoints** and **traces**.
Help system	Offering advice on instructions and example code
Syntax highlighting	Displays **different aspects of the language** in **different colours** to improve the code's **readability** and its **debugging.**
Project and file management facilities	A facility which **groups together** multiple files which are needed to develop a single program.

Deployment tool	A facility to take developed programs and 'package' them into **installation programs** which can be more readily distributed to other users.
Backup and version management	Facilities which create backups of written programs and can keep track of multiple versions of the same program during development. **CVS** (concurrent versions system) is an example of such a system.
Customisable environment	Facilities to customise the environment to suit the **preferences** of the developer; this may include **colours**, **font** and **font size**.

While some commercial programming environments cost many hundreds of pounds, there are a number of free alternatives that could be considered. For example, Sun's Java development environment is essentially free for use and can be readily downloaded from the Internet. However it is not really a novice's programming language.

An example of a modern development environment is shown in Figure 7.10.

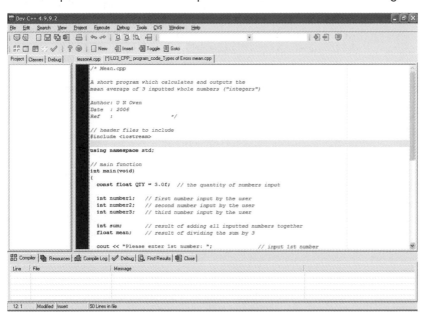

Fig. 7.10 A typical IDE, Dev-C++ ©Bloodshed Software, 2006

Coding the solution

In order to demonstrate the implementation stage of the development procedure, it will be necessary to select a couple of suitable programming environments. For contrast, we will select Microsoft Visual Basic® version 6.0 and Bloodshed Dev-C++.

Syntax

It is obviously beyond the scope of this book to teach you either the full Microsoft Visual Basic® or C programming languages; both would require books of their own to do the task justice.

However, it should be possible to discuss a few basic syntax ideas for each language, noting similarities and differences as we attempt to implement the Skateboarding case study.

In this section, we will limit our comparisons to:

- identifiers
- commenting
- pre-built functions.

(The full C and Microsoft Visual Basic® solutions are provided at the end of the section.)

Identifiers

You may recall our **data storage** quadrant from our requirements grid. If not, here it is again:

Data storage

Type of medal
Number of years
Total price
% Discount to be given
Medal price
Medal discount

The storage of data in a program is perhaps one of the most important considerations. Both C and Microsoft Visual Basic® can create **identifiers** – **sensible** and **meaningful names** which represent a **value**. There are two basic kinds of identifier:

- **variables** – a name with a value that **may** change
- **constants** – a name with a value that **cannot** change (it is fixed).

You might like to think of variables and constants like **boxes** in the computer's **memory** which can **store** different **values**. In order to store a value in such a box, it is necessary to know its **data type** – whether the value will be a number, letter, date, and so on. Both C and Microsoft Visual Basic® can store lots of different data types; unfortunately, the syntax is different for each.

Here is a **table of comparison**, showing how to set up the **identifiers** in each language:

Things to notice:

- C uses **semi-colons** to mark the **end of its statements**; Microsoft Visual Basic® **does not**.
- Variables are **prefixed**, with an **initial letter indicating** their data type (e.g. **iYears** is an **integer** – a whole number, one with no decimal places). This is **good practice** and is similar to a famous programming technique called **Hungarian Notation**.
- It is a common convention to write constants in **UPPERCASE**.
- Identifiers **cannot** contain **spaces** or **start** with a **number** in either C or Microsoft Visual Basic®.
- **Constants** are used to represent values that are **unlikely to change** while the program is running.

Identifier	Variable or constant	C syntax	Microsoft Visual Basic® syntax
Type of medal	Variable	char sMedal[10];	Dim sMedal As String
Number of years	Variable	int iYears;	Dim iYears As Integer
Total price	Variable	float fTotal_price;	Dim fTotal_price As Single
% Discount to be given	Variable	int iDiscount;	Dim iDiscount As Integer
Medal price	Variable	float fMedal_price;	Dim fMedal_price As Single
Bronze medal price	Constant	const float BRONZE_COST = 10.0;	Const BRONZE_COST As Single = 10#
Silver medal price	Constant	const float SILVER_COST = 20.0;	Const SILVER_COST As Single = 20#
Gold medal price	Constant	const float GOLD_COST = 40.0;	Const GOLD_COST As Single = 40#
Bronze medal discount	Constant	const int BRONZE_DISC = 5;	Const BRONZE_DISC As Integer = 5
Silver medal discount	Constant	const int SILVER_DISC = 8;	Const SILVER_DISC As Integer = 8
Gold medal discount	Constant	const int GOLD_DISC = 10;	Const GOLD_DISC As Integer = 10

Basic commenting

Both C and Microsoft Visual Basic® permit the use of **comments** or **remarks**. Comments are used to **document the solution within the code**. It is often called **self-documentation**, and, with the sensible naming of identifiers, goes a long way to making code **easier to read** and therefore easier to **understand**.

C has two basic commenting types: **single-line** and **multi-line.**

    // I am a single line comment

    /* I am
       a multi-line
       comment!

    */

Microsoft Visual Basic® tends to use just a single-line comment.

    ' I am a single line comment

Comments are **ignored** by the compiler; they are merely there to **explain the purpose** of the code.

Predefined functions

Both C and Microsoft Visual Basic® use predefined functions. A function is a **pre-written software component** that is called upon by the developer when they want to **perform a special task**.

An example of a **Microsoft Visual Basic® predefined function** would be:

    Number = Val (text)

The 'Val' function is used to get the numeric value of a piece of text (i.e. it converts '12' into 12) so that it can be used in arithmetic calculations.

An example of a C pre-defined function would be:

    System ("cls");

This simply clears the screen (in some versions of C this is the same as **clrscr();**).

C Implementation

The following program code represents the **final C language solution** for the Skateboarding case study, as tested using the **Bloodshed Dev-C++** development environment.

```
/* skate.c

    A program which calculates a membership fee for a local skateboarding company.

    The company has three levels of membership, bronze medal, silver medal and gold medal.

    Bronze: £10 per year, giving 5% discount on purchased goods
    Silver: £20 per year, giving 8% discount on purchased goods
    Gold: £40 per year, giving 15% discount on purchased goods

    The program allows the customer to enter the medal required and the number of years they
    require. The program then calculates and outputs the cost of membership and the correct
    discount the customer will receive on future purchases.

    Author: M Fishpool
    Date: January 2006
    Ref: Skateboarding */

#include <stdio.h>
#include <process.h>
#include <string.h>

int main()
{
    const float BRONZE_COST = 10.0;         // cost of a year of bronze membership
    const float SILVER_COST = 20.0;         // cost of a year of silver membership
    const float GOLD_COST = 40.0;           // cost of a year of gold membership
```

```c
const int BRONZE_DISC = 5;           // discount % of bronze membership
const int SILVER_DISC = 8;           // discount % of silver membership
const int GOLD_DISC = 10;            // discount % of gold membership

char sMedal[10];                     // medal required, input by user
int iYears;                          // number of years, input by user
float fMedal_price;                  // membership price of medal chosen
int iDiscount;                       // discount of medal chosen
float fTotal_price;                  // total price of membership required

printf("Skateboard Membership Calculator\n\n");
printf("Enter type of Medal: ");     // ask for medal type
scanf("%s",sMedal);                  // input medal
printf("Enter number of Years: ");   // ask for number of years
scanf("%d",&iYears);                 // input number of years

if (strcmp(sMedal,"bronze")==0)      // bronze medal wanted?
    fMedal_price = BRONZE_COST;
else
    if (strcmp(sMedal,"silver")==0)  // silver medal wanted?
        fMedal_price = SILVER_COST;
    else
        fMedal_price = GOLD_COST;    // gold medal wanted?
    //endif
//endif

if (strcmp(sMedal,"bronze")==0)      // bronze medal wanted?
    iDiscount = BRONZE_DISC;
else
    if (strcmp(sMedal,"silver")==0)  // silver medal wanted?
        iDiscount = SILVER_DISC;
    else
        iDiscount = GOLD_DISC;       // gold medal wanted?
    //endif
//endif

fTotal_price = iYears * fMedal_price;  // total price = year wanted x medal
system("cls");                       // clear the screen for output

/*   output headings, total price
and discount received
*/

printf("\n\nSkateboard Membership Calculator\n\n");
printf("Total price is GBP %6.2f\n",fTotal_price);
printf("Discount available will be %d percent\n\n",iDiscount);

system("pause");                     // wait for a keypress before ending
return 0;
}
```

Note: Minor modifications may be needed if a different C or C++ development environment is used.

Microsoft Visual Basic® solution

The following program code represents the **final Microsoft Visual Basic® language solution** for the Skateboarding case study, as tested using the **Microsoft Visual Basic® 6.0** development environment.

```
'skate.frm
'
'A program which calculates a membership fee for a local skateboarding 'company.

'The company has three levels of membership, bronze medal, silver medal 'and gold medal.

'       Bronze: £10 per year, giving 5% discount on purchased goods
'       Silver: £20 per year, giving 8% discount on purchased goods
'       Gold: £40 per year, giving 10% discount on purchased goods

'The program allows the customer to enter the medal required and the
'number of years they require.  The program then calculates and
'outputs the cost of membership and the correct discount the customer
'will receive on future purchases.

'Author: M Fishpool
'Date: January 2006
'Ref: Skateboarding

Dim sMedal As String                   ' medal required, input by user
Dim iYears As Integer                  ' number of years, input by user
Dim fMedal_price As Single             ' membership price of medal chosen
Dim iDiscount As Integer               ' discount of medal chosen
Dim fTotal_price As Single             ' total price of membership required

Const BRONZE_COST As Single = 10#      ' cost of a year of bronze membership
Const SILVER_COST As Single = 20#      ' cost of a year of silver membership
Const GOLD_COST As Single = 40#        ' cost of a year of gold membership

Const BRONZE_DISC As Integer = 5       ' discount % of bronze membership
Const SILVER_DISC As Integer = 8       ' discount % of silver membership
Const GOLD_DISC As Integer = 10        ' discount % of gold membership

Option Explicit

Private Sub Command1_Click()

    sMedal = Text1.Text
    iYears = Val(Text2.Text)

    If sMedal = "bronze" Then           ' bronze medal wanted?
       fMedal_price = BRONZE_COST
    Else
       If sMedal = "silver" Then        ' silver medal wanted?
          fMedal_price = SILVER_COST
       Else
          fMedal_price = GOLD_COST      ' gold medal wanted?
```

```
        End If
    End If

    If sMedal = "bronze" Then                ' bronze medal wanted?
        iDiscount = BRONZE_DISC
    Else
        If sMedal = "silver" Then            ' silver medal wanted?
            iDiscount = SILVER_DISC
        Else
            iDiscount = GOLD_DISC             ' gold medal wanted?
        End If
    End If
    fTotal_price = iYears * fMedal_price       'total price = year wanted x medal
    '
    ' Output the total price and discount received
    '
    Text3.Text = "Total price is GBP " + Format(fTotal_price, "0.00") + vbCrLf
    Text3.Text = Text3.Text + "Discount available will be " & iDiscount & " percent"

End Sub
```

Being a **RAD** environment, the Microsoft Visual Basic® solution also has the interface design (its **form**) to create. The basic design is shown in Figure 7.11.

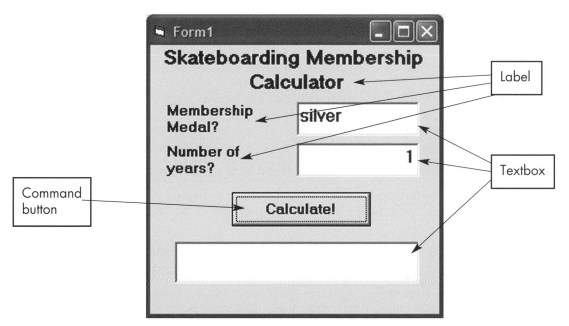

Fig. 7.11 The Microsoft Visual Basic® form design for the Skateboarding case study

Debugging

According to a famous anecdote, the word 'debugging' dates back to the mid-1940s when operators using an early computer system that had stopped working found a **dead moth shorting out various electronic components**. When being told of this, **Grace Hopper** (later to become a very celebrated female figure in computer science) was famously quoted as saying that it was the first computer '**bug**'. After that, the act of **finding** and **removing** errors from a program popularly became known as 'debugging'.

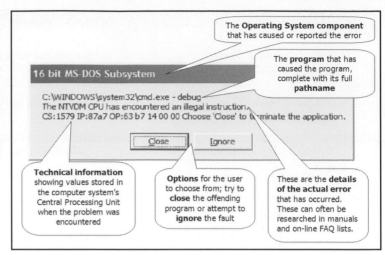

Fig. 7.12 Error message encountered at run-time in Microsoft Windows

In modern computing, bugs are obviously not physical, but are **mistakes which the programmer makes** while developing a computer program. Some errors occur at **compile-time**: these occur **before** the program is running (compile-time errors). Some errors occur at **run-time**: these occur **as** the program is running (run-time errors).

During compile-time there are two basic types of problems that can occur: syntax errors and semantic errors.

Syntax errors

In normal usage, syntax refers to the **grammatical structure** of a written or spoken sentence: in computing, it refers to the structure of instructions in a program which **cannot be understood by the compiler**. Typically, the developer has **spelt an instruction incorrectly** or **used the wrong symbol**.

Syntax errors are **fatal** and they **must all be fixed** before a program can be run.

Each **different programming language** has **its own syntax** which governs how it should be written. In order to reduce the number of syntax errors, it is necessary to learn the language thoroughly.

It should also be remembered that although a compiler **can spot errors**, they typically **do not fix them**: that's the job of the developer. If you have problems, asking for help and getting a fresh pair of eyes from a friend usually does the trick!

Less severe errors are often called **warnings;** these indicate a **potential problem** (e.g. losing accuracy of decimal places in a calculation), but do not stop the compilation process. It is usually optional (but recommended) that a developer fixes these. If left unchecked, **warnings can cause run-time errors to occur**.

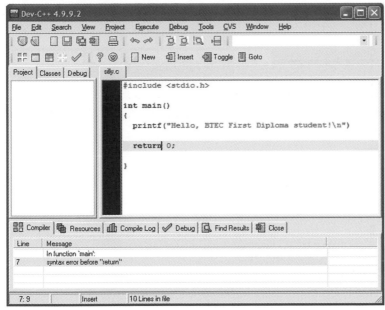

Fig. 7.13 A missing semi-colon creates a syntax error in this C program. But where?

Semantic errors

These errors are harder to detect as they are usually a result of mistakes in **logic** or **arithmetic.** As such, the compiler **does not tend to spot them**; the program **will run**, but probably **will not work as expected**.

The following is a typical semantic error, found in a simple C statement:

> fAverage = iNumber1 + iNumber2 + iNumber3 / 3;

The **syntax** of this line of code is fine. However, if this calculation were executed **it would not** find the **mean average** of the three numbers. **Can you see why not?** The answer is that the **meaning is wrong**; in order to find the mean average we would need to **add all three numbers together** and **divide their sum by 3**. A bit like this:

> fAverage = (iNumber1 + iNumber2 + iNumber3) / 3;

Can you spot the difference? This corrected statement has **bracketed** the variables being added together in order to ensure that the normal **BODMAS** rules of operation are overridden. If this was not performed, the computer would divide 'iNumber 3' by 3 and then add on iNumber1 and iNumber2. (For more on BODMAS, see Unit 10: Spreadsheet Software.)

It is because of such subtle differences that semantic errors are so much harder to debug.

Debugging tools

Fortunately, the modern developer has a number of different **tools** available to help them debug a program.

The most commonly used tools in a development environment are:

- traces
- breakpoints
- watches.

Each debug facility is designed to give information to the developer while the program is being developed and run.

Although the actual workings of debug facilities vary between development environments, the basic concepts remain very similar.

Traces

A trace is a simple mechanism which allows the developer to run a program **line-by-line** to see which lines of code are being executed as it proceeds. This is particularly useful when the code **branches** into different pathways, especially when selections (e.g. **if** statements) are being used. If the trace demonstrates **unexpected behaviour**, the developer can recheck their logic to see what has gone wrong.

Figure 7.14 shows an example of a trace in progress in Microsoft Visual Basic® 6.0.

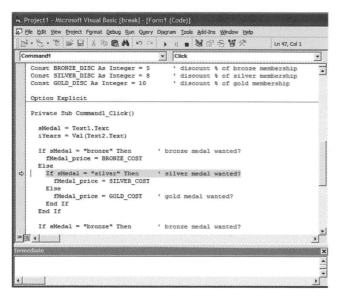

Fig. 7.14 Tracing through a line of Microsoft Visual Basic® program code

In Microsoft Visual Basic® 6.0, the trace facility (known as **Step into**) is activated by pressing the **F8** key or using the appropriate **toolbar icon** or **menu option** (as shown in Figure 7.15).

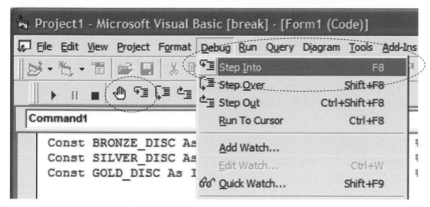

Fig. 7.15 How to start tracing in Microsoft Visual Basic®

Breakpoints

Tracing through a **long** program line-by-line to find an error is **laborious**. This is especially annoying if you know the first 50 lines or so are bug-free! Fortunately, most development environments have a facility called a **breakpoint**. A breakpoint is used to place a special

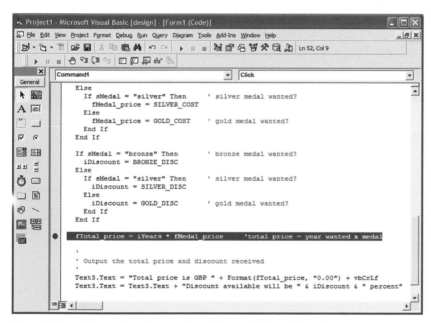

Fig. 7.16 Adding a breakpoint in a Microsoft Visual Basic® program

'break' marker in the program on a specific line of code. When the program hits this breakpoint when it is running, its execution is **temporarily halted**. From this point, the developer can either choose to trace **from this point onwards** (i.e. saving a lot of unnecessary tracing occurring **before** the breakpoint) or use a **watch**.

In Microsoft Visual Basic® 6.0, the breakpoint facility is **toggled** 'on' and 'off' by pressing the **F9** key or **clicking in the left-hand margin next to the desired line of code** (as shown in Figure 7.16).

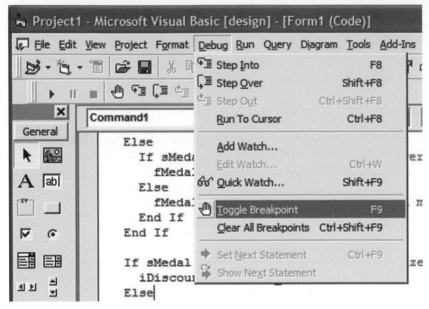

Fig. 7.17 How to toggle a breakpoint in Microsoft Visual Basic®

Watches

A watch is a very useful tool when debugging: it allows the developer to 'spy' on the **contents** of a variable while the program is running, typically during a **trace**.

The most common programming problem occurs when a developer is desperately trying to work out why **calculations** or **processes are not working as expected**. Of course, this is often because unexpected values are being stored in the variables. A watch facility allows us to **see the changes in variable contents** as different lines of the program code are executed.

In the example in Figure 7.18, the developer has added watches to **three specific variables** (fTotal_price, iYears and sMedal). This is achieved by using the **Debug** menu (as before) and naming the desired variables in a pop-up dialog box. As you can see, the values of the variables are shown after the program has hit a **breakpoint**.

Microsoft Visual Basic® also has the ability to let the developer **hover** the mouse pointer over a variable in the actual program code (while it is temporarily halted or in a trace). This rewards the developer by displaying a small **tool-tip**, showing the variable's current value. This can be done in addition to setting actual watches.

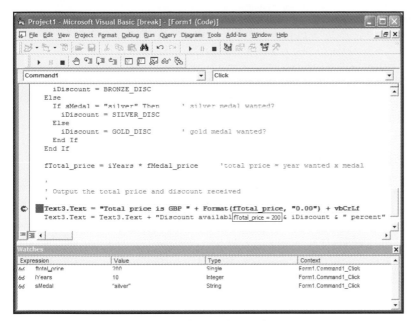

```
iDiscount = BRONZE_DISC
Else
   If sMedal = "silver" Then      ' silver medal wanted?
      iDiscount = SILVER_DISC
   Else
      iDiscount = GOLD_DISC       ' gold medal wanted?
   End If
End If

fTotal_price = iYears * fMedal_price      'total price = year wanted x medal
'
' Output the total price and discount received
'
Text3.Text = "Total price is GBP " + Format(fTotal_price, "0.00") + vbCrLf
Text3.Text = Text3.Text + "Discount availabl[fTotal_price = 200]& iDiscount & " percent"
```

Fig. 7.18 Watches in a Microsoft Visual Basic® program

Testing

Testing is the **quality control** procedure of the development process. Without testing there **is no guarantee** that the solution **works properly** or actually **meets the original needs** of the user, as defined in the original problem requirements.

Modern development processes are very complex, and as computer systems and their applications become even more intricate, so testing becomes more difficult to do quickly and completely. This is demonstrated by the number of 'bug-fixes' and 'patches' that can be downloaded from the Internet for programs that have already been released commercially by their developers, complete with a list of bugs and annoying errors. One technique is to release the program in a 'close-to-finished-but-not-quite' state and allow people to download it for evaluation. This is often called a **beta** release and is beneficial to both the developers and the customers: the customers get **free software** to use and the developers get an **unpaid workforce of testers**.

However, much **internal testing** is performed before even an early product is seen.

Test plan

The first stage in testing requires planning a suitable list of things to test. Not surprisingly, we call this a **test plan**. The most important thing to test is that the program meets the user's requirements; however, we also want to ensure that the solution is RARE:

- **reliable**: works repeatedly without unexpected problems
- **accurate**: works out calculations properly
- **robust**: works without crashing, particularly due to user mistakes when inputting data

- **efficient**: works as quickly as possible, using the best programming techniques and components.

A test plan should attempt to:

- check different **logical pathways** (e.g. selections and iterations)
- check **normal data** (data which makes sense and is likely to be input)
- check **extreme data** (data which is unlikely, but may be input)
- check **erroneous data** (data which makes no sense and may be input).

This can normally be achieved by collecting together a **suitable quantity and spread of test data** which will meet all these criteria. Of course, it is difficult to recommend what a 'suitable quantity' is in every possible scenario, but it is a good idea to ensure that particular checks are repeatable and do not just work out of 'luck'.

Expected and actual results

The best way to perform a test is to use a simple **trace table**. A trace table is a grid that records the **values entered** and **logical pathways used** when a program runs. Usually this is achieved by tracing the program code through **on paper**. This is often called a **dry run**. The values produced by this are called its **expected results**.

The same set of test data can then be tested on the live program. This will give the **actual results**. **Comparison** of the actual and expected results will give you an idea of how accurate your program is.

If the results are **similar**, this tends to suggest that the program is **correct** and works as expected. If the results are **different** (and you are confident in the paper solution and your calculations), it might indicate a problem somewhere in the code that has been keyed in; this is when the **debugging tools** become useful.

Trace table for Skateboard case study							
Test no.	sMedal	iYears	Medal selected?	sMedal_ price	iDiscount	Expected fTotal_ price	Actual fTotal_price in screen capture number...?
1	silver	1	silver	20	8	20.00	capture#1
2	gold	20	gold	40	10	800.00	capture#2
3	bronze	−1	bronze	10	5	−10.00 or Error?	capture#3
20	gold	A	gold	40	10	Error?	capture#4
21	mercury	2	gold	40	10	80.00	capture#5

A good addition to any trace is the use of **screen captures** to show the **physical results** of the program running.

The following table and figures (7.19–7.33) demonstrate the use of a trace table and some sample runs of the Skateboarding case study solution (shown both as C and Microsoft Visual Basic® solutions).

In the extract of the trace table shown above:

- Test #1 perfectly normal, using **normal data**
- Test #2 perfectly normal, using **extreme data** (20-year membership!)
- Test #3 perfectly normal, using **erroneous data** (−1 year membership!)
- Test #20 perfectly normal, using **erroneous data** ('A' year membership!)
- Test #21 perfectly normal, using **erroneous data** (invalid medal type – 'mercury')

Fig. 7.19 Microsoft Visual Basic®, test #1

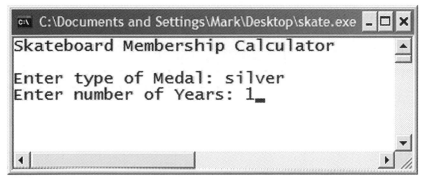

Fig 7.20 C, test #1

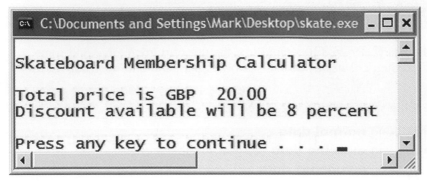

Fig 7.21 C, test #1

Test verdict?

Test #1 has performed as expected, indicating no problem.

Fig. 7.22 Microsoft Visual Basic®, test #2

Fig. 7.23 C, test #2

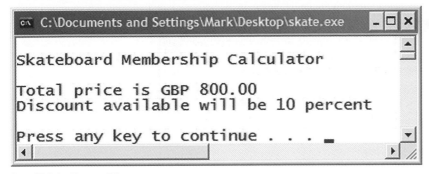

Fig. 7.24 C, test #2

Test verdict?

Test #2 has performed as expected (even with extreme data), indicating no problem.

Fig. 7.25 Microsoft Visual Basic®, test #3

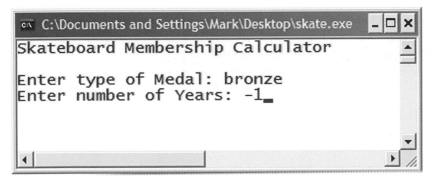

Fig. 7.26 C, test #3

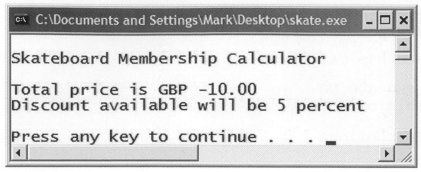

Fig. 7.27 C, test #3

Test verdict?

Test #3 has performed as expected (with erroneous data), but it makes no sense! In an **ideal design** it should **not** be possible to input a **negative** number of years. The solution is to use a technique called **validation** and usually involves the use of an **iteration**.

Fig. 7.28 Microsoft Visual Basic®, test #20

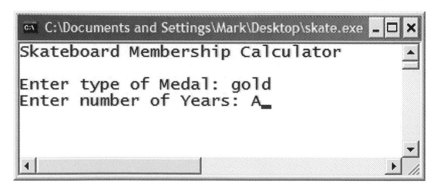

Fig. 7.29 C, test #20

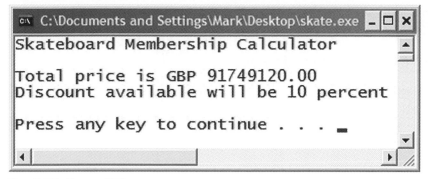

Fig. 7.30 C, test #20

Test verdict?

Test #20 has performed as expected (with erroneous data), but it has generated **different incorrect** results for **total price** in the C and Microsoft Visual Basic® solutions. Again, validation is needed to prevent the user from keying in bad data, in this case a non-numeric number of years.

Fig. 7.31 Microsoft Visual Basic®, test #21

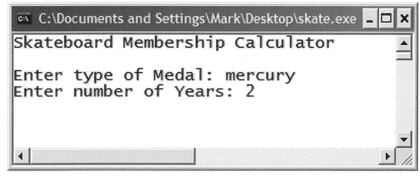

Fig. 7.32 C, test #21

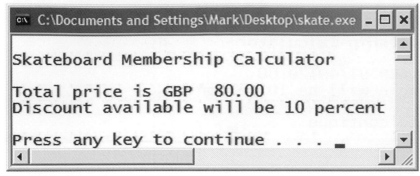

Fig. 7.33 C, test #21

Test verdict?

Test #21 has performed as expected (with erroneous data), but an error in the program logic has identified an invalid medal name ('mercury') as 'gold'. This has generated the correct results for 'gold'. Ideally, the 'mercury' input should have been rejected as an error.

Overall, the actual testing has performed as expected. Some improvements on validation can be recommended for future developments.

Documentation

Whether **printed** or in an **electronic format**, documentation is a vital aspect of any development process. Its importance cannot be underestimated.

There are essentially three forms of documentation:

- **internal documentation**: documentation actually inside the program code
- **user documentation**: documentation for the end-user, which explains how to actually use the program (e.g. a **user's manual** or **instruction guide**)
- **maintenance documentation**: documentation written by the programmer that explains the **technical aspects** of the solution. This is important should another developer (or even the same programmer) attempt to **expand** or **alter** the program in the future.

Let us take some time to examine each in turn.

Internal documentation

Programs should ideally be **self-documenting**. This can be commonly achieved using:

- **sensible** and **meaningful** identifier names
- good use of **comments**, written **in context** (i.e. describing what the line does in relation to the actual solution, not the syntax)
- good **indentation** and **layout**.

However, it should be remembered that if you are developing a program within an **organisation**, they will undoubtedly have specific **standards** that they use for **naming**, **formatting** and **approaches** to common problems. These standards are important; they ensure that solutions do not become 'too personalised', and that they can be worked on by any member of the organisation, should maintenance be required.

User documentation

User instructions are designed to be read by a **typical** person, not a developer. This is an important fact to remember! Accordingly, the user instructions should **avoid the use of technical terms or jargon**. Content may include:

* how to **install** the program (and **uninstall**)
* how to **start and end** the program
* how to **use** the program **properly**
* how to **resolve** problems that might occur (often called a **troubleshooting** guide).

Taking the user through a **typical example** of the program working is a good idea. Additionally, it is often advisable to keep instructions brief (**step by step** instructions are good), with **diagrams** or, better still**, screen captures**, to show the program actually working.

Maintenance documentation

This is technical documentation and, as noted, the **intended audience** is a **developer**. This means that programming terminology may be freely used, as long as it is sufficiently explained. Maintenance documentation may include:

* **overview of the original problem** in the developer's own words
* **technical description** of how the program works
* **fully self-documented** program listing
* **data dictionary** (a slightly less complex form of this is the **data table**) – an example data table for the Skateboarding case study would look something like the table shown on the following page, essentially describing all the **identifiers** in the solution
* an **evaluation** of the program (identifying its **strengths** and **weaknesses** and how well **it met the end-user's needs**)
* **future development** – an overview of **corrections** (of errors), **improvements** (to performance) or **expansions** (to functionality) that could be made.

Additionally, it is good practice for a developer to record (or **log**) **any changes** made to the program and what issues they addressed. These should be listed under **modifications**.

Identifier name	Variable or constant	Data type	Initial value	Description
sMedal	variable	String	-	medal required, input by user
iYears	variable	Integer (whole number)	-	number of years, input by user
fTotal_price	variable	Floating point (decimal)	-	total price of membership required
iDiscount	variable	Integer	-	discount of medal chosen
fMedal_price	variable	Floating point	-	membership price of medal chosen
BRONZE_ COST	constant	Floating point	10	cost of a year of bronze membership
SILVER_COST	constant	Floating point	20	cost of a year of silver membership
GOLD_COST	constant	Floating point	40	cost of a year of gold membership
BRONZE_DISC	constant	Integer	5	% discount of bronze membership
SILVER_DISC	constant	Integer	8	% discount of silver membership
GOLD_DISC	constant	Integer	10	% discount of gold membership

☆ **Activity**

Remember these problems that you solved using **pseudo code** and then a **visual design tool** of your own choice?

1. Calculating and outputting the mean average of three whole numbers input by a user.

2. Converting an input measurement in centimetres to inches (there are 2.54 cm per inch) and outputting the result.

3. Adding together two input whole numbers and asking the user to guess their sum. If the user is wrong, output the correct answer. If the user is right, output a 'congratulations' message.

You do? Good! Because now it is time to take your solutions and implement them, using an appropriate target programming language! If you have used storyboarding, it is recommended that you use Microsoft Visual Basic®. If you have used pseudo code, flow charts or structure diagrams, you can try using PASCAL, C, C++ or JavaScript.

QUIZ

1. After receiving a problem, what is the first thing you should do?
2. Rearrange the following developmental stages into the correct order (earliest first):
   TEST   DESIGN   DOCUMENT   MAINTENANCE   IMPLEMENT
3. Which four headers are used in a requirements list/grid?
4. Name the three software development constructs.
5. Name three commercial programming languages.
6. What is an IDE?
7. Give five features you might find in an IDE.
8. What is debugging?
9. Name three different debugging tools.
10. Which four qualities are we looking for when we test our solutions?
11. What are the three different classifications of test data that should be found in a good sample?
12. What is the difference between 'expected' and 'actual' results?
13. Which type of error is reported by a compiler: syntax or semantic?
14. Will a program compile if it has no comments?
15. Name three aspects of a program's implementation that improve its self-documentation.

ANSWERS

1. You should fully understand the problem before you attempt anything else!
2. DESIGN   IMPLEMENT   TEST   DOCUMENT   MAINTENANCE
3. Input, storage, processing and output
4. Sequence, selection and iteration
5. C, C++, Microsoft Visual Basic®, Visual Basic.NET, C#, Java™, JavaScript
6. An integrated development environment.
7. Text editor
   Compiler
   Debugging facilities
   Help system
   Syntax highlighting
   Project and file management facilities
   Deployment tool
   Backup and Version management
   Customisable environment
8. The act of locating and correcting errors or faults in a program
9. Trace, watch and breakpoints
10. A good program should be reliable, accurate, robust and efficient (RARE!)
11. Normal, extreme and erroneous
12. Expected results are what you predict your program will output. Actual results are what the program really outputs when it is run on the computer system.
13. Syntax
14. Yes; comments are optional and not needed by the compiler.
15. General layout and indentation, commenting and meaningful identifiers

COURSEWORK GUIDANCE

Programming can be one of the most frustrating subjects, but it is also one of the most enjoyable units because there is so much to learn and do!

To pass you will need to show a solid understanding of programming concepts, being able to describe a programming language (probably the one you are using in your school or college), use the tools of the language to develop a solution for a user and demonstrate that you can correct the code, using the language's own tools and techniques. You will also need to be able to document solutions and comment on how this should be done to meet organisational needs.

For the higher grades, you will need to justify the choices you have made in programming language and use of techniques, show that you can meet organisational standards, prepare technical documentation for your solution and evaluate your development procedures.

Unit links

This unit has direct links to the following:

Unit 2 Introduction to computer systems
Unit 3 ICT Project

Unit 8 Customising Applications Software
Unit 9 Database Software
Unit 10 Spreadsheet Software

●●●Further reading

Flanagan, D., *JavaScript Pocket Reference* (O'Reilly, 2002) ISBN: 0596004117

McBride, P., *Turbo Pascal Programming Made Simple* (Made Simple, 1997) ISBN: 0750632429

Wang, W., *Visual Basic 6 for Dummies* (Hungry Minds Inc. US, 1998) ISBN: 0764503707

Willis, T., Reynolds, M., Crossland, J. and Blair, R., *Beginning VB.NET* (Wrox Press Ltd, 2002) ISBN: 1861007612

Progress check

To record your achievement, simply tick the criteria awarded to you when each assignment is returned (you may be given three assignments for this unit, U7.01, U7.02 and U7.03 – the final column may not be used). There is a full copy of this grid available on the accompanying CD. The copy will also allow you to record your key skill achievement against Literacy, Numeracy and ICT objectives.

Assignment		Assignments in this Unit			
		U7.01	U7.02	U7.03	U7.04
Referral					
Pass					
	1				
	2				
	3				
	4				
	5				
	6				
	7				
Merit					
	1				
	2				
	3				
	4				
Distinction					
	1				
	2				
	3				

A completed sample of this document (for reference purposes) can be found at the back of Unit 1.

CUSTOMISING APPLICATIONS SOFTWARE

INTRODUCTION

The popularity of the personal computer (PC) has completely changed the way that people use computers. In the early days of IT, many companies had programs written especially for them in order to make their PCs generate the results they needed. These were called bespoke solutions and they relied on skilled developers to design and develop complex software, using programming languages such as BASIC, C or PASCAL.

Of course, many new and exciting custom-built solutions are still being programmed to meet customers' needs today. Even as you read this introduction, more bespoke programs are being created, using newer languages such as C++, Java and Microsoft Visual Basic®. As you probably know by now, these types of solution are covered throughout Unit 7: Software Design and Development in this book.

However, things have begun to change: improvements in the skills of the typical IT user have created a new breed of developer, one who uses commercially available applications, such as databases and spreadsheets, to perform basic customisations and automations. And perhaps more importantly, they can perform these operations without the need for traditional specialist programming skills.

This unit is designed to build on your basic understanding of such applications in order to explore ways in which you too can personalise familiar applications for particular individuals or optimise them for specific situations.

Reading through Unit 9: Database Software and Unit 10: Spreadsheet Software before you continue is helpful, but not necessary.

Learning outcomes

On completion of this unit you should:

1 understand why application software is customised

2 be able to customise application software

3 be able to create templates in application packages

4 be able to create macros and shortcuts in application packages.

RECORDING YOUR PROGRESS

In order to achieve each unit, you will complete a series of coursework activities. Each time you hand in work, your tutor will return this to you with a record of your achievement.

This particular unit has 11 criteria to meet: 5 Pass, 4 Merit and 2 Distinction.

- For a **Pass**: you must achieve **all** 5 Pass criteria.
- For a **Merit**: you must achieve **all** 5 Pass and **all** 4 Merit criteria.
- For a **Distinction**: you must achieve **all** 5 Pass, **all** 4 Merit **and both** Distinction criteria.

So that you can monitor your own progress and achievement in each unit, a recording grid has been provided (see the **Progress check** section at the end of this unit).

The following example describes a typical bespoke solution:

CASE STUDY: ESTIMATES FOR STEVE HODDER SKATEBOARDS

Steve Hodder runs a small skateboard shop. Among the product range are custom-built skateboards. Steve found producing the estimate for a new skateboard took lots of time. Estimates often had mistakes in the prices they quoted as they sometimes got their sums wrong. If a board was under-quoted the profit was reduced. If over-quoted, the customer often went to another shop with a better price.

One day he decided to get a program written to produce these estimates. The program lets him type:

- how many hours he expects the job to take
- colours and graphics for the skateboard
- how much the materials will cost
- the name, phone number and address of the customer.

The program prints out an estimate which can be given to the customer or posted in a window envelope (to save rewriting the address). This makes estimates look professional and they are also very quick to produce.

After using the program for a month, to test it worked correctly, Steve went back to the programmers to further develop the program so that a new version was produced to run on a computer in the shop. This allowed customers to enter their own details so they could explore the combinations of parts with how much their skateboard would cost.

Although the program cost them a lot of money it has paid for itself time and time again, as each job now has realistic profit and work is not lost from estimating too high a price. The new version has been a particular success as it frees up Steve's time and allows customers to explore at their own pace exactly what they require for their dream skateboard.

Bespoke programs like these are still written today for specialised areas where the **cost** and **time** involved in producing them is worthwhile because they make **complicated jobs** on the PC **simple** and **quick** for the user. However, the power and flexibility offered by modern applications in delivering basic customisation and automation could have created a similar solution for **far less cost** in **much less time**.

As you have just read, it may have been possible to **customise a spreadsheet application** to reliably calculate the same estimations as Steve Hodder's bespoke solution.

Here is a simple table comparing the two approaches:

	Typical bespoke program	**Customised application**
Example	Estimator program	Estimator spreadsheet
Set-up time	3 months	3 hours per template
Cost	£6000	£400
Ways it can be used	1	Many

As you can see, the main advantages to using the customised application approach are:

• quicker (the underlying application does most of the work)
• costs less
• spreadsheet application is more flexible and can be used for other tasks (e.g. displaying income graphs).

Once we have explored different customisation techniques, we will revisit Steve Hodder's estimation problem and outline a possible tailored solution, using some form of customised application.

So, why are applications customised?

The following section explains how an application may be **adapted** to suit **particular individuals** and **situations**, the benefits of doing so and the disadvantages that it may bring.

Types of customisation

There are many reasons why application software is customised, but generally they all make the user **more productive** or the computer **more enjoyable to use**.

Common types of customisation we can perform are explored below.

Default settings

Default settings control **how the computer behaves** if **no other changes are made**, for example, the folder which is used to store your saved documents or whether documents should be printed in landscape or portrait mode. This way the user does not have to waste time finding ways to make the computer work properly.

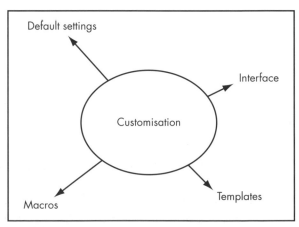

Fig. 8.1 Customisation overview

Default settings are there when the **program is started**. Most programs allow default settings to be changed so that they are still there the next time the program starts.

Microsoft® Word's default settings are very comprehensive and can be customised easily by the user. For example, you could customise the application to **ignore** spellchecking of Internet addresses and filenames (as has been selected in figure 8.2).

Menus and toolbars

Menus and **toolbars** are used to control applications, making them more **obvious** and **easy to find**. The defaults for these are usually good enough for most people; however, some users like to change these so that **popular actions** are **immediately accessible**. They might also choose to **hide options** they **rarely use** in order to **de-clutter the interface**.

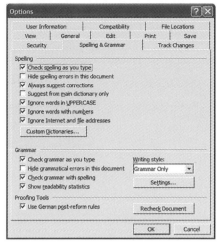

Fig. 8.2 The default Options tabbed dialogue box in Microsoft® Word

The menus are the words at the top of the application, for example, **File**, **Edit**, and so on.

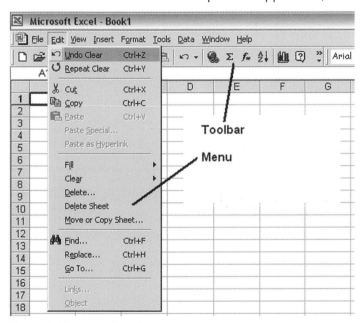

Fig. 8.3 Menus and toolbars

Toolbars are the **on-screen buttons** selected with a simple mouse click.

How to change a menu in Microsoft® Word

To customise the menu in Microsoft® Word, use the **Tools**, **Customise** menu option to see the dialogue box shown in Figure 8.4.

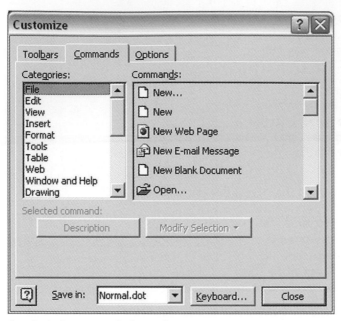

Fig. 8.4 Customise dialogue box

From here, a popular **command** can be **dragged to a menu** (as shown in Figure 8.5).

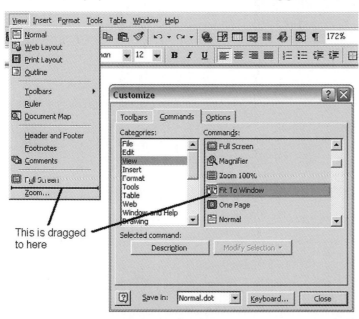

Fig. 8.5 Microsoft® Word menu change

To produce what can be seen in Figure 8.6.

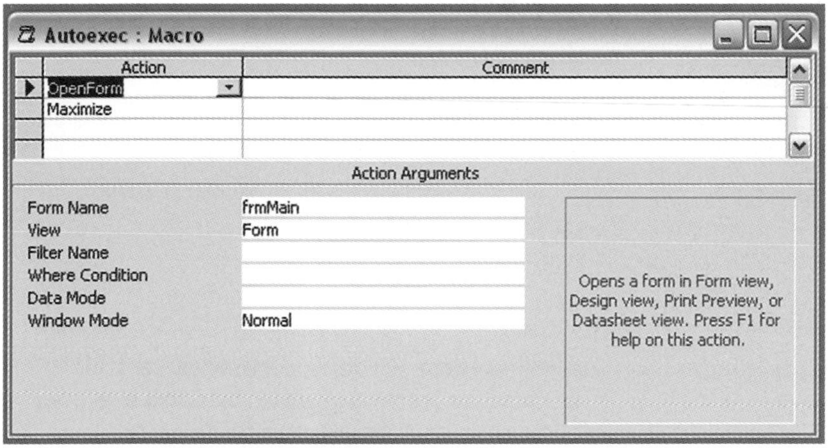

Fig. 8.6 The customised View menu

As you can see, the 'Fit To Window' option is now added to the View menu.

Additionally, it is possible to customise the interface by selecting a new toolbar to display (see Figure 8.7).

Toolbars can also display in two different ways:

- **floating** – appearing in their own 'window', which can be moved around the screen, floating over the text.
- **docked** – physically locked to the interface so that it cannot move.

The use of customised menus and toolbars reduces the number of keystrokes required of the user.

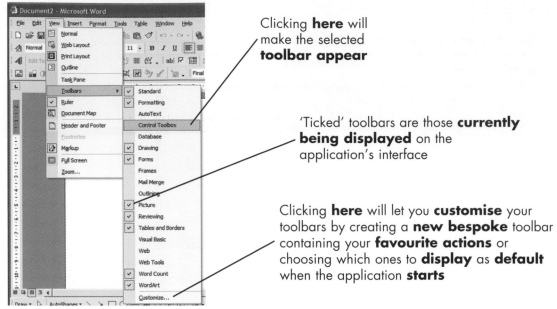

Clicking **here** will make the selected **toolbar appear**

'Ticked' toolbars are those **currently being displayed** on the application's interface

Clicking **here** will let you **customise** your toolbars by creating a **new bespoke** toolbar containing your **favourite actions** or choosing which ones to **display** as **default** when the application **starts**

Fig. 8.7 Selecting toolbars to display or hide

Templates

A **template** can be used for **every new document** that is created so that new documents start with **formatting** and **common words** already there. The template holds information such as whether the page is landscape or portrait, the fonts and font sizes to use, as well as any headers or footers that may be preferred.

How to create a template using Microsoft® Word

1. Create a new document.
2. Type in the words that are needed when the document starts. These are the words that will be the same in every document created with the template.
3. Add any graphics that are to be in every document created with the template.
4. Use the **File, Save As** menu option, give the template a name, then change the document type to **Template** and press the **OK** button.
5. Close the document.

How to create a template using Microsoft Excel®

1. Create a new spreadsheet.
2. Type in the words that are needed when a new spreadsheet is started.
3. Add any formulas that are to be in every spreadsheet created with the template.
4. Use the **File, Save As** menu option, give the template a name, then change the document type to **Template** and press the **OK** button.
5. Close the spreadsheet.

Forms to help data entry

Forms can be a very powerful way of helping the user **make the right choices**. The attributes of forms, like **user prompts**, for example, make them easy for users to understand. **Input boxes** and **navigation buttons** also help you to choose the right options and stay in a particular part of a program, or move to another one.

Forms can also contain useful **validation routines**, which check to see if input boxes are being completed correctly.

In the We Cell Phones example shown in Figure 8.8, the 'Quantity required' value **cannot** be left empty, have a '0' or be non-numeric.

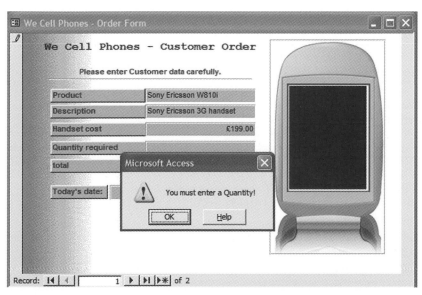

Fig. 8.8 We Cell Phones using validation in their forms

Wizards in Microsoft Access® (a popular database application) are themselves a series of **linked forms** that support you through a particular process. They are designed in such a way that you will remember to make choices at the right time, or move to a specific supplementary screen to make other choices.

Another advantage of using forms is that you can **simplify the user inputs** by creating **list boxes** for specific categories that **users can choose from**, rather than requiring them to key in information from memory (see Figure 8.9).

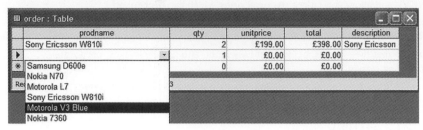

Fig. 8.9 A list box being used to assist data entry in Microsoft Access®

This will mean that when you use a **query** to search the data, you are **more likely to get accurate results**. Had the user keyed in the data and misspelt an input, the record may well have been omitted from a search.

A form can ensure that only one choice of word is made at a time, **making it easier** to, for example, count the instances of something in a database. For example: you have created a database to report technical problems. Consider the following complaints which have been entered by users:

Cannot log on
Can't log on
Log on doesn't work
System won't let me in!

All of the above **mean the same thing**. Unfortunately, when searching a database for instances of a particular fault, what will you key in to search for? Can't log on? Log on doesn't work? **The computer doesn't know** that they all mean the same thing, so they would be **treated as different faults**!

SCORECARD

+ Forms simplify complex processes, especially data entry

+ Forms can provide a list of limited choices for the user to select from

+ Forms have instructions and useful user prompts

+ Forms can be standardised by the organisation

+ User generally has less to write

+ Forms can be used to create a simple 'front-end' user interface for a more complex process

+ Forms can include validation, a process which can filter input for bad data.

− Forms which get too big are confusing!

Macros

A **macro** is a way of **running several** commands in an application, by pressing a button or selecting a menu option, to **automate actions** and **improve accuracy**.

A macro in Microsoft® Access is the list of **commands** or **actions** that use forms, reports or tables that have already been created in the database. Simple examples of Microsoft® Access macros include:

- printing reports
- performing searches
- opening forms and reports
- importing and exporting data.

Figure 8.10 shows an example of a Microsoft® Access macro.

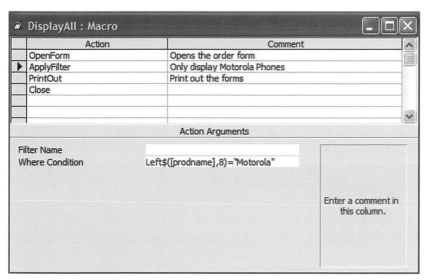

Fig. 8.10 A Microsoft® Access macro

This macro, which could be executed from a **single** button click:

1. opens the order form
2. applies a filter that includes only Motorola handsets
3. prints the filtered forms
4. closes the form.

A macro in Microsoft® Word or Excel® is a program, which produces a result for the user. This type of macro can be **recorded** by **remembering key presses** and **mouse clicks** or can be written by the user as program code (as shown in Figure 8.11).

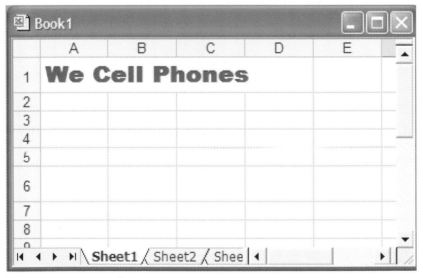

```
Book1 - Module1 (Code)

(General)                              Macro1

Sub Macro1()
'
' Macro1 Macro
' Macro recorded 1/04/2006 by WCP
'

'
    ActiveCell.FormulaR1C1 = "We Cell Phones"
    ActiveCell.Select
    Selection.Font.Bold = True
    With Selection.Font
        .Name = "Arial Black"
        .FontStyle = "Bold"
        .Size = 16
        .Strikethrough = False
        .Superscript = False
        .Subscript = False
        .OutlineFont = False
        .Shadow = False
        .Underline = xlUnderlineStyleNone
        .ColorIndex = 5
    End With
End Sub
```

Fig. 8.11 A Microsoft Excel® macro

This macro looks more complex as it is written in Microsoft Visual Basic® for applications (VBA) rather than the more straightforward macro language shown in the Microsoft® Access example.

Fig. 8.12 The macro is run in cell A1

If you look closely at Figure 8.11, you will see that this macro does the following:

1. It puts the text 'We Cell Phones' in the currently selected (**active**) cell.
2. It emboldens the font of the text.
3. It changes the font name to Arial Black.
4. It sets the colour of the text to blue (colour index '5').

This would enable the user to place the company logo anywhere on the spreadsheet, whenever the macro is run, rather than having to waste time with copy and paste or retyping and repeating the formatting.

SCORECARD

+ Macros can combine many complex actions into a single key press or mouse click
+ Macros can be used repeatedly
+ Macros can be recorded based on performing the task manually the first time
+ Macros can be used to do the boring, repetitive jobs
+ Macros are found in most Microsoft® Office productivity suites
- Macros can be complex to write
- Macros can be difficult to debug when they are not working properly
- To get the best out of macros requires a higher degree of technical skill

You **will be** expected to create macros with key presses, mouse clicks and simple options. This unit **does not** expect you to write complex code for a macro or to edit advanced code.

Short cuts

A **short cut** is a key press or menu option that starts a command **quickly** and **accurately**. This can make it much easier for the user, especially if the short cut is easy to remember (e.g. in Microsoft® Word, **CTRL + B** makes selected text **bold**).

Creating a shortcut in Microsoft Word®

Use the **Tools**, **Customise** menu option, then press the **Keyboard** button to see the dialogue box shown in Figure 8.13.

Select the **command** for the short cut, then **press the keys** that you want to start the short cut. As shown here, **Alt** with **Ctrl** and **W** will change the **zoom to page width**. To keep the short cut, use the **Assign** button. In this example, the changes are being saved to **Normal.dot** so they are available to new documents using this **default template**.

SCORECARD

+ Short cuts can be used to more directly perform actions that may require several mouse clicks and navigation of many different menus and dialogue boxes
+ Short cuts may be easier to remember than complex menu options
+ Short cuts could be standardised across different applications
- Keyboard short cuts may require difficult combinations of key presses, which are difficult for some users to perform

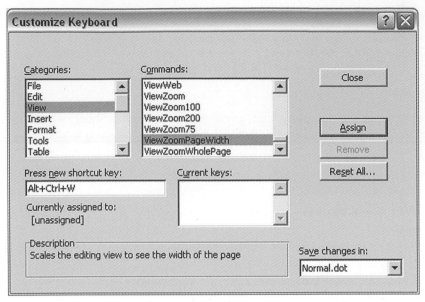

Fig. 8.13 Customising the keyboard

Benefits of customisation

Speed

Customisation can make using a computer a lot quicker by:

- **reducing** the amount of typing
- **reducing** the number of **menu choices**, making it easier for the user as they have **less to type** and **less to remember**
- **instantly finding** the right place in a document for some information to be entered
- doing **a number of actions** (such as a macro) with a **single** keypress or short cut.

Accuracy

As we have seen, customisation can help **accuracy** by controlling **data entry**. This makes it much harder for the user to enter bad data. This means that information generated by the program must be better, because the data the program has to deal with is better.

Many forms show the user the expected choices, making it much harder to choose something which is not valid. As we have seen, forms can also **validate** to make sure that data which is entered is accurate, and to reject bad data, which is obviously wrong. **Invalid data** might be:

- a date that is out of range, such as 31/2/07
- a National Insurance number which is out of range, such as YYW035578T, because the format of a NI number is two alphabetic characters, six numeric digits, one alphabetic character (alphabetic means letters in the range A–Z)

Ease of use

Customising application software can help ease of use in the following ways:

- starting documents with common words already typed into them
- automating key presses, so the user makes one choice, and then the customisation performs lots of actions
- using forms with buttons and easy controls for data entry
- selecting complex settings automatically.

Consistency of style

Many companies like to have **consistency of style**. Consistency of style means that different documents **look uniform and have a similar look and feel**, which reflects the company's identity. One of the ways this can be achieved is through the use of **standard templates**.

Standard templates are documents which are used when new documents are started. A template contains **formatting information**, such as **font types**, **colours**, **sizes**, **images**, and the words which are **always** in that type of document (this is sometimes called the **fixed content**). It may also contain auto-generated information, such as the date, time and the document and author's name.

Examples of templates include:

- memos for **internal communication**
- **letters** for posting out to clients
- **purchase orders**
- **emails**.

(For more on these types of document, please see Unit 1: Using ICT to Present Information.)

Disadvantages of customisation

Training required

Customising application software can bring many benefits. Training is required so users understand how the customisation helps them produce the results the company expects. But training costs the company money, because:

- the user is not at work and earning money for the company
- the user's workload has to be covered by another employee
- trainer time costs money.

Increased complexity of applications

Customising can also bring about an **increased complexity** to applications. This is because there is program code to make documents work that may need skilled and expensive developers to make any changes (if they are needed) and to solve problems with the way that code or templates work.

Human beings are very good at making decisions and adapting when things go wrong. Programs need to anticipate carefully everything that can happen; this makes them very complicated to write. Skilled programmers may be needed to get the most benefit from customisation, as they know how to test programs thoroughly and fix any complex errors that may occur.

Support needs

Most customisation is complex and will need support to ensure that any problems found using the application are solved. There are several kinds of support:

- **User training** is needed when the application is rolled out so users understand how to **get the most out of it**.
- **Bug fixing** to fix any code which gives errors when it runs. A bug fix might be to change the code so that a print feature such as 'setting paper to landscape' is added.
- **Maintenance** to improve code, because very often when people use code, they make a **wish list of features** they wish had been included to start with (e.g. the cursor defaulting to the first usable text box on a form when it appears).

Customising application software

Default settings

As you have learned, a default setting is the one that takes effect if nothing is changed by the user. An example of a default setting is the **printer**; if the user chooses **File**, **Print**, then clicks **OK**, the printer defaults will be used. These will include such things as:

- **orientation** – whether it is portrait or landscape
- **print quality** – whether it is high quality and slow, or fast with a lower quality
- **colour** or **black ink only**
- whether the pages are printed **double-sided** (duplex)
- which **order** the pages are printed (first-to-last or last-to-first).

Choice of printer

Many users have a choice of printer in their offices. Most computers in the modern workplace are attached to a network, which often has several remote printers available to users. Very often the choice of a printer is simply the closest one to where the user is working. But sometimes there is a practical choice for considering different types of printer (e.g. a laser for quick, cheap, black-and-white printing or an inkjet for slower colour printing). A customisation, such as a macro, could choose the **most appropriate printer** for the nature of the document.

The standard print selection dialogue box is shown in Figure 8.14.

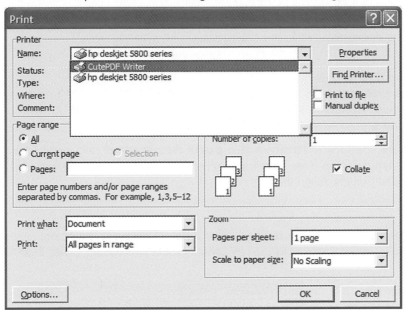

Fig. 8.14 Selecting a printer manually

However, this could be achieved using a simple macro. Figure 8.15 provides an example of doing just that in Microsoft Excel®.

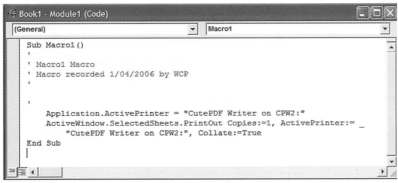

Fig. 8.15 Selecting a printer via macro

File storage locations

The file storage location is where a document is kept on the disk. In Microsoft Windows® XP, computers use the **My Documents** folder for saving work. Many users choose to create a separate folder to keep different types of work. In this situation, the user may find it convenient to set the **default file storage location** for their word processor to the **folder** where they do **the most work**. This will save a lot of time as they simply need to use **File**, **Save** or **Open** to reach documents in that folder.

When a user organises their disk space into **folders**, it makes it very easy to find their work again. This **also helps others** (e.g. if a team member were absent through illness and a document was needed urgently, a well-named folder structure would help others find the work quickly).

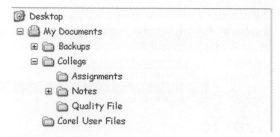

Fig. 8.16 A typical folder structure

Interfaces

An **interface** is the name we give to how the user **controls a program**. Every program has a **default interface**, which is easy to use and good enough for most users.

Customisation can **change** the interface to **remove the parts never used** and make sure that its **common features** (typically the ones most frequently used) are kept in plain view of the user, so they can easily and quickly select them.

Colour schemes

Many users change the **colour scheme** because they prefer different colours. The colour scheme can also be changed to make it easier to use, as some colours are easier to see than others.

The Microsoft Windows® operating system allows different users to log on to it and each user can then set their own colour scheme. This can make it simple and easy for users and others to see who is logged on to a computer.

Individual colour schemes are good because each user can have the colours they like, giving them more ownership of their workstation. Additionally, some users may have visual challenges which make certain colour combinations problematic; customising the colours to a more acceptable range can help.

Mouse settings

The mouse is a very important part of the computer as it is the most common way that users control the computer.

Fig. 8.17 Microsoft Windows® colour settings

There are three customisable settings which have the most impact on the user:

- Switch **primary** and **secondary** buttons, swapping left and right mouse buttons. Most users click the mouse button with their first or index finger; this means the primary mouse button is the left button for right-handed people or the right button for left-handed people.
- **Double-click speed** is very important, as many users double-click at their own speed. This setting should be the **normal speed the user does the double click**.

- **Mouse speed** – how **quickly** the **mouse pointer moves**. When the user moves the mouse on the desktop, this setting controls how far the mouse moves.

The **shape** of the mouse pointer may also be changed. Many users find working on a computer with their choice of mouse pointer more fun, especially if they are animated or cute!

Fig. 8.18 Mouse properties

Customising specific tools and functions

Custom dictionaries

This dictionary is used during spellchecking. The default dictionary is often good enough, but as the program is used, more words may be added to the dictionary to cover those used by the user (words which may be subject-specific, such as specialised words in chemistry or biology). The extra words in the dictionary make up the **custom dictionary**. Some applications create a custom dictionary which can be copied to another computer so that **specialised words** are available straightaway.

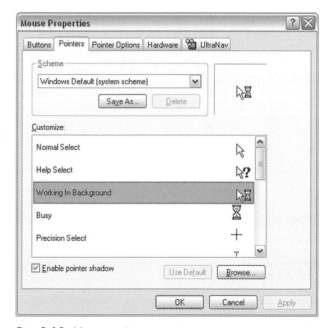

Fig. 8.19 Mouse pointers

AutoText

AutoText is a feature of word-processing packages such as Microsoft® Word, which recognises phrases that are used again and again. It anticipates the word and shows a prompt which can be selected to allow the application to automatically complete the phrase.

To set up AutoText in Microsoft® Word

1. Type in a word or phrase you use often.
2. Highlight the word or phrase.
3. Use the **Insert, Autotext, Autotext** menu option.
4. Press the **Add** button.

To use autotext in Microsoft® Word

1. Start typing the word or phrase you use often.
2. Word shows a prompt (see Figure 8.20).
3. Use the **Enter** key or **F3** to let Microsoft® Word finish the word for you, or keep typing to ignore and choose your own word instead.

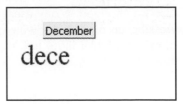

Fig. 8.20 Autotext

AutoCorrect

AutoCorrect is another feature of applications such as Microsoft® Word, where combinations of characters are **recognised**, even if they are **not quite** in the **right order**. AutoCorrect, as the name suggests, will replace the (slightly) incorrect spelling with the **right word** from the dictionary. For example, it will see 'adn' and replace it with 'and'.

AutoCorrect also converts **recognisable key presses** into **proper symbols**: (c) becomes ©, the copyright symbol, (R) becomes ®, the registered trademark symbol and :) becomes ☺, a smiley!

Setting up AutoCorrect

1. Use the **Tools, AutoCorrect** menu option to see the dialogue box shown in Figure 8.21.
2. Type your abbreviation (combination of characters) into the **Replace** box.
3. Type the phrase that will be used into the **Replace** box.
4. Press the **OK** button.

Templates

This section shows why templates are needed for applications such as:

- **word-processing** to be able to choose from **pre-prepared documents**, **saving time** with not having to type the words that are always there, such as **'yours sincerely'**

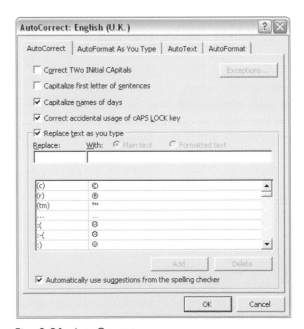

Fig. 8.21 AutoCorrect

- **spreadsheets**, to save time with not having to set **formatting** and **formulas** to produce calculation results
- **presentation** software, to keep **consistent style** between different slide shows.

The section also explains how to create templates for applications.

User need

The user need is an explanation of what the user requires from an application.

STATEMENT OF USER NEEDS

**Collaborative Convective Forecast Product
(CCFP-2005)**

Contents

Executive Summary
Preface
1. Introduction
2. The CCFP Forecast
3. Collaboration
4. Application
5. Training
6. Forecast Verification, Operational Assessment, and Feedback
7. Expectations of User Needs in the Outyears
8. Additions and Changes
9. Summary of Documentation Changes for CCFP-2005
References

Attachments

Fig. 8.22 Some sample user needs

Usually, the user need is identified in a document which carefully explains **what the user wants** from the new system as **part of their requirements**.

The user requirements is a **more detailed document**, which has sections for the user need and others parts of implementing a new system, such as:

- user needs to explain **what** and **why** the new system is wanted
- present system, to define the current hardware and software
- proposed **new customisation** to meet the user's needs
- proposed **hardware changes** to identify any new or different requirements.

User Requirements Document

1. Context of the project
2. Methodology
   2.1 System surveys.
   2.2 Site visits.
   2.3 User Requirements Workshop.
3. User requirements workshop
4. Annotated mock-up
5. Data issues
7. System requirements

Fig. 8.23 Some sample user requirements

Design

Template design is produced from the **user requirements** to **meet the user need**. The design needs to provide **all the features** required by the user to make sure that everything in the user requirements is **fully met**.

Features

Features in a template can include:

- The **use of logos** and **form fields**. Logos are a powerful method of showing the corporate identity. A logo is some sort of picture or image.
- **Form fields** can be used to bring values into a document from somewhere else. Form fields are quick and accurate for finding a specific place in the document, such as where the name or address needs to be entered. Automatically generated form fields can also be very useful for data such as the date or the name of the document (typically placed in the footer) when a document is printed.
- **Fonts** may be set in a template for **heading styles** and **normal text** so they are the right size and appearance for the document.
- **Paper** may be set to portrait or landscape.

Macros and shortcuts

This section shows why macros and shortcuts are needed for applications such as:

- word-processing, to be able to choose from pre-prepared documents, saving time with not having to type the words that are always there, such as *'yours sincerely'*
- spreadsheets, to save time with not having to set formatting and formulas to produce calculation results
- presentation, to keep consistent style between slide shows.

The section also explains, step by step, how to create simple macros for applications.

Creating macros

A macro is the name given to a **simple program in an application** which works with documents. Different application packages take different approaches to macros. Microsoft® Access macros are a list of commands or actions that are carried out with the database.

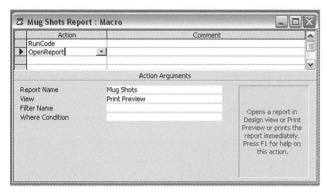

Fig. 8.24 Microsoft® Access macro 'mugshots'

Naming macros

A macro needs to be given a **sensible** and **meaningful** name, used to run the macro. Microsoft® Access macros are named when the macro is finished and saved. Microsoft® Word and Excel® macros are named when the macro is created.

To create a Microsoft® Word macro

1. Practise key presses to do actions the macro will record before you start.
2. Bring up the **Record New Macro** dialogue box.
3. Use the **Keyboard** button to give the macro a keyboard short cut.
4. Start recording the macro.
5. Use the key presses you practised.
6. Stop recording the macro.
7. To start the macro, use the keyboard short cut from step 3.

Creating a Microsoft® Word macro example

1. Start a new document.
2. Save the document as 'My First macro'.
3. Type in a word of your choice.
4. Use **Shift** with **Ctrl** and ← to highlight your word.
5. Use **Ctrl** with **B** to make your word bold.
6. Use **Ctrl** with **U** to underline your word.
7. Use → to move cursor to right of word.
8. Use **Ctrl** with **B** to turn bold off.
9. Use **Ctrl** with **U** to turn underline off.
10. Delete everything in the document.

11. Type your word again (it should not be bold or underlined).

12. You have now completed your practice key presses to do actions the macro will record before you start (step 1 in **To create a Microsoft® Word macro**).

13. Use the **Tools, Macro, Record New Macro** menu option to see the dialogue box shown in Figure 8.25.

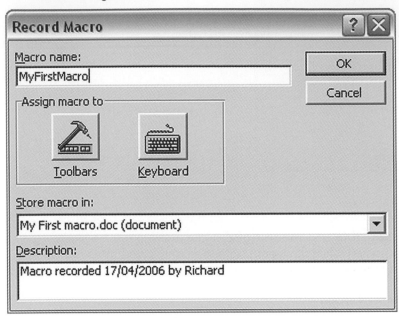

Fig. 8.25 Record macro dialog

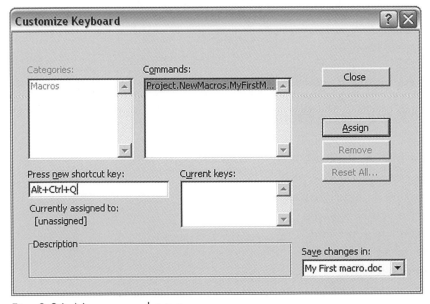

Fig. 8.26 New macro keypress

14. Type **MyFirstMacro** into the **Macro name** box.
15. Change **Store macro in** to **My First macro.doc (document)**.
16. Press the **Keyboard** button.
17. Set the short cut to **Alt** with **Ctrl** and **Q** (see Figure 8.26).
18. Press the **Assign** button.
19. Press the **Close** button.
20. The macro starts recording, you see the **Stop** button (as shown in Figure 8.27).
21. Use **Shift** with **Ctrl** and ← to highlight your word.
22. Use **Ctrl** with **B** to make your word bold.
23. Use **Ctrl** with **U** to underline your word.
24. Use → to move cursor to right of word.
25. Use **Ctrl** with **B** to turn bold off.
26. Use **Ctrl** with **U** to turn underline off.
27. Press the **Stop** button.
28. The **Stop** button disappears.
29. Save your document.
30. Delete everything.
31. Type a new word (it should not be bold or underlined).
32. Use **Alt** with **Ctrl** and **Q** to run the macro.

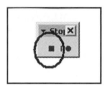

Fig. 8.27 Macro stop

Your word should now be bold and underlined.

Assigning macros

After a macro is **created** there must be some way of **starting** the macro, such as:

- A **toolbar button** is a good way of starting a macro using the mouse. A toolbar button is always on display, making it easy for the user to see.
- A **menu item** is a good way of starting a macro from the keyboard. A menu option can be seen by the user, so it is not difficult to remember.
- **A key combination** is the quickest way of using a macro, as the user does not need to take their hand off the keyboard to use it. Key combinations need to be learned, as there is nothing on the screen to remind the user which key combination is needed to start the macro.
- Using the **mouse to click** on a **button** in a form or document.
- Using the **mouse to click** on a **picture** in a form or document.

Storage of macros

The macro needs to be stored somewhere:

- Microsoft® Access stores macros as part of the **database**.
- Microsoft Excel® stores macros as part of a **worksheet**.
- Microsoft® Word stores macros as part of a **document** or in a **template**.
- Microsoft PowerPoint® stores macros as part of a **presentation**.

Use of macros in templates and documents

Templates are the starting point for every document, giving the application the basics of a new document such as paper orientation, font information, pre-typed words and similar.

A macro may be kept in a template or a document. For **most customisations**, the macros will be **kept in the templates**. This is so that when a new document is started, the **macros are there** and **ready** for the user to benefit from them.

Storing a macro in a document is less useful in most situations, as a document needs to be opened, then usually saved to a different filename so the original is not spoilt (when a template is used for a new document, then saved, the **File**, **Save as** dialogue box is shown, so the user selects a name for the document).

Storing a macro in a document is a good option for learners as it makes it much easier to move the document to another place, such as USB flash memory for working at home. Templates are less useful for using a macro on different computer systems as they need to be in the **correct folder** for the application to find them again. The correct folder is likely to be different for each system and can cause a lot of extra problems for the learner wanting to work on the macro in different places.

Testing macros

Every time a macro is produced, it needs to be tested. Testing works best with a plan (see Figure 8.28 for an example).

Test Plan

Application testing for: Customisation of Customer spreadsheet for SHS

Test reference number	Macro being tested	Type of test	Expected outcome	Actual outcome	OK or Action Required
1	printRange	Printing functions	Selected range printed	Printed	OK
2	printInvoice	Printing functions	Invoice printed	Invoice printed but missing footer	Add footer options
3	saveFile	Disk functions	Current File save to current directory	File saved	OK
4	eraseCustomer	Data functions	Customer data erased	Data not erased!	Check selected range
5	sortData	Data functions	Data sorted alphabetically (ascending)	Sorted in descending order!	Change sorting option
6	printQuery	Printing functions	Query printed	Printed	OK
7	printReport1	Reporting	Report1 printed	Printed	OK
8	printReport2	Reporting	Report2 printed	Report 3 printed!	Wrong report. Swap them!
9	PrintReport3	Reporting	Report3 printed	Report 2 printed!	Wrong report. Swap them!

Signed: Norman Hardy   **Date:** 10th July 2006

Fig. 8.28 Test plan

The test plan is one or more documents which **list the tests** that need to be carried out to ensure the macro works properly. The test plan is produced from the **user needs**, because the user needs explain **what is wanted** from the macro.

When the tests are run on the macro, the **results are written** into the document(s) to complete the documentation and to ensure the macro **works as expected**.

Creating shortcuts

A keyboard shortcut may be assigned to macro when the macro is first recorded (see Figure 8.29).

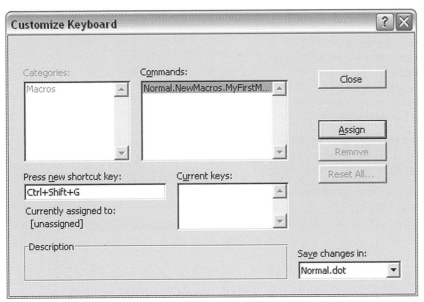

Fig. 8.29 Adding a keyboard shortcut to run a macro

The dialogue box shown in Figure 8.29 is reached by selecting the **Keyboard** button from the **Record New Macro** dialogue box in Microsoft® Word. The **Assign** button is used to keep the short cut.

Assigning shortcuts

Shortcuts may be assigned to **existing commands** inside an application or to **new macros**.

The Microsoft® Word **Customise Keyboard** dialogue box (shown in Figure 8.29) may also be used to change the existing keyboard shortcuts or assign new shortcuts. To do this, the **Tools**, **Customise** menu needs to be used to bring up the **Customise** dialogue box. From here, the **Keyboard** button can be used to show the **Customise Keyboard** dialogue box.

REVISITING THE CASE STUDY: ESTIMATES FOR STEVE HODDER SKATEBOARDS

By now we have seen a few different customisation techniques that could be used to create a similar solution by **tailoring commercial applications**. A possible approach could be to use **Microsoft® Access** to store **customer details**, their **customers job requirements**, **details of the stock** and **Steve's labour charges**.

A user-friendly **form**, acting as a front-end, could be used to let the customer's select colours and graphics for the skateboard, using simple **dropdown lists**.

A **macro** could then calculate the total cost of the materials and add Steve's charges. Another macro could then **transfer** this information to a **separate form** and **print it**.

The bill, designed using a suitable SHS **template**, would contain:

- SHS logo
- SHS address and contact information
- name, phone number and address of the customer
- details of the custom board
- how much the materials will cost
- Steve's labour charges
- final total, including VAT (value added tax).

The majority of this solution would mainly require customisation skills rather than detailed programming skills. Testing could be achieved by running the two solutions in parallel and seeing how the customised version fares against its more complex (and expensive) alternative.

It would also be possible to create a similar system by customising and automating a spreadsheet application such as Microsoft Excel®.

☆ Activity

Diskount Video Disks (DVD) have commissioned you to produce a database that contains a catalogue of all their products. The database will be created using Microsoft® Access and will be distributed to customers as a free CD they can pick up from store counters.

Before you start writing the database, DVD require some form designs for the database. Your task is to produce form mock-ups for the database, using pencil and paper or an application of your choice, such as Paint or Microsoft PowerPoint®.

QUIZ

Let us see what you have learned in this unit – test your knowledge and understanding by completing the crossword shown in Figure 8.30 (a copy can also be found on your companion CD).

Fig. 8.30 Crossword

Across
5. A way of running several commands using a button or menu option
6. The words at the top of an application, for example **File** or **Edit**
8. The name we give for how the user controls a program
9. When an application program is adapted to suit particular individuals and situations
11. Helps users when they create new documents to produce quick, consistent results
12. Helps users understand how a customisation works

Down
1. A file storage location
2. When a program rejects bad data
3. Improves or removes errors from code
4. When a program is tested and any problems found are corrected
7. Program written for a client
10. The on-screen buttons clicked with the mouse

ANSWERS

Across
5. Macro
6. Menu

8. Interface
9. Customisation
11. Template
12. Training

Down

1. Folder
2. Validation
3. Maintenance
4. Debugging
7. Bespoke
10. Toolbar

COURSEWORK GUIDANCE

To pass this unit you will need to demonstrate an understanding of software customisation. You can show your understanding by discussing advantages and disadvantages of customising software. Most of the evidence, however, will be practical: you will be asked to customise an application, produce templates, record and test macros and record and test keyboard short cuts.

The Merit criteria ask you to create templates and explain why they are useful. You are also asked to show that you can assign macros using different techniques and you are asked to explain the benefits of this.

The D2 grading criteria asks you to **Evaluate ways that macros can aid productivity**. Your evaluation should relate 'productivity' directly to users. The macros you use in your evaluation should be of real benefit to the users and your coursework should make it clear **how** the macros enable the users to be more productive in the **quantity** or **quality** of the work they produce. You should also evaluate the use of templates in capturing and presenting information. Again, your evaluation should relate directly to users.

Unit links

This unit has direct links to the following:

Unit 1 Using ICT to Present Information
Unit 7 Software Design and
          Development

Unit 9 Database Software
Unit 10 Spreadsheet Software

●●●Further reading

Harvey, G., *Excel 2003 All-in-one Desk Reference for Dummies* (Hungry Minds Inc. US, 2003) ISBN 076453758X

Lowe, D., *Word 2003 All-in-one Desk Reference for Dummies* (Hungry Minds Inc. US, 2004) ISBN 0764571419

Progress check

To record your achievement, simply tick the criteria awarded to you when each assignment is returned (you may be given three assignments for this unit, U8.01, U8.02 and U8.03 – the final column may not be used). There is a full copy of this grid available on the accompanying CD. The copy will also allow you to record your key skill achievement against Literacy, Numeracy and ICT objectives.

	Assignments in this Unit			
Assignment	**U8.01**	**U8.02**	**U8.03**	**U8.04**
Referral				
Pass				
1				
2				
3				
4				
5				
6				
7				
Merit				
1				
2				
3				
4				
Distinction				
1				
2				
3				

A completed sample of this document (for reference purposes) can be found at the back of Unit 1.

SPREADSHEET SOFTWARE

INTRODUCTION

Spreadsheet software has been developed specifically to allow users to **manipulate mainly numeric data**. It has functionality that allows the user to present this information in a number of different ways (e.g. tables, charts and graphs). Organised into rows and columns, the numbers can then be used in calculations, using **user-defined formulae** or **inbuilt functions**, or a combination of both.

One of the less obvious aspects of a spreadsheet is that because it contains rows and columns that can be sorted, indexed and ordered (as can data in a database); it can also **manipulate lists as a flat file database**. These lists can effectively be **managed** because they can be **searched, sorted and filtered** in the same way as data stored in a database.

This section will introduce spreadsheet terminology and provide an opportunity to understand the basic concepts of spreadsheets.

Learning outcomes

On completion of this unit you should:

1 understand what spreadsheets are and how they can be used
2 be able to create complex spreadsheets that use a range of formulae, functions and features
3 be able to use spreadsheets to present, analyse and interpret data
4 be able to check and document a spreadsheet solution.

RECORDING YOUR PROGRESS

In order to achieve each unit, you will complete a series of coursework activities. Each time you hand in work, your tutor will return this to you with a record of your achievement.

This particular unit has 7 criteria to meet: 4 Pass, 2 Merit and 1 Distinction.

- For a **Pass**: you must achieve **all** 4 Pass criteria.
- For a **Merit**: you must achieve **all** 4 Pass and **both** Merit criteria.
- For a **Distinction**: you must achieve **all** 4 Pass, **both** Merit **and** the **single** Distinction criterion.

So that you can monitor your own progress and achievement in each unit, a recording grid has been provided (see the **Progress check** section at the end of this unit).

Nature and purpose

Once data has been stored in a spreadsheet it can be manipulated in a number of different ways.

First, the data in a spreadsheet can be displayed in **rows** and **columns** as part of a **table** of information. Using the functionality of the software, however, it can also be displayed as **graphs** and **charts**. Take the following example of stock information for a skateboarding firm run by Steve Hodder (SHS): the table in Figure 10.1 shows how much stock they have in each sales category for the components that make up a skateboard, plus information about accessories; each category is then displayed as a total.

Shoes	£26,785
Trucks	£11,444
Decks	£9,238
Wheels	£14,516
Clothing	£38,570
Accessories	£4,597

Fig. 10.1 SHS stock information

This table tells the reader that the company has £4597 worth of skateboarding accessories, for example.

The same data could now be represented more visually using a **pie** or **bar chart**.

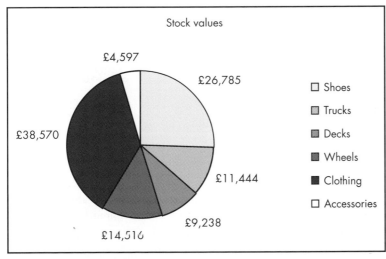

Fig. 10.2 Pie chart

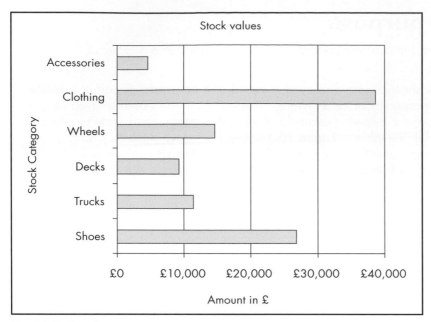

Fig. 10.3 Bar chart

The original data can also be **sorted**, into alphabetical order by category, or in descending order of stock value.

Accessories	£4,597
Clothing	£38,570
Decks	£9,238
Shoes	£26,785
Trucks	£11,444
Wheels	£14,516

Fig. 10.4 Ordered by category

Clothing	£38,570
Shoes	£26,785
Wheels	£14,516
Trucks	£11,444
Decks	£9,238
Accessories	£4,597

Fig. 10.5 Ordered by stock value

In this case, an alphabetical list by category might be useful if there are lots of entries in the table and the user wants to be able to find a specific category quickly. Alternatively, others in the organisation might want to know how much money there is tied up in stock. In this case, they would order the list in descending order of stock value and they would immediately be able to see which category accounts for the largest stockholding.

How the data stored in a spreadsheet will be viewed or presented will ultimately be decided by understanding how the information is going to be used.

A spreadsheet file itself, when opened as a new document has a set of **default options** (predefined settings which can be changed by the user), including the number of spreadsheet pages it contains (see Figure 10.6).

The default number of pages in the spreadsheet file shown in Figure 10.6 is three. Each spreadsheet is on its own **tab**, and clicking on the tab itself will allow the user to move between the different sheets. The combined spreadsheet pages in a file are known as a **workbook**.

Fig. 10.6 Spreadsheet tabs

Uses for spreadsheets

- **Industry** – used in manufacturing for analysing production information (e.g. an ice cream manufacturer would use a spreadsheet to compare ice cream production output on a week-by-week basis, maybe even comparing the same week across a number of years).

- **Sales departments** rely heavily on spreadsheets for **comparing** the performance of sales teams in different areas, and individual sales representative performance over weeks or months. They also use spreadsheets to **analyse** how well products are selling, using the spreadsheet's functionality to determine when they might have peaks in demand for a product, so that production can be informed to make more or less product to meet predicted demand.

- **Commerce** – financial organisations use spreadsheets to **forecast** future events. An example would be the use of a spreadsheet to predict future income based on a combination of factors, such as what is known and what might be (the 'what if' scenario).

- In general terms, spreadsheets are used to present information in such a way that the **relationships between different pieces of data can be clarified or interpreted.** An example here would be the idea of sales and production. Consider the following case study.

Gadgets for U Financial Statement			
	Sales	**Costs**	**Profits**
April 2005	£24,256.00	£13,098.24	£11,157.76
May 2005	£26,075.20	£14,080.61	£11,994.59
June 2005	£28,030.84	£15,136.65	£12,894.19
July 2005	£30,133.15	£18,381.22	£11,751.93
August 2005	£32,393.14	£19,759.82	£12,633.32
September 2005	£34,822.62	£21,241.80	£13,580.82
October 2005	£35,867.30	£21,879.06	£13,988.25
November 2005	£36,943.32	£27,707.49	£9,235.83
December 2005	£38,051.62	£28,538.72	£9,512.91
January 2006	£39,193.17	£29,394.88	£9,798.29

Fig. 10.7 Financial statement spreadsheet

Gadgets For U is a small production company making self-opening letter boxes. Adam Chandler, the Managing Director, is concerned that the company is slipping into overdraft with the bank. He discusses his concerns with the Sales and Production Managers, who have no immediate answers, although the Sales Manager says his statistics show that sales have been steadily increasing each month over the period in question. They speak to the Finance Manager, who produces the table of information shown in Figure 10.7.

Look at the above data – can you see anything obvious?

The Finance Manager cannot really detect anything from the table of figures and has created a chart (Figure 10.8) which consists of known sales each month, less known costs, which gives a profit figure.

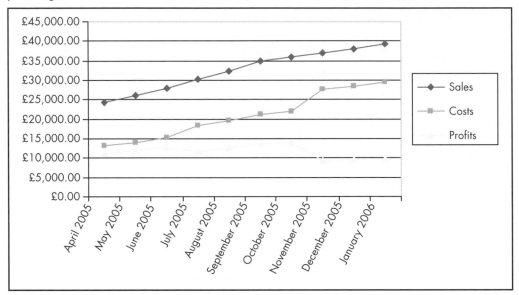

Fig. 10.8 Financial statement in graph format

This graphical representation of the situation makes it easier to identify where the points of interest are. By presenting the information in a different way, it is easier to **interpret the relationships between the different sets of data**. While there was a very slight fall in profits in July 2005 (even though sales were rising at that stage), there is a significant drop in profits of almost £5,000 in November 2005. Since then, profits have risen only minimally.

The Managing Director can now see that the Sales Manager is correct – sales have indeed risen steadily over the period. The sudden increase in costs in November is also visible, at the same time that profits slump. In reality, costs are made up of a number of factors and this still does not fully provide answers to the Managing Director's concerns. It does, however, give the relevant managers an indication of where they should look for the answers. The questions they now need to address are: 'Why did costs go up so dramatically in November 2005?' and 'Why have they continued to rise and not fallen again?'

Once such a spreadsheet has been developed to analyse a sequence or set of data, it can be used repeatedly, just by changing the relevant data. One such example would be to calculate the payroll for Gadgets for U employees.

When the spreadsheet is set up, with the names of the employees and the relevant columns to handle how many hours have been worked, basic pay rate, how much overtime, overtime pay rate, how much tax and National Insurance to deduct, the same spreadsheet could be reused each week. Thus, the only data that would need to be input each time would be the number of hours worked for each employee, and the output (the net salary) would be processed (calculated) automatically. This is an example of how a spreadsheet can be used to **repetitively and accurately perform calculations.**

Spreadsheet terminology

In general, all spreadsheet software uses the same terminology to refer to various aspects of the working environment. The most common terms used are **row**, **column**, **field** and **cell**. These are probably best explained by referring to a spreadsheet image:

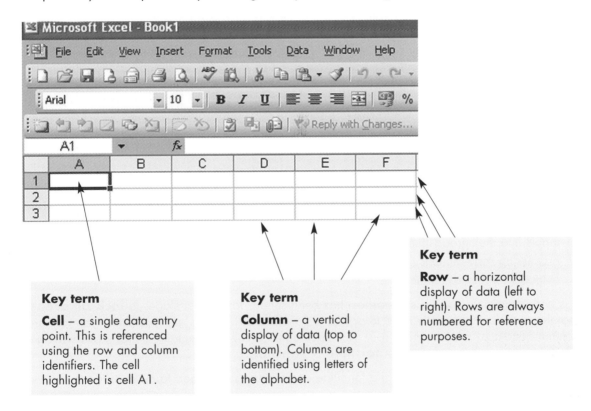

Key term

Cell – a single data entry point. This is referenced using the row and column identifiers. The cell highlighted is cell A1.

Key term

Column – a vertical display of data (top to bottom). Columns are identified using letters of the alphabet.

Key term

Row – a horizontal display of data (left to right). Rows are always numbered for reference purposes.

Fig. 10.9 A sample spreadsheet view

The term **field** is used in connection with spreadsheets to identify data of the same type. It we use the earlier example of the skateboard stock, the Category column would be considered a field, as would the Totals column. Often the field identifier becomes a column heading.

Understanding the concept of a **cell** is important in learning about spreadsheets because calculations use a **cell reference** in order to decide what detail to refer to.

Look at the following example:

	A	**B**	**C**
1	2	3	

In the example, cells A1 and B1 both contain an **integer** (whole number). In the cell referenced C1 we would like to display the answer to the calculation that adds 2 and 3 together. We know that the ultimate answer is to be 5! We now have three options:

- Calculate the answer manually and key the number 5 into cell C1
- Put a formula into cell C1 saying = 2+3 (add 3 to 2)
- Put a formula into cell C1 saying = A1+B1 (add the content of cell B1 to A1).

Clearly the first option is not suitable as it would be pointless using a software package and doing the hard work ourselves! While the second option would work, keying in the physical values (2 and 3) would reduce the functionality of the software. If you refer to the cells in the formula rather than to their actual numeric values, when the value inside one of the referenced cells subsequently changes, so will the answer! Therefore, if we have used a formula in cell C1 and we change the value in cell A1 from 2 to 5, the answer in cell C1 will automatically update to 8. So the third option above is clearly the most appropriate.

We will be working more with formulas in the next section.

User need

Spreadsheets need to be designed, paying attention to the **needs of the user**:

- purpose of the spreadsheet
- inputs into the spreadsheet
- processing requirements
- outputs from the spreadsheet.

It is not uncommon, once a spreadsheet has been set up, for the developer to **lock all areas** that the user does not really need to access (e.g. where the outputs are located, or the row and column headings) to prevent the user from keying into a cell accidentally, thereby overwriting what might have been a complex **formula** or **function**.

Before we really begin investigating formulae and functions, we need to make sure we understand the basic spreadsheet view.

Microsoft Excel®'s main screen looks like that shown in Figure 10.10.

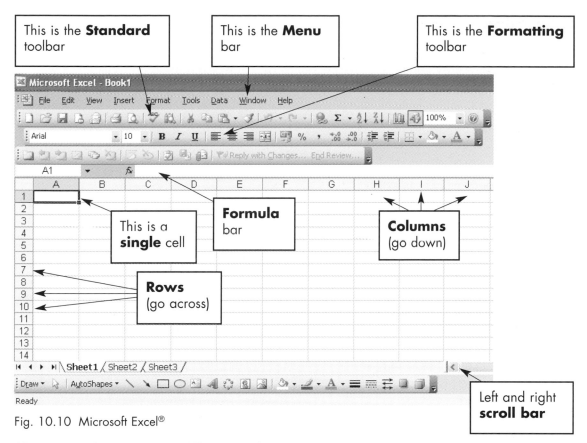

This is the **Standard** toolbar

This is the **Menu** bar

This is the **Formatting** toolbar

Formula bar

This is a **single** cell

Columns (go down)

Rows (go across)

Left and right **scroll bar**

Fig. 10.10 Microsoft Excel®

Formulae and Functions

First, it would be useful to differentiate between the concepts of a formula and a function.

Key terms

A **formula** is where the user creates a calculation using operators (plus, minus, divide and multiply) and cell references.

There are two types of **function: user-defined** and **inbuilt**. In basic terms they are exactly the same – they are complex calculations that can be used in a spreadsheet many times. They are usually named: for example, the SUM function totals a row or column of figures.

An **inbuilt** function is one which the user calls and uses from a library inside the software. A **user-defined** function is one that the user creates and names. For the purposes of this unit, we are only going to concern ourselves with formulae and inbuilt functions.

We also need to understand the difference between the cell's content and the cell's value. **Cell content** is any formula or function in the cell, whereas the **cell value** is the actual number or text (e.g. 26 or Hello or January).

We are now going to explore the **mathematical operators** available for use in spreadsheets, before we begin to develop complex calculations.

Formulae

Add

Addition is achieved by using the + symbol, much as you would if using a calculator. If we were going to use a calculator we would key in the following in this exact sequence:

6
+
2
=

This would give the answer 8.

Within the scope of a spreadsheet, however, we would insert the two numeric values into individual cells and use a formula to complete the calculation.

	A	**B**	**C**
1	6	2	

As suggested earlier, to add the two numbers together, we would simply key a formula in to the spreadsheet, into the cell where we want the answer displayed. In this case, that would be cell C1. The difference here is that we almost do the calculation backwards! The formula becomes:

=
A1
+
B1

Or in English: cell C1 equals (or takes the value of) the contents of cell A1 with the contents of cell B1 added to it.

	A	**B**	**C**
1	6	2	=A1 + B1

Having keyed the formula in to the cell, it is simply a case of pressing the **Enter key** to execute the formula.

Let us take this further. If we wanted to add the contents of four cells displayed in a row consecutively, the formula would look something like this:

	A	**B**	**C**	**D**	**E**
1	6	2	9	3	=A1+B1+C1+D1

Had the data all been held in a single column, the formula would have been modified as follows:

	A
1	6
2	2
3	9
4	3
5	= A1 + A2 + A3 + A4

There is a simpler way of executing this calculation, which we will see later in the chapter when we begin to look at **inbuilt functions**.

Subtract

Subtraction is achieved by using the − symbol. Again, it is the same symbol that we use on a calculator. To subtract 2 from 6, we need to modify the formula in the cell and replace the + symbol with a − one.

	A	B	C
1	6	2	= A1 − B1

In English: cell C1 equals (or takes the value of) the contents of cell A1 **less** the contents of cell B1.

Divide

Divide is achieved by using the **/** symbol. This is the first of the two spreadsheet operators that are different to those used on a calculator. When using a calculator we are used to employing the ÷ symbol. This, however, does not exist on a computer keyboard. The computer version is the forward slash symbol.

Just as with subtract, we merely need to replace the − operator with the / symbol.

	A	B	C
1	6	2	= A1 / B1

In English: cell C1 equals (or takes the value of) the contents of cell A1 divided by the contents of cell B1. This calculation will place the answer 3 into cell C1.

Multiply

Finally, multiply is achieved by using the * (or asterisk) symbol. On a calculator we would use ×. Just as with the previous examples, we need to replace the operator to change the nature of the calculation. For the purposes of this example we will use the same cells and the same data as seen previously:

	A	**B**	**C**
1	6	2	= A1 * B1

In English: cell C1 equals (or takes the value of) the contents of cell A1 multiplied by the contents of cell B1. The answer 12 will appear in cell C1.

These are relatively straightforward calculations and they are executed identically to the way that they would be done on a calculator. So, how would the computer handle this?

$$3 + 7 - 6 / 2$$

If you were using a calculator you would say:

3
Plus 7 is 10
Minus 6 is 4
Divide by 2 is 2.

If you keyed these numbers and operators into a calculator you would work this sum out and achieve the answer of 2. The computer, however, would not! The computer would calculate the answer as 7. Why?

As stated earlier, computers only work with logic, and as the computer would not necessarily understand how you would want the sum $3 + 7 - 6 / 2$ handled, a way of working with numbers like this has been programmed into the computer itself. This method of handling figures is known as **BODMAS**.

BODMAS

BODMAS stands for:

Brackets
Over
Division
Multiplication
Addition
Subtraction

This is applied to all mathematical calculations that a computer executes, so when our computer sees the sum $3 + 7 - 6 / 2$, this is how it calculates:

Are there any **brackets**?

No – move on.

Is there any **division**?

Yes – take the numbers on either side of the operator and work with them. The number 6 is divided by 2, to give the answer 3 and this replaces the original 6/2 in the sum.

The sum now reads $3 + 7 - 3$.

Is there any **multiplication**?

No – move on.

Is there any **addition**?

Yes – take the numbers on either side of the operator and work with them. The numbers 3 and 7 are added together to give 10 and this value replaces the original 3 + 7 in the sum.

The sum now reads 10 − 3.

Is there any **subtraction**?

Yes – take the numbers on either side of the operator and work with them. The number 3 is taken away from the number 10 and the answer is 7.

So – the computer returns the number 7 as the answer.

This is clearly not what we had originally intended with our sum 3 + 7 − 6 / 2. How do we use parentheses (brackets) to force the computer to view the sum differently? Remember, in the abbreviation that we learned earlier (BODMAS), **brackets must be handled first**.

By placing brackets in our sum, the computer will have to look at it differently.

(3 + 7 − 6) / 2

Let us look at how the computer will handle this:

Are there **brackets**?

Yes – inside the brackets are the following numbers:

3 + 7 − 6

Applying the rules of BODMAS, we need to do the addition bit before the subtraction.

3 + 7 is 10

The sum now reads 10 − 6.

10 − 6 is 4

We now replace all the numbers inside the brackets with the answer calculated above.

So (3 + 7 − 6) / 2 becomes 4 / 2.

We have dealt with the brackets. Is there any **division**?

Yes – 4 / 2 – the answer is 2.

Is there any **multiplication**?

No – the answer is still 2 – move on.

Is there any **addition**?

Yes, but as it was inside the brackets we have done it – the answer is still 2.

Is there any **subtraction**?

Yes, but as it was inside the brackets we have done it – the answer is still 2.

No more calculations? Then the answer is 2.

The most common formula in a spreadsheet is the **calculation of VAT**. VAT is a tax that is applied by the government to various products and services that we buy. Companies have a liability to pay any VAT they have collected on their sales to the government, but they are allowed to claim back VAT they have paid other companies for purchases they have made. It works something like this.

VAT on sales − VAT on purchases = Liability to government

However, if the VAT on sales is less than the VAT on purchases, then the organisation will receive a **rebate** (money back) from the government!

There are three VAT rates. These are currently as shown below, but they could change at any time:

- Standard rate: 17.5%
- Reduced rate: 5%
- Zero rate: 0%

Which rate the organisation applies to a sale is dependent on what the organisation is selling. The following are currently being charged at the **reduced rate**:

- domestic fuel
- installation of energy-saving materials
- grant-funded installation of heating equipment or security goods or connection of gas supply
- renovation and alteration of dwellings
- residential conversions
- women's sanitary products
- children's car seats.

The list of items that are **zero-rated** is huge, but here are some inclusions:

- clothing and footwear for young children
- charity advertising
- some education and training

- some exports
- some aspects of finance and security.

The rules are very complex, to say the least.

Regardless of which rate is applied, a spreadsheet developer will need to be able to calculate VAT, so that it is correctly added to an invoice prior to it being sent to a customer.

Let us work with some blank CDs being sold by Diskount Video Discs (DVD):

- A customer buys 10 CDs at 34 pence each.
- The subtotal for the invoice would be £3.40.
- VAT would then be added on top at 17.5% of the subtotal.
- This would be £3.40 * 17.5%, which would be 59.5 pence.
- We would now add the £3.40 and the 59.5 pence and come out with a grand total of £3.995 – rounded up to two decimal places (as we no longer have half pence) it would be £4.00.

Let us apply this to a spreadsheet.

	A	B	C	D	E
1	CDs	Cost	Subtotal	VAT	Grand total
2	10	0.34	=A2 * B2	= C2 * 17.5%	=C2 + D2

Each of the cells here contains a single-stage calculation.

Two-stage calculations (e.g. basic hours and overtime)

Although the above is a two-stage calculation (the subtotal is calculated, then the VAT, before the two are added together to form the grand total) we have created additional columns to handle each part of the calculation. A more common method of undertaking a **two-stage calculation** could be the calculation of a **gross salary** (that is, someone's wages before tax and National Insurance), where the employee earns two different rates, one for their basic hours and another rate for overtime. Let us look at the salaries of DVD employees. Commonly, overtime is paid at two rates: time and a half, and double time. This works out as follows:

- Basic rate: £5.00 per hour
- Rate at time and a half: £7.50 per hour
- Rate at double time: £10.00 per hour

The differentiation in the pay rate will be dependent on what has been agreed with the manager before the hours are worked.

So, if we were calculating the gross salary (or wage) for an employee, we would calculate his basic pay, followed by his overtime, which would then be added together to give his gross wage. For the purposes of this example, we will assume that he or she works 37 hours per week at basic rate, and has worked 4.75 hours at time and a half. What will happen here is that we will not create an additional column to calculate the basic salary and then the overtime, but key all the relevant data in to cells and do the entire calculation in one go:

	A	B	C	D	E
1	Basic hours	Rate	Overtime hours	Rate	Gross salary
2	37	5.00	4.75	7.50	= (A2 * B2) + (C2 * D2)

Notice the use of the parentheses (brackets) to help **organise** the calculation.

The ultimate answer in cell E2 would be £220.625, or £220.63 to two decimal places.

Compound interest

The best way to explain compound interest is to apply it. Let us imagine that you are going to invest £50 at an interest rate of 2% per month. At the end of your first month of investment, your money will have increased by 2%, from £50 to £51, as £1 is 2% of £50 and it is added on to your original investment. At the end of the second month you will again earn interest, but not £1 because that is 2% of £50 and you now have £51.

It is easier to see this in a spreadsheet:

	A	B
1	Original investment	£50.00
2	Month 1	£51.00
3	Month 2	£52.02
4	Month 3	£53.06
5	Month 4	£54.12
6	Month 5	£55.20
7	Month 6	£56.31
8	Month 7	£57.43
9	Month 8	£58.58
10	Month 9	£59.75
11	Month 10	£60.95
12	Month 11	£62.17
13	Month 12	£63.41

The formula that would have been keyed into cell B2 would have been:

= (B1 * 2%) + B1

The cell has been **copied** and **pasted** down the spreadsheet so that each cell offsets the cell reference by one as the copy and paste activity is executed. In cell B3 the calculation would read:

$$= (B2 * 2\%) + B2$$

Cell B4 would read

$$= (B3 * 2\%) + B3$$

Having set up this spreadsheet, how the original investment has grown will be seen automatically as the values increase as the 12 months are calculated:

	A	**B**
1	Original investment	£90.00
2	Month 1	£91.80
3	Month 2	£93.64
4	Month 3	£95.51
5	Month 4	£97.42
6	Month 5	£99.37
7	Month 6	£101.35
8	Month 7	£103.38
9	Month 8	£105.45
10	Month 9	£107.56
11	Month 10	£109.71
12	Month 11	£111.90
13	Month 12	£114.14

As you can see, the formulas are now starting to get quite complex! Let us move on to functions.

Functions

Most spreadsheet software contains a **library of functions** that you can use. To demonstrate functions, we are going to discuss some of the basic functions that are available in Microsoft Excel®. These include **statistical** functions and **logical** functions.

In the addition section earlier in the chapter, we considered how we would add up a series of consecutive cells (we saw this demonstrated with the data held in both a row and in a column).

	A	**B**	**C**	**D**	**E**
1	6	2	9	3	=A1+B1+C1+D1

A series of consecutive spreadsheet cells is known as a **range** and all of the statistical functions shown in this chapter use a range as part of the function structure. Statistical functions include Sum, Average, Min, Max, Count and Countif.

Sum

The **Sum** function automatically adds together the contents of all the cells included in the **range**. If we take the above example, to calculate the total we need to add A1 + B1 + C1 + D1. Using the Sum function, the formula is significantly shortened.

	A	**B**	**C**	**D**	**E**
1	6	2	9	3	=SUM (A1:D1)

The function literally means: E1 equals (or takes the value of) adding together all cells between A1 and D1 **inclusive** – so including the cells named in the range.

To use the Sum function the user has two options:

- Click the **AutoSum** icon, which is located on the Standard Microsoft Excel® toolbar.
- Key in the Sum into the cell.

Fig. 10.11

Keying a function or a formula into the cell is very straightforward. Using the AutoSum, on the other hand, requires some concentration! First, the user must access cell B14 (which is where the total is meant to appear).

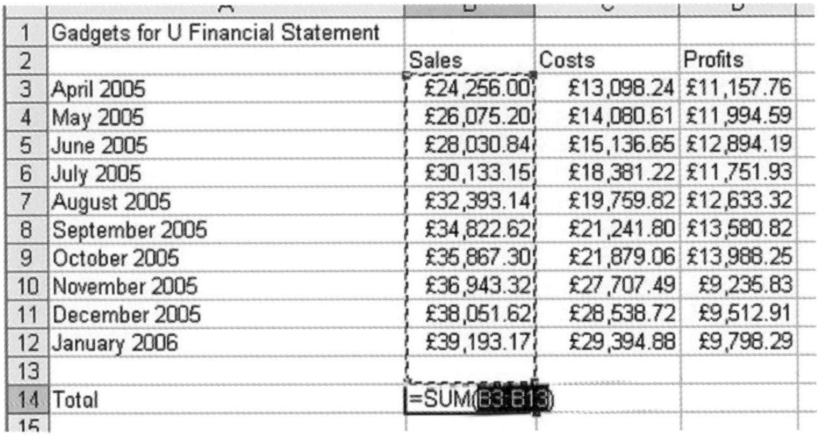

	A	B	C	D
1	Gadgets for U Financial Statement			
2		Sales	Costs	Profits
3	April 2005	£24,256.00	£13,098.24	£11,157.76
4	May 2005	£26,075.20	£14,080.61	£11,994.59
5	June 2005	£28,030.84	£15,136.65	£12,894.19
6	July 2005	£30,133.15	£18,381.22	£11,751.93
7	August 2005	£32,393.14	£19,759.82	£12,633.32
8	September 2005	£34,822.62	£21,241.80	£13,580.82
9	October 2005	£35,867.30	£21,879.06	£13,988.25
10	November 2005	£36,943.32	£27,707.49	£9,235.83
11	December 2005	£38,051.62	£28,538.72	£9,512.91
12	January 2006	£39,193.17	£29,394.88	£9,798.29
13				
14	Total	=SUM(B3:B13)		
15				

Fig. 10.12 AutoSum range

When the **AutoSum icon** is clicked, the computer will attempt to select the range on behalf of the user. It will look for continuous cells above or to the left of the sum. If the selection is **correct**, press the **Enter key**. If not, click into the start cell of the range and, holding down the left mouse button, drag down until the last cell has been covered, release the button and click Enter.

	A	B	C	D
1	Gadgets for U Financial Statement			
2		Sales	Costs	Profits
3	April 2005	£24,256.00	£13,098.24	£11,157.76
4	May 2005	£26,075.20	£14,080.61	£11,994.59
5	June 2005	£28,030.84	£15,136.65	£12,894.19
6	July 2005	£30,133.15	£18,381.22	£11,751.93
7	August 2005	£32,393.14	£19,759.82	£12,633.32
8	September 2005	£34,822.62	£21,241.80	£13,580.82
9	October 2005	£35,867.30	£21,879.06	£13,988.25
10	November 2005	£36,943.32	£27,707.49	£9,235.83
11	December 2005	£38,051.62	£28,538.72	£9,512.91
12	January 2006	£39,193.17	£29,394.88	£9,798.29
13				
14	Total	=SUM(B6:B8)		

Fig. 10.13 Selecting a particular AutoSum range

This technique for selecting a range will apply regardless of which function you use. Clicking and dragging across the range is the quickest way of identifying which cells are included in the sum.

Average

As with the Sum function, this function uses a range. However, there is no convenient icon for this. It requires the user to key it in.

The **Average** function takes all the cells in the range and does two things. First, it adds up all the cell contents like the Sum function does. It then goes one step further. It calculates how many cells there were in the range and divides the Sum by the number of cells in the range, to give the average.

Let us see how this works:

	A	B	C	D	E
1	6	2	9	3	=AVERAGE(A1:D1)

The computer adds: 6 + 2 + 9 + 3 = 20
It counts the number of cells in the range: 4
It divides 20 by 4 and returns 5

The answer 5 will appear in cell E1.

Min

The **Min** function finds the **lowest** (or minimum) value in the identified range.

	A	B	C	D	E
1	6	2	9	3	=MIN(A1:D1)

The computer will now search the range and find (and return) the lowest value. In this range the lowest value is 2.

Max

In the same way, the **Max** function finds the **highest** (or maximum) value in the identified range.

	A	B	C	D	E
1	6	2	9	3	=MAX(A1:D1)

Once again, the computer will search the range and, in this case, it will find (and return) the highest value. In this range the highest value is 9.

Count

The **Count** function literally counts the number of **non-blank** cells in the range.

	A	B	C	D	E
1		2			=COUNT(A1:D1)

Here the computer will simply return the number 1, as there is only one cell in the identified range (B1 contains the value 2).

Countif

The **Countif** function is a little more powerful, as it offers the user to count the number of cells in a range that meet a **certain criterion**.

	A	B	C	D	E
1	6	2	9	3	=COUNTIF(A1:D1,4)

To understand the function we need to take it apart:

= COUNTIF (A1:D1, 4)

- **Function** is the function's name (COUNTIF)
- **Range** is the range of cells to look at, including the named cells (A1:D1)
- **Criteria** is what exactly to look for (4)

If we apply the above function into cell E1, what will the computer return?

0! Because there is no cell that contains the value 4.

If we change the function, however, to read:

= COUNTIF (A1:D1, 6)

then the computer will return the number 1, because there is one cell in the range that contains the number 6.

If we modify the **data** in the range, but leave the function unchanged, we will get a different answer:

	A	B	C	D	E
1	6	2	9	6	=COUNTIF(A1:D1,6)

The computer will now return the result 2.

Adding cells to a range

One important thing that users should be aware of is what happens when cells are added to a range. If the user inserts a column between columns A and B, B and C or C and D, then the function will **automatically adjust** to **accommodate** the new column.

	A	B	C	D	E	F
1	6	2	10	9	6	=COUNTIF(A1:E1,6)

If, however, a column is added before column A or after column D, the function **will not** change. This function would still return the number 2.

	A	B	C	D	E	F
1	6	2	9	6	6	=COUNTIF(A1:D1,6)

To fix this, the user will need to **edit** the formula **manually** (changing the range), so that the answer will change to 3.

While there are many **logical** functions, for the purposes of this unit we are going to concentrate on the three most common ones: **IF**, **OR** and **AND**.

Once we start creating logical functions using **logical operators**, such as IF, OR and AND, our spreadsheet becomes even more powerful.

IF

IF functions (commonly known as IF statements) are used to select one action over another, dependent on a condition. For example:

If (it is cloudy today)
    Take an umbrella
Else
    Enjoy the sunshine

This is similar to the If ... Else statements you may have encountered in Unit 7: Software Design and Development.

All IF statements have the same structure:

IF (condition)
    Do **this** if **true**
Else
    Do **this** if **false**

Here is a spreadsheet example:

	A	**B**	**C**
1	3	19	=IF(A1>10, A1 + B1, 0)

which means in full:

if (A1 > 10)
    this cell becomes A1 + B1
else
    this cell becomes 0

Or, in English: if the content of cell A1 is greater than 10, return the answer obtained by adding cell A1 to cell B1, else return 0.

Looking at the data, what will the above function return?

The computer is not interested in the fact that cell B1 contains a value greater than 10 as B1 is not being checked in the condition. As such, the result that appears in cell C1 will be 0. However, if we **reverse** the values in A1 and B1, the answer will be 22 (19 + 3) because now A1 is greater than 10.

	A	**B**	**C**
1	19	3	=IF(A1>10, A1 + B1, 0)

OR

The **OR** operator allows the user to check **multiple cells**.

= IF(**OR**(A1<20,B1>5),A1+B1,0)

In English: IF the cell content of A1 is less than 20 OR the cell content of B1 is greater than 5, then add the contents of cells A1 and B1 together and return the result, else return 0.

The structure is:

IF (condition part A is true OR condition part B is true)
    Do this because one of them is true
Else
    Do this because they are both false

Look at the following example – what will the result be?

	A	B	C
1	21	7	=IF(OR(A1<20,B1>5,A1+B1,0)

Here, A1 is not less than 20 (so this will be false), but B1 is greater than 5 (so this will be true). The value 28 will be returned.

AND

The **AND** operator again allows the user to check multiple cells, but unlike the **OR** operator, where either part of the condition can be true for the condition to return the value of true, and thus execute the true part of the statement, with the AND operator **BOTH** parts of the condition must be true for the true part of the statement to be executed.

= IF(AND(A1<20,B1<5),A1+B1,0)

The structure is:

IF (condition part A is true AND condition part B is true)
    Do this because both of them are true
Else
    Do this because one or both are false

	A	B	C
1	**10**	**3**	=IF(OR(A1<20,B1<5,A1+B1,0)

Here, A1 is indeed less than 20 (so this will be true) AND B1 is less than 5 (so this will also be true), so the computer will add the two numbers together and return the result 13.

The results of all logical functions must be carefully checked because it is very easy to make a mistake. Test these carefully as part of a testing strategy.

Finally, you should have a basic understanding of **relational operator** symbols:

>   greater than
<   less than
=   equal to
>=   greater than or equal to
<=   less than or equal to

As we have seen, relational operators demonstrate the **relationship between two values** (e.g. 5>4, 4=4, 2<10).

Entering and editing data

In addition to being able to run formulae and functions, there are a number of additional factors that you should be aware of when it comes to entering and editing data.

Absolute and relative cell referencing

First, we need to understand what happens to **formulas** when they are **copied** and **pasted**.

Here is an extract from a small spreadsheet:

	A	B	C
1	3	19	22
2	11	17	28
3	42	26	68
4	106	33	139

What we actually did (having keyed data into cells A1 to B4), was to key the formula

= A1 + B1

into cell C1. We then copied and pasted the cells down. Thus, the formulas in column C are as follows:

	Formulas in column C
1	= A1 + B1
2	= A2 + B2
3	= A3 + B3
4	= A4 + B4

The formulas **adjusted themselves automatically to accommodate the changing row numbers**.

This is known as **relative** referencing, because as each cell is filled it automatically changes **relative** to the **last cell position**.

There are times, however, when **we do not want** the formula change like this. Look at the following example:

	A	B	C
1	3	4	12
2	11		44
3	42		168
4	106		424

Formulas in column C
= A1 * $B$1
= A2 * $B$1
= A3 * $B$1
= A4 * $B$1

In the above example, cell B1 contains a value which needs to be used in **every calculation**. If we do not apply **absolute cell referencing**, as we copy and paste the cells down column C, B1 will become B2, then B3, then B4 (just as the A column references have changed). Using the **$ (dollar) symbol** as part of the cell reference means that even when copied and pasted, that particular cell reference will **NOT** change.

Why use this functionality? Why use the cell reference B1 rather than simply keying in the value 4?

If we had hard-coded (= A1 * 4) into cell C1 and copied it down, while the cell reference would have changed and the value would not, had we then wanted to change the value 4 to 7 at a later date, we would have needed to **change every single formula** that contained the number 4. As it stands, we can simply **update the value in cell B1** and every calculation that relies on it will **update automatically**.

Autofilling cells

Spreadsheets also contain functionality to **automatically fill cells** when the series to fill the cells is **predictable**. Take the examples shown below.

A series of numbers. The numbers 1 and 2 had to be keyed into cells A1 and B1, they were then highlighted and dragged right. Notice the number in the small square that appears in column F2 – this shows what the last value will be when the mouse is released.

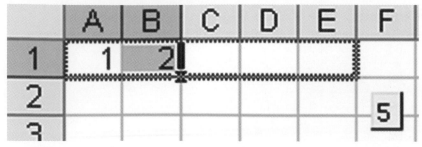

Fig. 10.14 Series demonstration (increase of 1)

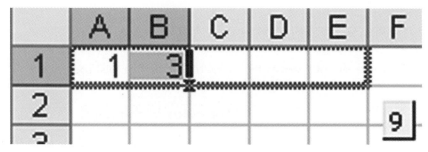

Fig. 10.15 Series demonstration (increase of 2)

Notice that here the numbers 1 and 3 have been input, and the series will complete:

1 3 5 7 9

The computer will automatically **predict** the values that need to be inserted.

This can also be done with **predictable text**, as shown in Figure 10.16.

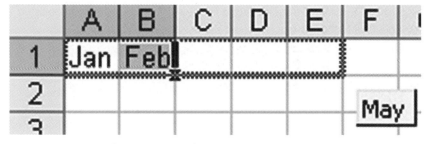

Fig. 10.16 Series demonstration (date)

Again, if gaps are left between the first two values, the computer will work out the series while observing the same gaps.

This is an incredibly useful function – what the user must ensure is that both the first and second values are highlighted *before* attempting to drag across.

Use of paste and paste link

Pasting cells is useful where the user wants the value (formula or function) from one cell to be copied to another cell.

The process is simple:

- **Select** the cell you want to copy.
- **Right-click** the mouse button.
- Select **copy** from the menu.
- **Move** to where you want the data to appear.
- **Right-click** the mouse button.
- Select **paste**.

This action will **only** copy the value from one cell into another. Although there are many different options for pasting cell information other than the actual value in the cell (using the **paste special** dialogue box), such as a **formula only** or a **cell format**, for the purposes of this unit we are only going to consider the **paste link** functionality.

There are times when we need to paste a value that has been calculated in a spreadsheet to another part of the spreadsheet, to be used in another calculation. Here is an example:

	A	B	Formula in Column B
1	John Weston Sales		
2	January	1,298	
3	February	2,597	
4	March	1,792	
5	Total Sales	5,687	= SUM (B2:B4)

	A	B	Formula in Column B
9	Hamid Aberah Sales		
10	January	2,421	
11	February	1,599	
12	March	2,331	
13	Total Sales	6,351	= SUM (B10:B12)

We now want to copy this data to another part of the spreadsheet so that we can give totals for our sales representatives over the three-month period.

	A	**B**	**Formula in Column B**
21	Sales for Jan – Mar 06		
22			
23	John Weston	5,687	= $B$5
24	Hamid Aberah	6,351	= $B$13
25	Total	12,038	= SUM(B23:B24)

What we have effectively done to achieve this is copy the contents of cell B5 into cell B23, and the contents of cell B13 into cell B24. We accessed the original position (cell B5 to start) and clicked to copy, but when we pasted the cell into cell B23, we did not simply paste, but used the **paste special** option on the menu to activate the **paste link**.

When we paste link, although we can see the **value** we have pasted, the underlying formula now contains the **absolute cell referencing notation**. This is known as **paste link**. This is useful, because if we change any of the original data for John Weston, in cells B2 to B4, or for Hamid Aberah in cells B10 to B12, not only the totals will update automatically, but the contents of cells B23, B24 and B25 will also update accordingly.

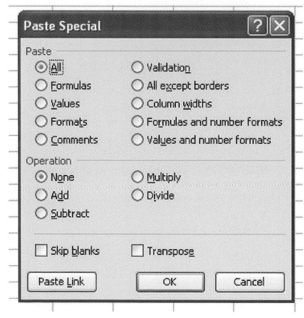

Fig. 10.17 Paste Special dialogue box

Linking cells between different spreadsheets or workbooks

Not only can we paste link within the confines of the same spreadsheet, we can **paste link** into **other spreadsheets** in the same workbook, and even into **different workbooks** entirely. All that changes is the formula.

For paste linking in the **same workbook**, the action is to copy the original cell, click on the spreadsheet where you want to paste the data, click on **paste special** and then on the **paste link** button. What you will now see is that the originating sheet reference has also been included in the formula:

=Sheet1!$B$5

If paste linking into a **different workbook**, the action is to copy the original cell, open the spreadsheet where you want to paste the cell, select the relevant destination cell, click on **paste special** and then on the **paste link** button. What you will now see is that the originating filename and sheet number have been included in the formula:

=[Name of File]Sheet1!$B$5

The advantage of using paste link functionality is if you need to **use data created in one spreadsheet in another workbook**. When you open the workbook that contains the link, the computer will automatically prompt you, reminding you that the spreadsheet contains cells linked to other spreadsheets and asking you to choose whether to update the spreadsheet or not. If you choose not to update the spreadsheet when opening it, it will still ask you the next time you open the file. If you have chosen to update the file, it will all happen behind the scenes.

Improving efficiency

Shortcuts (e.g. to aid movement around multi-sheet spreadsheet, to perform complex formatting)

One of the best ways to aid efficient movement around a single or a multi-sheet spreadsheet is for the user to **name a cell range** that s/he has to access frequently. To do this, you simply highlight the relevant cells, then click on the **Insert menu**, click on **Name** and then on **Define**. The dialogue box shown in Figure 10.18 will appear. It is now simply a case of naming the range by keying a name into the upper dialogue box (Names in workbook).

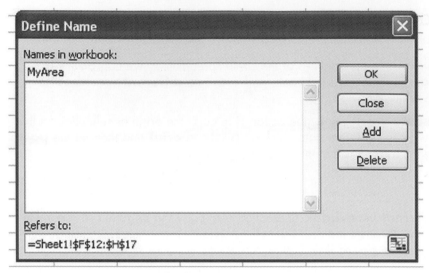

Fig. 10.18 Giving a range of cells a name

To move to the **named area** in the relevant spreadsheet, the user now just needs to select the relevant named range from the namebox, as shown in Figure 10.19 (A1).

When you click the dropdown symbol beside the **namebox**, all the **named ranges** will be **visible** (regardless of which spreadsheet they occur on). To move to the right place in whichever spreadsheet, simply select the relevant named range from the namebox.

When the computer moves to the relevant named range, it **automatically highlights all the cells included in the range**. This makes formatting easier because, as a user, you simply need to select the range from the namebox and click on any formatting choices you wish to make (such as defining the number of decimal places, changing the background colour, changing the font size, type or colour, etc.).

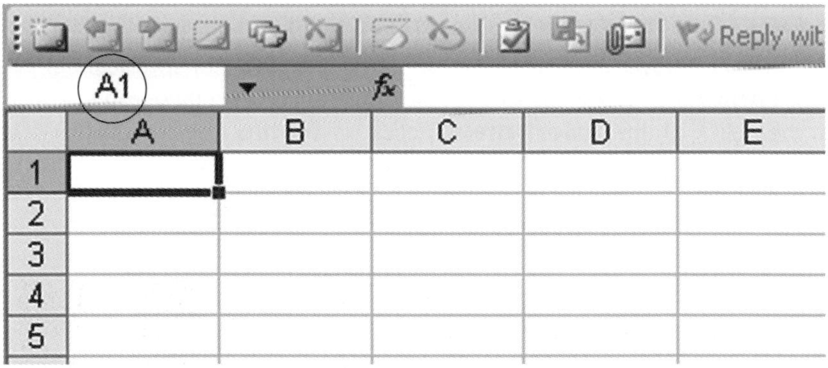

Fig. 10.19 The namebox

Combining information

As software suites such as Microsoft® Office have **complete compatibility** between the various applications within the product, it is extremely easy to copy and paste records from Microsoft® Access, a table of data from Microsoft Excel®, or a chart or graph into Microsoft® Word.

Using the **paste** functionality will merely copy whatever the original data was into the Microsoft® Word file. Pasting with **paste special** and **paste link** will enable the user to create linked files that will update automatically (or at least will give the user the option to update automatically) when a file is subsequently reopened.

The **cabinet** is the drive or memory device (such as a USB flash drive)

Each **drawer** represents a different folder in which the relevant files are stored

File management

At this juncture, now that we are potentially going to create multiple files, which may or may not be linked, it is time to consider the basic concepts of good file management.

In order to work efficiently with a computer, you **must** learn how to manage your data. In order to manage it effectively, you cannot simply rely on your memory (i.e. what name you gave a file and where you saved it). What

Fig. 10.20

you need to do is to make some logical decisions about your files, how they are named and where they are stored.

Imagine your computer as a huge filing cabinet – poor management would be the equivalent of placing all your documents/spreadsheets and database prints on top of the filing cabinet, without any real organisation. This diagram might help:

The filing cabinet is your storage device. It can be separated into different storage areas, each one named for easy identification. For example:

- Drawer 1 could contain all business documents for a specific client and be renamed SHS.
- Drawer 2 could contain documents for a second client, DVD.
- Drawer 3 could contain documents for client WCP.
- Drawer 4 could contain your personal documents, MyStuff.

To demonstrate the concept we will now create folders on the **root** (base) of a drive – in this case, the *root* of C:\. To create a folder, you have to work in the **My Computer** dialogue boxes. These can either be selected from the desktop (see icon in Figure 10.21), or from the Start menu.

In the address box below, you need to select the drive (or device) you wish to work with (Figure 10.22).

Fig. 10.21 My Computer icon on standard desktop

Fig. 10.22 Drive showing

To create a folder, right-click the mouse while holding it over the file list area. When the dropdown menu appears, click on **New**, then on **Folder**. It will ask you to name the folder.In Figure 10.22 you will see representations of the drawers, as seen on the filing cabinet image.

When **creating** and **saving** a file you would then place a file **within** the relevant folder. You choose which folder you wish to save to during the saving operation in your application. To ensure that your file ends up in the right folder, you make your drive, then folder selections in the **Save in** box at the top of the **Save As** dialogue box.

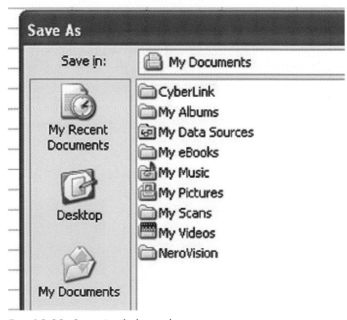

Fig. 10.23 Save As dialogue box

The file is then named and **OK** is clicked to complete the **save** action.

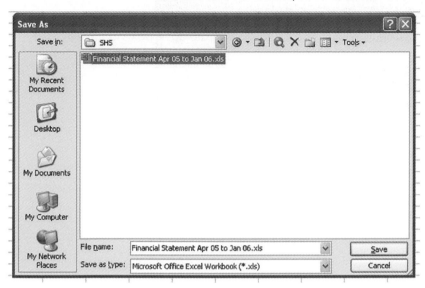

Fig. 10.24 Saving in the SHS directory

Notice that it has not been necessary to include the company's name in the filename because it is in the right **folder**.

The **full path** (location) of this file is:

C:\SHS\Financial Statement Apr 05 to Jan 06.xls

Presenting data

One of the most important aspects of spreadsheets is that the user needs to **lay out** and **format** the spreadsheet in a **consistent** and **professional** manner. To format a single cell or a range of cells, they first need to be highlighted, as formatting can only be undertaken on highlighted cells.

Spreadsheet software such as Microsoft® Excel includes a series of toolbars. The formatting toolbar has a series of icons that support some limited formatting options, such as:

* Font type
* Font size
* Embolden
* Italic
* Underscore
* Alignment (such as left, centre and right)
* Merging cells
* Currency formats
* Number formats
* Border, background colour and font colour options.

Fig. 10.25 Formatting toolbar

There are more options available if you access the formatting dialogue box via the **Format** menu, and click on **Cells**.

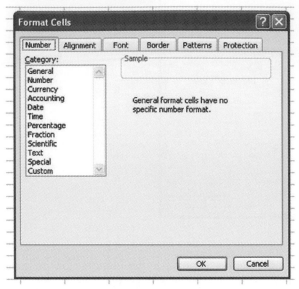

Fig. 10.26 Format Cells dialogue box

Explaining all the different options in their own right would be a book in itself. As such, what follows here is an overview of formatting options and decisions.

Appropriate data types and alignment

Text

Text is exactly what you think it is. It is any characters that have been input into a cell. Text is normally defaulted to align to the left of the cell. However, it can also be centred in a cell or right-aligned.

Text	Text	Text

Currency (or number)

Numbers can be displayed as **integers** (whole numbers), as **real numbers** (with decimal places) or as **currency** (again, with or without decimal places).

1	1.00	£1.00	£1

Regardless of which format is chosen, users should just make sure that they apply the format **consistently** across the data in the range.

Dates

There are a variety of date formats that the you can choose from and use.

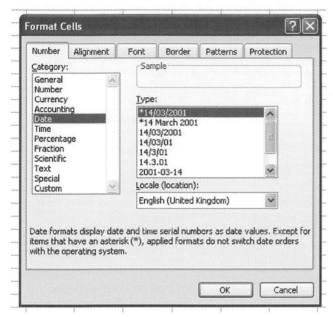

Fig. 10.27 Format Cells for date

Potential variations on dates are considerable, with **long dates**, **short dates** and **customised dates** on offer. If your setting is English (United Kingdom), as seen in Figure 10.27; the day will always precede (come before) the month. If, on the other hand, your setting is English (United States), many of the options will be reversed, with the month preceding the day, because that is traditionally how dates are represented in the USA.

Formatting cells

There may well be occasions when you want something in your spreadsheet to stand out. To this end there are a number of options you could choose, which allow you to **draw attention** to a specific cell or range of cells. As with other options, the cells to be affected need to be highlighted prior to making the relevant choices.

150.00	Background colour
175.00	Font colour
203.00	Shading (with a pattern rather than a colour)
262.00	Border

Of course, you could also apply these in any combination.

Other formatting

Having made the decision to display real numbers (those with decimal points), you need to decide the **number of decimal points** it is appropriate to display. If we are dealing with UK currency, for example, there is no point in displaying the data to more than two decimal places, as we do not have half or quarter pence, so £1.235 (one pound and twenty-three and a half pence) does not have any meaning; neither does £4.8825 (four pounds and eighty-eight and a quarter pence). However, some scientific calculations might depend on a high level of accuracy and a number of decimal places being displayed.

To format the number of decimal places, the most straightforward method is to click on the relevant icons on the formatting toolbar.

Increase   Decrease

Fig. 10.28 Formatting currency on the Formatting toolbar

All the user needs to do is to highlight the relevant numbers and then click on the **increase** and **decrease** icons, as shown in Figure 10.28. One click will remove or reveal another decimal place.

Merging cells

Merging cells is where you have a single piece of information that appears over a number of columns. It is most commonly required where you want to have a **heading displayed over a number of columns**. In the example below, the user has selected to display the heading over the first three columns.

SHS Financial Statement			
	Sales	**Costs**	**Profits**
April 2005	£24,256.00	£13,098.24	£11,157.76
May 2005	£26,075.20	£14,080.61	£11,994.59
June 2005	£28,030.84	£15,136.65	£12,894.19
July 2005	£30,133.15	£18,381.22	£11,751.93
August 2005	£32,393.14	£19,759.82	£12,633.32
September 2005	£34,822.62	£21,241.80	£13,580.82
October 2005	£35,867.30	£21,879.06	£13,988.25
November 2005	£36,943.32	£27,707.49	£9,235.83
December 2005	£38,051.62	£28,538.72	£9,512.91
January 2006	£39,193.17	£29,394.88	£9,798.29

Fig. 10.29 SHS Financial Statement

To achieve this effect, simply key the title into one of the cells. Then highlight all cells over which the title should be displayed and click on the **merge cells** icon (Figure 10.30).

Fig. 10.30 Formatting toolbar showing merge cells icon

Formatting charts

Shoes	£26,785
Trucks	£11,444
Decks	£9,238
Wheels	£14,516
Clothing	£38,570
Accessories	£4,597

Fig. 10.31 SHS Accessories data

To create a chart or graph, it is simply a case of highlighting the relevant detail in the spreadsheet and clicking on the **Insert menu** and then on **Chart**. The **Chart Wizard** will now take the user through a series of dialogue boxes containing a series of options. This includes whether or not to include a **legend**, for example (as shown in Figure 10.32).

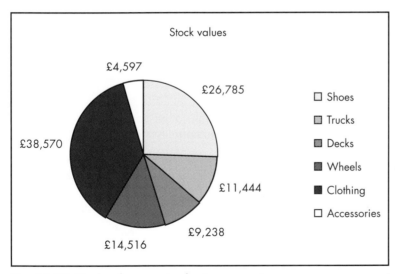

Fig. 10.32 Stock values as pie chart

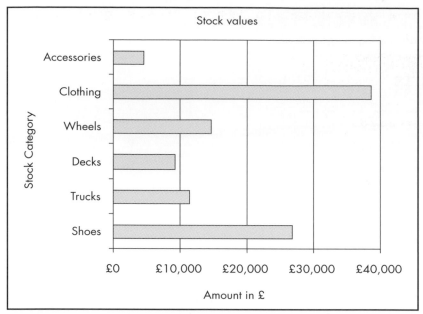

Fig. 10.33 Stock values as bar graph

The advantage of using the Wizard is that during the process you can view the choices made and how the overall chart will look, before committing to a specific chart type. In addition, you can choose whether the chart or graph should appear on the spreadsheet, or as a separate sheet in the spreadsheet workbook.

Any aspect of the chart (once it has been created) can be changed, including the axis on a bar or column chart, the titles and data labels (the legend can be added or removed, even after the Wizard has completed the chart).

The object can be moved – it can also be copied and pasted into other spreadsheets, or maybe even into a Microsoft® Word document, and the paste link functionality still applies.

The user should, however, exercise caution when **resizing** a chart or graph, as the image can become **distorted**. Making the object too small could also see some of the titles disappear, leaving data displayed without relevant titles or labels. Also, if the image is made too large, the writing can become blurred. The user must check that everything in the chart or graph is as it should be before saving or printing the image.

Choice of chart type

When using the Chart Wizard you can choose from a variety of charts to display the information. What the user must be aware of is how to select the right chart from the range of available alternatives. The most common four are listed below.

Pie charts are generally used where you want to visually represent some data as part of a whole. The pie is split into slices. The larger the slice, the more it represents of the whole.

Look at the example in Figure 10.34. This is the computer's own representation of the amount of free space and used space on a hard drive. It is accessed by right-clicking on the drive in My Computer.

As can be seen, the total capacity of the drive is 74.5 gigabytes, with 48.9 gigabytes used and 25.6 gigabytes free.

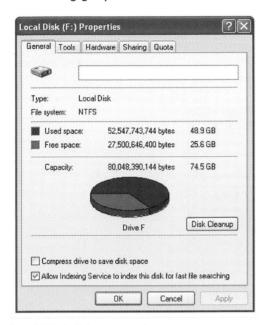

Fig. 10.34 Drive properties

Column charts – with vertical bars (upright) – are usually the common chart type which is offered as a default. These are useful for allowing users to visually compare columns of data.

Bar charts – with horizontal bars (flat) – are often used for comparing distances, for example. However, bar charts and column charts are actually interchangeable. (See Figure 10.3 for an example of a bar chart.)

Line graphs are good for comparing trends, as with the spreadsheet included earlier in this chapter (see Figures 10.7 and 10.8).

With any chart, users must check to ensure that the image actually **means something**. Please look at the image in Figure 10.35 and decide what you think it means.

In fact, this pie chart does not tell you

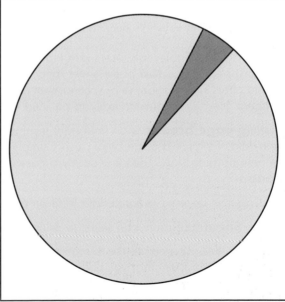

Fig. 10.35 A pie chart without annotation

anything. It has **no title**, **no key** and **no legend** – in fact, it is useless. This is a very common error made by users in creating such charts.

Formatting sheets

In addition to users being able to format individual spreadsheet cells and columns or rows of cells, the spreadsheet itself can be formatted in a number of ways. The sheet formatting options can be accessed through the **File menu** and by selecting **Page Setup**.

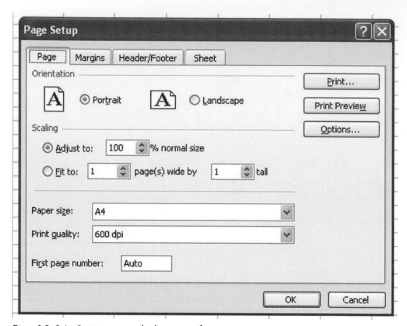

Fig. 10.36 Setting up whole page formats

On the Header/Footer tab, users can input either of these. A **header**, as you would expect, would appear at the **top** of the sheet, and a **footer** at the **bottom**. Information displayed in footers often includes: name of spreadsheet author, date of creation or modification and page numbers. Headers are more likely to be used for titles.

Inserting **page breaks** is an important technique to ensure that column or row titles stay with their data. To force a page break, users simply place the cursor into the cell where they want the new page to start. Then it is purely a case of selecting **page break** from the **Insert menu**.

Scaling can be used to force data to fit on a single page.

On the **Sheet** tab, users can select to print or not print the **gridlines** on a spreadsheet.

In order to fully appreciate the formatting options, it is best to experiment. For the purposes of this unit it is important that you have an understanding of what can be achieved.

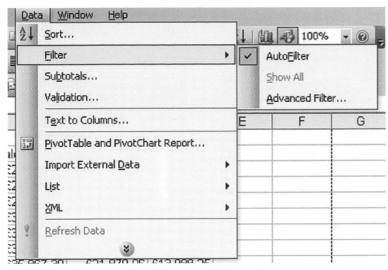

Fig. 10.37 Using the AutoFilter on a field or column

Analysing and interpreting data

Converting spreadsheet data to charts and graphs

It has already been suggested earlier in this chapter that being able to convert tables of data in a spreadsheet into charts and graphs is a useful way of representing data in a visually effective way. Experienced managers use both tables and charts to **analyse information** about their organisational performance.

Filtering and sorting lists

As discussed earlier in the chapter, spreadsheets also have basic database functionality. In order to filter and sort data easily, this functionality needs to be activated. To do this, you make the following menu choices – **Data, Filter** and activate **AutoFilter**.

This will change the visual appearance of your spreadsheet. This is because all columns that contain data will have now gained a **dropdown box** (see Figure 10.38).

2		Sales ▼	Costs ▼	Profits ▼
3	April 2005	£24,256.00	£13,098.24	£11,157.76
4	May 2005	£26,075.20	£14,080.61	£11,994.59
5	June 2005	£28,030.84	£15,136.65	£12,894.19
6	July 2005	£30,133.15	£18,381.22	£11,751.93
7	August 2005	£32,393.14	£19,759.82	£12,633.32
8	September 2005	£34,822.62	£21,241.80	£13,680.82
9	October 2005	£35,867.30	£21,879.06	£13,988.25
10	November 2005	£36,943.32	£27,707.49	£9,235.83
11	December 2005	£38,051.62	£28,538.72	£9,512.91
12	January 2006	£39,193.17	£29,394.88	£9,798.29
13				

Fig. 10.38 Using filtering techniques

When the dropdown box is activated, you can choose from a number of filtering and sorting options, or, alternatively, you can create your own custom filter (as shown in Figure 10.39).

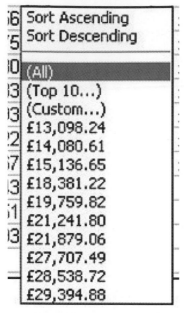

Fig. 10.39 Filtering options

Choice of methods for complex spreadsheets

Choosing which methods to apply to a complex spreadsheet will depend on what you are trying to achieve. Guidance has been given throughout this unit on the various techniques that the spreadsheet user has at his/her disposal. Experience of working with spreadsheets in general will also make choosing techniques appropriately much easier.

Checking

It is important from a spreadsheet development perspective to ensure that any spreadsheet is completely accurate and as efficient as possible. The spreadsheet should, thus, be **fully** checked.

Check formulae and functions work correctly

Checking calculations is a fundamental requirement for the spreadsheet developer. It is usual to check the results of calculations from functions and formulae using alternative methods. This usually means using a calculator or mental maths to check the results.

Sorting out errors

As far as formulae and functions are concerned, if there is an obvious error in syntax (the construction of the function or formula), the user will receive an error message. Often the software will give an indication of where or what the error is. As with developing databases, computer programs or projects, all testing of systems should be documented carefully. All calculations should be tested and the results recorded, along with any action that is required to fix the problems.

User requirements met

As with all other developmental projects, spreadsheets should be evaluated to establish how well they meet user requirements.

Documentation

User requirements

In Unit 3: ICT Project and Unit 9: Database Software it has been suggested that if you have developed an applications solution, you should really create a set of supporting documentation. This includes a **technical specification**, using traditional techniques such as **diagrams**, **data tables**, other **images** and **text**.

It is useful, to support a spreadsheet solution, if the user document is supplemented by a good technical document that particularly details the original **user requirements** and the **details of** any **formulae** and **functions** that the spreadsheet contains.

Detail of formulae and functions used

To this end, the most common document that is provided to support a spreadsheet is a formula print. This is chosen on the **Tools**, **Options** dialogue box, by checking the **Formulas** option (see Figure 10.40).

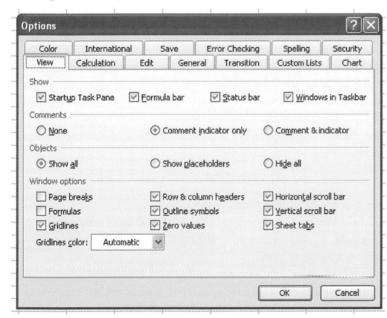

Fig. 10.40 Print options for spreadsheets

Care should also be taken to ensure that row and column headings are included on the print; otherwise it will not be clear where the formula or function is in the spreadsheet, and which other cell it is referring to. Selecting the row and column headings to be included on the print is on the **Sheet** tab on the **Page Setup** options.

QUIZ

1. What is a collection of spreadsheets in the same file called?
2. Name two different types of chart or graph.
3. What is the difference between absolute referencing and relative referencing?
4. What is a cell value?
5. Define a formula.
6. What does BODMAS stand for?
7. What is a two-stage calculation?
8. What is a data series?
9. Give an example of a data series.
10. What is a range?
11. What does the AutoSum do?
12. Name the three logical functions.
13. What does paste link do?
14. What is a file path?
15. Give three examples of cell formatting.

ANSWERS

1. A workbook
2. Pie chart, bar chart, column chart, line graph
3. With absolute referencing, any cells that have been identified with a $ symbol will not change when pasted to other cells. With relative referencing, when a cell is copied and pasted, the cell references change in relation to their last position.
4. The number or text in the cell
5. A formula is a sum that has been created using operators such as plus, minus, divide and multiply.
6. Brackets Over Division Multiplication Addition and Subtraction.
7. A two-stage calculation is where two different calculations are carried out at the same time in the same cell.
8. A data series is a range of values that are related to each other.
9. January, February, March or Jan, Feb, Mar or 1, 2, 3 or 1, 3, 5 (any valid series is acceptable)
10. A range is a series of consecutive cells.
11. The AutoSum automatically adds up a range of cells.
12. IF, AND, OR
13. Paste link is used when a figure in a spreadsheet (taken from another area of the spreadsheet or even another spreadsheet or workbook), is pasted with update functionality.
14. A file path is the drive and folder in which a file has been stored.
15. Background colour, font colour, shading, border

COURSEWORK GUIDANCE

To pass this unit you will need to demonstrate an understanding of how spreadsheets can be used. You will be expected to create a spreadsheet, formatting it appropriately and checking all aspects, including alignment, consistency and the results of formulae and functions.

You will need to show that you can make decisions about the presentation of data and how spreadsheets should be interpreted.

To show that you have gained significant knowledge, you will be asked to evaluate a solution and describe potential enhancements (Distinction criteria).

As with Unit 1: Using ICT to Present Information, Unit 3: ICT Project and Unit 7: Software Design and Development, the key issue with this unit is to make your solution look professional and presentable. Check your results carefully!

Unit links

This unit has direct links to the following:

Unit 1   Using ICT to Present Information
Unit 3   ICT Project

Unit 7   Software Design and Development
Unit 8   Customising Software Applications
Unit 9   Database Software

●●●Further reading

Harvey, Greg, *Excel 2003 All-in-one Desk Reference for Dummies* (For Dummies) (Hungry Minds Inc,US, 2003) ISBN: 076453758X

Heathcote, P., *ICT Projects for GCSE* (Payne-Gallway Publishers, 2002) ISBN: 1903112699

Heathcote, P., *Successful ICT Projects in Excel* (Payne-Gallway Publishers, 2002) ISBN: 1903112710

Heathcote, P., *Further Excel 2000–2003* (Payne-Gallway Publishers, 2004) ISBN: 1904467768

Progress check

To record your achievement, simply tick the criteria awarded to you when each assignment is returned (you may be given three assignments for this unit, U10.01, U10.02 and U10.03 – the final column may not be used). There is a full copy of this grid available on the accompanying CD. The copy will also allow you to record your key skill achievement against Literacy, Numeracy and ICT objectives.

Assignment		U10.01	U10.02	U10.03	U10.04
		Assignments in this Unit			
Referral					
Pass					
	1				
	2				
	3				
	4				
	5				
	6				
	7				
Merit					
	1				
	2				
	3				
	4				
Distinction					
	1				
	2				
	3				

A completed sample of this document (for reference purposes) can be found at the back of Unit 1.

NUMERICAL APPLICATIONS

INTRODUCTION

Every ICT practitioner needs to have some mathematical knowledge and to be able to apply it. This unit provides an introduction to a number of key mathematical skills and gives you opportunities to develop them. These skills can be applied to many different areas of ICT. This unit is vital in preparing for the further education needed to progress in a computing career.

The mathematical concepts introduced in this unit are chosen carefully to be relevant and useful. For example, the spreadsheet techniques will be used again and again, especially using equations and formulae.

Spreadsheet techniques (as shown in Unit 10: Spreadsheet Software) need an understanding of algebra – useful skills, especially if your ICT practitioner development is towards programming, where using variables is very similar to algebra.

Binary numbers are included in this unit because these numbers only use ones and zeros, which is how the computer operates. An understanding of binary is essential to get the most out of computers. Many error messages are based on binary and there are aspects of programming and setting up computers where a knowledge of binary is useful.

One of the great uses of ICT is to analyse information, which means that you, as an ICT professional, will need to understand statistics.

Very often, information from computer systems is presented as tables of numbers, which can be very difficult to understand and to find patterns in. You will learn how to convert these tables into charts and graphs, using spreadsheets.

Converting tables into charts or graphs involves choosing an appropriate type of chart or graph to show the data. You will need to develop your skills to enable you to use the computer to display and explain statistics.

The spreadsheet is a great tool for modelling situations, which can then be used to answer 'What if?' questions. You will learn how to do this, using spreadsheet equations and formulae to create models where different scenarios can be explored, such as, what if sales increase by 10%, or what if we employ another staff member?

The skills and techniques in this unit can be applied to claiming Application of Number key skills and will be a useful support for other units as well.

RECORDING YOUR PROGRESS

In order to achieve each unit you will complete a series of coursework activities. Each time you hand in work, your tutor will return this to you with a record of your achievement.

This particular unit has 11 criteria to meet: 5 Pass, 3 Merit and 3 Distinction.

For a **Pass**: you must achieve **all** 5 Pass criteria.

For a **Merit**: you must achieve **all** 5 Pass and **all** 3 Merit criteria.

For a **Distinction**: you must achieve **all** 5 Pass, all 3 Merit and **all** 3 Distinction criteria.

So that you can monitor your own progress and achievement in each unit, a recording grid has been provided (see the **Progress check** section at the end of this unit).

Calculations

You need to be able to carry out calculations using:

- **integers**, also known as whole numbers (e.g. 53 or 12)
- **decimals**, numbers with a decimal part (e.g. 5.3 or 12.26)
- **fractions**, part numbers shown as one number over another (e.g. ½ or ¼)
- **binary numbers**, numbers made up from ones and zeros (e.g. 00110111 or 01001001).

Integers and decimals

The number 245 is an integer, as **no part of the number is less than 1** (we call this a whole number). The position of each digit in a number shows the value of it:

100 column	10 column	1 column
2	4	5

So the number 245 means the number has 2 hundreds, 4 tens and 5 ones.

The values of the columns are all based on 10. (Our system of numbering is called base 10 or denary.) This table can be rewritten as:

10 to the power of 2	10 to the power of 1	10 to the power of 0
10^2	10^1	10^0
100 column	10 column	1 column
2	4	5

To the power of means how many times the number is multiplied by itself; so **10^2 means 10×10**, which gives 100. To the power of 0 is a special case that gives 1 for any number; for example:

- $10^0 = 1$
- $51^0 = 1$
- $2^0 = 1$

Decimal numbers have more columns to the right, separated from the integer part of the number with '.' which is called the **decimal point**. 24.53 is a decimal number as there is a **part of the number which is less than 1**:

10 column	1 column	Decimal point	$\frac{1}{10}$ column (tenths column)	$\frac{1}{100}$ column (hundredths column)
2	4	.	5	3

So the number 24.53 means the number has 2 tens, 4 ones, 5 tenths and 3 hundredths.

> **Key term**
>
> **Tenth**: if 1 was split into 10 equal parts, a tenth represents one of those parts.
>
> **Hundredth**: if 1 was split into 100 equal parts, a hundredth represents one of those parts.

The prevous table can be rewritten as:

10 to the power of 1	10 to the power of 0		10 to the power of −1	10 to the power of −2
10^1	10^0		10^{-1} or $\frac{1}{10}^1$	10^{-2} or $\frac{1}{10}^2$
10 column	1 column	Decimal point	$\frac{1}{10}$ column (tenths column)	$\frac{1}{100}$ column (hundredths column)
2	4	.	5	3

Fractions

A fraction is another way of writing a decimal number (e.g. 0.4 and 4/10 are the same number).

With a fraction, there are two numbers with a line in between. The first or top number (the **numerator**) denotes how many of the second or bottom number (the **denominator**) the fraction represents.

The bottom number shows how many parts 1 has been split into to make the fraction:

- ¼ (one-quarter): there are 4 of these in 1
- ⅕ (one-fifth): there are 5 of these in 1
- ¹⁄₃₂ (one-thirty-second): there are 32 of these in 1

Fractions are often used for the remainder when a number has been divided into another and the answer is not an integer (whole number). For example:

$26 \div 7 = 3\tfrac{5}{7}$ for this division, 7 divides into 26 three times ($3 \times 7 = 21$) giving a remainder of 5 ($26 - 21 = 5$), so the remainder is five-sevenths ($\tfrac{5}{7}$).

If both the numbers in a fraction are multiplied (or divided) by the same amount, the fraction still represents the same number, ⅕ and ²⁄₁₀ are equivalent (the same), as both top and bottom numbers have been multiplied by 2. Similarly, ⁹⁄₂₁ and ³⁄₇ are equivalent as both top and bottom numbers have been divided by 3.

Binary numbers

As mentioned earlier, an understanding of binary numbers is essential for ICT practitioners, as they help to recognise parts of a computer configuration and some error messages.

A computer is a **binary device**, with everything as **zero** or **one**. For example, the memory is made from millions of tiny points which have electricity (one) or no electricity (zero).

As we have seen in Unit 2: Introduction to Computer Systems, these tiny points are grouped together into eights, each called a **byte**. The patterns of ones and zeros in a byte can mean many things, such as an **ASCII code** to represent a letter of the alphabet:

0	1	0	0	0	0	0	1	= A

We find lots of ones and zeros difficult to read, so we usually convert the binary pattern in a byte to a denary number.

Binary numbers are numbers, but use **base 2** instead of the **base 10** we are used to. So, in the example above, the table can be redrawn as:

2^7	2^6	2^5	2^4	2^3	2^2	2^1	2^0	
128	64	32	16	8	4	2	1	
0	1	0	0	0	0	0	1	= 65

Every column where there is a 1 can be added together to calculate the binary number as a **denary (base 10)** number that we are familiar with: $64 + 1 = 65$.

So the binary number 01000001 means the number has no 128, one 64, no 32, no 16, no 8, no 4, no 2 and one 1, making 65.

Denary (base 10) numbers to binary

This method can convert a denary (base 10) number to binary, by subtracting the column headings. For example, for 35:

How many 128s in 35? Zero:

128	64	32	16	8	4	2	1
0							

= 0

How many 64s in 35? Zero:

128	64	32	16	8	4	2	1
0	**0**						

= 0

How many 32s in 35? One:

128	64	32	16	8	4	2	1
0	0	**1**					

= 32

Take the 32 from 35, so $35 - 32 = 3$

How many 16s in 3? Zero:

128	64	32	16	8	4	2	1
0	0	**1**	**0**				

= 32

How many 8s in 3? Zero:

128	64	32	16	8	4	2	1
0	0	1	0	**0**			

= 32

How many 4s in 3? Zero:

128	64	32	16	8	4	2	1
0	0	1	0	0	**0**		

= 32

How many 2s in 3? One:

128	64	32	16	8	4	2	1	
0	0	1	0	0	0	**1**		= 34

Take the 2 from 3, so 3 − 2 = 1

How many 1s in 1? One:

128	64	32	16	8	4	2	1	
0	0	1	0	0	0	1	**1**	= 35

To summarise, this method starts at the highest column of the binary answer:

- If the column is **bigger than the number**, **0** is written **into the column**, then the next lower column is looked at.
- If the column is the **same or smaller than the number**, **1** is written **into the column** then the **column heading is taken from the number, giving a new, smaller number**. The next lower column is looked at.

These are repeated until the lowest column of the binary answer is reached.

Addition

The number produced **when a number is added to another** (e.g. 1 + 3 = 4).

The **result** of an addition is called its **sum**.

Fig. 11.1 Addition

Subtraction

The number produced **when one number is taken away from another** (e.g. 5 − 3 = 2).

The number being taken away (3 in the example above) is called the **subtrahend**.

If the number being subtracted is larger than the number it is taken from, the answer is **negative** (a minus number) (e.g. 3 − 5 = −2).

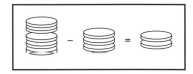
Fig. 11.2 Subtraction

Some people use a number line for additions and subtractions. To work out 3 − 5 using the number line in Figure 11.3, start on 3, count 5 to the left (subtraction is to the left, addition is to the right) to give the answer −2.

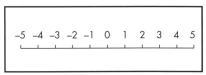
Fig. 11.3 Number line

Likewise, for −3 + 4, you start on −3, count 4 to the right, giving the answer 1, so −3 + 4 = 1; the same calculation can be written as 4 − 3 = 1.

The **result** of a subtraction is called the **difference**.

Multiplication

An operation **when a number is multiplied by another** (e.g. $4 \times 3 = 12$). Some people think of this as a number being added to itself by as many times as the other number; in this example, $4 + 4 + 4$ is the same as 4×3.

Fig. 11.4 Multiplication

The **result** of a multiplication is called the **product**.

Division

An operation **when a number is divided by another** (e.g. $6 \div 3 = 2$). Some people think of this as how many times a number can be subtracted from the other number, in this example, $6 - 3 - 3 = 0$ shows 3 can be taken away from 6 two times.

Fig. 11.5 Division

There are two symbols used to show division, $\div$ and $/$; so these two calculations are identical:

- $6 \div 3 = 2$
- $6 / 3 = 2$

Computers tend to use the forward slash ($/$), whereas we tend to use the common division operator ($\div$).

The **result** of a division is called the **quotient**.

Addition using decimals

The decimal place of each number must align e.g. $28.3 + 234.74$ is shown:

```
      2 8 . 3
  +   2 3 4 . 7 4
        1 1        (carry)
      2 6 3 . 0 4
```

The calculation starts from the right, 4 plus nothing gives 4.

Carry numbers are shown in the bottom line. $3 + 7$ gives 10, so 0 is written under this column, with a carry of 1 for the next column to left.

8 plus 4 plus 1 (the carry) gives 13, so 3 is written under this column, with a carry of 1 to the next column left.

2 plus 3 plus 1 (the carry) gives 6, so 6 is written under these, with no carry.

2 plus nothing gives 2.

So, $28.3 + 234.74 = 263.04$

Addition using fractions

Fractions need to be adjusted so they have a **common denominator** (the same number (divisor) under the line for each fraction to be added). The numbers above the line can then be added.

A common denominator can always be found by multiplying the bottom numbers together.

To add ⅔ and ⅕ together:

1. Find the common denominator by multiplying the bottom numbers together, $3 \times 5 = 15$
2. Adjust each fraction to the same denominator, ⅔ becomes ¹⁰⁄₁₅ (multiplied by 5) and ⅕ becomes ³⁄₁₅ (multiplied by 3)
3. Add the top numbers, showing the answer over the common denominator, ¹⁰⁄₁₅ + ³⁄₁₅ = ¹³⁄₁₅

To add ¼ and ⅔ together:

1. Find the common denominator by multiplying the bottom numbers together, $4 \times 3 = 12$
2. Adjust each fraction to the same denominator, ¼ becomes ³⁄₁₂ (multiplied by 3) and ⅔ becomes ⁸⁄₁₂ (multiplied by 4)
3. Add the top numbers, showing the answer over the common denominator, ³⁄₁₂ + ⁸⁄₁₂ = ¹¹⁄₁₂

Addition using binary numbers

When two binary digits are added, there are **three possible answers**:

$$
\begin{array}{cccc}
0 & 0 & 1 & 1 \\
= \quad \underline{0} & +\underline{1} & +\underline{0} & +\underline{1} \\
\mathbf{0} & \mathbf{1} & \mathbf{1} & \mathbf{10}
\end{array}
$$

These answers represent 0, 1 and 2 in binary.

Binary numbers usually have the same number of columns, but if these are different, they need to **align from the right**.

$$
\begin{array}{r}
0\,0\,1\,1\,0\,1\,0\,1 \\
+ \quad \underline{1\,0\,1\,1\,0\,0} \\
{}^{1\,1\,1\,1} \text{(carry)} \\
0\,1\,1\,0\,0\,0\,0\,1
\end{array}
$$

The calculation starts from the right, 1 plus 0 gives 1.

0 plus 0 gives 0.

Carry numbers are shown below the line. $1 + 1$ gives 10 (binary for 2), so 0 is written under this column, with a carry of 1 for the next column left.

0 plus 1 plus 1 (the carry) gives 10, so 0 is written under this column, with a carry of 1 for the next column left.

1 plus 0 plus 1 (the carry) gives 10, so 0 is written under this column, with a carry of 1 for the next column left.

1 plus 1 plus 1 (the carry) gives 11, so 1 is written under this column, with a carry of 1 for the next column left.

0 plus nothing plus 1 (the carry) gives 1, so 1 is written under this column, with no carry for the next column left.

0 plus nothing gives 0.

Many people convert their binary numbers to denary (base 10) to check their answers for these calculations.

	128	64	32	16	8	4	2	1	
	0	0	1	1	0	1	0	1	= 53 (32 + 16 + 4 + 1)
+			1	0	1	1	0	0	= 44 (32 + 8 + 4)
	0	1	1	0	0	0	0	1	= 97 (64 + 32 + 1)

Subtraction using decimals

When describing subtraction, it is useful to know the meaning of **subtrahend** and **minuend**. In the calculation 3 − 2, the 3 is the minuend and the 2 the subtrahend.

As with addition, the decimal place of each number **must align**.

    234.74
  + 28.3
      4.74

The calculation starts from the right. 4 minus nothing gives 4. 7 minus 3 gives 4.

4 minus 8 is clearly going to cause a problem, so we **need to borrow** 10 **from the next column to the left**, to increase the 4 to 14. Now we can say 14 minus 8, which gives 6.

Subtract 1 (30 becomes 20)
Borrow 10 (4 becomes 14)

    234.74
  + 28.3
    206.44

As we borrowed 10 from the next column to the left, we now need to **replace it** by reducing the 3 (effectively 30) to 2 (or 20), so that we can continue by saying 2 minus 2. This gives a 0.

Finally, 2 minus nothing (there is nothing in the first column below the 2) is 2.

So, 234.74 − 28.3 = 206.44.

Subtraction using fractions

Fractions need to be adjusted so they have a **common denominator** (the same number under the line for each fraction to be subtracted). The numbers above the line can then be subtracted. A common denominator can always be found by multiplying the bottom numbers together.

To subtract ⅙ from ¾ (i.e. ¾ − ⅙):

1. Find the common denominator by multiplying the bottom numbers together, $4 \times 6 = 24$

2. Adjust each fraction to the same denominator, ¾ becomes ¹⁸⁄₂₄ (multiplied by 6) and ⅙ becomes ⁴⁄₂₄ (multiplied by 4)

3. Subtract the top numbers, showing the answer over the common denominator, ¹⁸⁄₂₄ − ⁴⁄₂₄ = ¹⁴⁄₂₄

4. This answer can be simplified down by dividing both numbers in the fraction by 2, giving ⁷⁄₁₂

Subtraction using binary numbers

To subtract using binary we use the **two's complement method**. This works by making the subtrahend into a negative binary number (called the two's complement).

This can then be added in the same way that 5 plus −3 gives the answer 2.

To subtract 13 from 25 (i.e. 25 − 13), first find the two's complement of 13.

1. Convert 13 to binary

128	64	32	16	8	4	2	1	
0	0	0	0	1	1	0	1	= 13

2. Invert it (swap all the 0s to 1s and 1s to 0s)

1	1	1	1	0	0	1	0

3. Add 1 to the digit on the right of the binary number

	1	1	1	1	0	0	1	0	
+								1	
	1	1	1	1	0	0	1	1	= −13

Now the two's complement of 13 has been found it can be added to 25 to give the answer. During this part of the calculation, there should be an extra 1 carried to the left of the answer. This 1 is ignored.

		1	1	1	1	0	0	1	1		−13
+		0	0	0	1	1	0	0	1		25
		0	0	0	0	1	1	0	0		
1		1	1	1			1	1			carry

In this calculation, the answer can be seen by adding each column heading where there is a 1 in the column:

128	64	32	16	8	4	2	1	
0	0	0	0	1	1	0	0	= 12

$8 + 4 = 12$

If there is no 1 carried to the left of the answer, the answer is a negative number. Negative answers are in the two's complement form, so need to be converted back to see the number they represent by inverting then adding one.

To subtract 23 from 18 (i.e. $18 - 23$), first find the two's complement of 23:

1. Convert 23 to binary

128	64	32	16	8	4	2	1	
0	0	0	1	0	1	1	1	= 23

2. Invert it (swap all the 0s to 1s and 1s to 0s)

1	1	1	0	1	0	0	0

3. Add 1 to the digit on the right of the binary number

	1	1	1	0	1	0	0	0	
+								1	
	1	1	1	0	1	0	0	1	= −23

Now the two's complement of 23 has been found it can be added to 18 to give the answer. During this part of the calculation, there should be no extra 1 carried to the left of the answer, as the answer should be −5.

	1	1	1	0	1	0	0	1	− 23
+	0	0	0	1	0	0	1	0	18
	1	1	1	1	1	0	1	1	
									carry

In this calculation, the answer must be converted back from two's complement before it can be seen, by adding each column heading where there is a 1 in the column.

Invert it (swap all the 0s to 1s and 1s to 0s)

0	0	0	0	0	1	0	0

Add 1 to the digit on the right of the binary number

	0	0	0	0	0	1	0	0
+								1
	0	0	0	0	0	1	0	1

Calculate the answer by adding each column heading where there is a 1 in the column:

128	64	32	16	8	4	2	1	
0	0	0	0	0	1	0	1	= 5

$4 + 1 = 5$

So the answer is −5.

Multiplication using decimals

Multiplication using decimals is usually a calculation carried out in **three stages**.

First, one of the numbers is multiplied by each digit in the other number, each providing a part answer. These part answers are shifted to the left, according to the position of each digit.

Second, the part answers are added together.

To multiply 23.5 by 14.2 (i.e. 23.5 × 14.2), remove the decimal points and multiply as integers:

```
      2 3 5
    × 1 4 2
      4 7 0    ×2
    9 4 0 0    ×40
  2 3 5 0 0    ×100
          ı ı  Carry
  3 3 3 7 0    Add
```

The ×2 line multiplies 235 by 2, giving 470.

The ×40 line multiplies 235 by 40, giving 9400.

The ×100 line multiplies 235 by 100, giving 23500.

These are then added together to give the answer, 33370. We now put the decimal point back in. Do this by counting the number of digits after the decimal points in the original numbers (23.5 and 14.2); two digits. This means 33370 becomes 333.70 by moving the decimal point two places in from the left.

Multiplication using fractions

Fractions do not need to be adjusted before a multiplication.

To multiply ⅚ by ¾:

1. Multiply the top numbers together, $5 \times 3 = 15$
2. Multiply the bottom numbers together, $6 \times 4 = 24$
3. Show the answer, $\frac{15}{24}$ which simplifes to ⅝

Multiplication using binary numbers

This is very similar to multiplication using decimals, but is a lot simpler, as 1 and 0 are the only digits used in the calculation.

To multiply 35 by 10 (i.e. 35×10).

First, convert both numbers to binary:

128	64	32	16	8	4	2	1	
0	0	1	0	0	0	1	1	= 35
0	0	0	0	1	0	1	0	= 10

Then multiply the first number by each digit in turn of the second number, shifting the part answers to the left, according to which column each digit is in.

```
        00100011
      × 00001010
        00000000    ×0
       001000110    ×10
      0000000000    ×000
     00100011000    ×1000
                    Carry
     00101011110    Add
```

Many people would leave out the ×0 row, as zero added to the answer will not change it, and the calculation is easier to see with unwanted detail removed.

It is usual to check binary calculations by converting the answer back to denary (base 10) to confirm it produces the same answer as using denary.

$35 \times 10 = 350$

1024	512	256	128	64	32	16	8	4	2	1	
0	0	1	0	1	0	1	1	1	1	0	= 350

$256 + 64 + 16 + 8 + 4 + 2 = 350$

Division using integers

When describing division, it is useful to know the meaning of **dividend** and **divisor**. In the calculation 3 ÷ 2, 3 is called the dividend, and 2 the divisor.

Many people use a calculator to work out divisions, but it is still useful to understand how to divide using pencil and paper. This is called **long division**.

To divide 30123 by 3 (i.e. 30123 ÷ 3):

```
    1 0 0 4 1
3│3 0 1 2 3
 −3
  0 0 1 2
    −1 2
      0 3
      −3
       0
```

In this calculation we first find how many times the divisor, 3, is able to be divided into the first digit of the dividend. 3 divides into 3 one time, so 1 is written on the top line above the first digit of the dividend. 3 (3×1) is written underneath the first digit and taken away. There is no remainder, so a 0 is written:

```
    1
3│3 0 1 2 3
 −3
  0
```

We now find how many times the divisor, 3, is able to be divided into the next digit of the dividend. 3 divides into 0 no times, so 0 is written on the top line above the second digit of the dividend. The 0 of the dividend is copied down to the bottom row of the calculation:

```
    1 0
3│3 0 1 2 3
 −3
  0 0
```

We now find how many times the divisor, 3, is able to be divided into the next digit of the dividend. 3 divides into 1 no times, so 0 is written on the top line above the third digit of the dividend. The 1 of the dividend is copied down to the bottom row of the calculation:

```
    1 0
3│3 0 1 2 3
 −3
  0 0 1
```

We now find how many times the divisor, 3, is able to be divided into the next digit of the dividend. 3 divides into 12 four times, so 4 is written on the top line above the fourth digit of the dividend. 12 (3×4) is written underneath and taken away. There is no remainder, so a 0 is written:

```
        1 0 0 4 1
    3 3 0 1 2 3
    −3
      0 0 1 2
       −1 2
          0
```

We now find how many times the divisor, 3, is able to be divided into the next digit of the dividend. 3 divides into 3 once, so 1 is written on the top line above the third digit of the dividend. 3 (3×1) is written underneath and taken away. There is no remainder, so a 0 is written:

```
        1 0 0 4 1
    3 3 0 1 2 3
    −3
      0 0 1 2
       −1 2
          0 3
         −3
          0
```

So 3 can be divided into 30123, ten thousand and forty-one times.

Division using fractions

Fractions do not need to be adjusted before a division.

To divide ⅚ by ¾ (i.e. ⅚ ÷ ¾):

1. Invert the divisor, so ¾ becomes ⁴⁄₃
2. Multiply the fractions together, ⅚ × ⁴⁄₃
3. Show the answer, ²⁰⁄₁₈
4. Simplify the answer, ¹⁰⁄₉ or 1⅑

Division using binary numbers

The technique is the same as for division using decimals, except that it is a little simpler, as each stage of the calculation can only produce a 1 or a 0 as the result.

To divide 30 by 5 (i.e. 30 ÷ 5):

First, convert the denary numbers to binary:

128	64	32	16	8	4	2	1	
0	0	0	1	1	1	1	0	= 30
0	0	0	0	0	1	0	1	= 5

Remember, in this calculation the 30 is called the dividend and the 5 the divisor. All the 0s above the largest 1 can be disregarded in the dividend. This makes the calculation a lot easier to work out. So 00000101 becomes 101.

```
1 0 1 | 0 0 0 1 1 1 1 0
```

In this calculation we first find how many times the divisor, 101, can be divided into the first digit of the dividend. 101 divides into 0 no times, so 0 is written on the top line above the first digit of the dividend. And again, for the next two 0s:

```
        0 0 0
1 0 1 | 0 0 0 1 1 1 1 0
```

101 divides into 0001 zero times and into 00011 zero times:

```
        0 0 0 0 0
1 0 1 | 0 0 0 1 1 1 1 0
```

101 divides into 000111 one time. 101 is written underneath this and taken away. There is a **remainder**:

```
        0 0 0 0 0 1
1 0 1 | 0 0 0 1 1 1 1 0
           − 1 0 1
             0 1 0
```

The next 1 of the dividend is copied down to the bottom row of the calculation:

```
        0 0 0 0 0 1
1 0 1 | 0 0 0 1 1 1 1 0
           − 1 0 1
             0 1 0 1
```

We now find that the divisor, 101, divides into this 101 one time, so write another 1 above the line and subtract 101 from 101, leaving 000:

```
        0 0 0 0 1 1
1 0 1 | 0 0 0 1 1 1 1 0
           − 1 0 1
             0 1 0 1
             − 1 0 1
               0 0 0
```

We now bring down the last 0 and find that the divisor, 101, is able to be divided into the 0000 no times, so a 0 is written:

```
        0 0 0 0 0 1 1 0
1 0 1 | 0 0 0 1 1 1 1 0
           − 1 0 1
             0 1 0 1
             − 1 0 1
               0 0 0 0
```

So 101 can be divided into 00011110, 00000110 times.

These binary numbers can be translated back to denary to check the answer:

128	64	32	16	8	4	2	1	
0	0	0	1	1	1	1	0	= 30
0	0	0	0	0	1	0	1	= 5
0	0	0	0	0	1	1	0	= 6

$30 \div 5 = 6$

Remember, any time a binary calculation is made, the answer can be checked by converting each of the numbers to denary, which must give the same answer.

Calculations involving two or more steps

Some calculations involve a number of steps.

An example of that could be to work out the amount of paint needed to cover the walls in a room. In this calculation, the area of each wall needs to be worked out, then the areas added together. Finally, the coverage of the paint needs to be divided into the area of the walls to calculate how much paint is needed.

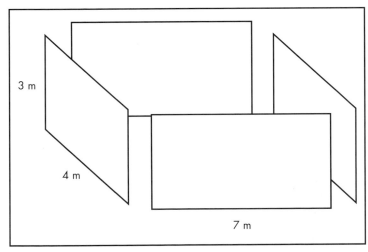

3 m

4 m

7 m

Fig. 11.6 Room

The area of a rectangle is calculated as one side multiplied by the other side, so for a wall in a room 7 m long and 3 m high, the area is 7 times 3, equalling 21 square metres. If another wall is 4 m long and 3 m high, the area of that wall is 12 square metres. Add these walls (remember there are two of each wall) together: 21 plus 21 plus 12 plus 12 gives 66 square metres. If the paint covers 6 square metres per litre, then the amount of paint needed will be 66 divided by 6, which equals 11 litres.

Numbers of any size

Very large and very small numbers are often shown in **standard form**. This is a way of **formatting a number** so it takes up **less space** and is **easier to understand**.

Standard form takes the **first three digits** of a number, with a **decimal point after the first digit**. The rest of the standard form is **10 to a power**. The power is how many times the decimal point needed to move to get to its position between the first and second digits.

2.35×10^{12} is the standard form of 2350000000000

Sometimes standard form is written with E instead of 10. E stands for **exponent**.

So $2.35e + 12$ is the same as 2.35×10^{12}.

Often standard form means that a lot of accuracy is lost, as numbers need to be rounded up or down to fit into the 3 digits. Here are some examples:

Original number	Standard form	From standard form
2344	2.34×10^3	2340
2345	2.34×10^3	2340
2345.1	2.35×10^3	2350
3456758	3.46×10^6	3460000
1298457687	1.30×10^9	1300000000

Notice how the third column in the table above shows the number from standard form. This is the number that can be obtained from the standard form. It is often quite different, because when the original number was rounded to standard form, the detail was lost.

Very small numbers are handled in much the same way, except that the power of 10 is a negative number. Here are some examples:

Original number	Standard form	From standard form
0.2344	2.34×10^{-1}	0.234
0.0002345	2.34×10^{-4}	0.000234
0.00023451	2.35×10^{-4}	0.000235
0.003456758	3.46×10^{-3}	0.00346
0.000000000001290457687	1.29×10^{-12}	0.00000000000290

You will see the standard form in Microsoft Excel® if a very large or small number is entered into a cell, as shown in Figure 11.7.

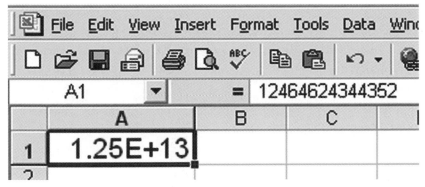

Fig. 11.7 Microsoft Excel® standard form

Microsoft Excel® does its best to fit the standard form into the size of the cell, so the number of decimal places in the standard form changes with the width of the column (see Figure 11.8).

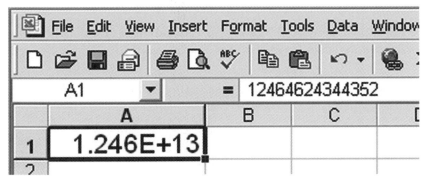

Fig. 11.8 Microsoft Excel® standard form 3dp

When Microsoft Excel® uses standard form to show a number, it still **keeps the original number in memory**, so **no detail is lost in calculations**.

Signed numbers

The sign of a number is + (plus) or − (minus), to show whether the number is **positive** or **negative**. If the number has no sign, it is taken to be positive.

As seen earlier, some people like to use a number bar to show how positive and negative numbers can be added or subtracted from each other (Figure 11.3). The number bar works by starting with one of the numbers, then counting right to add or left to subtract:

2 plus 3 equals 5

2 plus −3 equals −1

Approximation

Approximation can be used to check answers by giving a **rough result**.

This technique simply rounds numbers up or down to give a simpler calculation. If the answer to this simplified calculation is close to the answer of the actual calculation, then it is probably correct.

For example, 298×31 can be simplified to 300×30, giving 9000, which is quite similar to the actual answer of 9238.

Approximation is used to show:

- there are the right number of digits in the answer – in the example above, if the actual answer came out as 92380, then approximation would have shown it wrong
- a rough answer – if the actual answer came out as 1923, then approximation would have shown it is probably wrong.

Approximation is a technique to show that an answer **might be correct**; it cannot confirm that an answer is actually right. The real use of approximation is to identify when a calculation produces a wrong answer.

Fractions

Fractions and ratios are much the same thing, but shown in different ways.

A fraction shows a number above another number, with a line between them. This line is usually horizontal (flat), but is often shown in typed text as a forward slash.

The appearance of a fraction may be changed by multiplying or dividing both the numbers by the same amount. For example, $\frac{1}{3}$ is the same as $\frac{3}{9}$ (both numbers multiplied by 3) and $\frac{15}{45}$ (both numbers multiplied by 15).

Fractions are usually simplified, which means that both numbers are divided by whatever is needed to make them as small as possible. Thus $\frac{21}{28}$ would usually be written as $\frac{3}{4}$ (both numbers divided by 7).

If the top number (dividend) is larger than the lower number (divisor), the divisor is divided into the dividend to find out how many whole numbers the fraction represents, thus $\frac{50}{15}$ would be simplified to $\frac{10}{3}$ (both numbers divided by 5), then written as $3\frac{1}{3}$ (3 divides into 10 three times, remainder 1).

Ratios

A ratio shows a number before another number, with a colon (:) between them.

A ratio is a comparison expressed like a fraction, e.g. 2:1 boy/girl class ratio is the same as 2/1 or two boys to every one girl in the class.

Ratios are usually simplified, which means that both numbers are divided by whatever is needed to make them as small as possible. Thus 5:30 would usually be written as 1:6 (both numbers divided by 5).

Degree of accuracy

It is often useful to know the accuracy of a calculation. A high degree of accuracy is when the result of a calculation is **very accurate**.

A low degree of accuracy is when the result of a calculation is **very poor**. This happens when the figures used to produce the result are not very accurate.

For example, some statistics may be prepared to show the results from a survey. If 1012 people responded, then a high degree of accuracy would be obtained if 1012 was used in the calculations. A low degree of accuracy would result from 1000 being used instead, which would make the calculations easier to work out, but produce a less accurate result.

Extended calculations

Extended calculations have **several stages**, each producing a **part answer** which is then used in the **next stage** of the calculation.

Loans

Loans calculations find out **how much interest** is to be paid on a loan or **how much the repayments will be**.

These calculations are quite difficult to work out, so are usually produced using a spreadsheet. The spreadsheet allows formulae which use numbers typed into cells to show the required answers.

Depreciation

Depreciation is a calculation that finds out how **much something is worth after a set amount of time**. Depreciation is why the value of a second-hand car or motorcycle reduces as the vehicle gets older.

Depreciation is often used to work out the value of ICT equipment to an organisation. So if there is a 4-year capital write-off period, the equipment is worth the amounts shown in Figure 11.9.

This screenshot shows the calculations in cells B4 to B6 in the C column.

	A	B	C
1			
2			
3	Year 1	10000	
4	Year 2	7500	=B3 * 75%
5	Year 3	5000	=B3 * 50%
6	Year 4	2500	=B3 * 25%

Fig. 11.9 Capital write-offs

Pricing goods

Pricing goods can use a formula where the cost of the components, labour and a profit margin are brought together to work out the amount to be charged for goods.

Case study

Steve Hodder Skateboards is a small skateboard company. They use this formula to calculate the selling price of their custom-built skateboards:

(Cost of components + 10%) + (hours to build × £10)

So, if the components cost £20 and the board takes 2 hours to build:

(£20 + £2) + (2 × £10)

£22 + £20

Selling price: £42

Formulae

ICT practitioners are able to use formulae in spreadsheets, programs, databases and many other places where calculations are needed.

Algebraic formulae

Algebraic formulae can be used in spreadsheets and other software, to calculate:

- areas
- volumes
- wages
- currency conversion
- production costs
- quotations.

Areas

An area is the number that represents **how much surface something has**. This is useful for tasks such as estimating how much paint is needed for decorating a room.

The area will use the measurement **squared** (to the power of 2) as the unit, so if the sides are measured in cm (centimetres), then units will be cm^2; if the sides are measured in km (kilometres), then units will be km^2. This is because 2 figures are multiplied together to give the answer.

There are three simple calculations for area for different types of shape:

- Rectangle: base times the height
- Triangle: half the base times the height
- Circle: pi times the radius squared (pi is spoken as 'pie' and is a letter in the Greek alphabet (π) representing roughly $^{22}/_7$, which is used in circle calculations).

Area of a rectangle: the base is usually the bottom edge of the rectangle, 3 m in Figure 11.10. The height is usually the side edge of the rectangle, 2 m in this example.

The area is calculated as **base times height**, which is 3×2, giving 6 as the answer. Units should always be shown in the answer, so the area of this rectangle is 6 m².

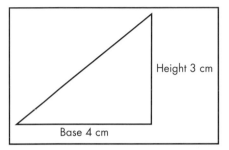

Fig. 11.10 Rectangle area

Area of a triangle: the base is usually the bottom edge of the rectangle, 4 cm in Figure 11.11. The height is how far the top corner is from the base line, 3 cm here.

The area is calculated as **half the base times the height**, which is $4 \times 3 \times 0.5$, giving 6 as the answer. Units should always be shown in the answer, so the area of this rectangle is 6 cm².

The height of this triangle is one of the sides because the angle between the base and the height sides is 90°, also known as a right angle. However, some triangles do not have a right angle, so an extra line needs to be drawn to find the height (as shown in Figure 11.12).

Fig. 11.11 Right-angled triangle

The height line makes an angle of 90° (a right angle) with the base line. Sometimes the base line needs to be extended, shown in Figure 11.12 with a dotted line.

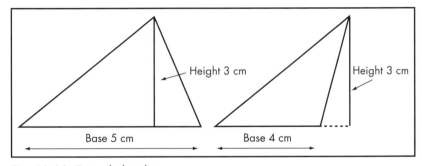

Fig. 11.12 Triangle heights

Key terms

An **angle** is formed at the meeting of two lines. The slant they form is measured in degrees. A 90-degree angle is called a **right angle**. Angles less than 90 degrees are called **acute**. Angles more than 90 degrees are called **obtuse**. Angles larger than 180 degrees are called **reflex**.

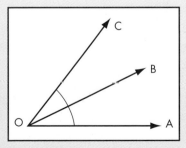

Fig. 11.13

Area of a circle: the area of a circle is calculated using the formula **pi times the radius squared**, which is often written as πr^2 where π represents pi and r represents the radius of the circle.

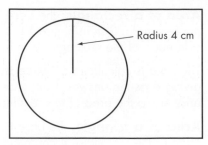

Fig. 11.14 Circle

In the circle in Figure 11.14, πr^2 becomes $\pi 4^2$, which becomes $\pi \times 16$, which is 50 cm^2 (rounded to the nearest whole number).

If you use Microsoft Excel® for calculating the area of a circle, there is a function, PI(),which returns the value of pi (see Figure 11.15).

Microsoft Excel® could also have calculated 4^2 using this formula, where ^2 means to the power of two (see Figure 11.16).

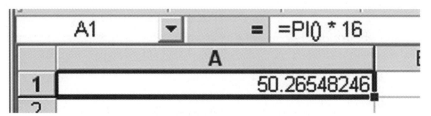

Fig. 11.15 Microsoft Excel® PI

Fig. 11.16 Microsoft Excel® PI with square

Volumes

A volume is the number that represents **how much space is inside something**. This is useful for tasks such as working out how much liquid can be held in a container.

The volume will use the measurement **cubed** (to the power of 3) as the unit, so if the sides are measured in cm, then units will be cm^3; if the sides are measured in km, then units will be km^3. This is because 3 figures are multiplied together to give the answer.

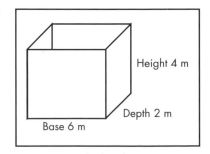

Fig. 11.17 Block volume

The volume is calculated by **multiplying the area of one end of the object by how deep it is** (the depth).

In the block shown in Figure 11.17, the volume will be the area of one end multiplied by the depth; this can be written as (area) $\times$ depth, which is $(6 \times 4) \times 2$ for this block.

This works out as (24) × 2, which is 48. The units need to be included, so the volume of this block is 48 m³.

In the shape shown in Figure 11.18, volume is the area of one end multiplied by depth; this can be written as (area) × depth, which is (base × height /2) × depth which is (8 × 5 × 0.5) × 2 for this shape (a **prism**).

This works out as (20) × 2, which is 40. The units need to be included, so the volume of this block is 40 cm³.

In the cylinder shown in Figure 11.19, the volume will be the area of one end multiplied by the depth; this can be written as (area) × depth, which is (πr^2) × depth. This becomes ($\pi 4^2$) × 3, which becomes (π × 16) × 3, which is (50) × 3 (with π × 16 rounded to the nearest whole number).

This works out as 150 for this cylinder. The units need to be included, so the volume of this cylinder is 150 cm³.

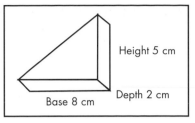
Fig. 11.18 Shape volume

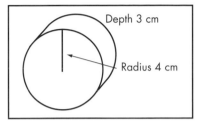
Fig. 11.19 Cylinder volume

Wages

One of the joys of working is payday! Unfortunately, the amount of money actually **received** is **not the same** as the amount of money **earned**. The difference between the amount earned (**gross pay**) and that received (**net pay**) is called the deductions.

Deductions will be for:

- Tax (also known as **PAYE**, pay as you earn)
- NI (**National Insurance**, contributions towards state benefits)
- **Pension** (if you are in a pension scheme).

The NI and pension deductions are a percentage of the amount earned. Tax deductions are complex, with three tax bands, depending upon how much is earned:

- Starting rate (10%) for up to £2,150 pa (per annum, that is, each year)
- Basic rate (22%) for between £2,151 pa and £33,300 pa
- Higher rate (40%) for more than £33,300 pa.

There is also a **tax code** that is allocated. This is an amount of earnings that is **tax-free**. Tax is paid when earnings **go above the tax-free allowance** (for the tax code). The tax code is a number followed by a letter, which is the type of code. The amount allowed is the number multiplied by 10, so a tax code of 450L shows an allowance of £4,500 pa.

If an employee earns a salary of £30,000, with a tax code of 475L:

Annual salary	£30,000.00
Monthly salary This is the gross pay	£2,500.00
Tax code 475L, annual allowance	£4750.00
Monthly allowance (£475 / 12)	£395.83
Taxable pay for month (£2,500 – £395.83)	£2,104.17
Amount of pay at starting rate (£2,090 / 12)	£174.17
Amount of pay at basic rate (£2,104 – £174.17)	£1,930.00
Starting rate tax (10% of £174.17)	£17.42
Basic rate tax (22% of £1,930.00)	£424.60
Tax to be deducted (£17.42 + £424.60)	£442.02
NI to be deducted (11% of (£2,500 – £420))	£228.80
Total deductions (£17.42 + £424.60 + £228.80)	£670.82
Take-home pay (£2,500.00 – £670.82) This is the net pay	£1,829.18

(All figures above rounded to two decimal places.)

These calculations are **simplified**. For accurate, up-to-date and detailed explanations of tax and NI, visit www.hmrc.gov.uk, which is the official **Inland Revenue** site.

Currency conversion

Currency conversion is a simple calculation where the amount you wish to convert is multiplied by the **currency conversion rate**.

The currency conversion rate changes all the time, according to how well the economies of the countries the currencies are from are performing. Up-to-date currency conversion rates can be seen in travel agents, on teletext and websites such as:
http://newsvote.bbc.co.uk/1/shared/fds/hi/business/market_data/currency/default.stm

If £1 buys $1.74515, then the currency conversion rate is 1:1.74515 (£:$), so £500 should buy $872.57 (500 × 1.74515), but in reality there is usually a **fee** to pay to whoever sells you the currency.

For this exchange rate, you can calculate the amount of pounds that can be purchased with dollars by dividing the currency conversion rate, so $500 should buy £286.51 (500 / 1.74515), but again, there is a fee to pay.

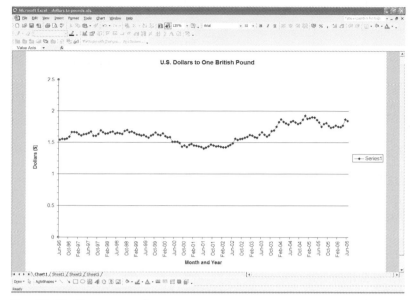

Fig. 11.20 Currency exchange rates

Production costs

Production costs can be calculated from the cost of the **material needed**, the **labour involved** in the manufacture and **fixed costs**, such as rent and the salaries of people not involved in production, such as sales and reception. Production costs also often include the cost of **delivering the products**.

The production costs will be used to find the selling price of a product by adding the desired profit margin to the cost.

Quotations

A quotation is produced to **provide a price for a job**. The quotation is usually compiled from the **costs of the labour and materials needed to complete the job**.

The profit in a quotation is usually from the cost of labour and a **mark-up** on the materials.

Use of variables

A variable is the name given in a program to a space in memory where a value can be kept. Algebraic formulae use letters to represent values; a program can use variables in the same way.

A program may be used to calculate the amount of paint needed to cover a wall. The calculation works by finding out the area of the wall, then dividing this by the paint coverage. This is the algebraic expression for the calculation:

$P = L * H / C$

where P = Paint needed, L = Length of wall, H = Height of wall, C = Coverage.

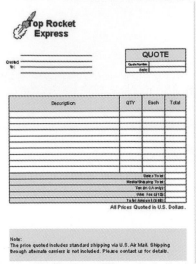

Source: http://www.smartdraw.com/
examples/form-invoice/business_quote.htm

Fig. 11.21 Business quote

A program could use variables named: PaintNeeded, WallLength, WallHeight, Coverage, to hold the numbers for each of these and to work out the amount of paint needed to cover the wall:

PaintNeeded = WallLength * WallHeight / Coverage

Statistical techniques

Most ICT practitioners understand and are able to use basic statistical techniques, as one of the fundamental uses of computers is to process data into information.

Data is the **raw information**. For example, data could be details of 10 million credit card transactions, which may be processed into information showing how many extra sales were made after a run of TV adverts. **Statistical techniques** are needed for this type of processing.

Numerical techniques

Some numerical techniques are needed to make sense of large amounts of data. These include mean, median, mode, rank, maximum, minimum, quartile and interquartile ranges.

Mean

The mean is a figure that many people call the average. It can be used to represent a range of numbers and is calculated by **adding all the numbers together**, then **dividing this total by how many numbers were added together**.

To find the mean of 3, 5, 6, 6, 7, 2, 9, 9, 1, 2:

1) Add the numbers together: 3 + 5 + 6 + 6 + 7 + 2 + 9 + 9 + 1 + 2 = 50

2) Divide by how many numbers: 50/10 = 5

3) The mean is 5

Median

The median is another number that can be used to represent a range of numbers. It is found by arranging the numbers into **rank order (lowest to highest)**. The median is the **middle** number.

To find the mean of 3, 5, 6, 6, 7, 2, 9, 9, 1, 2:

1) Arrange the numbers into rank order: 1, 2, 2, 3, 5, 6, 6, 7, 9, 9

2) Find the middle number, this range has an even number of items, so the middle number would be between 5 and 6

3) The median is 5.5

Mode

The mode is another number that can be used to represent a range of numbers. It is **whichever number is the most common**.

To find the mode of 3, 5, 6, 6, 7, 2, 9, 9, 1, 2:

1) Arrange the numbers into rank order: 1, 2, 2, 3, 5, 6, 6, 7, 9, 9

2) Find the number which is repeated the most; in this range there are three modes: 2, 6 and 9, as there are two of each

Rank

The rank is the **position of a number** in a range when they are **in order**.

To find the rank of 6 in this range 3, 5, 6, 6, 7, 2, 9, 9, 1, 2:

1) Arrange the numbers into order: 1, 2, 2, 3, 5, 6, 6, 7, 9, 9

2) The rank of 6 is 6, as it is six down from the beginning of the range

Quartile and interquartile ranges

One of the classic ways of showing data is the **cumulative frequency curve**. This curve is a very simple graph, with each point showing the total of everything below it.

The quartiles are flat (horizontal) lines drawn on the graph at the ¼ (25% or lower quartile) and ¾ (75% or upper quartile) values.

This graph shows that 25% of the sample lasted 24 years or less.

Other quartiles allow statements such as '25% of our visitors spent less than £12', or 'three quarters of the survey earned less than £25K'.

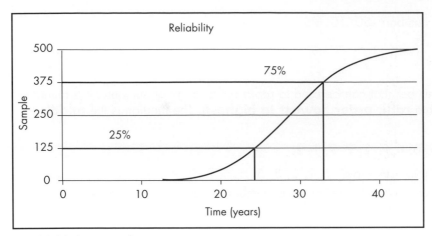

Fig. 11.22 Interquartile range

Maximum

The maximum number is the **largest number** in a range.

The maximum number in 3, 5, 6, 6, 7, 2, 9, 9, 1, 2 is 9.

Minimum

The minimum number is the **smallest number** in a range.

The minimum number in 3, 5, 6, 6, 7, 2, 9, 9, 1, 2 is 1.

Classification of data

Data is usually made up from millions of figures which are often difficult to understand in their raw form. **Classifying data** is often the first step towards making sense of all this detail. There are several ways of classifying data, including:

- collections
- tabulations
- frequency tables.

Collections

A **tally** can be used to identify **how often values are found** in a **data set** (see Figure 11.23).

Value	0	1	2	3	4	5	6	7	8	9	10	11	12	13	14	15
Frequency	0	0	10	5	10	0	7	1	0	6	0	10	3	0	0	1

Fig. 11.23 Tally

The tally totals shown above could be created by hand or may be the results of functions used in a spreadsheet or database to count similar values. These tally totals show there are no 0s or 1s, ten 2s, five 3s, and so on.

Data Checksheet

Processed being analysed: Handling returned computer parts

Information about: Goods returned by reason returned

Area/Location of data collection: Computer parts Warehouse no. 1

Data collection method: Inspect reason why were goods returned

Name: Mike Walker

Date	Incorrect	Warranty	Not to specification	Total
10/08/05	IIII	I	II	7
17/08/05	II	IIII	I	7
25/08/05	I	III	II	6

Fig. 11.24 Data checklist

Tallys can be created as data is recorded, as in the sheets shown in Figures 11.24 and 11.25.

Checksheet

Testing date: 13th July 2006

Manufacturing batch number: RKJ11

Number of defective "dead" pixels found on LCD Panel

	1	2	3	4	5	6	7	8	9	10	11	12	13	14	15
10															
								X							
5						X	X								
						X	X								
						X	X	X	X						
						X	X	X	X						
					X	X	X	X	X	X	X				
0					X	X	X	X	X	X	X	X			
Totals					1	2	6	7	4	4	2	2			

Fig. 11.25 Check sheet

Tabulation of large data sets

The tabulation of large data sets involves showing the data in a table to help simplify and explain it, such as the part table shown in Figure 11.26.

Data year	Number of records
1960	28,738
1961	24,281
1962	27,369
1963	20,760

Fig. 11.26

Frequency tables

A large data set is often processed into a frequency table, where ranges of values are counted. This might be part of a large amount of raw data, such as that shown in Figure 11.27

36.4	31.8	31.0	39.4	28.8	31.8	28.7	37.0	25.5	19.3	44.0	38.0	28.6
29.1	21.1	30.4	31.2	38.0	39.0	19.3	27.6	19.1	32.5	26.8	39.9	36.1
33.2	26.5	38.1	14.9	33.2	27.8	24.7	24.9	25.0	33.1	24.1	19.7	19.1
26.9	22.5	25.5	33.0	19.4	26.8	24.6	37.5	19.8	43.7	38.1	30.8	34.5

Fig. 11.27

which can then be shown as presented in Figure 11.28.

LENGTH	Frequency	Percent	Cumul. Freq	Cumul. Percent Frequency
$10<X<15$	6	1.2	6	1.2
$15<X<20$	35	7.0	41	8.2
$20<X<25$	93	18.6	134	26.8
$25<X<30$	155	31.0	289	57.8
$30<X<35$	130	26.0	419	83.8
$35<X<40$	57	11.4	476	95.2
$40<X<45$	24	4.8	500	100.0

Fig. 11.28

The table shows there are six items of data larger than 10 and less than 15, thirty-five items of data larger than 15 and less than 20, and so on.

Interpretation of graphical representations

If a picture is worth a thousand words, a graphical representation must be worth several million items of data! Graphical representations are among the most powerful methods of explaining data.

Pictograms

Pictograms include pie charts, bar charts and histograms.

Pie charts

A **pie chart** can be a great way of showing how something such as a sum of money has been divided up. The slices of the pie may have their percentage and value shown.

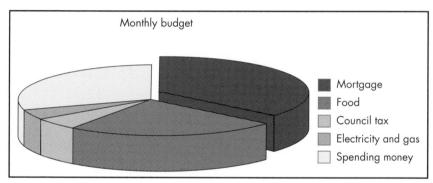

Fig. 11.29 Pie chart

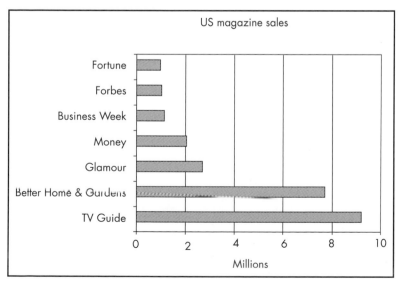

Fig. 11.30 Bar chart

Sometimes a slice is exploded to show it clearly, as with the mortgage above – useful if the written explanation of the pie chart refers to that slice.

Bar charts

Bar charts are a good way to show data that is not related numerically, such as sales of different magazines or newspapers.

The length of each bar represents the number of that item in the data set. A bar chart may have the bars shown vertically, often called a **column chart**.

Histograms

A histogram looks similar to a column chart, but there are no spaces between the bars, and each bar represents a range of values.

The histogram in Figure 11.31 shows how much **travel-time Americans endure**.

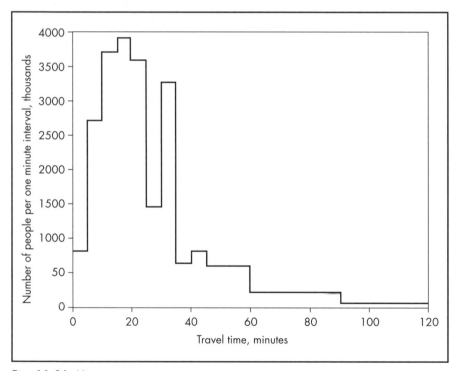

Fig. 11.31 Histogram

Interval	Width	Quality	Quality/width
0	5	4,180	836
5	5	13,687	3,723
10	5	18,618	3,723
15	5	19,634	3,926
20	5	17,981	3,596
25	5	7,190	1,436
30	5	16,369	3,273
35	5	3,212	642
40	5	4,122	824
45	15	9,200	613
60	30	6,461	215
90	60	3,435	57

Fig. 11.32 Histogram data

Line graphs

Line graphs include scattergrams, linear equations and frequency curves. (For the latter, see fig 11.22.)

Scattergrams

Scattergrams are often used when there is a rough or **approximate relationship between values**.

The scattergram is most useful when a **line of best fit** can be found which can then be used to **predict other values**.

In the scattergraph in Figure 11.33, SBP (systolic blood pressure) is plotted against age. There is a rough relationship between these, so a line of best fit can be drawn. The line of best fit tells us that the expected SBP for a 70-year-old is about 150, so that can be used as the basis of telling how normal the SBP reading is for someone aged 70.

Linear equations

A **linear equation** is the formula for a **straight line** in a graph.

Remember, Y is always the vertical axis, and X the horizontal, flat axis.

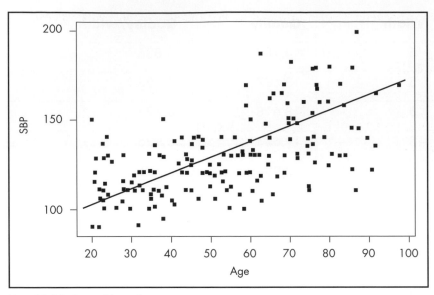

Fig. 11.33 Line of best fit

Every linear equation has the form Y = (X * Slope) + Constant.

The slope is found by looking at two points on the line, then dividing the difference between the Y values by the difference between the X values.

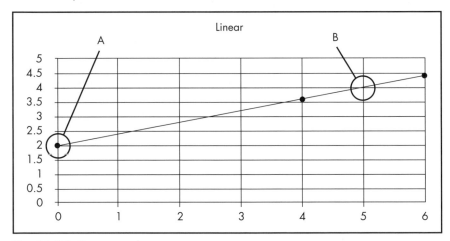

Fig. 11.34 Linear graph

In the graph in Figure 11.34, the constant is 2, where the line passes the Y axis at point A. The slope can be calculated from the two points, A and B.

The Y value for point A is 2, the Y value for point B is 4, so the difference between them is 2.

The X value for point A is 0, the X value for point B is 5, so the difference between them is 5.

The slope is the (difference between Y values) divided by the (difference between Y values), which is ⅖ or 0.4

Graphical data

As an ICT professional, you need to be able to present data graphically.

Creating a chart using Microsoft Excel®

Unit 10: Spreadsheet Software shows how to create some of the following:

- pie chart
- bar chart
- histogram
- scattergram
- linear graph
- frequency curve graph.

Appropriateness

There is little point in producing a chart or graph if it is not appropriate.

Choosing an appropriate type from the wide variety of charts or graphs available makes all the difference between the graphic becoming a pointless decoration or **helping to explain clearly the meaning of the data**.

The best type of chart is the one where it helps you to understand the data. Here are some broad guidelines:

- **pie chart**: how something such as a sum of money has been divided up
- **bar chart**: data not related numerically, such as sales of different products
- **histogram**: to represent a range of values, such as how much money is earnt by different age groups
- **XY line graph**: for data with two sets of numbers, such as a patient's temperature in a hospital against time
- **scattergram**: when there is a rough relationship between values, such as sales of a product against display size.

Context

Your charts and graphs should always be shown in the **right context**.

Do not include more than you need to get your understanding of the data explained to the reader of your document.

Every chart or graph should relate to the text around it so the reader can see both together, with each helping to explain the other.

Labelling

Labelling is crucial to **explain the meanings** of every chart and graph. Each should have:

- a title to name the chart or graph
- a name for the X-axis (flat, horizontal side)
- a name for the Y-axis (upright, vertical side)
- the scale identified, so it is clear that the numbers are as shown or represent thousands, millions, etc.

Scale

Always make sure the scale of the axes is right. The scale should be from the smallest to the largest values shown on the chart or graph. Figure 11.35 shows the wrong scale being used.

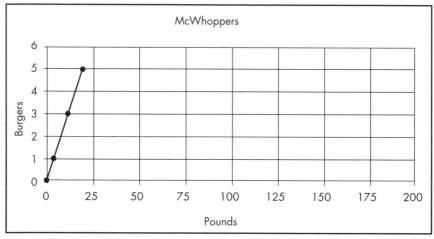

Fig. 11.35 Wrong scale

Communication

Never forget that the chart or graph is there to **communicate**, helping to explain a section in the document.

Make sure each chart or graph has a **definite purpose** and achieves that purpose by **showing the meaning of the data clearly**.

Interpreting graphs and charts

Interpreting graphs and charts is a skill that grows with practice and experience. Some ICT practitioners find it very easy, others have to work hard to do this.

When interpreting graphs and charts, look for:

- straight lines
- a value that is different
- how values are spread out.

Straight lines

A straight line shows there is a **direct relationship** between the numbers used for the X (flat) axis and the Y (vertical) axis.

A direct relationship means that if any point on an axis is chosen, then it is very easy to find out the **equivalent point** on the other axis.

In a simple example (represented in Figure 11.36), a burger chain sells their McWhopper burger for £3.86, so a straight line graph can be produced from the linear equation Y = 3.86X where Y represents how many burgers can be purchased for X pounds.

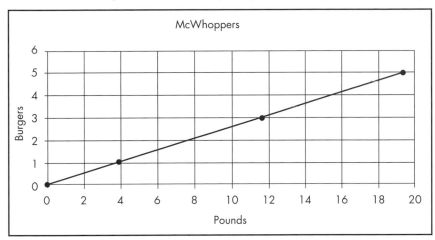

Fig. 11.36 McWhoppers

From the graph, you can see that £16 will get you 4 burgers!

Scattergrams

If a straight line can be found for a scattergram, then a relationship has been found between the axes.

A supermarket might produce a scattergram showing how quickly a product sells for different amounts of space on the shelf. The line of best fit will then estimate how much shelf space would be needed to reach desired sales.

Values that are different

Often in data it is the **different values** that are the most interesting.

Diskount Video Disks may find that sale of a particular series might increase for no apparent reason on the same day each week. A little market research may find that the preceding evening there was a repeat of a previous show which featured some popular actor or actress. The shop might then put up some posters to maximise this trend.

How values are spread

There is often interest in how values are spread. Sales of ice cream through the year will group together in summer, so production of ice cream will be towards making enough to sell during this period.

Using spreadsheets

Most ICT practitioners are able to use spreadsheets to **model calculations** involving **numeric data**. Spreadsheets allow quick and accurate models to be built which can be explored to see **what would happen if the numbers are changed**.

Features of a spreadsheet

Spreadsheets have many features which are covered in detail in many books. You may wish to buy a book for yourself or look in the library.

Features of a spreadsheet include:

- **graphical representation** of data by formatting cells and creating charts
- **inbuilt functions** to work out complex calculations easily
- tools, including **sort data**, **spellchecking**, and many more.

Graphical representation

Modern spreadsheets such as Microsoft Excel® are very graphical. The worksheet can be formatted with **colour**, **different fonts**, **images**, **lines** and in many other ways.

Data can be shown as a graph or chart by selecting the data, then pressing a button to start the chart wizard.

Inbuilt functions

An **inbuilt function** is a calculation that is built into the spreadsheet.

Many ICT practitioners use the **Insert**, **Function** menu option to place a function inside a Microsoft® Excel cell, as this method starts the **Paste Function Wizard**, which guides them through the process.

Fig. 11.37 Chart Wizard Icon

Inbuilt functions include:

- **Mean** to add a range of cells, then divide by how many cells had values
  =AVERAGE(A1:B12) shows mean of cells between (and including) A1 and B12
- **Mode** to find the most frequent number in the range of cells
  =MODE(A1:B12) returns the most common number in cells A1 to B12
- **Maximum** to find the biggest number in the range of cells
  =MAX(A1:B12) returns the largest number in cells A1 to B12
- **Minimum** to find the smallest number in the range of cells
  =MIN(A1:B12) returns the smallest number in cells A1 to B12
- **Countif** to find how frequently a number is in the range of cells
  =COUNTIF(A1:B12, 2) returns how many cells A1 to B12 contain 2

Tools

Modern spreadsheets include many tools to help the user, including:

- **Data sort**, to sequence the selected cells
- **Spellchecking** to highlight misspelled words
- **Auto Correct** to correct misspellings as you type.

Extended mathematical and statistical functions

There are many functions available in the spreadsheet, allowing complex calculations to be entered into cells using the name of the function.

Standard deviation

Standard deviation is a number that shows how **bunched up data is in a range**. **A small standard deviation** shows that **the data is close**; a **large standard deviation** that it is **spread out**.

The standard deviation can be found using the =STDEV(A1:B12) function (showing the standard deviation for the range of cells from A1 to B12 in this example).

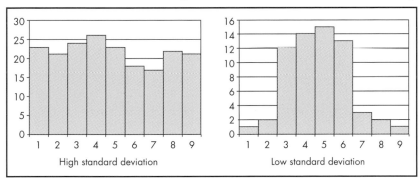

High standard deviation   Low standard deviation

Fig. 11.38 STD ranges

(For more on spreadsheet functions, see Unit 10: Spreadsheet Software.)

Slope

This function can be used with data used in a scattergram to show the slope of the best-fit line. The slope can then be used in a linear equation to predict values.

Benefits

The main benefits of using a spreadsheet are:

- **speed**, both in setting up the spreadsheet and in how quickly new results are calculated if numbers change in the spreadsheet
- **accuracy** of the results shown from calculations.

Modelling

Spreadsheets can be used to model real-life situations.

Many companies use spreadsheets to model production costs, including:

- the cost of running the premises
- the cost of materials
- the cost of labour (people).

What if forecasting can be applied to such a model?

- What if we produce 25% more product?
- What if we take on more staff?
- What if we increase our advertising?

The model will then quickly give answers to these questions. Remember, the answers given will only be as good as the calculations used in the spreadsheet, which in turn are only as good as the understanding of how the model works by the ICT professional who set it up.

(For a more detailed look at spreadsheets, refer to Unit 10: Spreadsheet Software.)

☆ **Activity**

Find out how much of the following currencies you can buy for £100:

1. US dollars
2. Euros
3. Japanese Yen

QUIZ

1. What is the numbering system which only uses 1 or 0?
2. What is the numbering system which only uses the digits 0 through to 9?
3. What is the software tool for modelling situations which can then be used to answer 'what if' questions?
4. What is the name given to whole numbers?
5. What number does 2^0 represent?
6. What number does 10^0 represent?
7. What number does 10^3 represent?
8. What number does 2^3 represent?
9. What number does 2^5 represent?
10. What answer do you get from $-2 + 5$?
11. What answer do you get from 6×7?
12. What answer do you get from $21 \div 3$?
13. What answer do you get from $28.1 + 574.51$?
14. What answer do you get from ⅔ + ½?
15. What answer do you get from ⅚ + ¾?
16. What answer do you get from $00010111 + 1001100$ (show your answer in both binary and denary)?
17. What answer do you get from ½ − ⅓?
18. What answer do you get from $01010111 - 101100$ (show your answer in both binary and denary)?
19. What answer do you get from 417×32?
20. What answer do you get from ⅜ × ⅔?
21. What answer do you get from 01010111×110 (show your answer in both binary and denary)?
22. What answer do you get from $3520 \div 5$?

23. What answer do you get from ¾ ÷ ⅔?
24. What answer do you get from 01010111 ÷ 110 (show your answer in both binary and denary)?
25. What is the standard form of 234456?
26. What is the area of the surface of a swimming pool which is 25 m long and 10 m wide?
27. What is the area of a triangle which is 5 m long and 10 m high?
28. What is the area of a circle which has a radius of 15 cm (use ²²⁄₇ to represent π if you are calculating by hand)?
29. What volume of water is in a tank 2 m long, 1.5 m wide and 0.8 m high when full?
30. What volume of air is in a prism 2 cm long, 3 cm wide and 0.6 cm high?
31. What volume of water is in a cylindrical tank 2 m radius, 3 m deep when full (use ²²⁄₇ to represent π if you are calculating by hand)?
32. What is the mean of 12, 24, 11, 12, 14, 12, 23, 12, 11, 12?
33. What is the median of 12, 24, 11, 12, 14, 12, 23, 12, 11, 12?
34. What is the mode of 12, 24, 11, 12, 14, 12, 23, 12, 11, 12?
35. For the linear equation, $Y = 2X + 7$, what is the value of Y if X is 3?
36. What type of graphic would you choose to show how something such as a sum of money has been divided up?
37. What type of graphic would you choose to show data not related numerically, such as sales of different products?
38. What type of graphic would you choose to represent a range of values, such as how much money is spent by different age groups?
39. What type of graphic would you choose to represent data with two sets of numbers, such as stretch against force?
40. What type of graphic would you choose when there is a rough relationship between values, such as sales of a product against display size?

ANSWERS

1. Binary (or base 2)
2. Denary (or base 10)
3. Spreadsheet
4. Integers
5. 1
6. 1
7. 1000 (10 × 10 × 10)
8. 8 (2 × 2 × 2)
9. 32 (2 × 2 × 2 × 2 × 2)
10. 3 (5 − 2)
11. 42
12. 7
13. 602.61
14. ³⁴⁄₃₅ (¹⁴⁄₃₅ + ²⁰⁄₃₅)
15. 1¹¹⁄₄₂ ((³⁵⁄₄₂ + ¹⁸⁄₄₂) gives ⁵³⁄₄₂)
16. 01100011 (binary) 99 (denary)

```
          128 64 32 16 8 4 2 1
            0  0  0  1 0 1 1 1 (23)
  +            1  0  0 1 1 0 0 (76)
            0  1  1  0 0 0 1 1 (99)
```

17. $\frac{5}{12}$ ($\frac{12}{21} - \frac{7}{21}$)

18. 01100011 (binary) 99 (denary)

```
     128 64 32 16 8 4 2 1
       0  0  1  0 1 1 0 0  (44)
       1  1  0  1 0 0 1 1  (invert)
  +                     1  (add 1)
       1  1  0  1 0 1 0 0  (2's complement of 44)

       1  1  0  1 0 1 0 0  (2's complement of 44, i.e. −44)
  +    0  1  1  0 0 0 1 1  (99)
       0  0  1  1 0 1 1 1  (55)
```

19. 13,344

```
        4 1 7
      ×   3 2
        8 3 4  ×2
     1 2 5 1 0  ×30
     1 3 3 4 4  Add
```

20. $\frac{3}{28}$ (($^{3\times}\frac{2}{8\times7}$) gives $\frac{6}{56}$ which simplifies when divided by 2)

21. 01111110 (binary) 126 (denary)

```
     128 64 32 16 8 4 2 1
       0  0  0  1 0 1 0 1 (21)
  ×    0  0  0  0 0 1 1 0 (6)
       0  0  1  0 1 0 1 0 (×10 binary)
       0  1  0  1 0 1 0 0 (×100 binary)

       0  1  1  1 1 1 1 0 (126)
```

22. 704

```
         0 7 0 4
     5 ) 3 5 2 0
       − 3 5
         0 0 2 0
           − 2 0
               0
```

23. $1\frac{1}{8}$ ($\frac{3}{4}$ × $\frac{3}{2}$ gives $\frac{9}{8}$)

24. 00000111 (binary) 15 (denary)

```
        0 0 0 0 1 1 1 1
1 1 0 | 0 1 0 1 1 0 1 0
        - 1 1 0
          1 0 1 0
          - 1 1 0
            1 0 0 1
            - 1 1 0
              0 1 1 0
              - 1 1 0
                0 0 0
```

128	64	32	16	8	4	2	1	
0	1	0	1	1	0	1	0	= 90
0	0	0	0	0	1	1	0	= 6
0	0	0	0	1	1	1	1	= 15

25. 2.34×10^5 (or 2.34 E 5)
26. 250 m² (25 x 10)
27. 25 m² (5 x 10 x 0.5)
28. 225 cm² ($\frac{2}{3}$ x 15² gives $\frac{2}{3} \times$ 225 gives $\frac{1575}{7}$)
29. 2.4 m³ (2 x 1.5 x 0.8)
30. 1.8 cm³ (2 x 3 x 0.5 x 0.6)
31. 37⅗ m³ ($\frac{2}{3}$ x 2² x 3 gives $\frac{2}{3}$ x 4 x 3 gives $\frac{264}{7}$)
32. 14.3 ((12 + 24 + 11 + 12 + 14 + 12 + 23 + 12 + 11 + 12) gives 143 then divide by 10)
33. 12 (arrange into rank order (11, 11, 12, 12, 12, 12, 12, 14, 23, 24) then find middle number)
34. 12 (most frequent number)
35. 13 (((2 x 3) + 7) gives (6 + 7))
36. Pie chart
37. Bar chart
38. Histogram
39. XY Line graph
40. Scattergram

COURSEWORK GUIDANCE

This unit is designed to introduce you to all the basic mathematical calculations you might be asked to perform as an ICT practitioner. As such, most of the evidence for this unit will require you to perform calculations.

However, there is also a requirement for you to demonstrate that you understand when one format is preferable over another.

The M1 grading criteria asks you to **select and use statistical techniques to meet a defined need**.

Your coursework should select appropriate statistical techniques to meet the defined need in your assignment, from any combination of: mean, median, mode, rank, quartile and interquartile ranges, maximum, minimum, tally charts, tabulation, frequency tables, pictograms such as pie charts, bar charts or histograms, line graphs such as scattergrams, linear equations or frequency curves.

The D1 grading criteria asks you to **justify the choice of statistical techniques for a given situation**.

Make sure you justify your choice of statistical techniques for the situation in the assignment, by explaining why your choice was appropriate.

Unit links

This unit has direct links to the following:

Unit 2   Introduction to computer systems
Unit 10 Spreadsheet Software

Further reading

Gaulter, B. and Buchanan, L., *Free Standing Mathematics Units: DATA Bk.2* (Oxford University Press, 2000) ISBN 0199147981

Selby, P. and Slavin, S., *Practical Algebra* (John Wiley & Sons Inc, 1991) ISBN 0471530123

Progress check

To record your achievement, simply tick the criteria awarded to you when each assignment is returned (you may be given three assignments for this unit, U11.01, U11.02 and U11.03 – the final column may not be used). There is a full copy of this grid available on the accompanying CD. The copy will also allow you to record your key skill achievement against Literacy, Numeracy and ICT objectives.

		Assignments in this Unit			
Assignment		**U11.01**	**U11.02**	**U11.03**	**U11.04**
Referral					
Pass					
	1				
	2				
	3				
	4				
	5				
	6				
	7				
Merit					
	1				
	2				
	3				
	4				
Distinction					
	1				
	2				
	3				

A completed sample of this document (for reference purposes) can be found at the back of Unit 1.

INSTALLING HARDWARE COMPONENTS

INTRODUCTION

Many ICT support technicians regularly install new hardware. Such hardware installations might be replacing a network card for connecting a computer to a network or just adding more RAM to make a computer's system run more smoothly. These tasks may be needed because a computer needs to be upgraded or because a critical part has broken.

This unit covers the skills and knowledge for such tasks. It is important for you to approach these tasks in a systematic and professional manner.

First you need to understand what installation or upgrade is required, and then prepare the resources that are needed to do this. These resources will include tools as well as the hardware itself.

Often there is a need to check information about the component, for example, to make sure the component will work with the existing operating system and other hardware.

This unit will also help you to understand the importance of health and safety, especially with regards to ESD (electrostatic discharge). This is why you have to earth yourself, as many computer components are damaged in this way.

ICT support technicians should also record the outcomes of their tasks and deal with associated documentation such as product registration.

Learning outcomes

On completion of this unit you should:

1 understand the reasons for and implications of the installation of hardware components
2 understand risks involved and precautions needed when installing hardware components
3 be able to install and test hardware components
4 know the procedures required on completion of an installation or upgrade.

Hardware components

This section helps you understand the reasons for and implications of installing hardware components.

Reasons

Reasons for installing hardware components include:

- routine maintenance
- fault repair
- new installation
- an upgrade.

Routine maintenance

Routine maintenance is where some work is carried out on hardware, even though it is not broken. This is so that **future problems can be avoided** by keeping the equipment in good order, in a similar way to servicing a car.

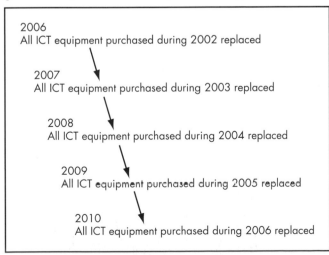

2006
All ICT equipment purchased during 2002 replaced

2007
All ICT equipment purchased during 2003 replaced

2008
All ICT equipment purchased during 2004 replaced

2009
All ICT equipment purchased during 2005 replaced

2010
All ICT equipment purchased during 2006 replaced

Fig. 12.1 Rolling replacement

Routine maintenance is often as simple as cleaning the equipment, as many problems can be caused when too much dust or dirt is inside the hardware.

Many organisations have a **rolling replacement programme** (see Figure 12.1), where old equipment is replaced with new in a structured way.

This means that regularly (usually every year) some of the equipment is replaced, next year some more, and so on. Rolling replacement programmes are often arranged so that by the end of each four-year period all the equipment has been replaced.

Fault repair

Installing new hardware components is a **common method of repairing faults** in ICT equipment. If a component fails, replacement is usually a quick, effective fix.

SCORECARD

Repairing components is quite unusual for several reasons:

- The cost of the time it takes a specialist to repair a component is often more than the cost of a new component
- The electronic circuits in many components are very tiny, making repairs difficult or impossible
- Repairing a component may introduce other faults
- Repaired components need to be thoroughly tested, which may require expensive specialised equipment and takes more time, making the repair even more expensive

Reasons for repairing components may include:

+ The component is expensive to replace
+ The component is rare, with a long wait for the replacement
+ A repair specialist is already employed by the organisation

---

New installation

A new installation is when new hardware components are installed to **replace all** of an existing system or where there is **no existing system**.

Upgrade

A hardware upgrade is when some or all of the hardware in a system is replaced with **better** and/or **newer** components. This is usually to enable the system to run **faster** and/or **run new software** that delivers **more functionality**. More functionality means that the system is able to perform tasks that it could not before the upgrade.

A new version of Microsoft Windows® often means that the hardware needs to be upgraded or the system slows down so much that there is no joy in using it. Users do not like to feel frustrated as they use their computers. If you have ever used a slow computer, you have probably felt the same way.

Implications

There are often implications to be considered when new hardware is installed. These may add to the cost and time needed to make the new equipment work properly.

Potential training requirements

There may be a **need to train users** how to use the new hardware.

Many new hardware installs bring in components which are familiar to users. A new PC is likely to be operated in much the same way as the PC it replaced.

Devices are less likely to be used in the same way, however, so users may need training to show them how to get them to work properly. A network switch from one manufacturer may have totally different controls from a network switch from another manufacturer.

Compatibility issues to be considered

In a perfect world, every component would work with every other component.

In the real world it is not quite like that. One obvious area where compatibility is vital is the match between **motherboard** and **processor**. The motherboard is the main circuit inside a computer system which connects together the processor (CPU, central processing unit), **RAM** (random-access memory), video system, disk drives and ports such as **USB** (universal serial bus).

Each **family of processors** uses a **different type of socket** to plug in to the motherboard. The wrong processor simply will not fit into the wrong sort of motherboard. Even when the processor fits into the motherboard, there may still be compatibility issues as the motherboard needs to provide exactly the right **power voltage** to the processor.

Another area where compatibility needs to be considered is **connecting peripherals**, such as the **keyboard** or **mouse**, to a system unit. Modern mice connect to the system unit through a **USB port**. If the mouse is an upgrade to an older system, there may not be a spare USB port, as the old mouse connected through the older **PS/2 port**, which is a totally different shape and size.

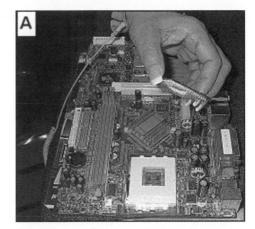

Fig. 12.2 Replacing a CPU

Fig. 12.3 CPU sockets

USB	Current connection for most peripherals, including mouse, keyboard, printer, scanner	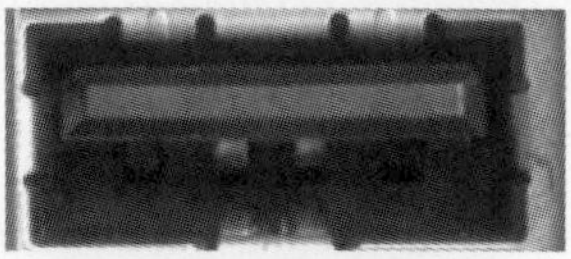 USB port
PS/2	Older connection for mouse and keyboard	 PS/2 port
Serial	Old connection for mouse and some printers	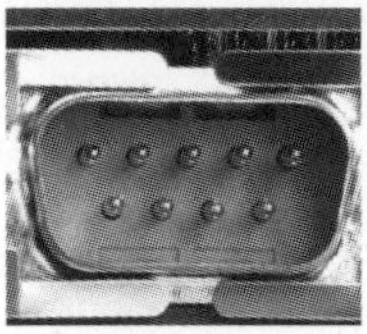 Serial port
Parallel	Old connection for printer and some scanners	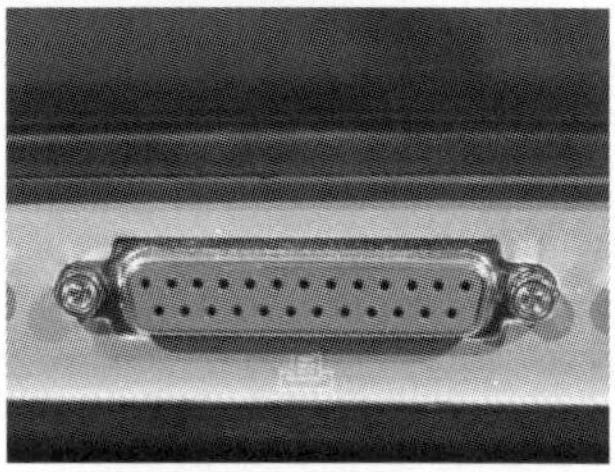 Parallel port

Fig. 12.4

Decommissioning of existing equipment

Decommissioning equipment means **taking it out of use**. Decommissioned equipment is often disposed of. Old kit has little value to an organisation, soaking up valuable storage space for no purpose.

The rolling replacement program operated by many organisations means that every piece of kit is replaced some time during a four-year period. Part of the **accounting system** tracks how much equipment is worth:

- 75% of the purchase price at the end of the first year
- 50% of the purchase price at the end of the second year
- 25% of the purchase price at the end of the third year
- 0% of the purchase price at the end of the fourth year.

So, as far as the organisation is concerned, the kit has served its purpose and is worth nothing at the end of the four-year cycle.

Sometimes old equipment can be sold to bring back some money to the organisation. Often the amount of money such equipment fetches is very small making it easier to throw the equipment away than to sell it (as administration and shipping costs may offset any profit).

There are companies that specialise in helping large organisations dispose of their old kit, by buying it cheaply then selling the equipment on. Another method used to sell equipment is through auctions.

If the equipment is thrown out, it will need to be disposed of properly, as many items of ICT equipment contain substances (such as nickel, cadmium and lead) that are damaging to the environment. Doing this properly and legally will actually cost the organisation money.

Consideration of user requirements

User requirements should be one of the main driving forces for purchasing new equipment. ICT systems are there to enable the users to perform their work, so any changes to these systems should be to enhance this.

The user requirements are typically written down in a document which clearly states what users require from their ICT systems. This document should be a central part of the thinking behind decisions to change hardware or other parts of the computer systems.

Service level agreements

A service level agreement (SLA) is an agreement **between departments** inside an organisation of **what each should expect from the other**.

For example, a helpdesk may have an SLA target to **resolve problems** within a **definite period**, such as two working days.

Purchasing a new type of equipment may have an effect on the SLAs, as the helpdesk will have little experience of the kit and solving problems may take longer, as it takes time to learn. Some problems may need to be sent to another place (e.g. the manufacturer), and it may take more time for the solution to the problem to return.

Benefits

There are many benefits to the gained from installing new hardware, including:

- **improved functionality**, as the system is able to carry out tasks it was not able to do before the upgrade
- **increased reliability**, as older systems are more likely to break down
- **faster systems** – new hardware is almost always faster than the equipment it replaces
- **better user satisfaction** from using up-to-date, fast systems.

Risks and precautions

When working with hardware you need to understand the **risks involved** and any **precautions needed** when installing the hardware components. Failure to understand these risks may result in injury to yourself and others, or even death. Precautions are also needed to ensure the hardware is not damaged during the installation.

Relevant health and safety guidelines and laws

As an ICT practitioner, you need to be aware of how the **law** relates to health and safety, as well as guidelines within the organisation where you work for safe working practices.

It is important that you work safely and protect the health of both yourself and other people inside the organisation.

Safe use of tools

Working with ICT equipment can be dangerous. There is risk in dealing with electricity and risk with using tools.

As an ICT professional you may be expected to use:

- **screwdriver** for removing and replacing screws to gain access to the inside of the computer and to remove and install components
- **anti-static wrist-strap** to remove electricity harmlessly from your body and to make sure components are not damaged by static electricity
- **multi-meter** to check that connections are not broken inside devices or cables and that voltages are in the right range and in the right places
- **cable tester** to check that network cables are wired up properly
- **crimper** to squeeze the plugs on to the ends of network cables
- **pliers** for holding or squeezing components together and picking small items such as screws out of cases and other places where they drop
- **mains-tester** to check that there is mains power (when wanted, such as into a device), or that there is no mains power (when not wanted, such as making sure a component is isolated from the mains before working on it).
- **continuity tester** to check that connections are sound and not broken.

Manual handling

Some ICT equipment is heavy and care must be taken not to strain or injure yourself by removing or positioning such equipment.

If the equipment is heavy and needs to be moved, you must seek help. **Never attempt to lift anything which looks as though it may be heavy**. It is very easy to injure your back through careless lifting and such an injury would be with you for the rest of your life.

Electrostatic discharge

There are two types of electricity: **current** and **static**. Current electricity is electricity from the **mains** or a **battery**. Static electricity **builds up on a surface** like your body.

Static electricity can slowly and gradually build up until there are thousands of volts on your body that need to be released. They are released when a route is found to earth. When such a route is found the electricity goes to earth very quickly. This is called an **ESD** (electrostatic discharge). If the route is through a sensitive electronic component, such as a network card, the component can be **damaged** and will **no longer work**.

It is important that static electricity is kept to the minimum and safely discharged before work is started.

Anti-static packaging

When new components are bought they should be packaged inside anti-static packaging. Anti-static packaging is usually a plastic bag, coated to reduce static electricity.

Components should be **kept inside** anti-static packaging until they are **ready to be installed**. Components that are removed from ICT equipment need to be kept inside anti-static packaging to keep them safe until the next time they get used.

Fig. 12.5 Anti-static packaging

Use of wrist strap

An **anti-static wrist-strap** can be used to avoid static damage to components with electronic circuit boards, such as network or video cards, or chips such as new RAM or a processor.

An anti-static wrist-strap fits around the wrist and has a **wire** which must be **connected to earth**. An earth can be the **chassis of a computer** (provided it is plugged into a mains electricity socket, but this is not recommended) or a **water pipe** (on a part of that is not painted).

Risks to systems

Any time equipment, especially ICT equipment, is repaired, upgraded or installed, there is a risk to the equipment, yourself and data. It is your responsibility, as an ICT professional, to do your best to minimise the risk to each of these.

Fig. 12.6 Wrist-strap

Damage to equipment

There are two types of damage which can occur to equipment:

- physical damage, such as a **crack**, **bent pin** or **snapping a component**. Great care must be taken when packaging components and installing them.
- electrostatic damage. Great care must be taken to keep components in anti-static bags until they are used and making sure there is no ESD allowed to ground through a component.

Fig. 12.7 damaged kit

Loss or corruption of data

The data is the most expensive part of any computer system. Data takes time to enter and time is an expensive commodity. Many companies rely on their computer data for lists of clients, money owed and all other aspects of the business.

Any computer system should have a **backup regime** (procedure) to make sure that if anything happens to data, there is something to go back to. As an ICT professional, you should make sure that a new complete backup is made before installing or upgrading components.

The restore routines of every backup system should be checked, as well as the backup routines, to make sure the data can be brought back if there is a problem.

> **Key term**
>
> The **backup regime** is a routine for making copies of data to magnetic tape or other media that can be kept safely away from the system.

The table below shows the grandfather-father-son regime used by many organisations, where three sets of tapes are reused for backups.

Week number	Tape used for backup	Name of tape 1	Name of tape 2	Name of tape 3
1	1	Son	Grandfather	Father
2	2	Father	Son	Grandfather
3	3	Grandfather	Father	Son
4	1	Son	Grandfather	Father
5	2	Father	Son	Grandfather
6	3	Grandfather	Father	Son
7	1	Son	Grandfather	Father

Loss of service

The **loss of ICT service** can be **very expensive**. Employees need to keep busy to earn the company money, customers must have their needs met, otherwise they will look elsewhere, invoices need to be chased to make sure that payments due to the company are made.

There is also the issue of **confidence;** customers expect companies to have ICT systems that work and may go elsewhere if they do not believe the computer systems are able to sustain the company.

Installations

You need to be able to be able to **install** and **test hardware** components for this unit. This section explains some of the issues around hardware installations.

Hardware

Hardware is the term given to describe any computer component. Some examples of the many types of hardware are:

- printer
- system unit
- network switch
- scanner.

Components

Components are the parts of a computer system such as memory chips, video card, CD-ROM, DVD, hard disk, network card, power supply unit (PSU) and processor.

Connectors and ports

Connectors and **ports** are where **components connect to a computer system**. Ports are the sockets where components plug in to the computer. Connectors are the plugs which fit into the ports.

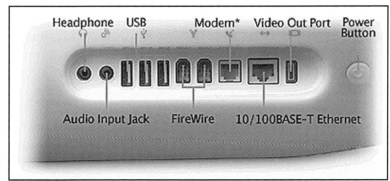

Fig. 12.8 Ports

It is important that connectors on new hardware are **compatible** with the ports on the existing hardware, otherwise they will not fit together and **will not work**.

Never force a connector into a port it clearly does not fit; you will most likely cause damage to both.

Power supply

The power supply unit (PSU) is the component that plugs in to the mains power supply and produces low-voltage electricity, which is needed to make the computer and components work.

Power supplies are rated by the watts they produce. The wattage is the amount of current (power) that comes out of the PSU. The PSU needs to produce enough wattage to allow the motherboard processor and other components to work properly (e.g. 350 watts).

Power supplies are potentially lethal and should not be taken apart or tampered with.

Specifications

Specifications are **data sheets** giving information about **how components work**. It is important that the specifications of the upgrade and other system components match.

Specifications are important to make sure that components will plug in to the correct ports and also to ensure that hardware works at the right speeds and voltages for each other.

Preparation tasks

Before an installation or upgrade can be carried out, some preparation is necessary.

Test selection

Equipment should **always** be tested to make sure it **works properly**. Examples of tests may be:

- A computerised till on a checkout may have a new scanner fitted. Some of the tests may need goods that can be scanned in to make sure the barcodes are picked up correctly.
- A laptop may have Centrino® to connect it to Wi-Fi wireless networks. One of the tests may be to have the Wi-Fi Wireless Access Port (WAP) (the transmitter/receiver) to broadcast its 'name' to help the laptop pick the signal up.
- A workstation may be fitted with a new CD/DVD re-writable drive. Some tests may use CDs that were written by the old drive to make sure the new drive can still read them. In addition a CD written by a new drive should be read by other drives to check the functioning of the new unit.

Test configuration

Often tests need to be configured to make them just right to check exactly the right component being tested.

If a laptop with an Intel® Centrino® wireless network connection is being tested, the Wi-Fi WAP may need to be configured so that the new laptop is added to the list of wireless devices that are allowed to connect to it. Without this configuration, the laptop could not connect, so any testing would be pointless.

A cable tester may need to be configured to test for the right type of cable. An example of this could be for network cabling which could be wired as cat 5 (category 5) to connect a computer to a switch (or hub), or as a crossover cable which connects a computer to another computer without a switch (or hub).

Reading instructions

It is important to read any instructions which come with a component. These instructions may be printed on paper or may be a 'read me' file on a CD or floppy disk which comes with the component.

Remember, the instructions are written by the people who design and make the components, so they usually give the **easiest** and **most effective** ways of **installing** the component and **making it work**.

It is often useful to look at the website from the manufacturer of the component for extra support if a component does not work as expected. Most manufacturer sites have support sections which include FAQs (frequently asked questions) covering common problems that people have using and installing the components.

Following procedures

Many organisations have procedures which are there to protect you, other users, its data, its customers and to maintain company standards. It is your responsibility, as an ICT professional, to find out which procedures are in place for your organisation and to make sure you follow them.

Safety check

You should make sure you work safely and do not leave a dangerous situation for other people. At the end of each job you should look back at it and see if there any safety issues which might need attention.

Remember, you have a **responsibility** under Health and Safety at Work legislation to make sure the workplace is **safe for yourself and other people**.

Obtaining resources

You must have the correct resources to be able to install an upgrade hardware. It is wrong to try to start an installation using **wrong or inappropriate tools**.

Sometimes you will need to get into a computer system to make changes and you must have sufficient rights to be able to do this. You must have enough **access rights** to be able to make the **configuration changes** needed to enable the hardware to work and to install the correct drivers.

Tools are resources which may be needed to **open up** a system, **disconnect** and **extract** old components and **install** new parts. The right tools need to be available. Without those, the installation may be impossible.

If the wrong tools are used, there may be damage caused. Trying to undo a screw with the wrong-sized screwdriver may result in the screw losing shape, making it very difficult to undo or tighten up. Using a wrong-sized screwdriver can be dangerous if it slips and cuts you.

Even the hardware to be installed is a resource that needs to be there, or the installation must fail!

Often hardware needs to have **configuration settings** made to function correctly. These settings are another resource needed for a **successful install**.

Check equipment is undamaged

It is very important when opening packaging to make sure that the equipment is **undamaged**. Any damaged equipment must be sent back to the supplier as it will be **covered by warranty** and should be **replaced** with a working version before being installed.

To carry on and try to make the damaged equipment work could **invalidate the warranty** and therefore cost the company extra time and money. Worse still, it could also cause damage to other connected equipment in the process.

Associated installation software

Many hardware components need **associated software** that must be installed for the upgrade or installation to work properly. Associated software are programs, in addition to the drivers, that are needed to allow the operating system to control the device.

Drivers are simply there so the operating system **recognises the hardware** properly and is **able to use it**. These are appropriate when hardware is installed into a system, as with a video card, or directly attached, as with a printer.

Associated software will be programs that help the users **get the most out of the hardware**. Examples of associated software include:

- a program to record sound that is bundled with a sound card
- a program to set up the firewall of a broadband router
- recording software with a CD-RW or DVD-RW drive.

Backing up data

Backing up data is often part of the preparation for a hardware installation as there is always a chance that things will go so wrong that the equipment **corrupts** or **loses data**. A backup will make a **copy** of the data to another place, so that even in the worst case scenario, **valuable data can be brought back**.

Too few organisations have a realistic understanding of how much their data is worth. A lot of companies would very quickly go out of business if they lost their data. One of the ways that loss of data can affect a company is if it has a list of clients who owe money to the company for goods or services provided. Without the list, it is very difficult to chase those clients for payment.

Remember, the method used to make a backup **must be tested** to prove it works.

Reassembling tasks

When reassembling components it is important to be sure to know **how to check** that they work properly.

Software installation

It is always very important to read the instructions when installing components, as the manufacturer should know how to best install them. Reading the instructions gives the ICT professional useful information, such as which software is required, and this is vital, as there are typically versions available for each type of popular computer system.

Many components require software which looks like **web pages** (HTML, the Hypertext Markup Language) to control the component settings (e.g. a firewall). Some components require an **install program** to run that installs the operating system driver and other software to help configure the component (e.g. a video card).

The point here is that **reading the instructions** is the **quickest**, **most effective way** of finding out how the install should be carried out.

It is also important to remember that sometimes the software must be installed **before the hardware is connected**, otherwise the installation will fail. Check carefully! Read the instructions.

New or upgraded component testing

You will need to find out how to **test** a **new** or **upgraded component** to confirm that it works properly. There is little use in inserting a component into a system, then hoping it will work. Components need to be tested.

To do this, the ICT professional finds out **how to test it**, to understand **what is required** from the component, and **how to prove** that has been achieved.

There should be a test plan for each installation to define what is expected and how to confirm these expectations are met.

Reconnection

Once the system has been reassembled it can be reconnected to the network and other peripherals. You need to make sure everything functions as it should. This should be part of a **test plan**. The best test plans are **structured** so the tests follow a **sequence**, making sure each stage of the installation works before moving on to the next part of the install.

Reconnection is one of these stages, as equipment can often work on its own, but gives problems when connected to the rest of the system.

Reassembling components

Reassembling components needs to be done carefully to make sure that no component is damaged and to ensure the components connect together properly. Always take care doing this. Keep your eyes open and do not use too much force with tools such as screwdrivers.

When reassembling, there should be no need for force to plug parts into other parts. Using force often means that there is something wrong, such as:

- one of the components is the wrong way round
- something is obstructing the connection, so it does not insert properly
- one of the components is at an angle

- something else needs to be taken out of the system to allow proper access to the connection
- the two items are not compatible!

Cleaning as required

When a system is dismantled it is a very good time to clean the components. Cleaning components is called **preventative maintenance** because this helps the system to work and eases future problems.

Many systems have a maintenance routine for this. A maintenance routine may be that every month the systems in different rooms are serviced. Often a maintenance routine is staggered, with a collection of systems serviced one week, another the next week, another the week after, and so on, then the routine starts again. This way, every system is **serviced regularly** and many problems are **prevented** before they have chance to start.

Safety check

Safety must always be in your thinking. When you deal with hardware and other components, be careful to not hurt yourself and to leave a safe environment for others.

Safety thinking needs to be from several different directions, such as being careful of:

- sharp edges which can cut you and others
- mains electricity that can kill you and others
- static electricity that can damage components
- heavy components that can damage you if lifted by yourself carelessly
- training cables that be tripped over, injuring yourself and damaging components
- safe positioning of equipment so it is not tripped over, likely to fall over or obstructing walkways or fire exits
- not positioned to give reflection or glare to users.

Not only is it good, considerate practice to keep the environment safe, but it is the law; the Health & Safety Act (1974) makes it illegal to make the workplace unsafe.

System testing

Testing the system is essential. You must always test a system before it is handed over to the user. You need to make sure that everything that has been changed or upgraded **works as expected**.

You must also make sure that the **system continues to work as it had previously**. Sometimes you will be able to do this, but often the user needs to be asked to make sure they can log on and use the computer as they would expect.

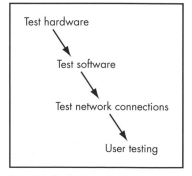

Fig. 12.9 System testing

Restoration of data

Restoration of data is when data is **brought back** from a **backup**.

Backups are essential, so that if anything goes wrong, there is a good version of data which can be restored to use.

It is vital that the restoration of data is practised to make sure that backups can be reused. You would be surprised at how many systems only try to restore data the first time that something goes wrong. If the restore does not work, all that precious data is lost. The restore should be carried out on a system that has never used the data before.

The point here is to **confirm** that the data **can still be used** after a disaster, before the disaster hits.

Configuration to end-user requirements

Once hardware or an upgrade is installed, you need to make sure that it is correctly **configured** for the end-user. To do that you need to look at the **end-user requirements** and make sure that the new equipment **matches** that.

Many organisations have procedures that use test plans to guide ICT practitioners, so that when the configurations are made there is a sensible, structured approach to confirming that all is acceptable. Often there is a 'sign-off' form that the end-user will complete to confirm that all is fine and that the upgrade is working and configured correctly.

File management

File management is an area concerned with **where** data and programs are kept on a network or a hard disk. Many organisations have **standards** for the names and storage locations of files. These standards are there to make it easier for users to do their work and for others to find files when they are needed in the future.

Few people stay in the same job all their life. Many people gain promotions within the organisation to other positions, or progress their careers by finding a better job in another organisation. In both these situations, another person will be allocated the workload, so will need to be able to find data files easily and identify which file is which from the filenames they have.

File management will also make sure that backups are kept of files, so if there is a disaster they can be brought back.

Naming files

Many organisations have standards for naming files. These standards make it very easy to identify files as the names are predictable. File naming is often used in a structured way to help identify documents. For example, **Parker-floorplan-rev3** could be used for the third revision of the floor plan for a client named Parker, just as **Kent-floorplan-rev2** could be used for the second revision of the floor plan for a client named Kent.

Files may be named according to **who creates them** or **what they are used for**. Filenames are often chosen so that the files group together when viewed.

Folder structures

Folder structures are vital to organise the data on the disk. Folders should be sensibly named and organised so that people can find work easily, especially as after a period of time it is very easy to forget what the file was called.

Folders may be on a local hard disk or on a network.

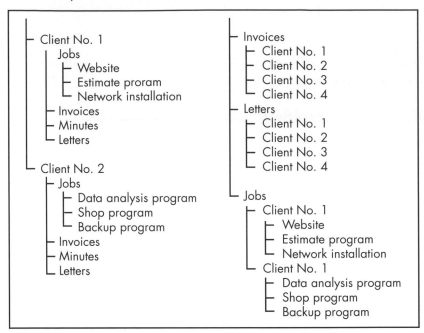

Fig. 12.10 Folder structures

Moving and deleting files

The ICT practitioner often has to move or delete files as part of the normal **housekeeping** on a computer system. Backups should be made regularly so the data is available if anything goes wrong. Files must be made available to other users who need to access them on the computer.

Files will be deleted as part of the housekeeping on a computer system when they are no longer needed. Often, when a project has been completed, the temporary working files are deleted for this reason.

Modern computer systems accumulate unwanted **temporary (.tmp) files**, which are left on the disk if a program crashes or a computer is turned off by the power switch on the case, rather than through the Start menu (e.g. as in Microsoft Windows™). These .tmp files should be deleted to help keep the computer running smoothly and reclaim usable disk space.

Default settings

A default is a **way the computer works** when **no other changes** are made. It is important that default settings are made after an installation to make sure the equipment works properly in the department where it is set up.

Many components are made for the American market and should be configured to work properly in the UK. An example of this is paper size; in the USA the common paper size is **Letter**, in the UK it is **A4**. The correct paper size should be the default so users have a better idea of what they are working with on their screen, and because if the paper size is wrong many printers (especially lasers) will wait for user intervention (by pressing one of the control buttons on the printer) before they will print the page. This can cause a wait for other users trying to print, as the page with the wrong paper size blocks the printer.

Another example of a default setting that is often missed is the keyboard layout. The US keyboard has @ as shifted 2; the UK keyboard has " as shifted 2. In this situation, a quick workaround is to use the key which has shown on the screen, as the operating system thinks those two keys are swapped round. The real solution is to enter the **Control Panel** and set the keyboard to the correct one.

As an ICT practitioner, you need to make sure that you do your best to make sure that the computer equipment is right for the people using it.

Testing

Every time a component is installed or upgraded it needs to be tested to make sure that it works properly. There should be a test plan to identify which tests need to be made to confirm the equipment is configured correctly.

Tools

There are many tools available to ICT practitioners to help test and monitor the running of computer hardware.

These tools include **utility software**, a type of program used to help you and the operating system find out what going on inside the computer, such as:

- **runtime analyser**: a program which is able to display the programs that are currently running on the computer and how they are performing
- **system information**: a utility showing the hardware configurations and running software

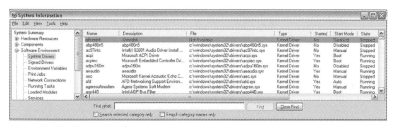

Fig. 12.11 System information

- **disk defragmenter**: a utility to bring files back together on the hard disk. As the disk is used, files get deleted, leaving gaps in the disk. When new data is saved to the disk, it will fill these gaps, but often the data is saved to several gaps in different places, as it does not fit into one. This is called **fragmentation**.

Specialist hardware tools may be used by ICT practitioners, such as:

- **power supply tester** to check that the PSU (power supply unit) produces the correct voltages
- **cable tester** to ensure that there are no faults in a network cable.

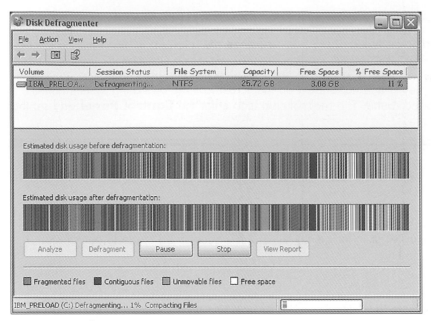

Fig. 12.12 Defragmenter

Gathering test information

When testing, you need to **gather test information** to find out **what happened** as the tests were run.

This information can be collected by **copying information** from the screen or it may be saved onto a disk as test data.

Some programs **dump** data onto the disk as a **log file**, recording what happened when the tests were run. Such a log file can be very useful as it may be loaded into a spreadsheet or other software, where **further analysis** can be carried out on it.

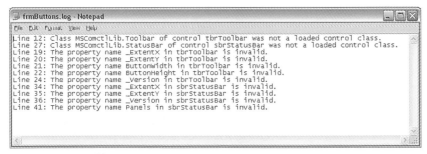

Fig. 12.13 Log file

The log file shown in Figure 12.13, was created by Microsoft Visual Basic® when it found errors loading a form that had been written as part of a program.

Validating information

It is usually best to run each test twice or more to **validate** the information each test produces. Obviously, if the second test match results are very different from the first test, the results are inconclusive and the tests need to be rerun until the results match.

There is little point in believing results which are obviously wrong. Rerunning tests until a consistent result is found will obtain the most accurate result possible.

Responding to test information

Very often the data from tests is **technical** and **complex**, so you need to understand how to **interpret error codes** and messages and to recognise inconsistent data. ICT practitioners often write programs which output messages that are meant to be understood by other ICT professionals, so can be difficult to read and understand. To help understand these, program documentation should have a section where error codes and messages are explained.

Testing needs to be carried out with the **appropriate documentation**.

Test information, once understood, will show whether the testing was successful or if the tests failed. Failed tests need to be responded to – they cannot and should not be ignored. Actions may be any combination of these:

*   tests are rerun to **confirm failure**
*   the cause(s) of failure **fixed**, with tests rerun to confirm now OK
*   the **test results are documented** and passed back to the **support section** for resolution
*   the problem is **escalated to a specialist** to resolve the problems.

Checking specification

Part of the testing may be to check the specification. For example, a computer may have a broadband connection which has been specified at 4 Mb per second; as an ICT practitioner, you may be asked to confirm the speed by running utility programs to check the data does move at that speed.

Other actions

It is important to know the **limits of your authority**, such as when to escalate a fault to your supervisor. There will be times when you have been asked to carry out a job, but do not have the experience or skills to complete it. If this happens, it is important to flag this rather than walk away from it and let somebody else find out later.

As an ICT practitioner, you will be part of a team, each member of which will have different expertise and experience. Jobs need to be completed. Any job beyond your experience will need to be passed on to a colleague who is able to deliver.

Installation procedures

Installation procedures include the planning implementation and tasks required on completion of the installation or upgrade.

Product registration

Registering a product is useful because it helps to **validate the warranty** and often **opens up support** from the producer to help with any problems found using the product.

Product registration methods

The main methods of registering a product are **online**, by **telephone** or by **post**.

Registering the product online is quick and effective. This method confirms the website for the product, produces instant registration and often gives access to support pages on the website for future problems.

Registering the product by post usually involves filling in a card which came with the product and posting it to the manufacturer.

Purpose and value of product registration

Product registration has purpose and value for both the manufacturer of the product and the organisation that bought it. The manufacturer finds out who buys their products, with information about purchasers. The organisation that buys a product benefits from registration because support is available to help with problems using the product, as well as receiving information about upgrades and new products which may be of interest in the future.

Importance of keeping receipts

A receipt is a **proof of purchase** and therefore very important. A warranty for a product commences at the date purchased. Many manufacturers need to see the receipt to **honour a warranty** claim on a product.

Communications

It is always useful to communicate with everyone who has a part in or who is interested in an installation or upgrade. If people are kept informed, they are less likely to complain as they know that progress is being made. Many complaints are made because people do not know what is happening, then guess that nothing is being done and that they have been forgotten.

Customer acceptance

Organisational procedures for many organisations need to have a user sign-off to confirm that an upgrade or support has been carried out effectively. This is called the **customer acceptance**.

Documentation

Documentation is the name given to the paperwork kept by an organisation. There are many types of documentation, including:

- **procedures** to make sure jobs are completed in the right sequence
- **user support requests** to have records of these and to ensure each request is met
- **supplier lists** to make ordering new equipment easier
- **known fixes to problems** so that they are easily resolved.

Purpose and importance of completing records

The purpose and importance of completing records relating to the installation includes:

- **time taken for the upgrade or installation** for charging the user department
- **purchase date** for warranty information
- **knowing which components are in which systems**, to help identify trends so that unreliable components are not purchased again
- **confirmation by the user that the work has been completed**, so the job can be removed from the support workload.

Technical manual update

Many well-organised ICT support departments keep **technical manuals** detailing **how to install components** and **fix problems**. These are very useful for both new and existing staff when a problem is encountered that has not been met by the technician before.

Updating these manuals is **essential**, as when new fixes are found for problems, they are then available if the problem is encountered again.

User manual update

User manuals explain to users of ICT systems how to operate their computers. When changes are made to an ICT system, the user manual should be updated so the information is kept **current** and **useful**.

Some organisations keep user manuals as ring binders to make it very easy to change pages. Often these pages are numbered by section (e.g. 1–12 or 2–3).

Logbook

A logbook is a **record of actions** that are taken. Logbooks may be for:

- a computer
- an ICT professional
- help desk requests.

 Activity

Produce a short presentation, explaining the risks to a computer system, with the measures that you would recommend to minimise the identified threats.

QUIZ

1. What is the term used to describe a program that regularly replaces all the ICT equipment in an organisation?
2. What is the term used to describe when some or all of the hardware in a system is replaced with better and/or newer components?
3. What is the term used to describe when a component works with the other components in a system?

4. What is the term used to describe the current connection for most peripherals, including mouse, keyboard, printer, scanner?
5. What is the term used to describe when equipment is taken out of use?
6. What is the term used to describe a document clearly stating what users require from their ICT systems?
7. What is the term used to describe an agreement between departments inside an organisation?
8. What is the tool used to squeeze the plugs on to the ends of network cables?
9. What is the device which removes electricity harmlessly from your body?
10. What is the tool used to check that connections are sound and not broken?
11. What is the term used to describe electricity from the mains or a battery?
12. What is the term used to describe electricity which can slowly and gradually build up until there are thousands of volts?
13. What does the term ESD stand for?
14. What type of software does the operating system use to recognise and use hardware?
15. What is the term used to describe recovering data from a backup?
16. What is the term used to name the most recent backup tape?
17. Name the law passed in 1974 to make unsafe workplaces illegal.
18. What is the name of the file created when a program dumps data onto a disk to record what happened when tests were run?
19. What helps to validate a warranty and open up support from the producer?
20. What is the name of a paper-based record of actions that were taken?

ANSWERS

1. Rolling replacement
2. Hardware upgrade
3. Compatible
4. USB (universal serial bus)
5. Decommissioning
6. User requirements
7. Service level agreement (SLA)
8. Crimper
9. Anti-static wrist-strap
10. Continuity tester
11. Current
12. Static
13. Electrostatic discharge
14. Drivers
15. Restore
16. Son
17. Health & Safety Act (1974)
18. Log file
19. Product registration
20. Logbook

COURSEWORK GUIDANCE

This unit requires you to demonstrate an understanding of the issues surrounding the practice of working with hardware. You will need to be able to describe situations in which new hardware should be installed.

You must show that you can identify Health and Safety risks prior to installation and be able to both install and describe the installation of components (ensuring that this is done safely) and test their functionality. These activities will also need to be documented.

With some hardware installations, software will also need to be installed and configured for an end-user.

Showing a thorough knowledge and understanding of risks to an organisation arising from the new installation of hardware components (and being to explain how these risks can be minimised) will contribute towards the Distinction criterion D1. Analysing potential problems that might occur during hardware component installation and providing possible solutions to these problems will meet the remaining criterion D2.

Unit links

This unit has direct links to the following:

Unit 2 Introduction to Computer Systems
Unit 6 Networking Essentials
Unit 13 Software Installation and Upgrade

As one of the two core units for this programme, it should be understood that this unit underpins all other units in the scheme.

Edexcel also show links to:

Unit 14 Technical Fault Diagnosis and Remedy
Unit 15 Providing Technical Advice and Guidance

This unit may NOT be done in combination with either Unit 22 or Unit 26.

●●●Further reading

Andrews, J., *A+ guide to Hardware: Managing, Maintaining and Troubleshooting* (Course Technology, 2003) ISBN: 0619186240

Mueller, S., *Upgrading and Repairing PCs*, 16th Edition (Que, 2004) ISBN 0789731738

Progress check

To record your achievement, simply tick the criteria awarded to you when each assignment is returned (you may be given three assignments for this unit, U12.01, U12.02 and U12.03 – the final column may not be used). There is a full copy of this grid available on the accompanying CD. The copy will also allow you to record your key skill achievement against Literacy, Numeracy and ICT objectives.

Assignment		Assignments in this Unit			
		U12.01	U12.02	U12.03	U12.04
Referral					
Pass					
	1				
	2				
	3				
	4				
	5				
	6				
	7				
Merit					
	1				
	2				
	3				
	4				
Distinction					
	1				
	2				
	3				

A completed sample of this document (for reference purposes) can be found at the back of Unit 1.

SOFTWARE INSTALLATION AND UPGRADE

INTRODUCTION

There are many jobs that an ICT support technician would perform as part of their daily duties, but perhaps the most common task they encounter is the installing of new software and upgrading of existing products.

Once upon a time, installation of a piece of software relied on having the appropriate set of floppy disks at hand – how things have changed! Modern installations can be achieved in an amazing variety of ways, but what is constant is the technician's need to ensure that the installation is appropriate, successful and fully meets the user's needs.

Learning outcomes

On completion of this unit you should:

1 understand software installation and upgrade processes
2 be able to prepare for an installation or upgrade
3 be able to install and upgrade software
4 be able to complete an installation or upgrade.

RECORDING YOUR PROGRESS

In order to achieve each unit you will complete a series of coursework activities. Each time you hand in work, your tutor will return this to you with a record of your achievement.

This particular unit has 10 criteria to meet: 5 Pass, 3 Merit and 2 Distinction.

- For a **Pass**: you must achieve **all** 5 Pass criteria.
- For a **Merit**: you must achieve **all** 5 Pass and **all** 3 Merit criteria.
- For a **Distinction**: you must achieve **all** 5 Pass, **all** 3 Merit **and both** Distinction criteria.

So that you can monitor your own progress and achievement in each unit, a recording grid has been provided (see the **Progress check** section at the end of this unit).

Key terms

Software installation: the process of loading software from an external media to a local computer system's backing storage so that it can be used.

Upgrade: the process of replacing an outdated piece of hardware or software with a more recent product in order to improve its performance, increase its functionality or fix existing compatibility issues or 'bugs'.

Software installation and upgrade processes

Why?

Installing new software or upgrading an existing program is not a step to be taken lightly! In order to do this successfully, the ICT practitioner has to be sure that the change is absolutely necessary.

As we have seen before, software has two separate categories:

- **systems software** – operating systems, disk utilities, anti-virus, firewalls, etc.
- **applications software** – word processor, spreadsheet, accounts, etc.

Knowing which category the desired software belongs to often provides a strong clue about the scale of the work that lies ahead; for example, systems software is often more difficult to install and get working than an application – it tends to be more complex and offer more challenges.

What factors contribute to the installation or upgrade of software?

The purchase of new hardware

Buying new hardware often brings problems. Existing software is designed to work with specific hardware, for example a PC. If a user decided to upgrade their hardware to an Apple iMac, the current Microsoft Windows® operating system and its applications would not run; the hardware is **not compatible**.

Equally, changes to specific hardware **components** may make existing software cease working; for example, a change of graphics card inside a PC might cause **incompatibilities** for a 3D modelling program.

The need for additional functionality

Often the user's needs have **changed** or just **grown** beyond the capabilities of the software they currently use. For example, they may have been happy to use a basic word-processing package to put a simple newsletter together, but as the newsletter becomes more complex, they consider purchasing a desktop publishing (DTP) program instead, as it offers a fuller set of features.

Wanting **additional functionality** is perhaps the most common reason to upgrade or install new software. Users who have legally registered certain types of software often upgrade on a regular basis to get the most recent version of the program.

An organisation's decision to change

Organisations often have a company-wide program of installation and upgrade, designed to 'roll out' changes to their employees' computer systems in a planned, controlled and systematic manner.

Perhaps two of the most common company-wide changes that are made are updates to office productivity suites (e.g. Microsoft® Office) and the operating system itself (e.g. upgrading to a new release of Microsoft Windows®). Performing changes on such a dramatic scale would be performed by a team of IT technicians proportionate to both the number of employees and the turnaround time required (i.e. more employees and a tight timeframe would mean more technicians).

The installation and upgrade process

Understanding the complete installation and upgrade process is best achieved using a simple diagram. As you can see, the process can be cyclical.

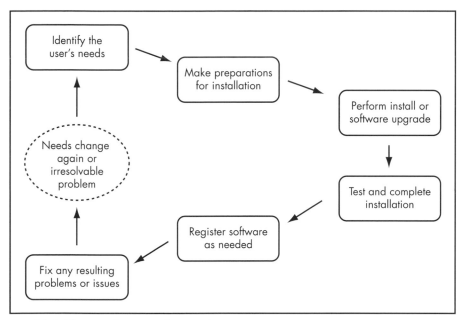

Fig. 13.1 The installation and upgrade process

Identifying the user's needs

Unless the request for new software has come from identified organisational needs, it is likely that it will be a direct request from the end-user. IT users often have a good idea of the software they would like to use to get a certain job done, but often are not experienced enough as practitioners to check the software's requirements or have the confidence to install themselves. Additionally, in most organisations user workstations are 'locked down' and, typically, common users without special privileges are unable to attempt software installation due to security settings made by the IT manager or system administrator.

Common procedures may exist within an organisation for requesting new software; this tends to be some kind of proposal which asks:

- Why is the software needed?
- What is the software called?
- How much does it cost?

- Is training required in order to use it?
- How will the software improve the work done by the user?

If these can be **justified** to a manager (and the **funds** are available), the software may be purchased. It is unlikely that a single employee would be given an upgrade, however, as this would make their data files potentially incompatible with their colleagues' software.

Make preparations for installation

The next step is to create a **checklist** (usually chronologically ordered), which can give a precise order to the actions required to perform the installation or upgrade. In an organisation it is likely that the IT services section will already have such a procedural checklist and it should be adhered to.

There are a number of things you need to know before you start.

1. Is this a **new installation** or an **upgrade** of an existing software package?

2. What are the installation requirements of the software?
   - Will it need **new hardware**?
   - [for an application] Will it need a **different operating system**?
   It is worth noting that these requirements can be:
   - **minimum** (enough to get the software running), or
   - **recommended** (to yield the best results).

3. By **when** is the installation (or upgrade) to be performed?
   - What timescale is involved?
   - Are there any limitations as to when this can be performed?

4. Is there is any **data** (or **user settings**) that needs to be **backed up** first?
   - If there is, **how much**?
   - **How** and **where** will it be backed up?

5. Is there a legal license to install the software?
   - Yes, 1 license per designated machine (a 'single license').
   - Yes, the installation is within 'site license' limits.
   - The software has been made available at no cost ('freeware').
   - The software can run on a network ('network license').
   - It is a time-limited version of the software ('shareware' on trial version).

6. **How** will the software be installed on to machine?
   - CD (compact disc)
   - DVD (digital versatile disc)
   - from a local file server
   - from the Internet
   - from a floppy disk or USB (univeral serial bus) flash drive.

7. Does the target computer system **permit** this type of installation (i.e. does it have the appropriate drive, port or connection)?

8. **How** will the installation be **tested**?

9. **How** will it be **activated** and/or **registered**?

10. What is the **procedure if problems** occur?
- try install/upgrade again
- attempt to find and repair the problem
- contact customer support
- uninstall the software.

Preparing answers to these questions will undoubtedly ensure that silly mistakes and errors are not overlooked before the actual install or upgrade commences.

Perform install or software upgrade

Installing new software is often performed because it **critically improves** an existing product or fills the organisational or user's need to expand into **new areas** of processing and creativity.

Upgrading is more complex, so let us start by examining why upgrades are released. Upgrades are released as:

- a **bug-fix**, essentially to **patch** errors in the original program code
- a **revised and expanded version** of the program, adding **new features** and (hopefully) **improved performance.**

Software companies typically release revised versions of their software when their older product has passed the mature (i.e. profitable) part of its lifetime and has started to decline in sales (and therefore profits). They may also do so to meet **new legal requirements** or **take advantage of new hardware**. It is also possible that it might incorporate **better security** – fewer **vulnerabilities** that virus writers may take advantage of.

Software packages often have **version numbers** which indicate the major and minor number of the product. A common example is shown in Figure 13.2.

```
C:\WINDOWS\system32\cmd.exe
Microsoft Windows XP [Version 5.1.2600]
(C) Copyright 1985-2001 Microsoft Corp.
```

Fig. 13.2 Microsoft Windows® XP shows its version number

This is the version number for a particular installation of Microsoft Windows® XP (Version 5.1. 2600). If we look at this in more detail, we see:

- operating system's name: Microsoft Windows® XP
- major version number: 5
- minor version number: 1
- build number: 2600

Large revisions to the operating system would change the **major** number. **Small revisions** to the operating system would typically change the **minor** number.

As you can see from the table below, Microsoft® earlier product updates had always kept to this basic pattern.

Operating system	Major.Minor.Build number
Microsoft Windows® 95 retail, OEM	4.00.950
Microsoft Windows® 95 retail SP1	4.00.950A
Microsoft Windows® 98 retail, OEM	4.10.1998
Microsoft Windows® 98 Second Edition	4.10.2222A
Microsoft Windows® Me	4.90.3000
Microsoft Windows® 2000	5.0.2195

Key terms

OEM (original equipment manufacturer) has different meanings: for an operating system like Microsoft Windows®, it implies that it is a copy sold to a computer system manufacturer (e.g. Dell) for installation on a new machine. For a hardware component (e.g. a hard disk), it is typically a retail version which is sold more cheaply as it usually has no drivers, manuals or nice retail box.

SP (service pack): generally, this is collection of updates, bug fixes and/or improvements to an existing program. However, rather than existing as a series of different updates, it is packed together in the form of a single installable package. Microsoft Windows® XP service packs 1 and 2 are good examples.

Incremental SPs contain only the fixes needed since the last SP.

Cumulative SPs are bigger because they also contain the contents from their predecessors.

Obtaining other users' experiences of new installations and potential upgrades is also a useful tool for the IT specialist. This can be achieved by simply comparing notes with colleagues or, more commonly in the twenty-first century, by visiting online **technical support forums** on the World Wide Web. Such forums often contain reports of **faults**, **experiences** and **suggested remedies**, which may help resolve a problem that has been encountered. Typically, the technician should feel comfortable posting new queries to such a resource, knowing that there is another person out there – somewhere – who has the answer.

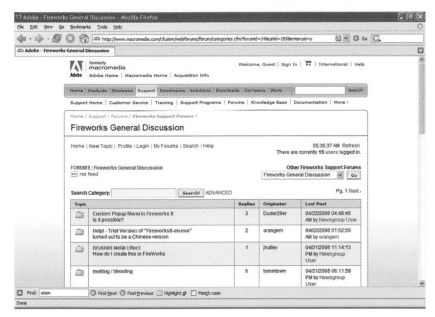

Fig. 13.3 A typical support forum

Preparation for an installation or upgrade

Once you are convinced that you have answered the questions on the checklist (as described earlier), it is possible to proceed.

You will have already:

- **backed up** any personal data or settings that are needed by the user
- **uninstalled** any older software that is no longer required
- made **recommendations** for any **hardware upgrades** that are needed (and installed these upgrades if it is within your job specification and ability to do so)
- **notified the user** of the approximate amount of time the computer system will be unavailable and, if possible, arranged another system as a temporary loan until theirs is ready for return.

By this stage you should have at your disposal:

- **the computer system** (with hardware suitably upgraded, if it was required)
- **the software package** to install or upgrade (this may be any physical media, an archived zip file or an Internet link for download – ensure that any installation files are checked for viruses before use)
- **installation/upgrade instructions** (this may be a printed document, electronic document or short 'readme.txt' text file)
- **proof of license arrangements**
- **activation information** (typically a selected user name, serial number or product key – product keys are often printed on manuals or on CDs, and for software purchased online

they may be emailed to the customer; additionally, if the activation is online (via website or email), a live Internet connection will be required; telephone activation is also commonly used, as is (to a lesser degree) postal activation)

- any **additional utilities** that you may need (e.g. archive software such as WinZip)
- any system **user names** or **passwords** needed to perform the task (e.g. Administrator account)
- **skills** and **experience necessary** to perform the task
- **enough time** to do the job **thoroughly**!

If this final checklist is complete, you should be ready to perform an installation.

Performing an installation or upgrade

The following example walks us through obtaining a new software package and installing it on a typical Microsoft Windows® XP computer system.

The software package in question is:

Macromedia Dreamweaver MX 2004, a popular web design package which is used to build professional websites.

The requirements for this package are:

- an **Intel® Pentium® III processor** or equivalent, **600 MHz** or faster
- **Microsoft Windows® 98**, **Windows® 2000**, **Windows® XP** or **Windows® .NET Server 2003**
- at least **128 MB** of available random-access memory (RAM) (**256 MB recommended**)
- at least **275 MB** available disk space
- a **16-bit** (thousands of colours) graphics card capable of **1024 × 768** pixel **resolution** or better (**millions of colours recommended**).

(Source: http://livedocs.macromedia.com/ dreamweaver/ mx2004/)

A quick investigation will reveal the target system's specifications:

- PC running Microsoft Windows® XP with Service Pack 2
- 2.0 GHz Athlon™ XP (2400+) CPU
- 512 MB of RAM

This information can be collected from the computer system while it is working. The easiest way to do so is by

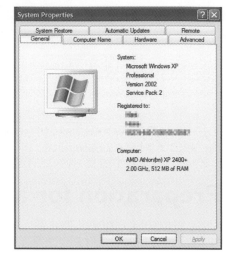

Fig. 13.4 System Properties tabbed dialogue

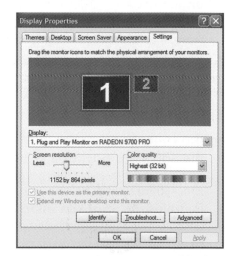

Fig. 13.5 Display Properties tabbed dialogue

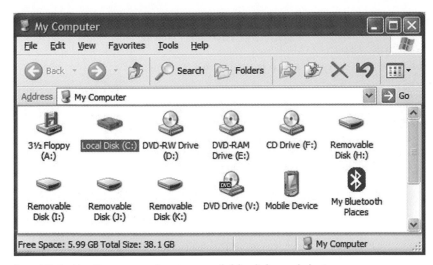

Fig. 13.6 My Computer, showing available disks and devices

selecting **Properties** by **right-clicking** on the **My computer icon** the desktop. The tabbed dialogue box shown in Figure 13.4 will appear.

- a Radeon® 9700 Pro with maximum resolution of 1280 × 1024 in 32-bit colour

The capabilities of the computer system's graphic card can be discovered using the **Display Properties** dialogue, which is accessed by **right-clicking** on the **desktop** and selecting **Properties** (see Figure 13.5).

The maximum available **screen resolution** and **colour quality** can be found here.

- Approximately **6 GB** of **free hard disk space**

More detailed information on the disk capacity and usage can be obtained in **Properties** by **right-clicking** on the primary **hard disk icon** on the desktop (this is usually called **C:**), as shown in Figure 13.6.

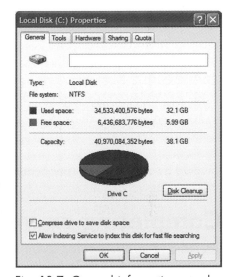

Fig. 13.7 General information panel for the hard disk

In Microsoft Windows® XP, a graphical representation of the chosen disk's usage will appear (see Figure 13.7).

Compatibility verdict?

A simple **table of comparison** can be drawn up which allows us to check the **compatibility** of the **software** and the **target computer system**.

Software requirements	Computer system specification	Verdict
At least 128 MB of available random-access memory (RAM) (256 MB recommended)	512 MB of RAM	👍
At least 275 MB available disk space	6 GB of free hard disk space	👍
An Intel® Pentium® III processor or equivalent, 600 MHz or faster	2.0 GHz Athlon® XP (2400+) CPU	👍
A 16-bit (thousands of colours) monitor capable of 1024 × 768 pixel resolution or better (millions of colours recommended)	A 17" monitor with maximum resolution of 1280 × 1024. A Radeon® 9700 Pro with maximum resolution of 1280 × 1024 using 32-bit colour.	👍
Microsoft Windows® 98, Windows® 2000, Windows® XP or Windows® .NET Server 2003	PC running Microsoft Windows® XP with Service Pack 2	👍

It would appear that the specification of the target PC is **acceptable** to **install** and **run** the required software.

Completing an installation or upgrade

Insert the Dreamweaver MX 2004 CD. The CD should autorun; if it does not explore the CD and **double-click** the Dreamweaver MX 2004 installer.exe icon. This should start the installation process (see Figure 13.8).

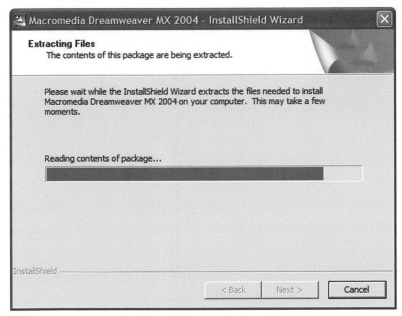

Fig. 13.8 Extracting the files necessary for installation

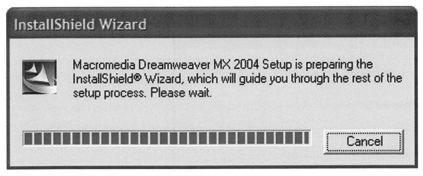

Fig. 13.9 Getting ready to run the setup program

Typically, a welcome dialogue is displayed, as shown in Figure 13.10.

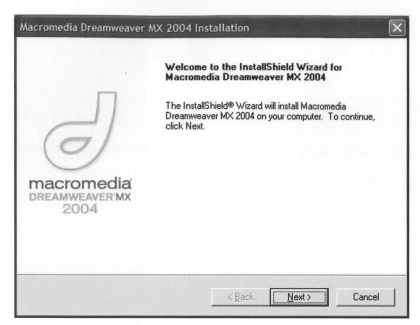

Fig. 13.10 The InstallShield Wizard starts

This is followed by the EULA, as shown in Figure 13.11.

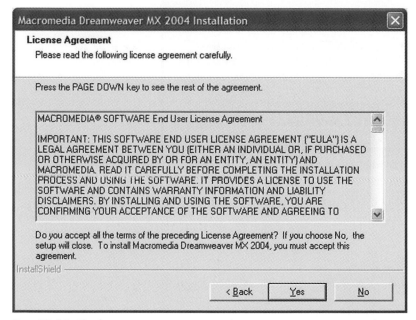

Fig. 13.11 The license agreement – you have to say yes to continue!

Refusal of the EULA normally **aborts** the installation process. It is very common (although not recommended) to skip to the 'Yes' button without reading the agreement. The recommended practice is to read through carefully and agree by pressing 'Yes'. If you are uncertain about any of the terms, it is worth querying this with a colleague or, in an organisation, your line manager or supervisor.

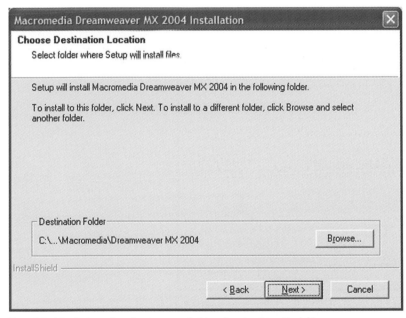

Fig. 13.12 Select the destination folder for the installed files

On a Microsoft Windows® operating system it is common to use a **default location** to install new software or upgrades. This is usually based in the **Program Files** folder of the main hard drive (C:):

C:\Program files\

It is common for a new application to create a folder for the SOFTWARE PUBLISHER (e.g. Macromedia):

C:\Program files\Macromedia

And then another sub-folder for the name of the software program being installed (e.g. Dreamweaver MX 2004):

C:\Program file\Macromedia\Dreamweaver MX 2004

During installation it is common for a program to ask the user to confirm which file types the user would like to associate. Here, Dreamweaver has suggested associating itself with all the common file types that would be used during web development. These can be selected and deselected as required, by checking or un-checking the relevant boxes (see Figure 13.13).

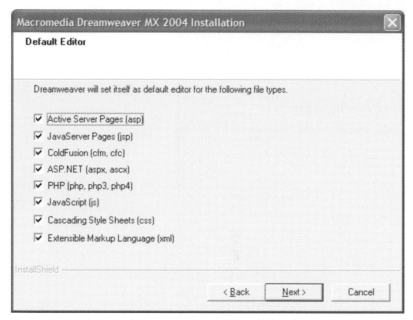

Fig. 13.13 Selecting the types of files to associate Dreamweaver with

It is common for the program to have an **Options** menu, which can add/delete associations if the user subsequently changes their mind.

Final check before installation starts

It is also quite common for an installation to give you one last chance to revise your settings before continuing (pressing **Back**).

Proceeding with the **Next** button (as shown in Figure 13.14) will start to copy and install the files as requested, the graphical **progress bar** and **percentage completion figure** giving a visual clue as to how much has been completed (see Figure 13.15).

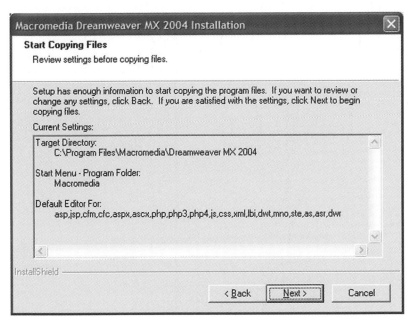

Fig. 13.14 A last-minute check before continuing

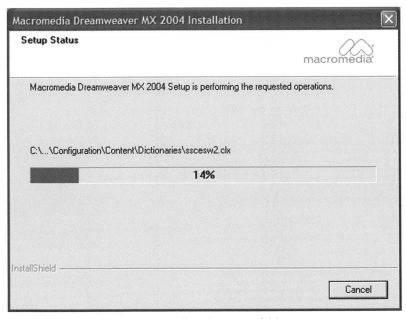

Fig. 13.15 The files start to install to the target folder

A successful installation may take quite a few minutes; this varies greatly depending on the **size** of the installation files and the **speed** of the hardware.

Success is usually denoted with a completion-style dialogue, as shown in Figure 13.16.

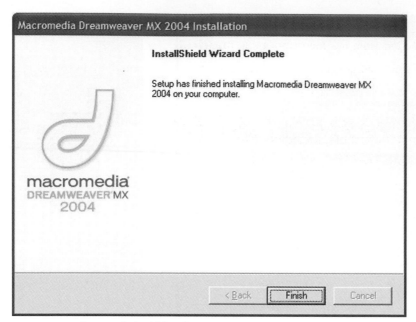

Fig. 13.16 The InstallShield finishes its work

Some installations may then load a helpful 'readme.txt' file or a web page (see Figure 13.17).

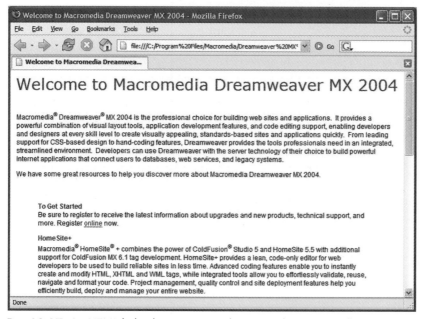

Fig. 13.17 An HTML help document may be opened automatically

Starting the program

The program can then be started from the new start menu **shortcut**.

Some programs require a quick configuration of user preferences the first time they are used (as shown in Figure 13.18).

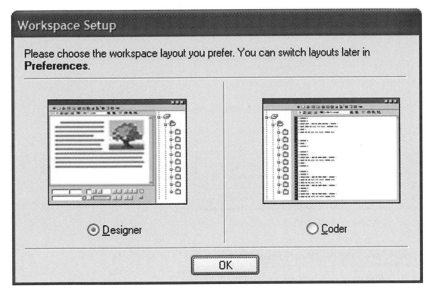

Fig. 13.18 User preferences are determined on first run of the software

Activation

The next stage is asking whether or not the program needs **activation**. In this case, activation would mean entering the **serial number** or **product key** that came with the package. The alternative would be to have a **fully working**, **non-activated** product as a **30-day trial**. Of course, after 30 days it would stop working and need to be **uninstalled**.

Choosing to enter the serial number is the correct course of action.

A dialogue will appear which will typically contain gaps that can be filled with the issued serial number. The printed serial number may appear as WWWW – XXXX – YYYY – ZZZZ. It is likely that this is keyed in without the spaces or hyphens.

If the serial number has been sent via an email, it should not be cut and pasted into the gaps, as some programs do not accept this method of input.

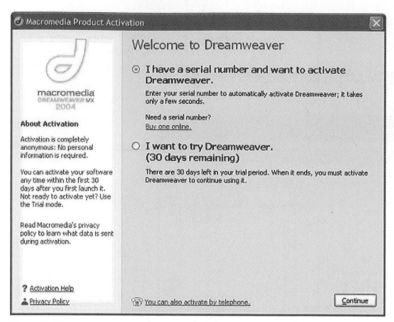

Fig. 13.19 A welcome message: activate or use as trial version

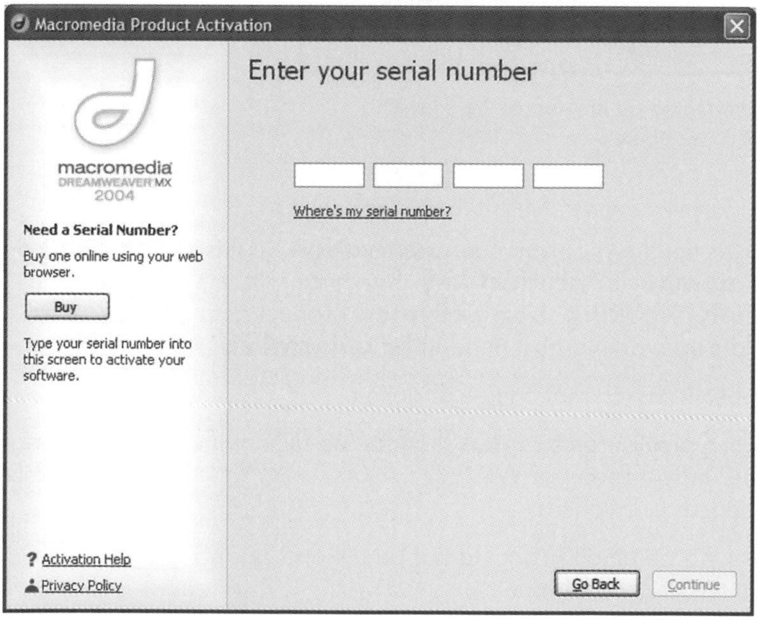

![Macromedia Product Activation - Enter your serial number]

Fig. 13.20 An activation box appears – it wants a valid serial number

Serial numbers should not be shared with other individuals; they are used to legally link the installed program with its purchase. However, it is possible that an organisation may use the same serial number for every installation they perform, depending on the terms and instructions of the license they have purchased from the software publishers.

After the serial number is entered, it is checked by the program to see if it is valid. An invalid serial will halt progress and will need to be re-keyed. Successful serial numbers are safely stored on the computer system's hard disk and will not need to be keyed again.

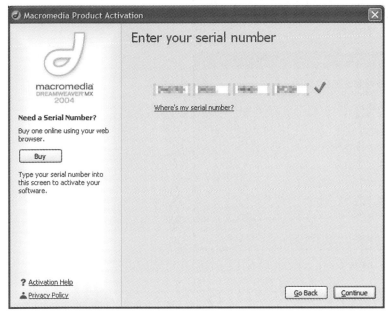

Fig. 13.21 A valid serial is entered and validated successfully

The next stage appears to be **registration**.

Registration

Key term

Registration is the **voluntary** process of sending a user's or organisation's information (e.g. name, email, location) to a software publisher.

SCORECARD

After registering, the publisher may:

+ Keep you informed of any upgrades
+ Offer deals on new products or services
+ Provide new bonus downloads
+ Send via email a lost serial number if reinstallation is required
| Provide limited technical support
+ Enter your name in a competition prize draw
+ Offer an extended warranty
− Pass your information on to other interested third parties, usually for marketing purposes

Note, for some software programs, the activation process is called registration.

These days, the most common way for registration information to reach the publisher is by being transmitted via the Internet, although some may permit postal or telephone registrations.

If you are uncertain at this time, you can usually decide to register at a later date or never register at all.

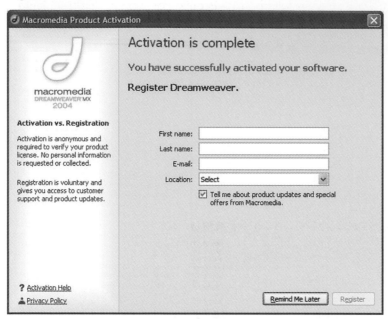

Fig. 13.22 Activation is complete: to register or not to register?

If your computer system has a firewall program present, it will undoubtedly detect the attempted transmission of your information from the new program, as shown in Figure 13.23.

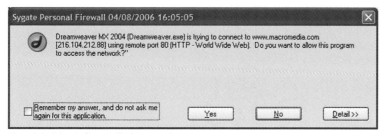

Fig. 13.23 A firewall detects the new program

If you want the program to be able to **transmit** and **receive data** over the Internet, the firewall must be set to **allow** such communication.

Testing

Perhaps one of the most important and overlooked stages of installation and upgrade is the actual testing. It is very common for an installation to proceed satisfactorily, but when the program is started it unexpectedly crashes or misbehaves. Technicians often forget to check this part of the process and find themselves called back and confronted by upset and confused end-users.

Testing contributes to the overall quality of service that the end-user receives.

How to test

This depends greatly on the software being installed and it is quite common for the technician to have problems when performing the testing, as they may not have the specialist IT user skills necessary. Generally, though, a technician is capable of testing some basic functionality common to all programs:

*   starting the program
*   creating a basic file
*   saving a basic file
*   loading a basic file
*   printing a basic file
*   quitting the program.

In Figure 13.24 a simple **web page** has been created.

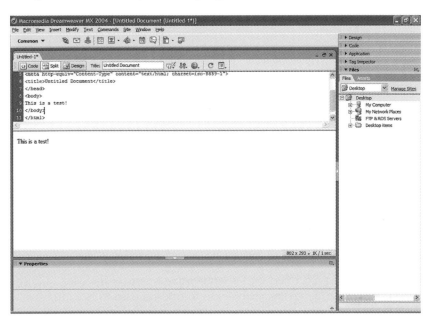

Fig. 13.24 Performing a simple test

This file is then saved and viewed from another application (in Figure 13.25, a web browser).

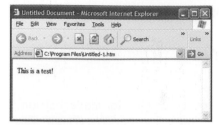

Fig. 13.25 The technician's test file

Other technical aspects that can be checked are that the application is reported correctly in the operating system's task manager (see Figure 13.26).

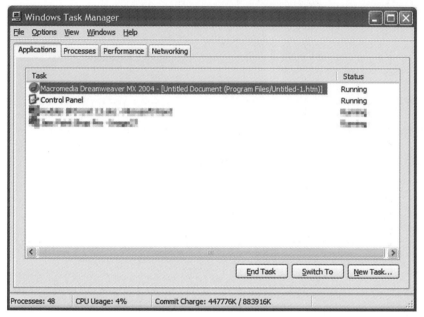

Fig. 13.26 Applications running in memory

And that the processes which contribute to the application are using a proportionate amount of computer system resources (e.g. RAM, CPU time), as can be seen in Figure 13.27.

Other functional tasks, ideally, should be performed by the end-user, as part of the user requirements check. A common occurrence is for the technician to ask the user to test the program for a specific period of time and report back any problems they encounter.

There will be two likely outcomes:

- Should the problems be serious in nature, the technician will return to investigate.
- If the end-user is satisfied by the installation and service provided, the job can be considered closed.

If serious problems cannot be resolved, it may be necessary to remove (or uninstall) the program from the computer system in question. This is important if the new installation or upgrade has also affected the function of pre-existing programs.

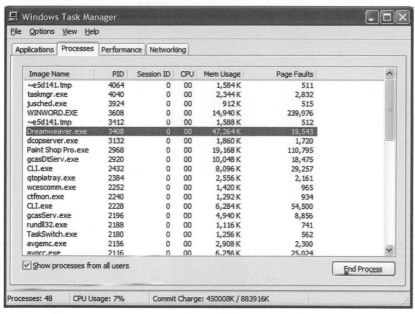

Fig. 13.27 Processes currently running in RAM

Uninstalling

In Microsoft Windows®, the removal of existing software is performed through the Control Panel's **Add or Remove Programs** applet.

Microsoft Windows® XP may show the Control Panel as presented in Figure 13.28.

Fig. 13.28 Control Panel, classic Microsoft Windows® view

Or as in Figure 13.29.

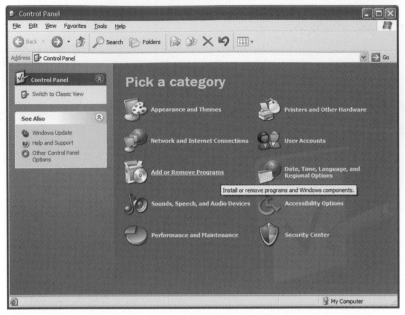

Fig. 13.29 Control Panel, Microsoft Windows® XP view

The **Add or Remove Programs** dialogue lists installed programs which can either be **changed** or **removed** (see Figure 13.30).

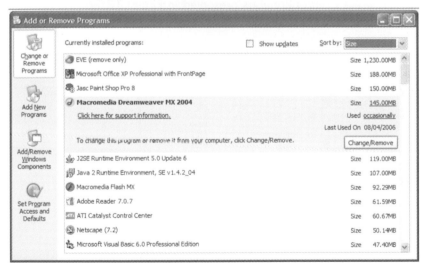

Fig. 13.30 Installed programs, ordered by size

Selecting to remove a program usually starts that application's **Uninstall** process, as can be seen in Figure 13.31.

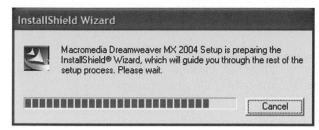

Fig. 13.31 InstallShield Wizard prepares to uninstall   Fig. 13.32 Choice of uninstalling or cancelling

A choice is then presented of whether to continue (see Figure 13.32).

Removing the software is usually a lot quicker than the original installation process. Although the program itself will be removed, it is common for data files it has created to remain behind. This data may require manual removal by finding and deleting the files individually.

Keeping records

Work records or **logs** of an installation or upgrade job are essential for good housekeeping and future reference (e.g. if the job has to be repeated elsewhere).

It is common practice for an organisation to specify what should be included in a technician's work records. Such records usually contain such information as:

- technician's name
- name of the software, its version, etc.
- type of preparation performed
- name of the end-user
- unique number of the target computer system
- date the installation/upgrade was performed
- any problems encountered (and their solutions)
- date the job was closed.

Communication

Communication between the technician and interested parties is vital at all times. Interested parties typically include:

- the end-user – to discuss **progress** and their needs (e.g. **training requirements**)
- the **technician's supervisor** – for guidance and technical advice
- the **software publisher** – to discuss technical issues requiring expert support and customer service.

Final procedures

This should include **safe storage** of relevant files, media or documentation. This may include:

- installation files
- original media, such as CD, DVD, floppy disks
- any documentation used (e.g. warranty, customer support arrangements)
- license agreements (although these may be held centrally by the IT manager)
- serial numbers.

Completion of a new installation and upgrade typically contributes to an IT department's SLA (service level agreement) between it and other departments in the organisation.

QUIZ

1. Name three reasons to install new software or perform an upgrade.
2. In order to justify a new software installation or upgrade, an employee will need to provide what details?
3. Which two 'levels' of system requirements are usually specified by new software?
4. What is an EULA?
5. Give two reasons why software updates may be released.
6. Which process is mandatory: activation or registration?
7. Give three advantages to registering software.
8. Give three ways to register software.
9. Why is testing important?
10. Give three examples of the kinds of details that should be included in a 'work record'.

ANSWERS

1. • New hardware is incompatible with existing software
   • User needs have changed
   • New functionality
   • To fix bugs present in existing software
2. • Why new software is needed
   • Name of software
   • Cost
   • If training will be required
   • How it will improve work
   • Minimum recommended
4. • End User Licence Agreement – the license to use the software as granted by the publisher to the user, stipulating rules on usage, copying and lending, etc.
5. • Bug fix or patch for current problems
   • To add new features
6. • Activation is mandatory
   • Registration may be voluntary
7. • Information on updates
   • Deals from publisher
   • New bonus downloads
   • Technical support
   • Extended warranty
   • Prize draws, etc.

8. • Online
   • Telephone
   • Post
9. • To ensure that the installation:
   • is stable and functionally correct
   • meets users needs.
10. • Technician's name
   • Name of software
   • Type of preparation performed
   • End user's name
   • Target computer system ID
   • Dates and times
   • Problems
   • Date the job was closed

 Activity 1

We Cell Phones are considering updating their administration PCs from Microsoft Windows® XP Pro to Microsoft Windows Vista® Professional Edition.

Research this new operating system and produce a short description of its **minimum** and **recommended** requirements.

 Activity 2

Steve Hodder (of SHS) has been advised to upgrade from Dreamweaver MX 2004 to Dreamweaver 8, but he is unsure that the extra expense is actually worth it.

In order to help him reach a decision, investigate the newer package and discover how it has been improved, what changes have been made and what (if any) new requirements the software has.

COURSEWORK GUIDANCE

In terms of theory, you will need to show an understanding of licensing and legal issues and be able to demonstrate knowledge about the processes involved in installing and upgrading software.

Practically, you will demonstrate the installation of various types of software, having suitably prepared to undertake the installation first. You will then need to show that you can test your installation.

For the higher grades you will need to be able to discuss issues such as the advantages and disadvantages of registering software, and also explain the problems that may occur during software installation.

Evaluating different types of software license and the issues around software piracy will need to be evidenced for a Distinction grade, along with an explanation of how the potential for problems during installation can be minimised.

Unit links9 This unit has direct links to txe following:

Unit 2 IntroductiGn to Computer Systems

Unit 3 ICT Project
Unit 5 ICT Supportink Organisations
Unit 12 Installang Hardware Components
Unit 17 *Security of ICT systems

●●●●Further reading

The Copyright Design and Patents Act 1988 www.copyrightservice.co.uk/copyright/

Many software manufacturer websites contain guidance on their products' requirements:

Adobe www.adobe.com

Macromedia www.macromedia.com (now also part of Adobe)

Microsoft® www.microsoft.com

Symantec www.symantec.com

Progress check

To record your achievement, simply tick the criteria awarded to you when each assignment is returned (you may be given three assignments for this unit, U13.01, U13.02 and U13.03 – the final column may not be used). There is a full copy of this grid available on the accompanying CD. The copy will also allow you to record your key skill achievement against Literacy, Numeracy and ICT objectives.

	Assignments in this Unit			
Assignment	**U13.01**	**U13.02**	**U13.03**	**U13.04**
Referral				
Pass				
1				
2				
3				
4				
5				
6				
7				
Merit				
1				
2				
3				
4				
Distinction				
1				
2				
3				

A completed sample of this document (for reference purposes) can be found at the back of Unit 1.

UNIT 16

MOBILE COMMUNICATIONS TECHNOLOGY

INTRODUCTION

From a technological standpoint, the spread of wireless communications devices, such as cellular telephones (mobiles), and the mainstream adoption of wireless connectivity in the IT industry have been both rapid and decisive.

This unit introduces you to the technologies involved, their common applications and just some of the ethical considerations of using mobile communications in the early twenty-first century.

Learning outcomes

On completion of this unit you should:

1 understand the characteristics and services of available mobile communications devices
2 understand the implications of mobile communications
3 be able to use mobile communications technologies to meet user needs.

RECORDING YOUR PROGRESS

In order to achieve each unit you will complete a series of coursework activities. Each time you hand in work, your tutor will return this to you with a record of your achievement.

This particular unit has 7 criteria to meet: 4 Pass, 2 Merit and 1 Distinction.

- For a **Pass**: you must achieve **all** 4 Pass criteria.
- For a **Merit**: you must achieve **all** 4 Pass and **both** Merit criteria.
- For a **Distinction**: you must achieve **all** 4 Pass, **both** Merit **and the single** Distinction criterion.

So that you can monitor your own progress and achievement in each unit, a recording grid has been provided (see the **Progress check** section at the end of this unit).

Available technologies

There are many different technologies available for wireless communication. Although it is useful to understand the underlying scientific principles involved in wireless communication, most devices can be investigated using simple terminology. The following section details the most common forms of mobile communication technology currently available.

Infrared

Key term

Infrared (often abbreviated to **IR**) is a form of electromagnetic radiation that has a wavelength longer than visible light, but shorter than that of microwaves. The discovery of infrared radiation is typically attributed to astronomer William Herschel in the early nineteenth century.

Modern IR data transmission is often used for short-range communication, typically between handheld devices such as mobile telephones and personal data assistants (**PDA**s), although it is probably more popularly used to change channels on a TV using a remote control!

IR data transmission works in the following steps:

1. The transmitting device sends a narrow beam of IR radiation from its light-emitting diodes (LEDs) towards a receiver. This light is invisible to the human eye.

2. This beam is **modulated** (turned on and off) to create a stream of digital data signals.

3. The receiver (usually a **photodiode**) then converts the beam back into electrical pulses, which it can then process into data.

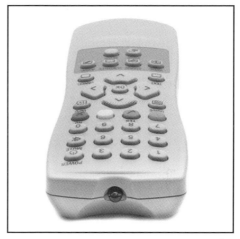

Fig. 16.1 An IR port on a remote control

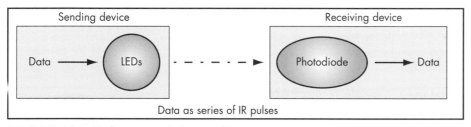

Fig. 16.2 How IR data transmission works

SCORECARD

- IrDA data standard has speeds up to 16 Mbps (slow compared to USB 2.0, working at 60 Mbps)
- IR typically has a **short range** (can be limited up to 2M for faster speeds)
- IR does **not penetrate** walls
- IR normally needs direct **line-of-sight** (LOS)
- Tried and tested technology

Other uses of IR

Originally developed by the National Aeronautics and Space Administration (NASA) and the military, Free Space Optics (FSO) is a newer communications application for IR, which uses more powerful laser-generated light to beam voice and data up to 10 km (6.2 miles), at speeds approaching 2.5 Gbps.

This is often used for high-speed gigabit Ethernet, where LOS communication is possible and is less expensive than actually laying optical fibre. Common applications could be for linking business premises or multiple campus buildings. It can also be **set up quickly**; an ideal tool for 'on the ground' disaster relief communications, where putting up cabled links is not practical or safe.

FSO solutions can experience interference from:

- **misalignment** – receiver and transmitter losing precise LOS due to movement
- **fog** – due to absorption, scattering or reflection by water droplets
- **rising heat** – also called **scintillation**, which alters the way light moves through the air
- **physical obstructions** – for example, birds flying through and 'breaking' the beam
- **beam wandering/spreading** – a growing weakness of signal over extended distances.

The IrDA® (Infrared Data Association) is a non-profit organisation, founded in 1993, which specifies worldwide standards for IR data transmission. Members include a number of high-profile companies which specialise in consumer electronics and telecommunications.

Bluetooth™

> **Key term**
>
> **Bluetooth™** is another wireless communication technology, originally developed by Ericsson in 1997.
>
> It is named after King Harald Bluetooth (Harold I of Denmark) and it is an IT industry specification for exchanging data between mobile devices (such as mobile telephones, PDAs), printers and notebook PCs, using a short-range radio frequency (2.4 GHz). Other common applications include hands-free kits for mobile telephone users.

Bluetooth™ can also be used to create secure **PANs** (personal area networks or piconet), since it can be used to connect PCs together for the purpose of exchanging data and resources.

The development of the Bluetooth™ technology is overseen by the Bluetooth Special Interest Group (**SIG**), which is comprised of over 2000 member companies, many of whom are well-known hardware manufacturers and specialists in telephone communications and consumer electronics.

Bluetooth™ requires little configuration by the user.

The secret behind Bluetooth™ is that once a Bluetooth™ device is enabled it actively **wants** to talk to other devices.

Fig. 16.3 The familiar Bluetooth™ logo. The logo is derived from Nordic runes for letters H and B.

When asked, a Bluetooth™ device will transmit its:

- **name** (typically manufacturer and model)
- **class** (type of device, e.g. mobile telephone)

- list of **available services**
- miscellaneous **technical information**.

Bluetooth™ devices also have a unique **48-bit address** which they can be identified by, although generally its name is used instead. This can cause problems sometimes, as a number of similarly named devices may be available in a small area.

The list of available services is perhaps the most useful piece of information transmitted because it tells the connected device which **types of request** it can make. For example, if a Bluetooth™ device says it supports 'File-based Object Exchange', it should be possible to **transfer data files** fairly painlessly. Likewise, devices that support 'Basic Printing' can be used to produce hard copies of electronic data sent via Bluetooth™ (e.g. printing text messages from a mobile telephone).

Fig. 16.4 A Bluetooth™ USB adaptor. This is designed to plug in to a notebook, typically giving the notebook access to other Bluetooth™ devices or a PAN.

Security

Although **authentication** (checking that the connection is **valid**) is not usually performed, it is possible to 'pair' Bluetooth™ devices using a personal identification number (**PIN**) or **passkey**. A Bluetooth™ PIN is usually a string of up to 16 alphanumeric characters. Both devices calculate and store a 'link key' from this PIN, and it must be re-authenticated with the other device before it can be trusted on subsequent reconnections. Optional **data encryption** can also be used to improve security.

Dealing with interference

As we shall see, Bluetooth™ shares the same frequency as other wireless networking products and more common household devices such as cordless telephones and microwaves. In order to avoid interference, the Bluetooth™ device 'hops' randomly between 79 different frequencies (between 2.402 GHz and 2.48 GHz) approximately 1600 times a second.

This process is called Frequency-Hopping Spread Spectrum (**FHSS**).

SCORECARD

- - Bluetooth™ support speeds up to 2.1 Mbps
- - Bluetooth™ range varies, depending on power of device (from 10 m, but can be up to 300 m)
- + Bluetooth™ can penetrate walls
- + omnidirectional – it does not require line-of-sight.
- + Bluetooth™ devices require little configuration
- + low power consumption, useful for preserving energy on mobile devices
- + trusted pairs can be created to improve security

Wi-Fi

The Institute of Electrical and Electronic Engineers (IEEE) is an international organisation that develops standards for different families of modern technologies. In particular, their 802 committee develops standards for local area networks (**LAN**s) and wide area networks (**WAN**s). A subsection of these standards, called 802.11, concerns the use of wireless networks.

Key term

Wi-Fi (wireless fidelity) is the name for the IEEE 802.11<u>b</u> set of standards, which detail wireless networks operating in the 2.4 GHz frequency, using a bandwidth of 11 Mbps.

Interoperability, one of the goals of the IEEE, is the ability for equipment made by **different manufacturers** to **work together** using a set of **agreed standards**.

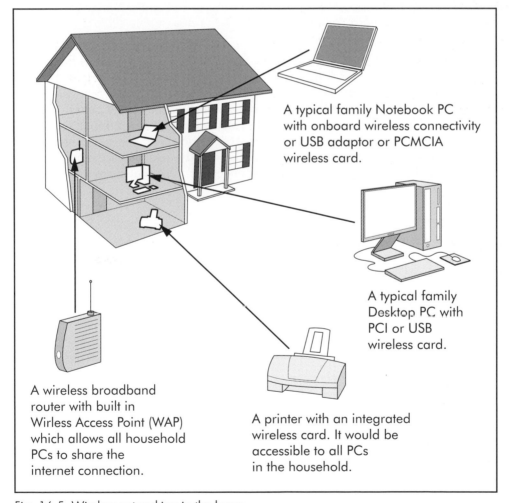

A typical family Notebook PC with onboard wireless connectivity or USB adaptor or PCMCIA wireless card.

A typical family Desktop PC with PCI or USB wireless card.

A wireless broadband router with built in Wirless Access Point (WAP) which allows all household PCs to share the internet connection.

A printer with an integrated wireless card. It would be accessible to all PCs in the household.

Fig. 16.5 Wireless networking in the home

Wi-Fi in the SOHO

Wi-Fi has become very popular recently, especially in small office, home office (SOHO) environments where traditional **cabled solutions** are **problematic**, **inconvenient** or **expensive** for the sake of ten or fewer computers/employees. Wi-Fi permits the creation of Wireless LANs (WLANs) and access to the Internet using easily integrated components that are sold on the high street.

The diagram in Figure 16.5 shows a typical Wi-Fi home set-up.

Wi-Fi at large

> **Key term**
>
> A recent phenomenon has been the installation of powerful WAPs in public places such as parks, train stations, fast food restaurants, hotel, airports, libraries and business centres. These WAPs create network **hot spots**, which can be used by an individual, with appropriate equipment such as a mobile telephone, PDA or notebook, to connect to the Internet.

In October 2005, Philadelphia, one of the largest and oldest cities in the United States of America, announced plans to build the biggest community wireless Internet system in the country. Philadelphia plans to create a hot spot which covers approximately 135 square miles. It is intended to attract citizens on a low wage as all they will be asked to contribute is $10. It is therefore not surprising that a number of telecommunication firms, who have invested heavily in more traditional cable or optical links, have spoken publicly against such community-based schemes.

In November 2005, the top 10 table for worldwide hot spots looked like this:

1	United States	32,350
2	**United Kingdom**	**12,608**
3	South Korea	8,923
4	Germany	8,742
5	France	4,145
6	Japan	3,041
7	Italy	1,730
8	Netherlands	1,714
9	Switzerland	1,510
10	Canada	1,392

(Source: Jiwire © December 2005)

And by venue:

1	Hotel / Resort	22,561
2	Restaurant	17,027
3	Store / Shopping Mall	13,288
4	Café	13,207
5	Pub	5,892
6	Other	4,484
7	Office Building	1,719
8	Gas/Petrol Station	1,483
9	Airport	1,207
10	Library	1,107

Wireless security

Data transmitted over a wireless network is, by its very nature, **insecure**. Unlike a wired solution, data is being broadcast freely through 'thin air'. It is therefore possible to **unlawfully gain access** to a wireless connection using appropriate hardware and software. In fact, this type of 'scanning' software can be downloaded freely from the Internet.

From 1999 original Wi-Fi solutions used a form of encryption called wired equivalence privacy (**WEP**). WEP is an **optional security** and, much to security professionals' disbelief, is often **not enabled as default** 'out of the box'.

Moreover, WEP uses a relatively **weak form of encryption**, which is easily cracked after a period of network observation. In fact, in a well-known demonstration, the Federal Bureau of Investigation (FBI) demonstrated WEP's weakness by attempting to hack it during a live demonstration: it took them just three minutes.

By 2003 a much improved standard, Wi-Fi Protection Access (**WPA**) was introduced to answer much of the criticism regarding WEP's robustness. A revised version, **WPA2**, followed a year later as part of the 802.11i standard.

Other standards for wireless networking

A sample of other notable implementations that exist within the 802 family follows:

802.11a: operates in 5 GHz frequency range, attracting less interference at faster 54 Mbps
802.11d: standards for country-to-country roaming
802.11e: incorporation of Quality of Service (QoS) to wireless network transmissions
802.11g: primarily for Wireless LANs operating in 2.4 GHz range, but at a faster 54 Mbps
802.11i: the introduction of enhanced security features (including WPA2)
802.11n: a task force (started in 2004) examining a theoretical speed increase to 540 Mbps.

Technology comparison

Technology	Transmission	Effective range
IrDA®	9600 bps – 16 Mbps	0–2 M
Bluetooth™	3 Mbps – 100 Mbps	10–100 M
Wi-Fi 802.11a	1 Mbps – 54 Mbps	45 M (indoors) – 90 M (outdoors) But depends on power of antennae used
Wi-Fi 802.11b	1 Mbps – 11 Mbps	45 M (indoors) – 90 M (outdoors) But depends on power of antennae used
Wi-Fi 802.11g	1 Mbps – 54 Mbps	45 M (indoors) – 90 M (outdoors) But depends on power of antennae used
Wi-Fi 802.11n	1 Mbps – 100 Mbps	45 M (indoors) – 90 M (outdoors) But depends on power of antennae used

Mobile (cellular) Telephones

By the early twenty-first century these have become an **absolute necessity** for most people, young and old. By 2004/2005 it had been estimated by the UK's Office of National Statistics that around 78 per cent of UK households had at least one mobile telephone, and this number has been increasing regularly since then.

Countless models are available, with many different designs, features and functions. Many have **games** (usually written in the programming language called **Java**™), many **play music** (e.g. MP3 files downloaded from a PC via a USB cable) and **video**.

In addition, nearly all mobile telephones feature highly customisable **user interfaces**, which mimic those of a standard PC's desktop, allowing the user to select different ring tones, wallpapers and animated screensavers. (For more on customisation, see Unit 2: Introduction to Computer Systems.)

Fig. 16.6 A modern mobile telephone

How mobile telephones work

Mobile telephones are essentially **radio transceivers** – they can **transmit** and **receive** radio waves, which may be converted into either voice or data messages, depending on the type of call. These radio waves are sent to other telephones via **base stations** (or **masts**). In larger geographical areas, it is necessary to divide coverage into a honeycomb of different **cells**. Each cell typically covers between 0.5 and 5 miles, and it is not uncommon for them to **overlap**.

As a user **moves** from area to area, the mobile telephone is **ordered** to move to a **new frequency** when a **new cell** is found with a **stronger signal** (as shown in Figure 16.8).

This **roaming** facility ensures that communication **remains constant**. A cell also has **switching facilities** to forward the connection to a public telephone network, so that calls can be made to traditional land lines. It is also possible to **roam** using another operator's cells.

Problems will occur, of course, if the area has **weak coverage** or no nearby cell at all; the user will either find they are **disconnected** or be **unable** to place a call. Sound familiar?

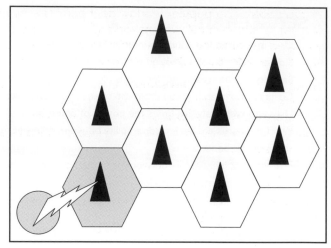

Fig. 16.7 Cell in use

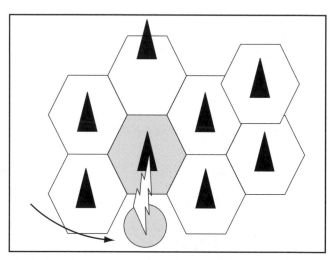

Fig. 16.8 User moves and another cell takes over with a stronger signal

GSM

Key term

GSM stands for Global System for Mobile communications, a popular standard used for mobile telephones in Europe and most of the world, giving it an installed user base of over 1.5 billion people. GSM communication has a **narrow bandwidth** and is generally used for **simple voice** communication.

Because GSM is so popular worldwide it permits easy roaming for its users: mobile devices can 'latch on to' different cellular networks while they are away from home. This facility has mainly developed because the GSM standard is said to be 'open'. **Open standards** encourage sharing and **interoperability** between different manufacturers and telephone companies.

Phones which rely on GSM standards are commonly called **2G** or **second-generation** handsets. This is because they use **digital signals** to communicate. Earlier mobile telephones had used **analogue signals** and are often referred to as **1G**, although they were never called this at the time. (See Unit 20: Telecommunications Technology, for more on digital and analogue signals.)

SIM card

A vital part of the GSM system is the **secure storage** of a subscriber's **user information**. This is achieved with the subscriber identity module (**SIM**), a small application that is often confused with the universal integrated circuit card (**UICC**) smartcard packaging it resides within.

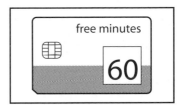

Fig. 16.9 A UICC – commonly known (incorrectly) as a SIM card

The UICC SIM application typically contains the following information:

- phonebook
- SMS (or text) messages
- location area identity (**LAI**)
- user preferences and settings
- international mobile subscriber identity (**IMSA**)
- integrated circuit card identifier (**ICCID**)
- 4-digit personal identification number (**PIN**) for security.

The LAI is used by a mobile telephone to **remember the last area** it was in before being switched off. This way, when the telephone is powered back on again, it does not have to perform frequency scanning for an available cell to reconnect.

The IMSA supplies the identity of the registered user to a GSM network. The ICCID uniquely identifies the actual ICCI package, and it is this number that is often printed on the ICCID SIM card.

Because a SIM is removable, it has become common practice for a user to move his or her details from handset to handset. Usually, the SIM has to be **linked** to the new telephone before it can be used, although some telephone operators block this by performing a **SIM-lock** – preventing a telephone from using a different SIM to the one it was **originally supplied with**. In some countries, SIM-locking is illegal, in others it is mandatory.

IMEI

The actual mobile telephone handset is identified by yet another number, its **IMEI** (international mobile equipment identity). Stolen telephones can be permanently blocked by identifying their IMEI and adding them to a centralised boycott list called the Central Equipment Identity Register (CEIR).

Attempting to unblock or change a telephone's IMEI is against the law in the UK, as detailed in the Mobile Telephones (Re-programming) Act 2002.

A simple way of finding out a device's IMEI is by dialling ***#06#**

SMS

> **Key term**
>
> **SMS** stands for Short Message Service, but is more popularly known by the common verb **texting**. SMS is a data service which allows a mobile telephone user to compose short text messages and send them to another user. It is also possible to send SMS texts via the Internet.

SMS works by sending the message to an SMS Centre (**SMSC**), using a protocol called Short Message Peer to Peer (**SMPP**), which then attempts to relay the message on to the desired target.

If the recipient's telephone is not switched on or the attempt fails, a retry might be attempted by the SMSC, depending on the settings used. SMS is said to use **best effort** delivery – this means that delivery is **not guaranteed**, and it is indeed possible that some messages **may never reach** their destination.

Fig. 16.10 example SMS text

SMS messages can contain:

- simple text
- ringtones
- pictures for logos and wallpapers
- over-the-Air (OTA) programming.

OTA programming is often sent by a telephone company to send **additional configuration settings** for **new services** that the user has requested, for example, Multimedia Messaging Service (**MMS**).

GPRS

Also known by its fuller name general packet radio service, **GPRS** is an extension available to GSM devices which permits additional data transmissions along unused cell bandwidth. GPRS is often seen as a step between 2G and 3G technology, and so has been informally called **2.5G**.

Unlike 2G telephones, which use permanent **circuit-switching**, GPRS uses **packet-switching** techniques to provide additional services such as internetworking for Wireless Application Protocol (**WAP**) and MMS. MMS permits the sending and receiving of media-rich data such as pictures, animations and music.

Packet-switching vs circuit-switching

In **circuit-switching** a **permanent connection** is made between the sending and receiving devices while the communication is ongoing; it is a fixed **point A to point B** connection.

Fig. 16.11 Circuit-switching

In **packet-switching** the data is **split up** into a number of different packets. In theory, packets can then travel to the destination device **through different routes**, being **reassembled** in the **correct order** at the other end. The actual path taken by the data usually reflects the **fastest** and **most reliable** route.

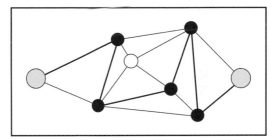

Fig. 16.12 Packet-switching

3G

Key term

Third-Generation or **3G** technology is often exemplified by the addition of **higher speed data** applications to the standard voice services. As such, it has been described by some operators as like 'having broadband for your phone'.

Video telephony (the ability to see the caller as the call is being made) is perhaps the most popular selling point of the technology, but Internet access, email, GPS navigation and music downloads are also strong contenders.

3G technology is **not** a unified standard; there are four main implementations:

- UMTS (Universal Mobile Telephone System)
- CDMA 2000 (Code Division Multiple Access 2000)
- TD-SCDMA (Time Division-Synchronous Code Division Multiple Access)
- W-CDMA (Wideband CDMA).

By 2006, the following UK telecommunications operators use W-CDMA in order to support 3G devices and services:

- Hutchinson 3G UK ('3')
- T-Mobile
- Vodafone
- Wave Telecom
- Orange
- O2
- Manx Telecom

Fig. 16.13 A typical 3G mobile telephone demonstrating video telephony

(Source: 3Gtoday © March 2006)

In countries such as Japan, where adoption of 3G is quite advanced, the **older GSM market** is effectively in **rapid decline**. Such trends are expected to follow in the rest of the world, as **technology**, **services** and **pricing** all improve.

Licensed vs unlicensed

Technologies such as Bluetooth™ and Wi-Fi usually operate in the **unlicensed** 2.4 GHz frequency.

Cellular technologies operate on **licensed** frequencies: 2G GSM is either allocated 900 MHz (O2, Vodafone) or 1.8 GHz (T-Mobile, Orange); 3G is allocated 2.1 GHz.

> **Key term**
>
> If a frequency is **licensed** it is **regulated** by an appointed government body. In the USA this body is called the Federal Communications Commission (**FCC**); in the UK this same function is performed by **Ofcom**, the Office of Communications. In the UK, Ofcom is also responsible for **auctioning** specific chunks of the **radio frequency spectrum** for **commercial use**.

Regulations vary from country to country, but generally they ensure a **minimum of interference** and **reliable service**.

If frequency is unlicensed then it is available for **anyone to use**, but there is no guarantee that any device will perform at **peak performance** due to possible **interference**.

Social, moral and ethical implications

In addition to understanding the various technologies which support mobile communications, it is important to think about **how** these devices have changed **our behaviour**, and the new **personal challenges** to our **conduct** that they represent.

Key terms

Ethics: 'the science of morals in human conduct' (Oxford English Dictionary)

Morals: '. . . [The] concern with the distinction between good and evil or right and wrong; right or good conduct' (Princeton University)

Social changes

Socially, the advent of mobile communications has **changed** the way that **people talk** to each other. Increasingly, contact is made electronically through mobile telephone SMS or instant messaging through PDAs, rather than meeting in person. Modern mobile telephones and PDAs also provide facilities to **send and receive email**. This has necessitated the introduction of an **abbreviated form of language**, often referred to as **TXTing**.

Key term

TXTing has developed from the online chat channels (such as IRC – Internet Relay Chat), where brevity of typing is essential. This is particularly important when the device's input device is limited (e.g. a mobile telephone's primarily numeric keypad) and keying in relies on laborious multiple presses of the same key.

TXTing uses a combination of abbreviations, numbers as words and symbols to create short but informative messages. Here is a simple example:

cu l8r m8 soz I 4gt :(

Which really means:

See you later, mate. Sorry I forgot. (I'm really unhappy about this!)

As you can see, this is a **large reduction in keying** and also manages to give **emotional context** to the message being sent. (For more on texting, see Unit 1: Using ICT to Present Information and Unit 5: ICT Supporting Organisations.)

Some mobile telephones use a system called **predictive text input** (or **T9®**), which recognises the sequence of characters input and makes suggestions about the most likely word the user is about to type.

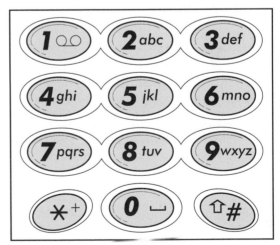

Fig. 16.14 The by now familiar mobile telephone keypad

Studies in 2004 at London's City University showed that concerns about **negative effects** on **spelling** and **grammar** due to TXTing were mainly **unfounded**, although it was noted that regular TXTers had a tendency to be more concise and less colourful in their written descriptions. Whether this is a good or bad thing is somewhat open to debate. You may have your own view!

Mobile gaming has also become popular, with the both advent of Java games on mobile telephones and handheld games consoles which have Bluetooth™, infrared or Wi-Fi connectivity. The Sony® PSP (PlayStation Portable) and the Nintendo® DS (Dual Screen) permit players to challenge other players, both in close proximity and over the Internet, using suitably configured Wireless Access Points.

Fig. 16.15 Nintendo DS © Nintendo 2006

As with all online gaming, it offers the possibility of seeking new alliances (and friendly rivalries) which are not restricted by country borders, religion or politics.

Moral concerns and ethical problems

Hacking

Wireless connectivity brings the risk of malicious interference (or **hacking**) to the forefront as the need to hijack **wired** systems is no longer necessary.

Mobile communication devices generally have a somewhat poor reputation for security. Although it is certainly not uncommon for a poorly protected device to be exploited by someone less scrupulous in order to gain services or data, it is often a case of poor installation or configuration on the part of the user or technician.

Theft of services

If left unsecured, wireless services (such as hot spots) can be connected to by other users, effectively **stealing bandwidth** from the user who is paying for the service. More importantly, they could theoretically **steal data** or **download dubious material**, which would get traced back to the user to whom the service is registered.

Sometimes connections to another user's wireless network is accidental; however, there are many common terms used to describe more purposeful actions that could be seen as morally wrong.

Key terms

Sniffing: the process of using a sniffer program to monitor data traffic which is being communicated over a network, in order to gain access information. Dangers occur when data is sent unencrypted.

Wardriving: the activity of driving around with a mobile communications device and looking for unsecured wireless hot spots for connection.

Warchalking: the activity of marking unsecured wireless hot spots for other users to connect to. Sometimes this is done physically (e.g. on a wall), other times the location is posted on a website.

In the UK, a case of bandwidth theft has been dealt with in a court of law. In July 2005 a West London man was fined £500 and sentenced to 12 months' conditional discharge for hijacking another person's broadband connection. Formerly, he was charged with 'dishonestly obtaining an electronic communications service' and 'possessing equipment for fraudulent use of a communications service'.

Again, there is a question here: just because the mobile communications technology makes this possible, should it be done? Is it not okay to get something for free? Is it not the registered user's fault for not securing their services properly? These are all good questions. But again, it all depends on the individual's **morals** and **sense of ethics** as to whether they will take advantage.

Identity theft

As discussed elsewhere (particularly Unit 17: Security of ICT Systems), identify theft is a growing concern. The use of mobile communication devices does not improve the situation, as they are easy to steal and then be used fraudulently. Additionally, they often carry personal information (e.g. a PDA) which could be used to perpetrate an unlawful act.

Institutions that store personal data about their clients and employees (e.g. financial, medical or educational records) should be particularly careful about wireless security.

Responsibilities

Both mobile communications **users** and **administrators of wireless systems** have **responsibilities** to secure their equipment.

For a **mobile telephone** user:

- Ensure wireless connectivity is off (e.g. Bluetooth™) when not in use.
- Use passkey technique for trusted pairing when using Bluetooth™.
- Do not store personally sensitive information on the device.
- If the telephone is stolen, report it so that it can be blocked.

For a **Wi-Fi network**:

- Place a firewall between the wireless network and the main LAN.
- Change to a less powerful antenna to scale down transmission.
- Use 802.11a, which uses the less busy 5 GHz band.
- Use encryption (WPA is better than WEP).
- Change the default administration password on network devices.
- Routinely change any user passwords.
- Do not broadcast the SSID (Service Set Identifier) – the network's 'name'.
- Use MAC filtering to only permit trusted devices to connect.

Community effects

Communities in general can **benefit from** – and be **concerned about** – the **implications** of increased mobile communication. Perhaps the most common concern of mobile communications has been the **alleged link** between **mobile handsets**, **base stations** and **serious illnesses** (such as cancer).

As for masts, the Independent Expert Group on Mobile Phones (**IEGMP**) reported back in 2000 that 'no evidence to conclude that mobile phone base station emissions posed any risk to health, as exposures to the emissions were expected to be at a small fraction of the guideline levels set by the International Commission on Non-Ionizing Radiation Protection (**ICNIRP**)'.

For **mobile handsets,** the results seem somewhat **mixed** and **inconclusive**. Here is an extract from an article on the BBC News website, posted 3 March 2006:

> A laboratory study concluded last year that radio waves from mobile phones do harm body cells and damage DNA.
>
> However, the European Union-funded Reflex research did not prove such changes were a risk to human health.
>
> The UK government-commissioned Stewart report in 2000 concluded there was no evidence of harm associated with using mobile phones.
>
> (Source: http://news.bbc.co.uk/1/hi/health/4771080.stm)

Recently there have been several cases of masts being moved after complaints or petitions from local people living near them, but the reasons stated by the companies involved tend to cite acknowledgements that they should not have been placed in residential areas in the first place.

Another community-based phenomenon is that of **community wireless**, an initiative where certain business or residential areas, or cities, create wireless connectivity for their inhabitants, typically funded through sponsorship, advertisement or low-cost charges. The general view is that wireless connectivity is as much a basic human right as running water, gas or electricity.

In late 2005, Google Inc., best known for its search engine technology and services, put a bid in to blanket San Francisco with free wireless high-speed Internet access in direct response to Mayor Gavin Newsom's request for a service suitable for supporting its 760,000 residents. Despite ongoing worries over privacy, the offer was seriously contemplated and is now going forward in a collaborative effort between Google, EarthLink, Tropos Networks and Motorola.

Such Municipal Wireless Networks (MWNs) are likely to become more common in the next few years, as mobile communication devices become even more popular and wireless infrastructure increases.

How to communicate with a mobile device

The following example demonstrates how to **link a mobile telephone to a PC** using a simple **Bluetooth**™ wireless connection. It will also walk you through a **simple file transfer**.

The following equipment is needed:

- mobile telephone with Bluetooth™ capability
- PC with operating system that supports Bluetooth™ devices (e.g. Microsoft Windows® XP)
- Bluetooth™ USB adaptor.

Fig. 16.16 Sony
Ericsson T630

Fig. 16.17 Bluetooth™ USB adaptor

Follow these steps carefully:

1. **Power on** PC.
2. **Log on** to PC as **Administrator** (to enable suitable security rights).
3. **Switch on** mobile telephone.
4. **Enable Bluetooth**™ **function** on telephone.
5. **Insert Bluetooth**™ **adaptor** into an **unused USB port**. The icon shown in Figure 16.18 will be displayed on the **system tray** part of Microsoft Windows® XPs **task bar**.

   You should recognise this from earlier – the **Bluetooth**™ logo. This is usually the sign that the Bluetooth™ device is **connected**, **recognised** and **active**.
6. We will now try to add the mobile telephone to the PC's list of known Bluetooth™ devices.

   Double-click the **Bluetooth**™ **icon**.

   The dialogue box shown in Figure 16.19 will appear.
7. Click **Add** button.
8. The dialogue shown in Figure 16.20 will now appear.

Fig. 16.18 Microsoft Windows® XP system tray

Fig. 16.19 PC's Bluetooth Devices dialogue

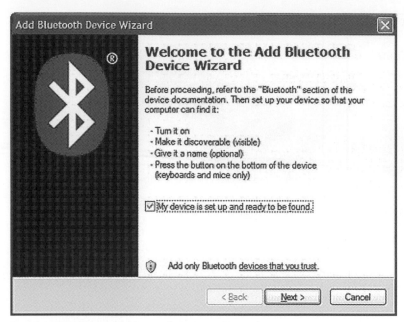

Fig. 16.20 PC's Add Bluetooth Device Wizard

Follow the instructions presented. Then ensure that the **checkbox** is **ticked** and click **Next** button.

9. After a short time spent searching the local vicinity for a Bluetooth™ device, the new device should appear (see Figure 16.21).

Fig. 16.21 New devices are shown

The mobile telephone should have been **discovered. Click on it** to select it and press **Next** button.

10. The dialogue shown in Figure 16.22 should appear.

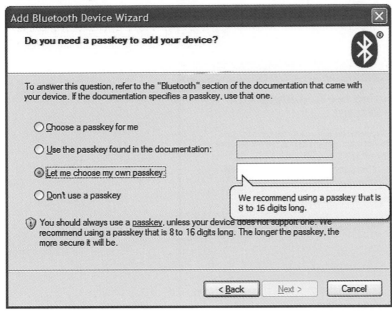

Fig. 16.22 Passkey selection

We can now choose own our **passkey** to **secure** the **Bluetooth**™ **pairing**. Enter a **suitable passkey** (e.g. 19921995) and press **Next** button.

11. The dialogue shown in Figure 16.23 will appear.

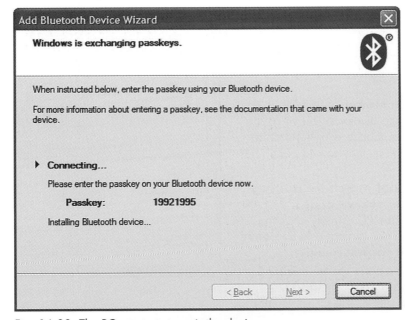

Fig. 16.23 The PC attempts to pair the devices

The mobile telephone should also be prompting the user to **accept** the named device which is contacting it ('MARK2'); **please do so**.

12. The mobile telephone will then ask you to **enter** the **passkey** into the **handset**, using the **alphanumeric** keypad. **Please do so**.

If the **passkey matches**, the information shown in Figure 16.24 will appear on the PC monitor screen.

Fig. 16.24 The PC lists the paired devices' services

The mobile telephone should also now add 'MARK2' to its list of known devices.

This list is remembered, so it should not be necessary to repeat this pairing process set-up on future connections.

You may also notice that a number of 'bubble' dialogues appear above the Bluetooth™ icon as the **various services** that the mobile telephone offers are **discovered** by the PC as they talk to each other.

Note: If the passkeys **do not match** the **pairing will fail** and an error message will appear on both the mobile telephone and the PC. Simply click the **Back** button on the PC's error dialogue to try again, ensuring that you type the passkey carefully.

13. You should now see the dialogue shown in Figure 16.25, confirming the known device ('T630').

14. Now the Bluetooth™ connection is active, it should be

Fig. 16.25 The PC now lists the paired device

possible for the PC to use **any of the services** that the Bluetooth™ mobile telephone is **offering** (and vice versa). A simple example is a **file transfer** from the PC to the **mobile telephone.**

15. **Right-click** on the **Bluetooth**™ **icon** and select the **Send a file** menu option. The dialogue shown in Figure 16.26 should appear.

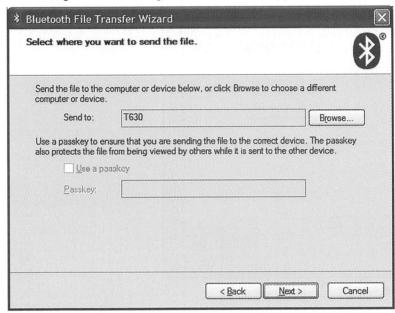

Fig. 16.26 The PC's Bluetooth File Transfer Wizard

16. Click **Next** button and the Browsing dialogue box will appear (see Figure 16.27).

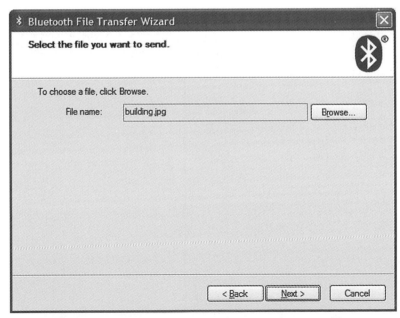

Fig. 16.27 The PC's Bluetooth File Transfer Wizard wants a file

Click the **Browse** button.

17. The familiar Microsoft Windows® XP 'File open' dialogue will appear (as shown in Figure 16.28).

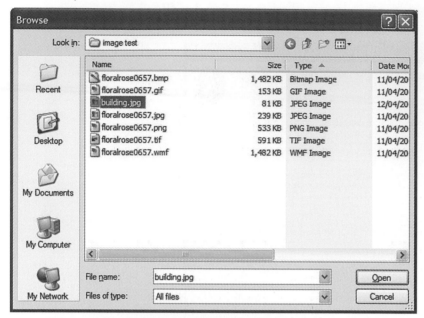

Fig. 16.28 Microsoft Windows® XP's File Open dialogue

Select the file you wish to transfer and click the **Open** button.

18. The file will be confirmed (as shown in Figure 16.29).

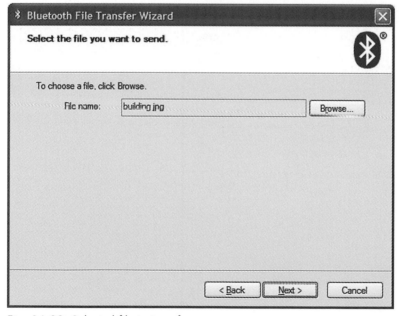

Fig. 16.29 Selected file to transfer

Click the **Next** button.

19. After connection has been made, the mobile telephone will then ask the user to accept the image.

Once you click the telephone's **accept** button, progress bars should appear on both the mobile telephone's display and the PC monitor screen.

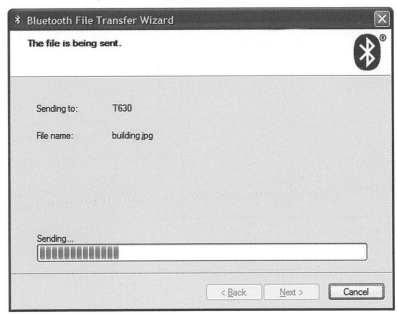

Fig. 16.30 A sending progress bar

20. When the file has been **successfully received** into the mobile telephone's 'My pictures' library, the **on-screen confirmation** shown in Figure 16.31 should appear on the PC.

21. Check the transfer by viewing the picture on the mobile telephone.

22. Remove the T630 device from the PC's devices list.

23. Disable the mobile telephone's Bluetooth™ facility.

Note: Bluetooth™ activity does contribute to the mobile telephone's battery drain.

24. Safely remove the Bluetooth™ USB adaptor from the PC.

Fig. 16.31 Completion notification of the successfully sent file

QUIZ

1. Describe the basic features that define:
   a. 1G
   b. 2G
   c. 2.5G
   d. 3G
2. What is a wireless hot spot?
3. What are the top three venues where you might find a wireless hotspot?
4. Which has lower power consumption – Bluetooth™ or Wi-Fi?
5. What is SMS?
6. What is MMS?
7. What is OTA?
8. What is bandwidth theft?
9. Which Wi-Fi encryption technique is better – WEP or WPA?
10. Bluetooth™ devices are paired using a _____ ?

ANSWERS

1. a. 1G – analogue signals
   b. 2G – digital signals
   c. 2.5G – GPRS and packet switching
   d. 3G – high-speed data services, e.g. Internet access, video telephony
2. Physical area which has connectivity via a wireless device
3. Hotel/resort

Restaurant

Store/shopping mall

4. Bluetooth™

5. Short Message Service – the ability to send short text messages to other mobile telephone users

6. Multimedia Messaging Service – an expanded message service including pictures, sounds, music and video

7. Over-the-air programming – update settings sent to mobile telephones via SMS

8. Illegally using someone else's wireless connectivity

9. WPA

10. Passkey

 Activity 1

The local branch of Diskount Video Discs (DVD) has four administration PCs which need to be networked together to enable the sharing of files and resources. Unfortunately, their current high street premises are rented and they are forbidden to install cables.

Draw up a shopping list for a suitable wireless network solution that can link these PCs together.

 Activity 2

Steve Hodder from SHS has £250 to spend on a new 3G mobile telephone, which he intends to purchase from We Cell Phones (WCP). Produce a comparison of three different commercially available models that he could consider for this price.

 Activity 3

Try connecting a Bluetooth™ device (e.g. a mobile phone) to a PC and sending data (such as a file) from the device to the PC.

Write step-by-step instructions on how this was achieved so that another user could successfully accomplish the same goal.

COURSEWORK GUIDANCE

To pass this unit you will need to show that you understand the basic concepts of the mobile telecommunications industry. You need to be able to describe technologies, standards, licensing and wireless networking issues, as well as discussing the advantages and disadvantages of using different technologies.

You will need to compare different technologies and evaluate at least three (for a Distinction).

In practical terms, you will need to be able to set up and configure two different devices.

Showing an understanding and appreciation of the social, moral and ethical implications of using such technologies is also a requirement for a pass. These concepts are developed within the Merit criteria, where you are asked to explain how these issues should be addressed.

Unit links

This unit has direct links to the following:

Unit 1	Using ICT to Present Information
Unit 2	Introduction to Computer Systems
Unit 5	ICT Supporting Organisations
Unit 12	Installing Hardware Components

Unit 17	Security of ICT Systems
Unit 20	Telecommunications Technologies

Edexcel also shows links to the following:

Unit 6	Networking Essentials

●●●●Further reading

Breire, D. and Hurley, P., *Wireless Home Networking for Dummies* (Hungry Minds Inc. US, 2003) ISBN: 0764539108

Davis, H., *Absolute Beginner's Guide to Wi-Fi Wireless Networking* (Que, 2004) ISBN: 0789731150

Hannsman, U., *Pervasive Computing: The Mobile World* (Springer-Verlag Berlin and Heidelberg GmbH & Co K, 2003) ISBN: 3540002189

Vos, I. and de Klein, P., *The Essential Guide to Mobile Business* (Prentice Hall PTR, 2001) ISBN: 013093819X

FSO Alliance http://www.wcai.com/fsoalliance/

Hutchison 3G UK ('3') http://www.three.co.uk/

IrDA® http://www.irda.org/

Jiwire Hot Spot finder   http://www.jiwire.com/

MOA – Mobile Operators Association   http://www.mobilemastinfo.com/

Mobile technologies www.becta.org.uk/mobiletechnologies/

Motorola http://www.motorola.com/

Nokia http://www.nokia.com/

O2 http://www.o2.com/

Ofcom – Office of Communications http://www.ofcom.org.uk/

Orange http://www.orange.co.uk/

Siemens http://www.benqmobile.com/

Sony-Ericsson http://www.sonyericsson.com/

Stewart Report http://www.iegmp.org.uk/report/text.htm

T9 (predictive text) http://www.t9.com/

The Bluetooth SIG website http://www.bluetooth.com/

T-Mobile http://www.t-mobile.co.uk/

Translate it! http://www.transl8it.com/

Vodafone http://www.vodafone.co.uk/

Wi-Fi Alliance http://www.wi-fi.org/OpenSection/index.asp

Wi-Fi Alliance Worldwide Hot Spot Finder http://wi-fi.jiwire.com/

Magazines:

Mobile News

What Mobile

Progress check

To record your achievement, simply tick the criteria awarded to you when each assignment is returned (you may be given three assignments for this unit, U16.01, U16.02 and U16.03 – the final column may not be used). There is a full copy of this grid available on the accompanying CD. The copy will also allow you to record your key skill achievement against Literacy, Numeracy and ICT objectives.

		Assignments in this Unit		
Assignment		**U16.01**	**U16.02**	**U16.03**	**U16.04**
Referral					
Pass					
	1				
	2				
	3				
	4				
	5				
	6				
	7				
Merit					
	1				
	2				
	3				
	4				
Distinction					
	1				
	2				
	3				

A completed sample of this document (for reference purposes) can be found at the back of Unit 1.

INDEX

Please see below for the single-user licence associated with the CD-ROM. If an institution requires an institutional licence, so that copies can be made onto a network or more than once computer simultaneously, please contact btecfirstenquiries@hodder.co.uk

ELECTRONIC END USER SINGLE USE LICENCE AGREEMENT

BTEC First for ICT Practitioners CD-ROM (the 'CD-ROM'**)** published by Hodder and Stoughton Limited (HS) under its Hodder Arnold imprint.

NOTICE TO USER:
THIS IS A CONTRACT. BY ACCESSING THIS CD-ROM YOU AND OTHERS TO WHOM YOU ALLOW ACCESS TO THE CD-ROM ACCEPT ALL THE TERMS AND CONDITIONS OF THIS AGREEMENT.

Upon your acceptance of this Agreement, HS grants to you a non-exclusive, non-transferable licence to view and save the files contained on the CD-ROM, subject to the following:

1. Use of the CD-ROM. **You may only save one copy of each separate PDF file on the CD-ROM onto the hard disk or other storage device of only one computer**. If the computer is linked to a local area network then the PDF files must be saved in such a way so that they cannot be accessed by other computers on the same network. You may make a single back-up copy of the CD-ROM (which must be deleted or destroyed on expiry or termination of this Agreement). Except for that single back-up copy, you may not make or distribute any copies of the CD-ROM, or use it in any way not specified in this Agreement.

2. Copyright. The PDF files on the CD-ROM are protected by Copyright Law. Except as stated above, this Agreement does not grant you any intellectual property rights in the contents of the CD-ROM as sold. All moral rights of artists and all other contributors are hereby asserted.

4. No Warranty. The CD-ROM is being delivered to you AS IS and HS makes no warranty as to its use or performance except that the CD-ROM will perform substantially as specified. HS AND ITS AUTHORS AND SUPPLIERS DO NOT AND CANNOT GIVE ANY WARRANTY REGARDING THE PERFORMANCE OR RESULTS YOU MAY OBTAIN BY USING THE CD-ROM OR ACCOMPANYING OR DERIVED DOCUMENTATION. HS AND ITS AUTHORS AND SUPPLIERS MAKE NO WARRANTIES, EXPRESS OR IMPLIED, AS TO NON-INFRINGEMENT OF THIRD PARTY RIGHTS, THE CONTENT OF THE CD-ROM, MERCHANTABILITY, OR FITNESS FOR ANY PARTICULAR PURPOSE. IN NO EVENT WILL HS OR ITS AUTHORS OR SUPPLIERS BE LIABLE TO YOU FOR ANY CONSEQUENTIAL, INCIDENTAL, SPECIAL OR OTHER DAMAGES, OR FOR ANY CLAIM BY ANY THIRD PARTY (INCLUDING PERSONS WITH WHOM YOU HAVE USED THE CD-ROM TO PROVIDE LEARNING SUPPORT) ARISING OUT OF YOUR USE OF THE CD-ROM.

5. Entire liability. HS's entire liability, and your sole remedy for a breach of the warranty given under Clause 4, is (a) the replacement of the CD-ROM not meeting the above limited warranty and which is returned by you within 90 days of purchase; or (b) if HS or its distributors are unable to deliver a replacement copy of the CD-ROM you may terminate this Agreement by returning the CD-ROM and associated textbook within 90 days of purchase and your money will be refunded. All other liabilities of HS including, without limitation, indirect, consequential and economic loss and loss of profits, together with all warranties, are hereby excluded to the fullest extent permitted by law.

6. Governing Law and General Provisions. This Agreement shall be governed by the laws of England and any actions arising shall be brought before the courts of England. If any part of this Agreement is found void and unenforceable, it will not affect the validity of the balance of the Agreement, which shall remain wholly valid and enforceable according to its terms. All rights not specifically licensed to you under this Agreement are reserved to HS. This Agreement shall automatically terminate upon failure by you to comply with its terms. This Agreement is the entire and only agreement between the parties relating to its subject matter. It supersedes any and all previous agreements and understandings (whether written or oral) relating to its subject matter and may only be amended in writing, signed on behalf of both parties.